Truth, Justice and Reconciliation in Colombia

The signing of the peace agreements between the Fuerzas Armadas Revolucionarias de Colombia—Ejército del Pueblo (FARC—EP) and the Colombian Government in late November 2016 has generated new prospects for peace in Colombia, opening up the possibility of redressing the harm inflicted on Colombians by Colombians.

Talking about peace and transitional justice requires us to think about how to operationalize peace agreements to promote justice and peaceful coexistence. This volume brings together reflections by Colombian academics and practitioners alongside pieces provided by researchers and practitioners in other countries where transitional justice initiatives have taken place (notably Bosnia and Herzegovina, South Africa, Sri Lanka and Peru). This volume has been written in the south, by the south, for the south.

The book engages with the challenges that lie ahead for future generations of Colombians. Rivers of ink have dealt with the end goals of transitional justice, but victims require us to take the quest for human rights beyond the normative realm of theorizing justice and into the practical realm of engaging how to implement justice initiatives.

The tension between theory—the legislative frameworks guaranteeing human rights—and practice—the realization of these ideas—will frame Colombia's success (or failure) in consolidating the implementation of the peace agreements with the FARC-EP.

Fabio Andrés Díaz Pabón is a Colombian political scientist. He is a Research Associate at the Department of Political and International Studies at Rhodes University in South Africa and a Researcher at the International Institute of Social Studies, Erasmus University Rotterdam, Netherlands. Fabio works at the intersection between theory and practice, and his research interests are related to state strength, civil war, conflict and protests in the midst of globalization. In addition to his academic publications, his analysis has been published by *Al Jazeera*, *Time*, *The Conversation*, *Los Angeles Times*, and *Warscapes* among others.

Europa Perspectives in Transitional Justice

The *Europa Perspectives in Transitional Justice* series from Routledge, edited by Professor Tim Murithi, provides a platform for innovative research and analysis of concepts, strategies and approaches to dealing with the past in deeply divided societies worldwide. The series encourages multidisciplinary scholarship on issues relating to reconciliation and how it is enhanced by efforts to promote redress and achieve socio-economic justice. The series aims to provide an invaluable resource for academics, policymakers, peace practitioners, researchers and all those interested in issues relating to addressing the deep-seated divisions within countries and communities. It also aims to propose forward-looking recommendations on how to achieve societal transformation.

The series comprises individual and edited volumes which provide analysis of transitions taking place at the global, regional and country levels, as well as engaging with thematic issues in the broad field of transitional justice and reconciliation.

Tim Murithi is Extraordinary Professor of African Studies at the Centre for African Studies, University of the Free State, and also Head of the Justice and Reconciliation in Africa Programme at the Institute for Justice and Reconciliation in Cape Town, South Africa. He has more than 21 years of experience in the fields of peacebuilding, governance, international justice and security in Africa. He sits on editorial boards and advisory panels for the Journal of Peacebuilding and Development, African Journal of Conflict Resolution, the Africa Peace and Conflict Journal and the journal Peacebuilding. He is author and editor of eight books; in addition he has authored more than 75 journal articles, book chapters and policy papers.

South Africa's Struggle to Remember
Contested Memories of Squatter Resistance in the Western Cape
Kim Wale

Truth, Justice and Reconciliation in Colombia
Transitioning from Violence
Edited by Fabio Andrés Díaz Pabón

For more information about this series, please visit: www.routledge.com/Europa-Perspectives-in-Transitional-Justice/book-series/ECPTJ

Truth, Justice and Reconciliation in Colombia
Transitioning from Violence

Edited by
Fabio Andrés Díaz Pabón

LONDON AND NEW YORK

First published 2018
by Routledge
2 Park Square, Milton Park, Abingdon, Oxon OX14 4RN

and by Routledge
711 Third Avenue, New York, NY 10017

Routledge is an imprint of the Taylor & Francis Group, an informa business

© 2018 Fabio Andrés Diaz for selection and editorial material; individual chapters, the contributors

The right of Fabio Andrés Diaz to be identified as the author of the editorial material, and of the authors for their individual chapters, has been asserted in accordance with sections 77 and 78 of the Copyright, Designs and Patents Act 1988.

All rights reserved. No part of this book may be reprinted or reproduced or utilised in any form or by any electronic, mechanical, or other means, now known or hereafter invented, including photocopying and recording, or in any information storage or retrieval system, without permission in writing from the publishers.

Trademark notice: Product or corporate names may be trademarks or registered trademarks, and are used only for identification and explanation without intent to infringe.

First edition published 2018

by Taylor & Francis Books

Europa Commissioning Editor: Cathy Hartley

Editorial Assistant: Eleanor Simmons

British Library Cataloguing in Publication Data
A catalogue record for this book is available from the British Library

Library of Congress Cataloging in Publication Data
A catalog record has been requested for this book

ISBN: 978–1-85743-865-9 (hbk)
ISBN: 978–1-315-14837-3 (ebk)

Typeset in Times New Roman
by Taylor & Francis Books

Contents

List of illustrations	vii
List of contributors	viii
Acknowledgements	xii

Transitional justice and the 'Colombian peace process' 1
FABIO ANDRÉS DÍAZ PABÓN

PART I
The Quest for Peace 13

2 Conflict and peace in the making: Colombia from 1948–2010 15
FABIO ANDRÉS DÍAZ PABÓN

3 The peace process with the FARC—EP 34
CARLO NASI

4 The emergence and consolidation of transitional justice within the realm of Colombian peacebuilding 50
MARCO ALBERTO VELÁSQUEZ RUIZ

5 The Transitional Justice Framework agreed between the Colombian Government and the FARC—EP 66
CAMILA DE GAMBOA TAPIAS AND FABIO ANDRÉS DÍAZ PABÓN

PART II
The Challenges 85

6 From transitional justice to post-agreement rural reform: many obstacles and a long way to go 87
ROCÍO DEL PILAR PEÑA HUERTAS

7 Creole radical feminist transitional justice: An exploration of Colombian feminism in the context of armed conflict 102
LINA M. CÉSPEDES-BÁEZ

8 From combatants' boots: Reincorporation and reconciliation 118
DIANA ACOSTA-NAVAS AND CARLOS FELIPE REYES

9 Historical memory as symbolic reparation: Limitations and opportunities of peace infrastructures as institutional designs 136
ELIANA JIMENO

10 Enhancing reconciliation in the Colombian Truth Commission by embracing psychosocial tasks 154
NATALIA TEJADA V

11 Transmission in times of transition: Intergenerational approaches to Colombia's violent past and present 168
ARIEL SÁNCHEZ MEERTENS

PART III
The Lessons 187

12 Rethinking the Colombian transition to peace through the South African experience 189
JERÓNIMO DELGADO CAICEDO AND
JULIANA ANDREA GUZMÁN CÁRDENAS

13 Transitional Justice in Peru: Lessons for Colombia 205
JEMIMA GARCÍA-GODOS

14 Bosnia and Herzegovina: The challenges and complexities of transitional justice 220
LOUIS FRANCIS MONROY-SANTANDER

15 The quest for justice in post-war Sri Lanka 235
SHYAMIKA JAYASUNDARA-SMITS

16 A long walk for justice 250
FABIO ANDRÉS DÍAZ PABÓN

Index 263

Illustrations

Figures

2.1	Emergence and demobilization of armed groups in Colombia (1948–2010)	17
4.1	Legal Evolution of Transitional Justice in Colombia	51
5.1	Components of the integral system for truth, justice, reparation and guarantee of non-repetition in Colombia	69
5.2	How does the special jurisdiction for peace in Colombia work?	77
11.1	Municipalities where data was collected	170
11.2	Students' Sources of War Knowledge	176
11.3	Imagined Geographies of Violence—The places associated with war	178
11.4	Causes of Conflict According to Students	180
11.5	Main Actors of Armed Violence in Colombia According to Students	181
11.6	Students' Views on the Peace Process	181

Tables

6.1	Estimations of dispossessed land in Colombia	88
9.1	Mechanisms of Victims' Participation in Colombia	145

Contributors

Fabio Andrés Díaz Pabón is a Colombian political scientist. He is a Research Associate at the Department of Political and International Studies at Rhodes University in South Africa and a Researcher at the International Institute of Social Studies in the Netherlands. Fabio works at the intersection between theory and practice, and his research interests are related to state strength, civil war, conflict and protests in the midst of globalization. In addition to his academic publications, his analysis has been published by *Al Jazeera*, *Time*, *The Conversation*, *Los Angeles Times*, and *Warscapes*, among others.

Diana Acosta-Navas is a PhD candidate in Philosophy at Harvard University, recipient of the Edmond J. Safra Center Graduate Fellowship for the academic year 2017–18. She holds a BA in Philosophy from the University of Los Andes, and an MA from the National University of Colombia. She conducts research in the intersection of political philosophy and philosophy of language. Her investigation focuses on institutions that empower vulnerable members of society by enabling them to perform actions with their speech: most prominently, truth commissions and affirmative consent policies. Diana has taught a variety of courses at different institutions, including the National University of Colombia, Universidad del Rosario, Harvard College and the Harvard Kennedy School.

Lina M. Céspedes-Báez is a Colombian lawyer who graduated from Universidad del Rosario (Colombia). She obtained a Master's Degree in Gender Studies at Universidad Nacional de Colombia, and an LL.M. with a concentration in international law from Cardozo School of Law (Yeshiva University). She was awarded a Fulbright Scholarship to pursue her doctorate degree in law in the USA. From 2014 to 2015 she was a doctoral fellow at the Institute for Global Law and Policy at Harvard University's law school. In 2016, she received her doctorate degree with honours from Temple University. She also holds a specialized degree in Tax Law from Universidad del Rosario. She is currently the Vice Dean of Universidad del Rosario Law School.

Jerónimo Delgado Caicedo holds a BA in Government and International Relations (Universidad Externado de Colombia), an MA in Economic, Political and International Affairs (Universidad Externado de Colombia—Université Paris IV Paris-Sorbonne) and a PhD in Geography (University of Cape Town). He is Co-ordinator of African Studies, Universidad Externado de Colombia, and a Consultant for the Africa Office at the Colombian Ministry of Foreign Affairs. He has been actively involved in South–South Co-operation initiatives on Conflict Resolution with the Colombian Ministry of Foreign Affairs and the Colombian Agency for Reintegration.

Camila de Gamboa Tapias is an Associate Professor at the Centro de Estudios Interdisciplinarios sobre Paz y Conflicto, Universidad del Rosario, Bogotá. She obtained her law degree at the Universidad del Rosario and received her MA and PhD from Binghamton University (SUNY). Her specialist research areas include democracy, transitional justice, moral sentiments and memory. She has written numerous articles on transitional justice and political philosophy. She is the editor of the special edition of *Revista Estudios Socio-Jurídicos* entitled 'Justicia transicional: memoria colectiva, reparación justicia y democracia', and of the book *Justicia Transicional: teoría y praxis*, edited by Universidad del Rosario. Currently she is writing a book on Colombia and transitional justice. She is the Vice-President of *La Sociedad Colombiana de Filosofía* and a member of the General Assembly of *La Comisión Colombiana de Juristas*.

Jemima García-Godos (Dr Polit. in Human Geography) is Associate Professor at the Department of Sociology and Human Geography, University of Oslo. Her research focuses on state-society relations and transitional justice, victim reparations and victims' rights in post-conflict societies, particularly in Colombia and Peru. Her publications include *Transitional Justice in Latin America: The Uneven Road from Impunity towards Accountability* (Routledge, 2016) co-edited with Elin Skaar and Cath Collins, and *Transitional Justice and Peacebuilding on the Ground: Victims and ex-combatants* (Routledge, 2013) co-edited with Chandra L. Sriram, Olga Martín-Ortega and Johanna Herman.

Juliana Andrea Guzmán Cárdenas holds a BA in Government and International Relations (Universidad Externado de Colombia) and is an MSc candidate in International Affairs (Columbia University–Universidad Externado de Colombia). She has researched at the Observatorio de Política y Estrategia en América Latina at the Instituto de Ciencia Política Hernán Echavarría Olózaga (ICP) and was formerly Academic Co-ordinator at Foros Semana. She has also been part of the research team at the Centre of African Studies at the Universidad Externado de Colombia and is currently Senior Associate at the Berkeley Research Group.

x *List of contributors*

Shyamika Jayasundara-Smits is a lecturer in Governance and Conflict at the International Institute of Social Studies (ISS), Erasmus University Rotterdam, Netherlands. She is also a member of the research group Governance, Law and Social Justice. Her research interests cover issues in governance, state-building, peace and conflict. Shyamika holds a PhD in Development Studies from ISS, Erasmus University Rotterdam, an MA in Conflict Transformation from the Eastern Mennonite University, Virginia, USA and BA (Honours) in International Relations from the University of Colombo, Sri Lanka. She has also received specialized training in Peace Research from Oslo University, Norway. Shyamika is a former Fulbright Fellow and has experience of working in academia and with governmental, non-governmental and civil society organizations in Sri Lanka, Suriname, the USA, Germany, and elsewhere in Europe.

Eliana Jimeno is an international consultant and a peace practitioner on peacebuilding, memory and symbolic reparations. She has a bachelor's degree in political science from Universidad del Rosario, Bogotá, and an MA in International Peace and Conflict Resolution from American University. Eliana's current professional and academic focus is on public policy design, institutional strengthening and capacity building, in particular the role of local authorities in the implementation of peacebuilding programs.

Louis Francis Monroy-Santander is a Colombian PhD researcher currently working at the University of Birmingham in the United Kingdom, focused on the study of international state-building and its impact on reconciliation practices in post-war Bosnia-Herzegovina. Having done extensive research fieldwork in Bosnia as well as Kosovo, he has developed an interest in UN peacebuilding operations and their impact on societies subject to international peace interventions. He is funded by the Economic and Social Research Council (ESRC) of the UK.

Carlo Nasi is associate professor of the Political Science Department at the University of Los Andes, where he was director of graduate programmes between 2002 and 2010. He has conducted research and published various texts on conflict resolution, civil war and democratization in Colombia, El Salvador and Guatemala. He was a Hamburg Fellow and a MacArthur Associate at the Center for International Security and Cooperation (CISAC) at Stanford University. He holds a PhD in Political Science from the University of Notre Dame.

Rocío del Pilar Peña Huertas is a lawyer, PhD and professor at the Universidad del Rosario in Bogotá, Colombia. She is a researcher and (since 2013) the academic coordinator at the Observatorio de Restitución y Regulación de Derechos de Propiedad Agraria. Her work focuses on public policy, transitional justice, human rights and agrarian rights. She is the editor of the journal *Revista Estudios Socio-Jurídicos*. She has co-authored several books about the role of judges and human rights in Colombia.

List of contributors   xi

Carlos Felipe Reyes holds BA degrees in Law and Economics from the University of Los Andes (Colombia) and MA degrees in Public Policy and Urban Planning from Harvard University. Carlos has been advisor to the Colombian Minister of Health and Social Protection and to the Director of the National Planning Department. His research has focused on the relation between national and local governments in health and education.

Ariel Sánchez Meertens holds a PhD in anthropology and a Master's degree in Conflict Studies and Human Rights (Utrecht University). He recently completed a postdoctoral fellowship at the Universidad Nacional de Colombia and serves currently as an advisor to Bogotá's Memory, Peace and Reconciliation Center. Ariel also worked at the Administrative Department of the Civil Service as an advisor on pedagogy of the peace accords between the Colombian government and the FARC—EP. As a Marie Curie Fellow he taught at the University of Ulster in Northern Ireland and at Utrecht University. His work focuses on memory, education and transitional justice mainly in Colombia and Sri Lanka.

Natalia Tejada V. is a Colombian psychologist with more than 10 years of experience designing and implementing psychosocial support programmes and peacebuilding initiatives with victims of armed conflict, child soldiers, and vulnerable populations in urban and rural settings. She has also published on related topics in Colombia. Natalia currently works as a consultant with the Social Development Global Practice at The World Bank Group in Washington, DC, and with the Colombian Government on initiatives of mental health and psychosocial support in post-conflict settings. Natalia holds an MA in International Peace Studies from University of Notre Dame, USA, an MA in Brief Strategic Psychotherapy from the Centro di Terapia Strategica in Arezzo, Italy, and graduated as a psychologist from University of Los Andes in Colombia.

Marco Alberto Velásquez Ruiz is a Colombian lawyer (Pontificia Universidad Javeriana, 2005), and holds a PhD in Law (Osgoode Hall Law School, York University, Canada, 2016) and an LL.M. in International Law (Graduate Institute of International and Development Studies—IHEID, Switzerland, 2010). In addition, he has been consultant to various national and international organizations. Currently, Marco is an Auxiliary Magistrate at the Colombian Special Jurisdiction for Peace. He has lectured and researched on international law, human rights, transitional justice and peacebuilding.

Acknowledgements

Books are not easily brought together without the help of many people, and this edited volume is no exception. This book would have not been possible without the support of institutions, individuals and academics from the global South.

The idea for this book emerged in a conversation with Tim Murithi from the Institute of Justice and Reconciliation in South Africa regarding the need for discussions written from the global South with regards to transitional justice that engage the challenges of the South from a southern perspective, and to amplify the voices of those living in the places that we write about, rather than objectifying them in books and texts. This conversation incepted and guided the development of this book.

The Political Sciences Department at the University of Los Andes in Colombia facilitated the fieldwork in that country which supported the final review of the many chapters. Special thanks are owed to Laura Wills and Carlo Nasi, as well as to Ana Teresa Chacón and Hernando Romero for their support.

The Research Department of Rhodes University in South Africa, and especially Jaine Roberts, supported the final revision of the volume. Vera Chapman Browne's and Jennifer Thorpe's assistance in supporting the final review and the style-setting of the text was invaluable.

Cathy Hartley and Eleanor Simmons of Taylor & Francis shepherded the entire process of the production of the volume with excellent administrative support.

Manuel Guerrero created all the diagrams and figures which illustrate key concepts and contextual data presented by different authors in their chapters; his work was extremely helpful.

I would like to acknowledge the generosity of Chirrete Golden, the Colombian street artist who allowed the use of his work 'Mural por la memoria y los desplazados en Colombia' (Mural for the memory and the internally displaced population in Colombia) as the book cover. I would also like to thank Roberto Romero Malagón for permitting the use of his photograph of this mural for the book cover.

The dedication and effort from all the contributors to this volume was central to this project. Their speed, rigour and responsiveness were outstanding, and supported the completion of this project in a remarkably short amount of time. All remaining errors are mine.

1 Transitional justice and the 'Colombian peace process'

Fabio Andrés Díaz Pabón

The signing of the peace agreements between the Fuerzas Armadas Revolucionarias de Colombia—Ejército del Pueblo (FARC—EP) and the Government of Colombia in late November 2016 has generated new prospects for peace in Colombia, opening up the possibility of redressing the harms inflicted on Colombians by Colombians.

The negotiation process and the agreements have been explicit about the importance of justice and the prioritization of victims. In fact, the negotiation agenda established the topic of justice for victims as central to the peace process. Other elements of the agreements relate to land, demobilization, disarmament and reintegration of cadres, illicit crops and illicit drugs, and political participation.

The agreements regarding victims and justice present a roadmap for a journey towards a more peaceful environment. They signal the intention and commitment of actors to reach this goal, but institution building and specific policies and programmes to implement these agreements are necessary to achieve it. Statehood and peace have never been built by decree; they are built by institutions, bureaucrats, and by government policies that are consistent across time.

Peacebuilding and state-building must not be seen as processes which are disconnected from justice. The strengthening of institutions, endowments, processes, and practices that realize the agreements signed in a peace process will condition the possibility of justice agreements being implemented. They also affect citizens' perceptions of the credibility of their state.

For this process of state-building and for the consolidation of a justice framework to take place successfully, institutions and the state apparatus must assess the gaps between the commitments contained in the agreements and the realities of the country. This ensures that institutions can be designed to implement procedures and processes accordingly. If we are talking about peace and justice seriously we need to think about **how** to operationalize peace agreements, otherwise we risk pursuing armchair justice in favour of real justice, and using the peace agreements and their transitional justice frameworks as hollow rhetorical tools rather than pathways to peace.

Transitional justice is a broad label that refers to a series of different interim arrangements applied in post-agreement scenarios, with different outcomes (De Greiff, 2012). In the case of Colombia, the idea of transitional justice has been embraced as the primary framework through which the victims and perpetrators of the Colombian conflict will be engaged, and as the mechanism for the provision of justice and redress (Gobierno de Colombia y FARC—EP, 2016).

Transitional justice as a field of practice and study in intra-state conflicts is fairly new (less than 40 years old); claims with regard to what must be done in transitional justice initiatives thus seem, in some cases, to be driven by normative claims rather than by evidence (Teitel, 2000). Because of this, the process of making transitional justice initiatives a reality remains a great challenge in practice (Fischer, 2011). Determining how best to operationalize transitional justice in the context of the frailty of the state —a natural context to a post-conflict scenario—is thus no easy endeavour.

Reflecting on the challenges related to the idea of justice within the Colombian agreements is vital. The implementation of the agreements on transitional justice can cement (or fail to) a social covenant to reassert the legitimacy of the Colombian state in its territory after more than 50 years of internal war and violence. Being aware of the challenges ahead of implementing the agreements with regard to transitional justice is as important as achieving the agreements themselves.

What has been agreed on in Colombia is neither good nor bad *per se*. It constitutes an opportunity, a roadmap, and a framework for attempting to consolidate state legitimacy within the country. This volume distances itself from debates regarding what justice is, what justice should be, and how should it be implemented. Instead, the focus is placed on **how** what has been agreed to relates to the implementation of the transitional justice initiatives, and what challenges they will face in their implementation in relation to the victims' needs in the Colombian context.

It is these challenges that this volume considers. It focuses on identifying the challenges facing the implementation of the objectives of the transitional justice component of the peace agreement between the FARC—EP and the Colombian Government. By reflecting rigorously on some of the challenges to be encountered in realizing this vision of justice, this work hopes to inform the debate on what is required to bring justice to the victims of the Colombian conflict in accordance with the peace agreement and the transitional justice frameworks it establishes. A full understanding of these challenges should inform the implementation strategy and practice for the peace agreements.

This volume will explore the following challenges with respect to the conception and implementation of the transitional justice framework in Colombia: reconciliation, memory, education, land, gender, demobilization and reintegration.

This reflection is led by Colombian academics and practitioners, in partnership with researchers and practitioners in other countries where transitional justice initiatives have taken place (notably Bosnia and Herzegovina,

South Africa, Sri Lanka, and Peru). This volume has been written in the south, by the south, for the south.

Transitional justice: Tensions and challenges of a field in the making

In modern peacemaking processes aiming to move countries away from civil war and internal conflict, it is common to see provisions for justice arrangements made as part of peace negotiations. These are commonly referred to as transitional justice mechanisms. Transitional justice has become a more popular approach to post-conflict reconstruction in the case of civil wars and internal conflicts since the late 1980s when Latin American dictatorships transitioned from dictatorial regimes towards fuller democracies (Sriram, 2010; Sriram, 2000).

The prevalence of transitional justice in 'modern' peacebuilding is illustrated by the fact that transitional justice initiatives now tend to be integrated into peace negotiations in order to facilitate post-conflict peacebuilding (Kostic, 2012). State-building initiatives, combined with mechanisms to deal with past atrocities, are expected to lead to stability and reconciliation (De Greiff, 2012). Transitional justice as part of peace agreements aims to establish channels to determine accountability for war crimes, to individualize responsibility, and to generate a comprehensive view of violent pasts (Kostic, 2012). The measures and mechanisms created to achieve these ambitious objectives constitute transitional justice: the addressing of human rights violations via the establishment of tribunals; truth commissions; lustration; reparations; and political and societal projects aimed at fact-finding, reconciliation, and remembrance (Fischer, 2011).

A number of debates and tensions exist within the field and practice of transitional justice: notions of justice—retributive or reparative—compete; international jurisprudence, institutions and norms often contrast with national and local legal frameworks; institutions and cultural practices, each of which may be employed to differing degrees, shape the transitional justice process; and finally, the end of the process is contested—should transitional justice establish truth, or deliver retributive justice? The Colombian peace process illuminates each of these debates and demonstrates the possibility of moving beyond the dichotomies implied in these debates to achieve a more holistic process.

Traditionally within the field of transitional justice the policy options for reparation, retribution, and restoration have been seen as mutually exclusive and debated in opposition to each other. This has limited the potential for transitional justice processes to be perceived and operate as an integral approach for peacebuilding, able to consider different needs and alternatives. One of the main examples of this opposition is the debate of peace versus justice: a legalist approach advocates for an emphasis on criminal justice in order to deter future human rights violations, while those in favour of focusing on peace agreements may allow élites related to the conflict to be included in post-conflict scenarios (Fischer, 2011).

The field of transitional justice evolved from an initial legalistic view, focused on processing war crimes, and extending its aims and objectives to include a broader and transformative dimension (Teitel, 2000). Transitional justice mechanisms must support institutions seeking justice to redress aggressions, whilst also supporting future good governance (Andrieu, 2010) and the consolidation of institutional legitimacy and the rule of law (Betts, 2005). These multiple objectives have driven the implementation and design of transitional justice initiatives towards a more comprehensive interpretation of the field. Recent transitional justice initiatives combine provisions that aim to improve accountability and adherence to the rule of law, reform institutions, and rebuild trust. These mechanisms are believed to provide for reconciliation while consolidating justice and reparations (Fischer, 2011).

The objectives of the transitional justice framework contained in the agreements established between the Colombian Government and the FARC—EP relate to access to justice, the definition of a justice system that serves the Colombian society, and its contribution to reparation. Hence, the agreements combine elements of both restorative and retributive justice. In doing so, the agreements aim to create a system with the objectives of justice, restoration, reparation, and non-repetition (Gobierno de Colombia y FARC—EP, 2016).

The agreements between the FARC—EP and the Colombian Government pursue a third way in comparison to other agreements on justice for victims, by not applying the dichotomy of retributive and restorative justice. The agreements include a series of elements that combine reparation, retribution, and restoration of the rights of the victims. The Colombian agreements appear to constitute an example of what is referred to in the literature as a 'hybrid' justice system (Sriram, 2010). The 'local versus international' debate frames another set of opposing ideas within the transitional justice field. When transitional justice mechanisms are implemented, they are in some cases applied in accordance with international rules and standards to the detriment of local and national rules and practices. Where this is the case, tensions and legitimacy gaps may be created. This is especially true for communities that had no access to formal systems of justice before conflict emerged (as is common in weak states) and depended on customary law but that post-conflict are required to pursue justice and reconciliation processes outside of this through institutions shaped by international rules and standards. The introduction of new laws, institutions and trials that are perceived to be alien structures can be cause for concern and can be seen as colonial instruments. The literature refers to this privileging of the international over the local as the 'liberal' co-option of customary law and local forms of justice. These initiatives are commonly encountered as removed or distant, and often fail to support sustainable peacebuilding initiatives (Andrieu, 2010).

This should not make of local initiatives of justice a romantic goal for justice in opposition to international frameworks per se. Their advantages lie on the capacity of allowing a context-sensitive operation, empower citizens and link the processes of transitional justice with the experiences and realities of communities (Lederach, 1997).

However, local frameworks are not exempt of their own challenges. In some cases, "local" justice frameworks and customs ignore the rights of women, minorities and LGBTI communities, making of local initiatives means reproduction of existing inequalities through a local/localized "justice" system. Also there is the risk of spoilers, former warlords or remaining armed actors manipulating this process for their benefit (Hirblinger, 2017). Thus, assuming that local/localized processes are better than international processes can be a simplified description of the challenges of implementing these initiatives at a local level (Mac Ginty & Polanska, 2015).

The transitional justice framework contained in the agreements established between the Colombian Government and the FARC—EP speaks to local realities and necessities, and it relates to the international jurisprudence set by the Rome Statute of the International Criminal Court. The agreements were shaped by the interplay between international jurisprudence on human rights (and the obligations/restrictions imposed on nations by international treaties in this regard) as well as the demands of national legislation and context.

Another dilemma that often arises in discussions around transitional justice relates to the role that 'truth' and the role truth and reconciliation commissions, as opposed to trials and courts, can play in reconciliation. Truth commissions have been presented as viable alternatives to trials and prosecutions and as effective mechanisms for countering denial about human rights abuses. Truth has the potential to provide partial redress for victims, contributing to healing and reconciliation (Fischer, 2011). In addition, it is argued that truth commissions can promote public dialogue (Sriram, 2010). However, critics of truth commissions assert that revealing the truth about human rights violations can become an impediment to reconciliation as it can also promote animosity, reopen wounds, and increase political instability (Skaar, 2013). Some academics are in fact sceptical of the very idea that truth-telling mechanisms in themselves can bring healing and maintain peace in a post-conflict society (Mendeloff, 2004). Another critique to the use of truth commissions is the fact that these commissions often lead to the creation of official, state-sanctioned versions of a violent past. This can impose particular versions of the conflict, often making the multiplicity of individual experiences and interpretations of an armed conflict less visible (Andrieu, 2010). Where this happens, it creates controversy regarding whose truth is presented by truth commissions when these processes are undertaken (Loyle & Davenport, 2016).

The task of implementing transitional justice mechanisms as part of peace processes and agreements is riddled with different dilemmas. These dilemmas are inherent to the transition from war to peace, and in moving from agreements to practice, and require decision-making on how to proceed and effectively achieve justice in accordance with the requirements of particular contexts. Context-specific requirements relate to the actors and the histories of the particular contexts that suffered violence and war. Framing discussions about transitional justice as centred merely on theoretical dichotomies and debates will illuminate the type of initiatives undertaken, but may also obscure reflection on the capacity of the agreements and the instruments set in place to achieve peace and to incorporate the voices of the victims. A strong focus on the context/s in which the transitional justice process will be undertaken is necessary for the latter.

We must not forget that transitional justice is a mechanism that is used to deal with pasts comprised of mass human rights violations within reconciliation and peacebuilding processes in contexts of state weakness and fragility. The prefix transitional is not given loosely, and we need to reflect on how to effect these transitions to take place. This requires researchers to see transitional justice through a peacebuilding and a process lens, and not solely from a human rights perspective (Andrieu, 2010). Transitional justice is thus likely best served by a toolset that allows for the combination of different mechanisms to achieve these ends (De Greiff, 2012). The final goal of transitional justice is peace, and that is where our focus should be oriented.

Transitional justice in the 'international' context: restorative and retributive debates meet the Colombian agreements

The decision about what justice means also depends on whom the justice system is focused on: the perpetrator (amnesty, prosecution, and lustration) or the victim (financial compensation, truth telling, and memorialization[1]).

In the case of Colombia, the agreements reveal a holistic model of restoration and retribution. On the side of restoration, the Colombian example uses an existing legal framework defined by the existing Victims' Law. The Victims' Law establishes a mechanism for repairing the harm done to victims by different actors in the conflict (Gobierno de Colombia, 2011). In addition, some of the agreements hint at a reparative role for the perpetrators of crimes, in that they outline a possible role for the latter in activities such as de-mining processes,[2] the participation of victimizers in illicit crop eradication programmes, and the construction of infrastructure projects by perpetrators. Such activities can be seen as a twofold mechanism that is both retributive and reparative (Gobierno de Colombia y FARC—EP, 2016).

The agreements between the Colombian Government and the FARC—EP may break new ground in relation to the abandonment of the dichotomy of international/national/local definitions and standards of justice, reaching a middle ground that is able to comply with national needs and international standards, and that incorporates notions of both restorative and retributive justice.

In combining elements of restorative and retributive justice, and in bridging international and local understandings and standards of justice, the agreements outline a system that aims toward justice, reparation, and non-repetition, and which serves as a guideline for institutionalizing this process. However, its implementation will prove challenging.

The legalistic language of the agreement can be seen to give preponderance to penal sentences. It does not clarify how the reparative aspects of the agreements speak to the needs of the victims. This is as a result of the fact that the previous peace processes, and the institutions which emerged from them, were not as focused on the needs of the victims. The 'what', but not the 'how', is clearly stated. The work to operationalize and implement the plans to reach the objectives defined by this transitional justice framework is left to the existing institutional structures. This transitional justice approach, being holistic and multiple in its aims, is different to the previous peace processes that gave rise to the existing institutional framework. The existing institutions are thus not necessarily well equipped to implement the current transitional justice process or to achieve its aims. Reflection is necessary to determine how the existing institutions need to be adapted in order to perform the functions that they will be called upon to provide. In addition, the lack of clarity on the process of integration of the special jurisdiction for peace with the integrated system of truth, reparation, and non-repetition leaves the role of the victims in this process open to interpretation (see Chapter 5). This ambiguity regarding how the process will be grounded has been met with concern by some sectors of the Colombian polity and the international community (Amnistía Internacional, 2016).

A complex institutional setting complicates the system designed for truth, reparation, and non-repetition in the peace agreement. This institutional layout reflects the intersection of a series of mechanisms and institutions that should bring a comprehensive understanding of restorative justice, reparation, and retributive justice and its connection to the wider peace process. The transitional justice process that is taking place aims to recognize the rights of the victims beyond the peace agreement with the FARC—EP (victims from paramilitaries, the armed forces, and other operating guerrillas will have access to the benefits under this framework).

According to the agreements signed in Bogotá, human rights abuses will not be the object of pardons or amnesties or alternative judicial punishments. It is worth noting that this jurisdiction will be applied to both citizens and fighters responsible for crimes within the Colombian conflict. It can thus become a framework for bringing justice for atrocities committed by both the FARC—EP and the Colombian Government forces (Alto Comisionado para la Paz, 2016).

The role of victims in the Colombian agreements seems to be more pronounced than in other transitional justice initiatives. The framework includes clauses that are orientated towards a victim-focused justice, supporting truth and reconciliation initiatives rather than a functioning as a simple punitive device. However, victims did not participate directly in negotiating the agreement, although the negotiations were informed by the views and needs of a group of 60 victims, which met once with the negotiation teams of the FARC—EP and the Colombian government in Havana to represent the voice of more than eight million victims (Verdad Abierta, 2014). As the agreements did not involve the victims' consent or approval it could be claimed that their participation was more aesthetic than real. Within the context of a patriarchal society the extent of meaningful participation by indigenous groups; Afro-Colombians; lesbian, gay, bisexual, transgender, and intersex (LGBTI) minorities; and women in the implementation of the agreements remains to be seen.

Transitional justice is part of an agenda for change. It is necessary, yet not sufficient in itself, to achieve change (Sriram, 2010). The capacity of the state to implement this agenda will define its success. This is something already demonstrated in Colombian history; it has proved difficult and challenging to fulfil the promises made in previous peace initiatives (Amnistía Internacional, 2012).

Structure of the book

To reflect on these questions regarding the challenges facing the transitional justice process within the wider Colombian peace process, the volume is structured in three sections. The first section deals with the background of the Colombian conflict and previous peace attempts. The second is concerned with the challenges of transitional justice with regard to forced displacement, land, gender, reconciliation, the demobilization of former combatants, memory, and the intergenerational transmission of the history of the Colombian armed conflict. The third section focuses on the lessons for Colombia from transitional justice initiatives in Peru, Bosnia and Herzegovina, Rwanda, and South Africa.

The book begins with a brief history of the conflict and of previous peace processes, making the case that the current peace process is best understood in relation to the wider historical process of state consolidation and successive peace attempts in Colombia (see Chapter 2). The current peace process and the agreements reached with the FARC—EP are the outcome of an effort that involved several peace processes over the last three decades. This longer historical process explains, informs, and guides the current peace process with the FARC—EP, as Nasi notes in Chapter 3.

The Colombian Government has implemented and experimented with a diversity of measures in pursuit of justice and transitional justice in Colombia. These developments have occurred in line with the evolution of the field of transitional justice. As Velázquez notes in Chapter 4, initiatives including justice in peace processes are not new in Colombia and have taken different forms, such as amnesties, pardons, restitution, and reparation programmes. The current agreements with the FARC—EP are an evolution of these previous experiences.

The volume proceeds to present and discuss in detail the agreements between the FARC—EP and the Colombian Government and its transitional justice component. Transitional justice agreements are anything but simple mechanisms, and Colombia's is no exception. As Gamboa and Díaz argue in Chapter 5, the agreements present a model that can be seen as the intersection of the international demands and the national needs for transitional justice.

With this background established, the volume proceeds to analyse the challenges facing the implementation of these transitional justice mechanisms in a country still in transition. The analysis of the challenges with regard to the implementation of the agreements and their success is informed by an analysis of the capacity of and the challenges faced by Colombian institutions in previous peace initiatives and as well as the current context. There is a multiplicity of elements that should be considered in relation to the initiatives for transitional justice in Colombia, but given the restrictions of what can be discussed in a book, the debate in this text will be centred on land, gender, demobilization, reconciliation, the role of truth and memory, and education.

Challenges encountered in relation to policies regarding land and its restitution in Colombia are discussed in two chapters. In Chapter 6, Peña Huertas discusses a series of challenges seen in the implementation of previous initiatives. These difficulties are part of a structural problem present in previous initiatives undertaken by the state to deal with the land issue. Initiatives for peace and justice operate in the context of a political economy where institutions are often weak, underfunded and overstretched.

The volume proceeds to reflect on the insights gained through a gendered lens. As Céspedes argues in Chapter 7, particular understandings of gender in relation to transitional justice initiatives can, in fact, overshadow other types of victimization, and misinform other policy initiatives, as she demonstrates is the case with policies responding to land dispossession and their impact on women. The particular biases of a narrow gender perspective are entrenched in much of the transitional justice field, where gender is considered primarily or only as it relates to sexual abuse. This can lead to policy and implementation blind spots, leaving a great deal of the victims in Colombia ostracized. At least 50% of the victims of the Colombian conflict are women.

There are victims and victimizers. We speak of cadres as perpetrators, but rarely do we see also see them as victims. Cadres have been represented in public discourse as dangerous animals, lurking in wait to attack their fellow citizens. However, in most cases, cadres have been also victims of war, and their role within a transitional justice framework as it links to reconciliation and reintegration into society should not be overlooked. Citizens that have been pushed to fight against each other should be seen as humans who were pushed towards warfare, unless we assume a Hobbesian vision of humanity. Acosta and Reyes reflect in Chapter 8 on how justice, reconciliation, and reintegration can cohabit. Supporting initiatives where former victimizers can play their role in restitution and reparation, whilst helping former victims become able to transcend their own victimization in a post-agreement setting as both victims and perpetrators are reintegrated into society, can promote transitional justice. As reconciliation is a relational concept, we cannot expect to achieve reconciliation without the victimizers.

The volume proceeds to reflect on the tensions between justice, memory, and education, and the possibilities for transitional justice mechanisms to support memory, history, truth, and reconciliation exercises. Doing so might entail challenges for Colombia, as Jimeno presents in Chapter 9. An analysis of justice and memory processes highlights the tensions between local and national actors and agendas, and the tensions between mandated versions and processes of memorialization in practice. Tejada takes this reflection forward in

10 *Transitional justice and the peace process*

Chapter 10, through discussion of the work of the truth commission for Colombia in the light of the transitional justice mechanisms which have been established. Tejada explores whether these can, or cannot, promote reconciliation. Finally, Sánchez, in Chapter 11, interrogates the understanding of the links between memory and education in an analysis of how education interacts with, creates, and re-creates narratives and understandings of the conflict.

However, the Colombian experience and the challenges facing the implementation of its transitional justice framework are not wholly unique. It is important to reflect on and understand the challenges faced in comparable experiences and practices elsewhere in the world, as this can inform Colombia's path forward. The experiences of South Africa, Peru, Sri Lanka, and Bosnia and Herzegovina are thus brought to the fore to inform reflection on the challenges that transitional justice will face in Colombia. Colombia will most likely not travel the same path as these countries, but can learn from the challenges they faced and the response they mobilized in the implementation of their transitional justice initiatives.

In Chapter 12, Delgado and Guzmán reflect on the lessons demonstrated by the case of South Africa regarding advancing a new social covenant against the backdrop of a broad failure to adequately tackle structural issues such as inequality and effective reparation for the victims of the apartheid regime. García-Godos reflects on the experience of Peru, and outlines how the dangers of the politicization of transitional justice mechanisms can affect the credibility of transitional initiatives and their institutions, weakening their mandates and enfeebling the possibility of justice in Chapter 13. The experience of the conflict in Bosnia and Herzegovina then presents the dangers of elevating imposed versions of transitional justice that are internationally legitimate, but perceived as too far removed from the citizens, thus creating a sense of illegitimate justice, as Monroy-Santander argues in Chapter 14. Finally, the case of Sri Lanka warns us against the instrumental use of transitional justice mechanisms as a way to fulfil a checklist of what needs to be done in the eyes of the international community. As Jayasundara-Smits argues in Chapter 15, we must be aware of the danger of making transitional justice mechanisms a totem that allows countries to claim their liberalness and openness, while sweeping aside the needs of the victims.

In all of these cases, and in past transitional justice experiences in Colombia, challenges have emerged most forcefully in the practice, rather than in the theory. The framework set into place by the peace agreements and their implementation in Colombia opens up a new opportunity and constitutes a junction between two possible scenarios. In the first scenario, the implementation of transitional justice mechanisms is beneficial and important in improving Colombian democracy, creating a series of public policy instruments with the potential to increase the legitimacy of the state, and recognize the human rights of the victims of the conflict. The second scenario is shaped by the looming risk of other armed groups, and a virulent opposition to the peace agreements and transitional justice. These 'spoilers', and failures of the institutional framework of transitional justice, could undermine and oppose the objectives of peace in Colombia, leaving Colombia with the agreement, but a weak justice and a general discontentment with peace.

The Colombian case can serve as a valuable case study through which to explore strategies to deal with human rights violations and build peace, while considering the challenges these objectives entail. To reflect on the practical challenges related to the implementation of the agreements regarding transitional justice and human rights in Colombia in light of the experiences of Colombians on the ground, as well as those related to the nature of pertinent institutions and their capacity to realize the human rights of Colombians affected by the conflict, is thus a point of departure from which to inform contributions towards peace—the aim of transitional justice.

The following chapters should thus be seen as an engagement with the challenges ahead for Colombia as a nation in its foreseeable future. However, if we discuss transitional justice as part of peacebuilding it is vital that academics, politicians, activists, and international organizations transcend their discourse and address how to implement changes in order to build peace, given these challenges and these frameworks. Rivers of ink have dealt with the end goals of transitional justice, but victims require us to take the quest for human rights beyond the normative realm of theorizing justice and into the practical realm of engaging how to implement justice initiatives.

The tension between theory—the legislative frameworks guaranteeing human rights—and practice—the realization of these ideas—will frame Colombia's success (or failure) in consolidating the implementation of the peace agreements with the FARC—EP.

Notes

1 Memorialization can be understood as a cultural approach to confronting a traumatic past through practices of remembrance, representation and commemoration where communities come to terms with a difficult event through means of expression such as novels, films, music, performances, monuments or museum exhibitions. (Obradović-Wochnik, 2013).
2 Since 1990 it is estimated that more than 11,000 people have died or been injured by landmines. 38% of the victims are civilians and 62% are members of the armed forces. 80% of the victims have been injured and 20% died (Dirección para la Acción Integral contra Minas Antipersonal, 2015).

References

Alto Comisionado para la Paz, 2016. *ABC Jurisdiccion Especial para la Paz*, [Online] Available at: www.altocomisionadoparalapaz.gov.co/oacp/Pages/informes-especiales/jurisdiccion-especial-paz/index.html [Last accessed 30 September 2016].
Amnistía Internacional, 2012. *Colombia: La Ley de Victimas y Restitucion de Tierras*. Madrid: Amnistía Internacional.
Amnistía Internacional, 2016. *La situación de los derechos humanos en Colombia—9 de Febrero de 2016*. s.l.: Amnistía Internacional.

Andrieu, K., 2010. Civilizing peacebuilding: transitional justice, civil society and the liberal paradigm. *Security Dialogue*, 41(5), pp. 543–601.

Betts, A., 2005. Should approaches to post-conflict justice and reconciliation be determined globally, nationally, locally? *The European Journal of Development Research*, 17(4), pp. 735–752.

De Greiff, P., 2012. Theorizing Transitional Justice. In *Transitional Justice. NOMOS LI. Yearbook of the American Society for Political and Legal Philosophy.* New York: New York University Press, pp. 31–77.

Dirección para la Acción Integral contra Minas Antipersonal, 2015. *Víctimas de Minas Antipersonal.* [Online] Available at: www.accioncontraminas.gov.co/estadisticas/Paginas/victimas-minas-antipersonal.aspx [Last accessed 25 October 2015].

Fischer, M., 2011. Transitional Justice and Reconciliation: Theory and Practice. InH. J. Giessmann, B. Austin & M. Fischer, eds. *Advancing Conflict Transformation: The Berghof Handbook II Edition.* s.l.: Opladen/Farmington Hills: Barbara Budrich Publishers, pp. 406–424.

Gobierno de Colombia y FARC—EP, 2016. *Final Agreement to End the Armed Conflict and Build a Stable and Lasting Peace.* [Online] Available at: www.altocomisionadoparalapaz.gov.co/procesos-y-conversaciones/proceso-de-paz-con-las-farc-ep/documentos-y-comunicados-conjuntos/Documents/comunicado-conjunto-60-23-septiembre-2015.pdf [Last accessed 20 June 2017].

Gobierno de Colombia, 2011. *Ley de Victimas y Restitucion de Tierras.* [Online] Available at: www.centrodememoriahistorica.gov.co/descargas/ley_victimas/ley_victimas_completa_web.pdf [Last accessed 20 June 2017].

Hirblinger, A., 2017. *Preventing Violent Conflict through Community-based Indicators.* Caux: Inclusive Peace and Transition Initiative.

Kostic, R., 2012. Transitional justice and reconciliation in Bosnia-Herzegovina. Whose memories, whose justice? *Sociologija*, 54(4), pp. 649–666.

Lederach, J. P., 1997. *Building Peace: Sustainable Reconciliation in Divided Societies.* Washington, DC: United States Institute for Peace Press.

Loyle, C. E. & Davenport, C., 2016. Transitional Injustice: Subverting Justice in Transition and Postconflict Societies. *Journal of Human Rights*, 15(1), pp. 1–24.

Mac Ginty, R. & Polanska, M., 2015. When the Local Meets the International. *Global Trends: Prospects for World Society*, pp. 193–208. [Online] Available at: www.global-trends.info/fileadmin/Globale-Trends/beitraege_kapitel/gt-2015_en.pdf [Last accessed 24 January 2018].

Mendeloff, D., 2004. Truth-Seeking, Truth-Telling, and Postconflict Peacebuilding: Curb the Enthusiasm? *International Studies Review*, 6(3), pp. 355–380.

Obradović-Wochnik, J., 2013. Silent dilemma of transitional justice: silencing and coming to terms with the past in Serbia. *International Journal of Transitional Justice*, pp. 1–20.

Skaar, E., 2013. Reconciliation in a transitional justice perspective. *Transitional Justice Review* 1(1), pp. 2–50.

Sriram, C. L., 2010. Beyond conflicts and pursuing accountability: beyond justice versus peace. In O. Richmond, ed. *Palgrave Advances in Peacebuilding: Critical developments and approaches.* Basingstoke: Palgrave Macmillan, pp. 279–293.

Teitel, R. G., 2000. *Transitional Justice.* Oxford: Oxford University Press on Demand.

Verdad Abierta, 2014. *Victimas en La Habana: los que fueron y los que faltaron.* [Online] Available at: www.verdadabierta.com/procesos-de-paz/farc/5555-victimas-en-la-habana-los-que-fueron-y-los-que-faltaron [Last accessed 27 September 2017].

Part I
The Quest for Peace

2 Conflict and peace in the making
Colombia from 1948–2010[1]

Fabio Andrés Díaz Pabón

Introduction

This chapter discusses the evolution of the Colombian conflict and the existence of peacebuilding initiatives with different groups as part of the process of consolidation of statehood in Colombia since 1948. Both war and attempts at peace-making in Colombia have coexisted since 1948 (Palacios, 2012).

To understand the coexistence of peace initiatives and the active pursuit of violence in Colombia, we need to understand the violence beyond the broad narrative that the Colombian armed conflict is essentially a fight between the Fuerzas Armadas Revolucionarias de Colombia—Ejército del Pueblo (FARC—EP)[2] and the Colombian state. Various groups with different agendas overlap in each of the different provinces of Colombia, making this understanding imprecise. Colombia is a country in which different armed groups have exerted violence in the same territory: paramilitaries, Ejército de Liberación Nacional (ELN)[3], Ejército Popular de Liberación (EPL)[4], Bandas Criminales (BACRIM)[5], Autodefensas Gaitanistas de Colombia (AGC)[6], organized armed groups, and drug traffickers are some of the labels used to describe some of the organizations still operating in the country alongside the FARC—EP dissidents.

Thus broader understanding is necessary to reconsider accounts that depict the violence which has taken place in Colombia since 1948 as solely FARC—EP related. Several violent conflicts, peace attempts, and agreements have taken place with other groups in the last five decades (López Hernández, 2016). Colombia has signed at least nine peace agreements with different groups since the 1980s. This has all taken place while violence was ongoing in the country (López Hernández, 2016; Palacios, 2012).

Recent scholarship on the Colombian conflict presents a more nuanced description of the violence in Colombia and an understanding of the 'greyscales' that enable the mix of illicit crops, drug trafficking, state weakness, guerrilla groups, peace processes, peace agreements, and the prevalence of violence and warlordism to emerge almost simultaneously in the same territory (Romero, 2003; Duncan, 2006; González González, 2014).

The emergence of the FARC—EP could be defined as the outcome of the transformation of a particular self-defence force. In fact, it can be argued that some of the founding FARC—EP members were victims of the 'political' violence in Colombia between 1920 and 1950 (Sánchez Gómez, 1988). In a way, the FARC—EP is the offspring of the failure by the state to deliver justice to all their citizens and its incapacity to achieve a monopoly of violence in the country (Comisión Histórica del Conflicto y sus Víctimas, 2015; Corporación Observatorio para la Paz, 2009; Aguilera, 2014). Other authors argue that the dynamics of violence that co-created the FARC—EP were actually a continuation of the existing partisan violence before 1948 (Meertens & Sánchez, 1983; Molano, 1994). The birth and the origins of the FARC—EP are a matter of academic debate; the fourteen different accounts of the origin of the conflict in Colombia presented by the historical commission of the conflict of Colombia are proof of this (Comisión Histórica del Conflicto y sus Víctimas, 2015).

The state has sought to end the violence either by negotiation or by military defeat both before and after the emergence of the FARC—EP. However, these attempts to consolidate the power of the state have been obstructed by some sectors that have benefited from the conflict at a national or local level, thus fuelling the violence. The tension between war and peace is a constant of modern Colombian history (Palacios, 2003; Gutiérrez Sanín, 2014).

This chapter presents a brief summary of the Colombian conflict, and of previous peace processes that took place in the country after 1948. The history of Colombia and its violence is analysed considering the peace negotiations, peace attempts, military offensives, and the demobilization initiatives that involved multiple armed groups during the tenure of successive governments in the country between 1948 and 2010.

This interval can be characterized as comprising two main periods: 1948 to 1991, and 1991 to 2010. The initial period of 1948–1991 can be considered as that of the emergence of the modern form of violence in Colombia: the period begins in 1948 with violent initiatives throughout the country following the assassination of Jorge Eliécer Gaitán and ends with the establishment of a new political covenant in the 1991 Constitution. The period of 1991 to 2010 can be considered a period of transformation, between the enactment of the new constitution and the 2012–2016 peace process with FARC—EP (see Chapter 3). The 1991–2010 period saw multiple peace processes and several demobilizations. At the same time, counter-responses by armed actors and local élites against the democratic openings of the 1991 Constitution and the peace agreements signed in this period were observed.

The emergence of left-wing guerrillas and the 1991 Colombian Constitution

The emergence of violence in modern Colombia saw its inception in the period known as 'La Violencia' (the violence), a wave of inter-party violence

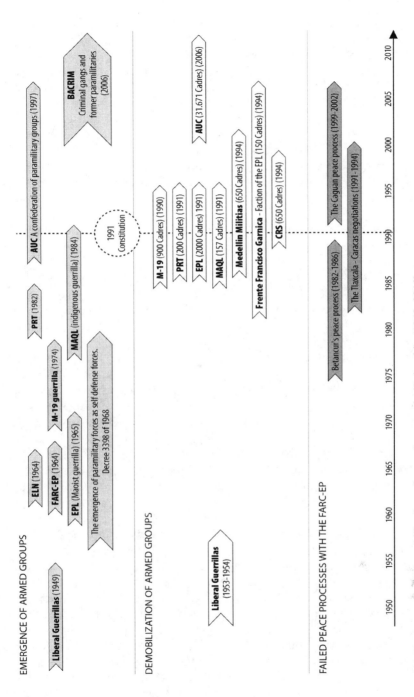

Figure 2.1 Emergence and demobilization of armed groups in Colombia (1948–2010)
Source: Own elaboration.

between 1948 and 1958 in which almost 2% of the population of the country was assassinated (Palacios, 2003). This process led to the rise of multiple liberal guerrilla groups and armed right-wing groups.

The period between the emergence of the guerrillas and the passing of the 1991 Constitution can be understood as having three main phases. Between 1948 and 1964 bipartisan violence transmuted into a rural war and gave rise to the left-leaning guerrilla movements that are still in existence today. The period between 1964 and 1982 was marked by the first attempt by the state to defeat the left-wing guerrillas militarily, some overtures towards negotiation processes which failed, the end of the National Front duopoly, and the Government of Julio César Turbay Ayala (1978–1982) and its counter-insurgency policy. Finally, the period between 1982 and 1991 is characterized by the emergence of the state's first official attempt to negotiate a peace deal with FARC—EP and other guerrilla groups: this met with a degree of success while failing in other respects. The period ended with the drafting of the 1991 Constitution.

From 'the violence' to the emergence of a rural war: 1948–1964

As a response to La Violencia, several armed groups (which lacked any centralized or structured organization) proliferated across the countryside; against a background of increasingly violent clashes, the '*pájaros*' (Conservatives) and guerrillas (Liberals) emerged as 'self-defence' groups (Palacios, 2003). Violence took a stronger partisan line after the election of President Mariano Ospina Pérez (1946–1950), and was expressed in the recurrence of pogroms by Conservatives on Liberals and their reprisals, and in calls by Catholic priests across the country for their congregations to support the Conservative Party, condoning violence against Liberals from their pulpits, and in some cases participating actively in that violence. Not only had the Government sought a political cleansing of their opponents from the state bureaucracy, but the state also turned a blind eye when violence targeted Liberals (Meertens & Sánchez, 1983). This practice continued and escalated during the government of Laureano Gómez (1950–53) whose incendiary rhetoric brought the country closer to a civil war (Palacios, 2012). The irresponsibility of the Government and its authoritarian actions triggered a peaceful *coup d'état* and ushered in a military regime promoted by politicians from both parties who wanted to stop the civil war (Palacios, 2003).

The assumption of the presidency by Gen. Gustavo Rojas Pinilla in June 1953, at the head of a military administration, brought the offer of an armistice to the liberal guerrillas, and the promise of both peace and the monopoly of violence within the country. The military regime promised to be a neutral holder of the monopoly of violence, as other institutions—such as the police—were seen as biased by significant segments of the population. The promise of peace came in the form of an amnesty that was to be warranted by the military rule, taking place between 1953 and 1958. Indeed, both the Pinilla Government, and the military junta that followed (after the *coup d'etat* of 1957 that ousted Pinilla) managed to demobilize several of the liberal guerrilla groups (Meertens & Sánchez, 1983; López Hernández, 2016).

After 1958, a bipartisan duopoly called the National Front (which was to last until 1974) emerged as a solution to the violence, which both traditional political parties had employed as a means to achieve political power. Under the arrangement, both parties were to participate in government alternately. Violence was greatly reduced under the National Front, but this political agreement between the Conservatives and the Liberals failed to allow for the entrance of new political parties into the system, or to guarantee the safety of citizens beyond the bipartisan violence (Molano, 1994). It also overlooked the violence to which some of the demobilized liberal guerrillas were subjected, which led to the belief that the state would not honour agreements and the promise of peace for former fighters, and that peace would not be warranted by the state (Meertens & Sánchez, 1983).

In the meantime, the Cold War winds were blowing: the Cuban Revolution and the fear of the spread of communism across Latin America also influenced Colombian politicians and their fears. It was feared that the remaining self-defence groups that had not demobilized were liable to become instruments of socialist interests and act as the seeds of a Cuban-style revolution in Colombia (Pizarro Leongómez, 2011). In the Colombian Congress there was a strong partisan debate about the prevalence of some groups bearing arms, and whether and how they constituted a threat for the Colombian state. In fact Senator Álvaro Gómez claimed at the time that areas such as Marquetalia (where one of the peasant self-defence forces was located) constituted an affront to state sovereignty and were in fact 'independent republics' (Gutiérrez García & Marín Suárez, 2013). As a consequence, the Government decided to act to abort the possibility of a left-wing guerrilla force emerging in the country. A military campaign unfolded in 1964 to some degree of tactical success, uprooting existing groups identified as potential seeds of communist revolution in Colombia. However, the campaign failed strategically, as it in fact accelerated the birth of the Marxist guerrilla movement, radicalized other organizations, and informed a narrative of a repressive state that was not to be trusted.

From the birth of the guerrilla movements to the end of the security statute: 1964–1982

The late 1960s and the decade which followed were dominated by the military response of the Colombian Government to the rise of 'new' armed groups and the transformation of old groups; this period also saw the entrance of new elements that further complicated the Colombian conflict: drug trafficking and paramilitary forces.

As early as 1965, the government of León Valencia (1962–1966), recognizing the challenges of controlling the totality of the Colombian territory and informed by fears of the spread of communism, issued Decree 3398, which established a legal framework to support the creation of self-defence groups that could be armed in order to defend the state against the feared guerrillas and spread of communism in the country (Meertens & Sánchez, 1983; Palacios, 2012). During this period there were no formal peace offers from or to any guerrilla groups, and initial attempts to tackle the guerrillas were mediated by military operations. Different governments took different approaches. The administration of Carlos Lleras Restrepo (1966–1970), for example, passed Law 48 of 1968, which defined the legal framework for the consolidation of self-defence forces, and pursued a military approach to combating armed groups. The latter policy was continued by the government of Misael Pastrana Borrero (1970–74), and included military operations such as Operation Anorí in 1973, in which the ELN was nearly destroyed. The objective of the state was to reclaim the monopoly of violence in the territory through force.

Yet, in this period, more armed groups were born: the EPL in 1965 and the Movimiento 19 de Abril (M-19) in 1974 (Palacios, 2012). The EPL was of Maoist origin and emerged as the radicalization of some members of the Colombian Communist Party, following debates around the Sino-Soviet split (Vargas Velásquez, 2000). The M-19 took its name from the date of the allegedly fraudulent presidential elections of 1970.[7]

Meanwhile, drug trafficking was becoming established within Colombian society, as the permissive stance of some political leaders allowed for an influx of money from drug trafficking into the economy and political system, and the legalization of drug lords' incomes (Pécaut, 2013). During this period (1974–1982) private self-defence groups (some of them the same self-defence forces created during the 1960s) merged their hatred of guerrilla groups with the funding from drug traffickers, large landowners, cattle growers and emerald traders—creating the seeds of a future 'paramilitarism' in the country (Gutiérrez Sanín & Barón, 2005).

The governments of the 1960s established a legal framework that allowed for the emergence of counter-insurgency self-defence forces.[8] In contrast, the 1970s brought increased confusion around the legal regulation of these forces. The absence of the state monopoly of violence, conjoined with the interests of drug traffickers and local élites, allowed for different groups to project their own military force in different parts of the country (García-Peña Jaramillo, 2005; Romero & Valencia, 2007). In some respects the Colombian state turned a blind eye, as the armed forces saw these groups as allies in their fight against the guerrillas (Ronderos, 2014). The government of Alfonso López Michelsen (1974–78) made attempts to start peace negotiations with the ELN, but failed to start a formal process.

President Turbay (1978–1982) was elected toward the end of the decade, and established the highly repressive 'security statute', under which the Government adopted a militarized response to the rise of guerrilla groups. This response commonly included human right abuses, torture, and disappearances across the country (Ramírez Bacca & Marín Arenas, 2015). Interestingly, in addition to a martial approach, the Turbay Government attempted the start of a negotiation process with the FARC—EP in 1981; however this process failed to formalize.

From martial law to peace and the promise of a social covenant: 1982–1991

In 1982 the newly-elected government of Belisario Betancur Cuartas (1982–1986) led a fresh attempt to build a peace process with the guerrilla forces, but encountered a series of obstacles related to the growth of paramilitaries and drug trafficking within the country. In facing this challenge, the Betancur Government adopted a different approach to solving the violence in Colombia. During this period, the state considered a new peace process with the guerrillas. While peace processes were previously understood as processes of amnesties, or demobilizations, no formal peace negotiations had previously been undertaken with the left-wing guerrillas. The infrastructure and the institutions for peace started to be built in this period.

The Government's first attempt at a peace process with the FARC-EP was expressed in the La Uribe agreements signed in 1984.[9] A ceasefire was also agreed with the EPL, the Movimiento de Autodefensa Obrera (ADO)[10] and the M-19.[11] The agreements were weak in their implementation, as the state lacked either the experience or the capacity to verify, arbitrate, and implement the agreements. However, they allowed for the emergence of the Union Patriótica (UP)[12] party and the introduction of the political expression of the FARC—EP's agenda into mainstream politics. Despite the promise offered by the agreements, the Government argued that the FARC—EP used the ceasefire they established to grow militarily. At the same time, the armed forces did not honour the ceasefire, and members of the UP were massacred in face of the indifference of state institutions (Palacios, 2012). Trust was not established, thus processes were not successful.

In the 1980s the country also found itself fighting not only guerrillas, but also drug traffickers. In 1979 the Turbay Government signed a Treaty of Extradition with the USA, permitting that country to extradite Colombians indicted in US courts.[13] Following this, increased pressure from the US Government, and the 'war on drugs' paradigm it pursued, led in turn to greater pressure being placed on drug cartels by the Colombian Government in the 1980s. This in turn unleashed a violent response from these groups (Matthiesen, 2000). This new battlefront for the state was evidenced by the assassination of the Justice Minister, Lara Bonilla, in 1984, and the perception that the state was besieged by this violence was highlighted by the 1985 attack by the M-19 guerrillas on the Palace of Justice in Bogotá (where Colombia's Supreme Court was based).

The administration of Virgilio Barco Vargas (1986–1990) continued the efforts for peace, notably with the M-19 group (most of these meetings were secret, and were not official), while the UP gained ground politically, winning several posts in municipalities and some seats in the Senate and the Congress

(Cepeda, 2006). In 1988, the M-19 kidnapping of the leader of the Conservative Party (the son of former President Gómez) mobilized political support and public opinion in favour of a peace process. The inclusion of the Movimiento Armado Quintín Lame (MAQL)[14], the EPL, the Partido Revolucionario de Trabajadores de Colombia (PRT)[15], the Corriente de Renovación Socialista (CRS—a faction of the ELN)[16], and the Comandos Ernesto Rojas in different peace processes contributed to a broader (yet incomplete) national peace process. This process still failed to include the ELN and the FARC—EP.

Yet, the signing of these agreements, as well as the peace agreements with the M-19, signalled the possibility of peace in the 1990s. The electoral campaign for the presidential election in the 1990s reflected a state that was trying to attain peace and change, but was under siege from different actors. The assassination of three presidential candidates (Galán of the Liberal Party, Jaramillo of the UP, and Pizarro of M-19) showed that instability and continued conflict was desirable for some groups such as paramilitaries, drug traffickers and even some members of the establishment.

The progress towards peace and the creation of an initial institutional framework for peace during this period culminated in a reform that changed the outdated constitution of 1886, the 1991 Constitution (Cárdenas et al., 2006; Banks & Alvarez, 1991; Uprimny, 2003). Facilitated by the peace process, the 1991 Constitution served to provide a framework which allowed, among other things, the recognition of the rights and entitlements of indigenous and Afro-descendant communities, the creation of mechanisms for political participation and the reassertion of a multi-party democracy.

The 'end of history': the 1990s, 9/11 and Uribe

Many considered that an encompassing and ambitious constitution would finally afford space for a stronger social covenant in Colombia, and while the FARC—EP and the ELN were not part of the 1991 constitutional assembly process, the promise of a more open state and the possibility of peace were tangible. In addition, international developments such as the collapse of the Soviet Union and the promise of the 'end of history' brought dramatic transitions that could support peace in Colombia (Fukuyama, 1989).

However, hopes for the consolidation of peace in Colombia were countered by the response of right-wing groups and politicians against the 1991 Constitution; the encroachment of illicit drugs as the fuel for the Colombian conflict, which allowed left-wing armed groups to survive the demise of the Soviet Union and escalate confrontations;[17] and a series of unexpected consequences of democratization in the country, such as the co-optation of political posts across the territory by paramilitaries (López Hernández & Ávila Martínez, 2010; Gutiérrez Sanín, 2014).

This period saw two formal attempts to achieve peace with the FARC—EP: one during the administration of César Gaviria Trujillo (1990–1994), and another during that of Andrés Pastrana Arango (1998–2002). Thereafter, the successive administrations headed by Álvaro Uribe (2002–2006 and 2006–2010) pursued a military approach towards peace with the guerrillas.

From hope to the emergence of the FARC—EP as an electoral force: 1991–98

Following the signing of the new constitution in 1991, and given that some groups demobilized successfully, the government decided to increase pressure on other guerrillas to force them to negotiate. The government therefore attacked former safe havens of the guerrillas that had not accepted its offers of a peace process (Corporación Observatorio para la Paz, 2009). However, the effects of this strategy appeared to be limited.

Whereas the peace processes at the beginning of the 1990s facilitated the demobilization of several guerrilla groups (notably the M-19, the MAQL, the CRS and the EPL), the outcomes of these processes were not homogeneous: the paths of the cadres of these organizations varied after their demobilization. The M-19, MAQL, and the CRS cadres followed a largely successful reinsertion process. In contrast, the EPL and several of its cadres returned to warfare to feed the ranks of paramilitary groups.

Several elements explain the recidivism of the EPL cadres in comparison with the other groups who demobilized in the early 1990s. Among these were the lack of options for demobilized cadres, the weak institutional capacity of the demobilized groups to undertake initiatives for their cadres, and the incapacity of the state to provide security for demobilized cadres. In the case of the EPL the most notable factor was the terror campaign unleashed by the FARC—EP[18] that saw demobilized EPL cadres as either traitors or competitors for the political control of the provinces of Urabá and Córdoba. The assassination of hundreds of former EPL cadres between 1991 and 1995 by the FARC—EP (Comisión Interamericana de Derechos Humanos, 1999)[19] pushed former EPL cadres to join other armed groups, and inflamed the violence in these provinces.

As noted, the policy of the Gaviria Government was not solely military; it also attempted a joint peace process with the ELN and the FARC—EP, with negotiations taking place in Venezuela and Mexico. The initial approaches managed to define a ten-point agenda, and a series of preliminary agreements, including agreement on mechanisms for verification (one of the weaknesses of the previous peace process). These negotiations were overshadowed by the doubt (or lack of commitment) by the FARC—EP regarding the possibility of reaching an agreement and a peace process. The negotiations broke down after the kidnapping of a former minister by the EPL and his subsequent death in captivity.

With the arrival of the government of Samper (1994–98), the focus of the state and the military forces was dispersed by the internal crises of legitimacy of the presidential figure within the country. As the president's campaign received money from drug traffickers to support his presidential bid (El

Espectador, 2016), Samper lost credibility and legitimacy both inside and outside the country. The involvement of drug money in financing the victory of Samper added to the prevalent challenge of drug trafficking and production, and the existence of armed contenders continued to challenge the state's monopoly of violence. As a result, the armed forces distrusted the government because of the role of drug money in his election. This allowed the FARC—EP and paramilitaries to expand thanks to the resources they accrued from illicit crops and illicit drugs, and their taxation. Hence there was significant growth of the FARC—EP and the paramilitaries during this period (Duncan, 2006; Pécaut, 2008).

The weakness of the state and the strength of contesting armed groups was evident in the increase in the extent and intensity of military operations undertaken by the FARC—EP. The military offensive of the FARC—EP led the government to abandon several military outposts, which reduced the military presence in several areas of the country (Palacios, 2012). Hundreds of soldiers were lost on the battlefield, and hundreds more kidnapped by the FARC—EP.

The strength of paramilitary forces also increased during this period. While paramilitaries developed an institutional framework in the late 1960s, their greater encroachment into the Colombian conflict was facilitated by Law 356 of 1994, which normalized the possibility of the privatization of security by different actors (which was termed *convivir* [20]) in those areas of the country where security was precarious.[21] This growth of paramilitary activity was facilitated by existing institutional links between paramilitary forces and regional élites who shared common goals related to counterinsurgency warfare, creating a symbiosis between paramilitary groups and some regional leaders across the country (Gutiérrez Sanín, 2014).

In addition to this process, there was a resurgence of the violent response by élites to the democratization process of the 1991 Constitution. The repressive and violent backlash against democratic overtures by actors that do not want to lose their privileges in a context of violence became a characteristic feature of the Colombian State, which explains why democratic openings in Colombia have been frequently been followed by violence and repression (Gutiérrez Sanín, 2014).

Paramilitaries took advantage of the vulnerability of city-based Colombians, who felt cornered by the guerrillas in the face of the weakness of the Colombian armed forces. They gained public support and political credibility beyond the regions where they had influence through a successful advocacy and media campaign (Ronderos, 2014). However, by 1997, when the Constitutional Court of Colombia declared the law that rendered the creation of the *convivir* organizations unconstitutional, the damage was already done. Their growth, expansion, and co-optation of local institutions had already taken place, furthering the entry points for private armed groups formed in the 1980s into the state apparatus (Romero & Valencia, 2007).

This period (1991–98) also saw a reconfiguration within armed groups. After 1997 the different paramilitary groups affiliated under the Autodefensas

Unidas de Colombia (AUC)[22]. Their members (paramilitaries and drug cartels) used their private armies as part of their economic and political strategies in different parts of the country (Llorente & Deas, 1999). Their affiliation presented a more homogeneous façade and enabled them to communicate a more coherent discourse beyond their illegal activities.

In this context, the Samper Government decided to negotiate with the guerrillas to release kidnapped soldiers and police officers. This was not a peace process, but a prisoner release/exchange.

In the presidential elections of 1998, the candidate elected by Colombians was the one who appeared to be the closest to starting a negotiation process with the FARC—EP. This made the FARC—EP and the debates around their existence central to Colombian politics, transforming the FARC—EP into a deciding factor in the next elections.

Elections, war and peace: 1998–2002

President Pastrana was elected with a strong public mandate to achieve peace with the guerrillas (Pastrana Arango, 2013). A new peace negotiation with the FARC—EP began in 1999 and ended in 2002. This failed. Contrary to what might be assumed, this was not related to international political dynamics and the terrorist attacks of 11 September 2001 in the USA, but rather it was determined by the internal dynamics of the process.

From the outset, the peace process was laden with problems regarding the nature and the structure of the negotiation itself. As the negotiations were held without a ceasefire, every military action by the guerrillas undermined the credibility of the process (Corporación Observatorio para la Paz, 2009). Colombians could not cope with the dissonance of peace conversations while military actions were taking place.

There were also paradigmatic differences between the actors at the negotiation table, as well as different time frames and logics that clashed. For the Government, the peace process was conceived in terms of fulfilling the mandate given to Pastrana by Colombians, whereas for the FARC—EP, the peace process was taken as proof of their strength, evident from their bringing the state to a negotiation table through sheer force. Both actors sought to achieve peace, but their logics around peace and envisioned endgames were completely different.

A series of additional elements complicated the negotiations. One of these was the existence of a demilitarized zone as the size of Switzerland that the FARC—EP used as a tactical 'safe haven'. As noted, FARC—EP kidnappings of civilians, and constant attacks on police stations and military bases across the country, led many to regard the peace negotiations as dissonant with the actions of the FARC—EP. During this period the paramilitary forces continued an aggressive political and military campaign, exploiting the public sentiment against the FARC—EP (Bonilla, 2012). The campaign depicted the paramilitaries as defenders of the rule of law and the state, while their military actions resulted in massacres and, as the consequence of the clashes to dislocate the guerrillas from several areas in the country, caused forced displacement to spike.

The peace process was mired in its preliminary stages. The mere definition of a negotiation agenda was troublesome, demonstrating a lack of either commitment or knowledge of the management of a negotiation process. For example, in the three years of negotiations the parties failed to establish a verification commission, or determine a friendly third party to solve disputes in the process (Palacios, 2012).

For many Colombians, these years are remembered as years under siege. This sense, and the successful media campaign deployed by paramilitaries, increased the existing public sympathy toward the paramilitaries among some sectors of the Colombian élites, following the logic that 'the enemy of my enemy is my friend' (Ronderos, 2014). During this period, paramilitaries managed to influence and co-opt several political posts across the country, consolidating their power and encroaching themselves into the Colombian political system.

This was an unexpected outcome of the 1991 Constitution. The constitution provided for decentralization in order to allow representation to inform public policy. However, the co-optation and manipulation of local, regional, and national politics by power players with weapons and money from drug trafficking was not anticipated (López Hernández & Ávila Martínez, 2010; Gutiérrez Sanín, 2014).

This peace process came to an end when the FARC—EP hijacked a commercial airplane and kidnapped a member of Congress who was aboard. However, in spite of the fact that the FARC—EP was seen as an enemy by society, its influence on the next electoral campaign remained central. Politicians focused on the ideas of war and peace, and sought ways to appear supportive of peace but tough on the FARC—EP. Uribe came to power by giving voice to the frustration of Colombians towards the FARC—EP.

All-out war and peace: 2002–2010

From the beginning of the 2002 presidential campaign, Uribe adopted the approach of former president López Michelsen of the early 1980s—that the guerrillas had to be obliged, by force, to negotiate. This was not a new strategy and was reminiscent of the approach undertaken by the administrations of Turbay, Barco, and Gaviria.

The Uribe Government's approach to solving the conflict differed greatly from the unpopular peace process of its predecessor. The Uribe Government became involved in another peace process—not with left-wing forces, but with the paramilitaries (Pardo Rueda, 2007). This peace process, which was undertaken between the Colombian Government and the AUC, involved a demilitarized zone and an ill-defined ceasefire, and managed to garner the support of the Organization of American States (OAS). The process has been widely criticized, however, its implementation created a series of institutions and structures related to demobilization, disarmament, and reintegration (DDR), as well as the first modern attempt in Colombia to establish a transitional justice framework.

The new Government improved several security indicators as a result of the de-escalation of confrontations with the paramilitaries, and the tactical retreat by guerrillas to the fringes of the state in response to the latter's military offensive. Expressed under Uribe, the capacity of the state to reassert its military might is partially the legacy of the 'Plan Colombia' campaign pursued by the Pastrana Government.

It is ironic that the improved security indicators in this period were achieved while the number of internally displaced Colombians skyrocketed (Ibáñez Londoño, 2011). Security might have improved for some, but not for all Colombians. By the end of Uribe's first term the failures of the peace process with the paramilitaries emerged (Pardo Rueda, 2007). In addition, and thanks to the legal framework that instituted a transitional justice framework as part of the peace process with the paramilitaries, the denunciation of the alliances between paramilitaries and politicians started to become visible. A standing symbol of the reach and the connivance between paramilitaries and a sector of the political establishment in these years is the standing ovation that the leaders of the paramilitary received in the Colombian capital Bogotá in 2004. At that time, paramilitaries claimed to have influence over some 30% of the Colombian Congress (López Hernández & Ávila Martínez, 2010).

One could argue that, in fact, one of the lessons of the Uribe Government was the acknowledgment by some sectors of Colombian society of the costs for human rights and democracy incurred in pursuit of an all-out war strategy. The international community and local organizations began to criticize the human rights violations taking place within the country as a product of the military campaign. At the same time, the failures of the peace process with the paramilitaries became evident. New 'paramilitary' groups, now labelled 'emergent bands', appeared in the locations of former paramilitary groups, recycling their repertoires and capacities almost perfectly. As the guerrillas retreated, the paramilitaries and their offshoots expanded.

In spite of this, the increased perception of security across the country enabled Uribe to be easily re-elected for a second term in 2006. He achieved this after modifying the 1991 Constitution to enable presidential re-election. However, the extension of his political mandate started to compromise the separation of powers between the legislative, the executive, and the judiciary in Colombia, as the 1991 Constitution did not include checks and balances in the case of re-elections.

Uribe continued his security policy in his second term. The government facilitated a discourse whereby the members of armed groups were referred to as terrorists, and Uribe was able to ostracize his political opponents by labelling them as supporters of terrorist groups (Tickner & Pardo, 2003;

López de la Roche, 2014). Simultaneously, a nationalist discourse emerged, and the glorification of armed forces was common. Advertisements appeared in television, radio and printed media, which touted the victories of war and military operations, and the possibility of winning the war was latent in media coverage. This world view was bolstered by strategic victories, such as the killing of the FARC—EP's military commander and its 'Chancellor', as well as military operations which resulted in the liberation of several people who had been kidnapped by the FARC—EP. These operations became useful propaganda instruments for the Government to show its successes. The nationalist, almost chauvinist, environment made opposition to the government extremely difficult (López de la Roche, 2014).

The effective propaganda, and the marginalization of opposition, masked worrying signs. The assassination of civilians, later claimed to be guerrillas or paramilitaries, by members of the armed forces showed the risks of an all-out war to institutions: between 2002 and 2008 around 4,000 civilians were murdered by the armed forces and then later presented as guerrillas or paramilitaries (Human Rights Watch, 2015). These events came to be known in Colombia as the *falsos positivos* (false positives). The Government put pressure on the military forces to demonstrate results under an incentive system that equated success with the number of casualties caused to the different illegal groups. The system of rewarding those military units that achieved higher casualties against the guerrillas or the paramilitaries[23] caused some military units in different regions of the country to resort to the assassination of civilians in the search for rewards and promotions.

In addition to this, accusations of nepotism and corruption came to surround the Uribe Government, which nevertheless attempted to modify the constitution once again to support Uribe's serving a third term. The attempt was aborted by the Colombian Constitutional Court, which ruled that a second consecutive re-election was against the Colombian Constitution. Still, a securitization policy and the continuation of the Uribe administration's approach proved important for Colombian citizens, since Uribe's Minister of Defence, Juan Manuel Santos, was elected as President under the expectation that he would maintain the approach initiated by Uribe. Once again the existence of the FARC—EP defined the campaign and the selection of the incumbent into the Colombian presidency.

The quest for peace: The Colombian state and its history

As seen above, the history of Colombia can be described as a country at odds with itself. Attempts at reaching peace with different armed groups have been a constant element in the history of the country for the last 70 years. For the last four decades the state and its institutions have sought to end the conflict in Colombia by either force or negotiation. The multiple peace processes and formal and attempted negotiations involving different guerrillas and paramilitary groups across the country are proof of these attempts. Despite different governments having managed to sign peace agreements with several organizations, and to demobilize a considerable number of fighters, a great paradox emerges: peace agreements have not been enough to stop the emergence and continuity of armed organizations within the Colombian state. The continuation of war and violence in Colombia has been facilitated by the incentives of illegal drug trafficking, the multiplicity of armed actors and interests in different territories, the difficulty faced by the state in operating at the fringes of its territory, and the challenge of consolidating a national covenant able to incorporate and embrace different local elites as part of a national project.

The Colombian democracy—the longest-running in Latin America—is belied by many features not typically associated with democracy: more than 7m. citizens becoming internally displaced persons (IDPs) as a result of the violence, giving it the highest IDP population of any country in the world as of 2017 (UNHCR, 2017); nearly 1m. assassinations since 1985 (Unidad para las Victimas, 2017); the death of more than 50,000 combatants; the closure of political opportunities to political parties not aligned with the liberal or conservative élites; the assassination of blossoming political parties; the assassination of three presidential candidates in a single presidential campaign; and the stifling of dissent that opposed either radicals, the Government, or local élites (Gutiérrez Sanín, 2014). This is part of the political economy of Colombia that can be illustrated by its history. Colombia is a case study that challenges the categories or conceptions of what a democracy is and how it should operate (Gutiérrez Sanín, 2014).

Between 1948 and 2010 the Colombian democracy saw several efforts undertaken in the search for peace. Different Colombian governments have pursued peace. This quest, as well as the resilience of violence, has prevailed across time and been illustrated by the failures of previous attempts at peace with the FARC—EP and other groups. The peace negotiation with the FARC—EP that started in 2012 can thus be seen as the continuation of the history of successes and failures of the Colombian state in the search for peace. Its emergence is the outcome of a process in the making for four decades, which resulted in a mutually damaging stalemate between the warring parties and an interest by the élites of both the FARC—EP and the Colombian Government in undertaking a negotiation. This created the space and conditions for the negotiation between the Santos Government, and the FARC—EP between 2012 and 2016 (see Chapter 3).

Although the FARC—EP is recognized as the biggest armed organization challenging the power of the state, the demobilization of cadres from the FARC—EP will not mean that all the violence in Colombia will disappear overnight. Paramilitary groups, drug traffickers, and other armed groups will present challenges to the success of the 2016 peace agreement and to the state's ability to assert its monopoly of force in the country. The peace process with the FARC—EP has meant that the state has greater flexibility to allocate its resources against the remaining armed organizations, so it may oblige them to submit to the state, or to facilitate a negotiation/surrendering process. However, this will require the state to establish government functions in those places where armed groups prevailed in the past, which may prove a challenge to state capacity. The provision of justice and other public services is necessary if the state is to take the opportunity to contest these other organizations and realize its sovereignty.

Notes

1. The author would like to express his gratitude towards Francisco Gutiérrez Sanín for his help in the development of this chapter. His contributions to previous versions of this document and his insights for the development of the text were invaluable.
2. Revolutionary Armed Forces of Colombia—People's Army.
3. National Liberation Army.
4. Popular Liberation Army.
5. After the peace process with paramilitaries in the early 2000s the Government proscribed the used of the word paramilitary and started to use the acronym of BACRIM (criminal organizations) to designate organizations that were formerly described as paramilitaries.
6. Gaitanist Self-defence Forces of Colombia.
7. In which the former military dictator Rojas Pinilla lost the election to the Conservative candidate, Misael Patrana.
8. By means of Decree 3398 of 1965 and Law 48 of 1968.
9. The Uribe agreements should not be confused with the surname of former president Uribe (2002–2010). These agreements were signed on 24 March 1984 in the municipality of La Uribe (Meta province). The agreements provided for a ceasefire, and a procedure that would allow the transition of the FARC—EP into civilian life, a series of development initiatives in areas affected by violence, as well as an official statement of commitment from the state to combating paramilitarism.
10. Labour Self Defence Movement.
11. On 24 August 1984 in Corinto (Cauca province) and El Hobo (Huila province), a ceasefire was signed in order to facilitate the discussion around the reforms that would help to constitute a future peace process.
12. Patriotic Union.
13. Agreement ratified by Law 27 of 1980.
14. Quintin Lame Armed Movement.
15. Revolutionary Workers' Party of Colombia.
16. Socialist Renovation Stream. This was a faction of the ELN which considered that the armed struggle was no longer viable and opted for political contestation versus the state.
17. Some argue, however, that before this time, the left- wing guerrillas were not actually dependent on financial or logistical support from the USSR.
18. A sub-group of the ELN and a dissident faction from the demobilized EPL also took part in this campaign.
19. This included several massacres, such as those that took place in Filipinas, Las Moras, San Rafael, La Lolita and La Chinita.
20. Coexistence or cohabitation, in English.
21. During this period at least 529 rural cooperatives were created in 24 provinces within the country, which involved at least 15,300 citizens (Verdad Abierta, 2013).
22. The United Self-Defence Forces of Colombia was a 'federal' organization of right-wing groups that in some cases included landlords, industrialists and cattle farmers

looking to defend themselves from the guerrillas; in other cases it involved groups operating at the borders of legality, such as the emerald miners and traders, and in other cases it involved drug traffickers, and right-wing armed groups—the legacy of the big cartels of the 1980s.

23 There are other examples on how these 'body-count' indicators created perverse incentives. Notable examples are the assassination of civilians in the Vietnam War (Daddis, 2011), and more recently the use of these indicators in the war against drug cartels in Mexico (Ahmed & Schmitt, 2016).

References

Aguilera, M., 2014. *Contrapoder y justicia guerrillera. Fragmentación política y orden insurgente en Colombia (1952–2003)*. Bogotá: Universidad Nacional de Colombia, Debate.

Ahmed, A. & Schmitt, E., 2016. *Mexican Military Runs Up Body Count in Drug War*. [Online] Available at: www.nytimes.com/2016/05/27/world/americas/mexican-militarys-high-kill-rate-raises-human-rights-fears.html [Last accessed 14 November 2017].

Banks, W. C. & Alvarez, E., 1991. The New Colombian Constitution: Democratic Victory or Popular Surrender? *The University of Miami Inter-American Law Review*, pp. 39–92.

Bonilla, J. I., 2012. Periodismo, guerra y paz. Campo intelectual periodístico y agendas de la información en Colombia. *Signo y Pensamiento*, 21(40), pp. 53–71.

Cárdenas, M., Junguito, R. & Pachón, M., 2006. Political institutions and policy outcomes in Colombia: The effects of the 1991 constitution. *IDB Working Paper No. 203*, February, pp. 1–92.

Cepeda, I., 2006. Genocidio político: el caso de la Unión Patriótica en Colombia. *Revista Cetil*, 1(2), pp. 101–112.

Comisión Histórica del Conflicto y sus Víctimas, 2015. *Contribución al entendimiento del conflicto armado en Colombia*, Bogotá: Comisión Histórica del Conflicto y sus Víctimas.

Comisión Interamericana de Derechos Humanos, 1999. *Tercer Informe sobre la Situación de los Derechos Humanos en Colombia—Capítulo IV.* [Online] Available at: www.cidh.org/countryrep/colom99sp/indice.htm [Last accessed 11 November 2017].

Corporación Observatorio para la Paz, 2009. *Guerras inútiles: una historia de las FARC*. Bogotá: Intermedio.

Daddis, G. A., 2011. *No Sure Victory: Measuring US Army Effectiveness and Progress in the Vietnam War*. Oxford: Oxford University Press.

Duncan, G., 2006. *Los señores de la guerra: de paramilitares, mafiosos y autodefensas en Colombia*. Bogotá: Planeta.

El Espectador, 2016. *'Cartel de Cali financió a Ernesto Samper y hasta pagó su absolución'*. [Online] Available at: www.elespectador.com/noticias/judicial/cartel-de-cali-financio-ernesto-samper-y-hasta-pago-su-articulo-638171 [Last accessed: 21 September 2017].

Fukuyama, F., 1989. The end of history? *The national interest*, Issue 16, pp. 3–18.

García-Peña Jaramillo, D., 2005. La relación del Estado colombiano con el fenómeno paramilitar: por el esclarecimiento histórico. *Análisis político*, 18(53), pp. 58–76.

González González, F. E., 2014. *Poder y violencia en Colombia*. Bogotá: CINEP.

Gutiérrez García, D. J. & Marín Suárez, J. F., 2013. Violencia estatal en Colombia, ¿legítima o ilegítima? *Pensar Historia*, Issue 2, pp. 37–48.

Gutiérrez Sanín, F., 2014. *El orangután con sacoleva: cien años de democracia y represión en Colombia (1910–2010)*. Bogotá: IEPRI.

Gutiérrez Sanín, F. & Barón, M., 2005. Re-stating the state: paramilitary territorial control and political order in Colombia (1978–2004). *Crisis States Programme Working Papers*, September, pp. 1–36.

Human Rights Watch, 2015. *El rol de los altos mandos en falsos positivos: Evidencias de responsabilidad de generales y coroneles del Ejército colombiano por ejecuciones de civiles*. [Online] Available at: www.hrw.org/es/report/2015/06/23/el-rol-de-los-altos-mandos-en-falsos-positivos/evidencias-de-responsabilidad-de [Last accessed 22 June 2017].

Ibáñez Londoño, A. M., 2011. El desplazamiento forzoso en Colombia: un camino sin retorno hacia la pobreza. *Cuadernos Geográficos*, 48(1).

Jimeno, R., 1989. *Noche de lobos*. Bogotá: Siglo Ventiuno Editores.

Llorente, M. V. & Deas, M. D., 1999. *Reconocer la guerra para construir la paz*. Bogotá: CEREC.

López de la Roche, F., 2014. *Las ficciones del poder: patriotismo, medios de comunicación y reorientación afectiva de los colombianos bajo Uribe Vélez (2002–2010)*. Bogotá: IEPRI.

López Hernández, C. N., 2016. López, C. *"Adiós a las FARC¿ Y ahora qué." Construir Ciudadanía, Estado y Mercado para Unir a las Tres Colombias*. Bogotá. Debate.

López Hernández, C. N. & Ávila Martínez, A. F., 2010. *Y refundaron la patria: de cómo mafiosos y políticos reconfiguraron el estado colombiano*. Bogotá. Debate.

Matthiesen, T., 2000. *El arte político de conciliar. El tema de las drogas en las relaciones entre Colombia y Estados Unidos, 1986–1994*. Bogotá: FESCOL.

Meertens, D. & Sánchez, G., 1983. *Bandoleros, gamonales y campesinos: el caso de la violencia en Colombia. El Ancora, 1983*. Bogotá: El Ancora.

Molano, A., 1994. *Trochas y Fusiles*. Bogotá: El Ancora.

Palacios, M., 2003. *Entre la legitimidad y la violencia: Colombia 1875–1994*. Bogotá: Editorial Norma.

Palacios, M., 2012. *Violencia pública en Colombia: 1958–2010*. Bogotá: Fondo de cultura económica.

Pardo Rueda, R., 2007. *Fin Del Paramilitarismo: es Posible su Desmonte?* Bogotá: Ediciones B.

Pastrana Arango, A., 2013. *Memorias olvidadas*. Bogotá: Editora géminis.

Pécaut, D., 2008. Las FARC: fuentes de su longevidad y de la conservación de su cohesión. *Análisis político*, 21(63), pp. 22–50.

Pécaut, D., 2013. *La experiencia de la violencia: los desafíos del relato y la memoria*. Bogotá: La Carreta.

Pizarro Leongómez, E., 2011. *Las FARC (1949–2011): de guerrilla campesina a máquina de guerra*. Bogotá: Grupo Editorial Norma.

Ramírez Bacca, R. & Marín Arenas, L. D., 2015. Seguridad e Ideología en Colombia, 1978–1982: análisis crítico del discurso de Julio César Turbay Ayala. *Anuario de Historia Regional y de las Fronteras*, 20(2), pp. 241–269.

Romero, M., 2003. *Paramilitares y autodefensas: 1982–2003*. Bogotá: Instituto de Estudios Políticos y Relaciones Internacionales (IEPRI), Editorial Planeta Colombiana.

Romero, M. & Valencia, L., 2007. *Parapolìtica: La ruta de la expansión paramilitar y los acuerdos políticos*. Bogotá: Intermedio Editores.

Ronderos, M. T., 2014. *Guerras recicladas*. Bogotá: Aguilar.

Sánchez Gómez, G., 1988. *Guerra y política en la sociedad colombiana*. Bogotá: El Ancora Editores.

Tickner, A. B. & Pardo, R., 2003. En busca de aliados para la" Seguridad Democrática" La política exterior del primer año de la administración Uribe. *Colombia internacional*, Issue 56/57, pp. 64–82.

Tokatlian, J. G., 2004. Una reflexión en torno a Colombia, 1999–2002: ¿Negociación para la paz o proceso para la guerra? *Foro Internacional*, pp. 635–655.

UNHCR, 2017. *Tendencias Globales sobre refugiados y otras personas de interés del ACNUR*. [Online] Available at: www.acnur.org/recursos/estadisticas/ [Last accessed 22 June 2017].

Unidad para las Victimas, 2017. *Registro Unico de Victimas*. [Online] Available at: http://rni.unidadvictimas.gov.co/RUV [Last accessed 22 June 2017].

Uprimny, R., 2003. The constitutional court and control of presidential extraordinary powers in Colombia. *Democratization*, 10(4), pp. 46–69.

Vargas Velásquez, A., 2000. La democracia colombiana tratando de salir de su laberinto. *Reflexión Política*, 2(3).

Verdad Abierta, 2013. *Las Convivir, motor de la guerra paramilitar*. [Online] Available at: www.verdadabierta.com/justicia-y-paz/juicios/5009-las-convivir-motor-de-la-guerra-paramilitar [Last accessed 21 September 2017].

Wills, M. E., Sánchez Gómez, G. & Gutiérrez Sanín, F., 2006. *Nuestra guerra sin nombre: transformaciones del conflicto en Colombia*. Bogotá: Norma.

3 The peace process with the FARC—EP

Carlo Nasi

The long journey to a negotiation

When the government of President Juan Manuel Santos (2010–2018) decided to attempt a new peace negotiation with the Fuerzas Armadas Revolucionarias de Colombia—Ejército del Pueblo (FARC—EP) guerrillas, it was aware that such a course of action entailed high risks. Previous governments had failed consistently in their attempts to reach a bargained solution with the FARC—EP. On two occasions, during the governments of Belisario Betancur (1982–1986) and Andrés Pastrana (1998–2002), failure to achieve an agreement was due to the fact that the FARC—EP negotiated only tactically (in order to attain short-term military and political benefits instead of seeking to end the war). Even if both governments share part of the blame for such failures, the FARC—EP never considered renouncing war in the first place during these negotiations (Bejarano, 1995; Pizarro Leongómez, 2011; Nasi, 2009).

The government of President Virgilio Barco (1986–1990) did negotiate with several rebel groups that eventually turned in their weapons (see Chapter 2), but was unable to start peace negotiations with FARC—EP (Pardo, 2004; García Durán, 1992). In fact, Barco's government demanded that any rebel organization willing to start peace negotiations should first declare a unilateral ceasefire (and comply with it for a few months), which would be interpreted by the government as a sincere peace gesture. The FARC—EP announced a ceasefire but then (unlike other rebel groups) did not comply with it, so the negotiation with them never started (Ramirez, 1991). Later, the government of President César Gaviria (1990–94) held short-lived peace talks in Venezuela and Mexico that ended in deadlock. At the time, the FARC—EP had demanded that the government undertake deep structural transformations of the Colombian polity and economy, which was at odds with the fact that a legitimate and popularly elected National Constituent Assembly had just drafted a new political constitution in the context of a successful peace negotiation with other rebel groups (Palacios, 2012).

Given previous experiences, it seemed that any peace negotiations with the FARC—EP were doomed to fail. In addition, the gradual involvement of this rebel group in drug-trafficking activities led different governments, analysts, and most Colombian citizens to believe that the FARC—EP had mutated into a greedy criminal enterprise, which sought rents and riches instead of the ideological agendas ostensibly espoused (Nieto, 2001).

In 1998 the government of President Pastrana made yet another attempt to reach a peaceful settlement with the FARC—EP. In order to sit at the bargaining table, the government had to abide by a precondition demanded by FARC—EP, consisting of the demilitarization of five municipalities (an area corresponding to 42,000 sq km—approximately the size of Switzerland). Whereas the FARC—EP had argued that demilitarization was necessary in order to have a 'safe space' from which to conduct the peace talks, the demilitarized area turned out to be a safe haven where the rebel group engaged in all sorts of illegal activities. Furthermore, after three years of intermittent negotiations, and amidst increasing levels of violence between both actors, the government and the rebels had not even agreed upon a single item in a long and complex bargaining agenda (Nasi, 2009).

It seemed that both the government and the rebels had negotiated solely for tactical reasons (as part of a military strategy aimed at defeating the opponent). Although it failed to reach a negotiated peace, Pastrana's government was able to set the stage for turning the tables against FARC—EP through 'Plan Colombia', a programme that was aimed at strengthening Colombia's institutional and military capacities.[1]

In 2002, after Pastrana's peace negotiations with the FARC—EP broke down, Álvaro Uribe, a right-wing populist politician who promised to fight back and eventually militarily defeat the FARC—EP, was elected president (he was re-elected in 2006 to serve a second term). President Uribe's election followed the restructuring and strengthening of the Colombian army through Plan Colombia, which allowed the government to undertake a sustained military offensive against the rebels (Isacson, 2010).

Plan Colombia helped the Colombian government to regain the upper hand in the war vis-à-vis the FARC—EP. In fact, before Uribe's election, the FARC—EP had attained unprecedented strength. At its peak the FARC—EP was comprised of nearly 20,000 combatants and had expanded its territorial control across various regions, especially in Colombia's southern provinces (Granada, et al., 2009). Uribe's government contained the rebel's expansion. While never attaining a decisive military victory, the government was able to weaken the FARC—EP (Granada, et al., 2009), and this hard-line policy became very popular in Colombia.

When President Santos was elected in 2010 for his first term in office, he was expected to continue with Uribe's legacy of dealing with the FARC—EP solely in military terms, particularly given that he had supported this approach when he was Uribe's Minister of Defence. However, two years after taking office, Santos started a negotiation process with the FARC—EP, which prompted a furious reaction by former President Uribe and a number of right-wing politicians, who accused the government of 'high treason.' But why did Santos opt for a bargained solution in the first place?

President Santos was aware that attaining a decisive military victory over the FARC—EP would be both very costly and extremely difficult. Colombia's vast territory, thick forests, inaccessible mountains and porous frontiers had always provided the rebel group with plenty of safe havens. In addition, the FARC—EP had demonstrated a great deal of resilience during five decades of armed conflict. In spite of the fact that Colombia never approached a truly revolutionary situation, the FARC—EP seldom (if ever) experienced a shortage of recruits and funds. High levels of unemployment and poverty in various rural regions, coupled with a precarious state presence in different areas, played into the hands of the FARC—EP. The FARC—EP had also become a *de facto* authority in some regions, providing some form of order and justice to locals, which helped them recruit followers (Pizarro Leongómez, 2011).

While Uribe's government was able to push the rebels back to rural areas and regain control of various territories, this was a far cry from victory. The FARC—EP did suffer heavy casualties, but survived and changed their tactics. By reverting to small-scale guerrilla tactics, the rebel group was able not only to better resist the government's offensive, but also to recover the military initiative in some parts of the country (Fundación Ideas para la Paz, 2013).

In any event, the improvement in the military capacities of the Colombian armed forces facilitated by *Plan Colombia* produced a sense of vulnerability in the leadership of the rebel group: for the first time ever, the Colombian armed forces were able to capture and kill not only rank-and-file guerrillas and mid-level commanders, but also some of the top FARC—EP commanders. In particular, the Colombian military killed the FARC—EP's second in command, Luis Edgar Devia Silva (also known as Raúl Reyes) in 2008, then his replacement, Víctor Julio Suárez Rojas (alias Mono Jojoy) in 2010, and later the top commander Guillermo León Sáenz Vargas (alias Alfonso Cano) in 2011. The war became increasingly costly for the FARC—EP, which must have spurred internal debates in the rebel group about the convenience of prolonging an insurgency that had not led to revolution in over fifty years (Corporación Observatorio para la Paz, 2009).

Conversely, President Santos decided to start peace negotiations when it became clear that not even Plan Colombia had sufficed to defeat the FARC—EP on the battleground, and that the all-out strategy entailed significant costs in terms of the legitimacy of the state. More than 4,000 civilians had been assassinated by the Colombian armed forces during the counterinsurgent campaign (Human Rights Watch, 2015). Negotiating with the rebels was a rational course of action, since the war was yielding diminishing returns and the U.S. government was gradually scaling down its military aid to Colombia. At the same time, due to Plan Colombia (and the military plans which succeeded it) any prospects of taking power by force had vanished altogether for the FARC—EP. After enduring successive severe military blows and realizing that the war was no longer profitable enough (nor leading to any meaningful political ends), the rebel group and its leadership must have considered it prudent to seek a way out of the conflict through politics.

Deciding on the correct timing to approach the FARC—EP was, however, not an easy decision. The FARC—EP's top commander, Alfonso Cano, had been proposing a peace process since the beginning of Santos' tenure in 2010 (El Tiempo, 2010). However, President Santos was not convinced of the feasibility of sitting at the negotiation table, and was also pressured by Uribe (and by rightist elements within his own party) to not change course.

After the killing of Alfonso Cano in 2011, President Santos concluded that the situation was ripe for seeking a bargained solution. In fact, the FARC—EP was enduring internal turmoil, determining Cano's replacement and reconsidering its options. It was then that Santos approached the new top leader of the FARC—EP, Rodrigo Londoño Echeverri (also known as Timochenko), with the proposal to secretly explore peace talks. The peace process started when Timochenko agreed to start a dialogue.

Peace negotiations and the importance of rules and procedures: Lessons from the past

To avoid placing the negotiation process in the public spotlight, and anticipating high political costs in the event that it failed, President Santos opted to conduct secret pre-negotiations. Although it seemed that FARC—EP leaders had good reasons to look for a way out of an increasingly costly war, this did not necessarily mean that the government and the rebel group could agree on the terms of a peaceful settlement.

Thus, President Santos formed a commission headed by his own brother, Enrique, in order to secretly meet with FARC—EP delegates and explore the actual possibility of reaching a peaceful solution (Santos Calderón, 2014). After six months of pre-negotiations, this commission crafted a procedural framework, which provided a roadmap for the upcoming negotiations (Oficina del Alto Comisionado para la Paz, 2012). This document specified the basic rules of the negotiations, which included:

First, negotiating abroad, specifically in Cuba. This provision was important, because the most recent peace negotiation with FARC—EP, under the government of Pastrana, had taken place in Colombia, under conditions that entailed costly concessions for the government.

Santos avoided repeating such a mistake. No areas within the country were to be demilitarized and it was agreed that the negotiations would not be conducted in Colombia, but abroad. Cuba, a country respected by the rebels, was chosen as the site where the peace negotiations would take place.

Second, limiting public participation and media involvement. On previous occasions, little attention was paid to the role of civil society in the negotiations. Indeed, when the Pastrana government peace negotiations deadlocked, the government had agreed with the FARC—EP to 'democratize the peace talks', that is, to invite Colombians of all walks of life to submit proposals in order to 'reach the peace' in the so-called public hearings (*audiencias públicas*). Many citizens ended up proposing all sorts of reforms on different topics.

However, this only heightened confusion and produced further delays in the peace talks (Nasi, 2009). The Pastrana government and the FARC—EP never defined a procedure to sort out, accept, or discard the citizens' proposals, which continued to accumulate. The parties never specified how this procedure would lead to peace, or how it would link with the bargaining agenda. Complexity was increased, rather than decreased, by this process. To complicate matters even further, too many aspects of the negotiations were disclosed to the public, which fostered posturing and grandstanding by politicians and FARC—EP delegates.

In contrast, during Santos's tenure the negotiation team clarified from the start that the government and the FARC—EP shared the main responsibility for finding a way out of the armed conflict. Citizens' inputs would be allowed, but they would only play a secondary role. It was also emphasized that negotiations would be confidential, meaning that disclosure to the public would only occur in due time. Negotiating would take place on bilateral, confidential terms, with the active support of Cuba, Venezuela, Norway, and Chile (that acted as guarantors of the negotiation process). This corrected yet another procedural error committed in past negotiations with the FARC—EP.

Third, negotiating without a ceasefire. In response to the specific political conditions of Colombia, the negotiation team opted to negotiate in the midst of war, which was a risky decision. In fact, the ongoing violent confrontation between the government and the guerrillas caused grave tensions at the bargaining table, to the point that some political groups even demanded that President Santos should stop negotiating or should 'respond blow by blow to the terrorists' (El Heraldo, 2014). But the government chose to negotiate in the midst of war, because a premature ceasefire could have accrued a military advantage to the FARC—EP and could have strengthened the accusations of opposing politicians that Santos was surrendering the monopoly of force by the state. Therefore, during the peace negotiations the armed forces continued to fight the FARC—EP.

Fourth, negotiating under the rule that 'nothing is agreed upon until everything is agreed'. This norm provided an incentive for reaching comprehensive peace accords, rather than partial agreements. Indeed, no partial agreements reached by the parties, regardless of their merits, would ever be implemented by themselves. This principle also allowed the negotiation to advance on less contentious topics, fostering progress in several topics without necessarily stalling the negotiations.

Finally, negotiating a limited agenda. The parties agreed on a limited number of topics to be included in the agenda. Again, this was a way to correct past mistakes. During the 1998–2002 failed peace negotiation, the Pastrana government did not set limits to the bargaining agenda, with the result that it eventually included 67 topics concerning all sorts of political, social, and economic transformations (Nasi, 2009). Pastrana's negotiating team conveyed the false impression that 'anything and everything' was negotiable, which was at odds with the fact that the bargaining table was extremely slow in showing any results. Failure to reach any agreement after three years of negotiations ultimately came as no surprise.

President Santos, instead, even before sitting at the bargaining table, agreed with the FARC—EP on an agenda that made it clear that the peace negotiations would not entail a 'negotiated revolution'. The FARC—EP was not in a position to demand anything close to this, since the rebel group never threatened the stability of the regime and was unpopular throughout Colombia.

The bargaining agenda included six topics, whose rationale, breadth and scope will be discussed in the next section: 1) agrarian reform, 2) political rights, 3) drug trafficking, 4) victims and transitional justice, 5) end of the conflict, and 6) implementation of the accords.

It is important to emphasize which topics were excluded by the bargaining agenda: it was clear from the start that the negotiations would not substitute the Colombian democracy with some other kind of socialist regime, nor that the capitalist economic system would be overhauled: changes in the financial sector or the abolition of private property were excluded from the bargaining agenda. The agenda also did not mention a restructuring of the Colombian military and police: due to the context of the negotiations, it was unthinkable to let the FARC—EP demand institutional reforms of the Colombian armed forces. It was a modest bargaining agenda that entailed a few important—albeit far from radical—concessions to the rebels and that recognized the advances made in the 1991 Constitution.

The peace accords and the prospects of attaining a sustainable peace

The peace negotiations between the government of Santos and the FARC—EP officially started in late 2012 and ended with the signing of a peace accord on 26 September 2016. Whereas there was fast progress during the first year and a half of the negotiations (in which the parties mostly debated policies related to rural reforms, deepening democracy, and dealing with drug trafficking), the dialogue slowed down and suffered a deadlock when the parties approached specific concessions to the FARC—EP and guarantees of compliance by the government, as well as the discussion on the topic of victims and transitional justice. The 'definitive' peace agreement was signed in a public ceremony in Cartagena on 26 September 2016.

However, due to sustained critiques by former President Uribe and other political sectors who questioned the legitimacy of the agreements and the negotiation process, President Santos had decided that Colombians should have the final word on the peace accords through a plebiscite that was held on 2 October 2016.

The plebiscite and its vote were intended to foster the legitimization of the negotiation process and the mandate given to President Santos for achieving peace. However, defying all polls and predictions, and partly due to a successful negative campaign by Uribe's supporters that massively spread misinformation through the media (Revista Semana, 2016b), the low popularity of Santos's government, a deep distrust in the FARC—EP by Colombians, and the difficulties inherent in communicating the content of a 300-page agreement to the population, a majority of Colombians rejected the peace accords.

In order to preserve the legitimacy of the peace process, President Santos was forced to renegotiate the peace accords with the FARC—EP, introducing many of the concerns of those who were opposed to the agreements. A tense period followed, during which, firstly, the government negotiating team met with former President Uribe and various other politicians and social and religious leaders who had opposed the peace accords, in order to hear and collect their objections to the accords. Then there was a renegotiation of the accords with the FARC—EP in order to change some parts of the peace agreements (La Silla Vacia, 2016).

It is worth noting that even though the FARC—EP could have vetoed all (or most) of the proposals for changing the content of the peace accords, the rebel group chose not to do so, hoping to create a stronger consensus in favour of the accords. Indeed, implementing any peace accord is very difficult; implementing it with the majority of the population against it is nearly impossible. The FARC—EP exercised its veto power only on a few occasions, when the rebel group perceived that some proposed changes threatened its vital interests (for example, with regard to proposals aimed at limiting its political participation following the demobilization of FARC combatants).

When renegotiating the terms of the peace agreement with the FARC—EP, the government's negotiation team acted as a broker, fostering various changes in the peace accords as long as they did not derail the agreements. Whereas it was important to introduce some changes in the accords, the goal of achieving peace was equally important.

The government and the FARC—EP signed a new agreement in Bogotá on 24 November 2016. Predictably, despite the fact that both sides included a number of important modifications in the accords, this did not translate into unanimous support for the new peace accords, or lead to a change of position by those who had opposed the agreements form the start. Part of the opposition was defused, but former President Uribe and his followers maintained a radical stance denouncing that the government and the rebels had only introduced 'cosmetic changes' in the accords (El Colombiano, 2016).

Santos next faced the dilemma of submitting the new accords to some form of popular ratification. Given that the previous accords had been rejected in a plebiscite, it was important to probe whether most Colombians endorsed the new peace agreements. However, carrying out a new plebiscite was both costly and risky: even if there had been a number of popular mobilizations throughout the country in favour of peace, a new plebiscite might have deepened polarization and given the opponents of the peace process another opportunity to spoil the negotiations. In a worst-case scenario, the government risked losing a plebiscite for a second time in a row, something that would have meant ruining the peace process.

Eventually, Santos opted for a safer option. His government inquired with the high courts whether ratification by Congress could be considered as some form of 'popular ratification', considering that Congressmen had been popularly elected (Revista Semana, 2016a). When the courts supported the idea of ratification by Congress, the government went ahead, taking advantage of its majorities in Congress. Congress swiftly ratified the accords on 1 December 2016 (BBC Mundo, 2016).

This opened the way for a new stage in the peace process: implementation. As at late 2017 the implementation of the peace accords was taking place, and it was difficult to anticipate whether it would lead to a sustainable peace, as this is something which can only be assessed in the long term. At the same time, however, one can bring forth some ideas on the foreseeable effects of the accords.

Regardless of the content of the accords, they do imply the termination of a long-standing insurgency by the FARC—EP. Although certain other rebel groups and other illegal armed actors (which are primarily engaged in drug-trafficking) will not simply disappear because of the signing of a peace accord with FARC—EP, bringing an end to the FARC—EP's insurgency constitutes a milestone that will, by and large, bring a major share of the violence to an end.

With regards to the various topics of the peace accords, it is worth mentioning that the accords include a modest—albeit very important—agrarian reform. This issue is significant because the FARC—EP has been (at least primarily) a rural phenomenon. Colombia has a long history of forceful dispossessions of the lands of peasants and a track record of failed agrarian reforms (Machado, 2009), which partly explains the rise, proliferation, and endurance of insurgencies. Even though the claim that the FARC—EP represents (or is supported by) a majority of Colombian peasants is ludicrous, most of the FARC—EP's social support comes from specific rural areas. For the FARC—EP, an agrarian reform programme has been central to its politics and identity, as shortly after its foundation, the rebel group proposed such an initiative (Ferro & Uribe, 2002).

The peace agreements mention the creation of a land fund for distributing terrains to landless and land-poor peasants, which aims to contribute to redress past injustices (see Chapter 6). However, this is not a radical or revolutionary rural reform programme. The peace accords do not include expropriations of large landowners, nor do they set any limits to large rural landholdings (Colombian rural landholdings are technically not limited by size). Rather, the government is expected to buy land and also use land owned by the state (the so-called *baldíos*) in order to redistribute them to peasants, especially in the areas most affected by the armed conflict.

The formalization of land titles is expected to complement this policy. Land ownership in Colombia's rural areas is defined by a high degree of informality, as nearly 60% of owners lack land titles. The creation of special tribunals to resolve disputes over land property will be useful in promoting formalization and defusing conflicts. In addition, the government is expected to make substantial development investments in those rural areas that have been affected the most by war, assisting peasants with credit and technical aid to improve the productivity of rural areas. As such the agreements can be read as a rural development plan, rather than as a rural revolution agenda.

The accord on political rights includes a mix of measures aimed at improving the protection of the rights of opposition parties and the creation of broader avenues for political participation. One should mention that Colombia has maintained democratic procedures for decades, and that no government has legally banned any opposition parties.

At the same time though, opposition parties have endured different types of exclusions due to various structural barriers. For instance, between 1958 and 1974, the Frente Nacional (FN or National Front), a power-sharing agreement aimed at stopping La Violencia[2], restricted access to government to parties other than the Liberals and the Conservatives (Sánchez, et al., 1984). When the FN ended, Liberal and Conservative politicians largely succeeded in prolonging this power-sharing agreement into the late 1980s by resorting to informal understandings. Only with the Constitutional Reform of 1991 was the FN fully dismantled, which allowed the election of hitherto marginalized political groups.

Even more troublesome than the FN has been the violent exclusion of some political parties that seemingly threatened the status quo. For instance, in the mid-1980s, in the context of the peace process between the administration of President Belisario Betancur and FARC—EP (which ended in failure), this rebel group formed a political party, the Unión Patriótica (UP), to participate in electoral contests (Dudley, 2008). However, the UP did not function as a regular party, but formed part of the FARC—EP's strategy to take power by combining both legal and illegal means (the so-called 'combination of all forms of struggle').

This led to a very violent reaction by rightist groups, in particular by some regional élites that believed that the UP threatened their political status and promoted the FARC—EP's revolutionary agenda (Romero, 2003). These élites sponsored right-wing paramilitary groups, which, sometimes in collusion with the Colombian military, virtually annihilated the UP in a short space (Romero, 2003; Dudley, 2008).

Even if the FARC—EP has also been guilty of killing scores of politicians belonging to different political parties, the extreme violence endured by the UP finds no parallel in Colombia: from the mid-1980s many politicians and supporters of the UP were threatened and killed by rightist militias, to the point that this party was forced out of the electoral competition in the 1990s.

Counter-intuitively, in spite of the annihilation of the UP, in those same years Colombia gradually became a relatively safer place for other left-wing political parties. Colombia experienced an effective democratic opening following President Barco's partly successful peace processes of the late 1980s and the early 1990s, and the crafting of a new constitution in 1991. As various guerrilla organizations handed in their weapons and formed legal political organizations (see Chapter 2), these parties made important democratic inroads. Since 2003 the Polo Democrático Alternativo, a political party which includes both former guerrillas and politicians from the left (not necessarily connected with rebel groups), was able to elect Bogotá's mayor[3] three times in a row. It has become clear that left-wing parties can compete in electoral contests and win elections without their candidates being killed.

However, due to the precedent concerning the systematic killing of UP members, the importance of broadening political participation is vital for the FARC—EP. Furthermore, in spite of the democratic opening of the early 1990s, various social movements have been repressed and several human rights defenders have been killed by either private militias or even the state's coercive apparatus (Human Rights Watch, 2013). There is still plenty of room for deepening democracy in Colombia, as assassinations of social and political leaders are still common in the country.

The accord on political rights will offer greater guarantees to opposition parties and social movements, such as the creation of a statute for opposition parties (something that has been non-existent in Colombia), removing legal obstacles for the creation of new political parties, improving access to mass media for opposition parties, and introducing a series of measures to improve the transparency of the elections and strengthen social movements. The FARC—EP will also receive specific incentives: they will be granted 10 seats[4] in Congress (five in the Senate and five in the House of Representatives) in the elections of 2018 and 2022, regardless of the electoral results. In addition, the political party formed by the FARC—EP will be funded by the state and will be allowed to use a series of mass media tools in order to disseminate its message.

These specific agreements have been very controversial in Colombia. Former President Uribe and other sectors have opposed the peace process, as they consider that FARC—EP leaders, especially those responsible for gross human rights violations, should not be allowed to have any political positions. On the other hand, supporters of the agreements consider that granting the FARC—EP 10 seats in Congress constitutes some sort of compensation for the massacre of UP members. Furthermore, many consider that guaranteeing the FARC—EP—for a limited time—a few seats in Congress is a fair price that Colombians should pay if the rebel group is expected to lay down its weapons for good. This is an important incentive for the FARC—EP to make the transition from violence to politics.

The accord on illicit drugs includes various provisions aimed at curbing the production, trafficking, and consumption of illicit drugs. This agreement, however, includes a great deal of wishful thinking. In fact, a variety of criminal groups (besides the FARC—EP) are involved in drug trafficking and many peasants throughout the country cultivate illegal crops independently of the presence of the FARC—EP in their territories. Drug production and trafficking is an international industry that transcends the FARC—EP.

This accord includes provisions related to policies that have been implemented in the past in the 'war against drugs' that have not been particularly successful (Pardo, 2004). They aim to target peasants, drug traffickers and drug consumers, each in a differential manner. Peasants who cultivate illicit crops would be helped by the government to substitute them with legal ones. Drug addiction will be approached as a public health issue, and the consumption of drugs would be considered as a medical problem rather than a criminal offence. Finally, drug traffickers would be dealt with using the repressive apparatus of the state.

The foreseeable effects of the drugs policies included in the peace agreements are hard to assess. In the renegotiated accords it became clear that in order to enjoy the benefits of transitional justice, the FARC—EP is expected to provide information about the illegal economies in the regions where their units were active and exercised effective control over territory and the population. The new agreements also state that there will be no amnesty if drug-trafficking-related offences were for the personal enrichment of guerrillas (Goebertus Estrada, 2016).

A looming risk is that the so-called criminal gangs (*bandas criminales*, or BACRIM) will take over drug production in regions formerly controlled by FARC—EP. As long as the government will not be capable of offering alternatives of employment and wealth generation that replace the avenues created by drug production and trafficking, and will not be able to reassert state presence in these areas, Colombia will never become a country free of illicit drugs.

In any event, the accord is significant because the FARC—EP will change from being an organization involved in drug trafficking and drug production to a legal organization that is expected to sever all its ties with the production and commercialization of illicit drugs. The FARC—EP is expected to help the government in the fight against drug trafficking by providing information, and also supporting the state to reach the areas where it has been absent.

Another element of the agenda negotiated with the FARC—EP concerns victims and transitional justice (see Chapter 5). The government stated from the very beginning of the process that the negotiation would be centred on protecting the victims' rights (Rettberg, 2013). In 2011, before the peace process started, the Santos government issued a law aimed at compensating millions of victims of Colombia's armed conflict (Congreso de la República de Colombia, 2011). Even if it will be very difficult to redress all the victims' rights—considering the high number of victims of the conflict—this is essential for healing the wounds caused by the war, to deter the emergence of new armed groups, and to consolidate the role of the Colombian state. Both the state and the FARC—EP are expected to undertake restorative actions in relation to the victims in order to ameliorate or repair some of the damage caused in the course of war (Goebertus Estrada, 2016).

The FARC—EP, as well as the other actors involved in the Colombian war, has committed plenty of hideous crimes throughout fifty years of confrontations. Fighters of the Colombian conflict are responsible for numerous homicides, kidnappings, bombings, rapes, and the forced displacement of communities among other violations. Granting a blanket amnesty to the guerrillas was not a feasible option for negotiators, as Colombia had ratified the Rome Statute of the International Criminal Court.

But FARC—EP leaders had made the point that various politicians and entrepreneurs were (also) culprits in the Colombian war, as their institutions were responsible for atrocities. The FARC—EP also stated that they would not become the first guerrilla organization in the world to end up in jail after signing a definitive peace accord (El Espectador, 2015). This debate seemed intractable, and its resolution required finding a delicate balance between peace and justice.

After a prolonged deadlock on this issue, an ad-hoc committee of lawyers was formed in order to help both parties deal with the dilemmas of Transitional Justice (Pizarro Leongómez & Valencia, 2009). This committee crafted a formula, which seemed to be in accordance with the letter of the Rome Statute, but did not necessarily imply sending the FARC—EP leaders to jail. According to this formula, those guerrillas and actors in the conflict who had committed gross human rights violations and confessed all wrongdoings will have an 'effective restriction of freedom' (in a place other than in jail). Those actors who confessed all wrongdoings but not in a timely manner will spend some years in regular jails, and those actors who are reluctant to confess their crimes and later found guilty by the Colombian courts will spend up to 20 years in jail (Oficina del Alto Comisionado para la Paz, 2016).

As with most transitional justice formulas, this accord emphasizes that serving justice is not only about retribution, but implies other mechanisms such as truth-telling and reparations to victims (see Chapter 5). There is little doubt that this accord entails some degree of impunity: perpetrators of gross human rights violations will get off the hook with light sentences, which has spurred bitter debates in Colombia.

After the parties resolved the impasse related to transitional justice, the negotiations focused on the measures that were necessary to ensure the implementation of the agreements, and also on the specific rules of the disarmament, demobilization and reintegration (DDR) process. However, the negotiations deadlocked when the parties approached these points. In fact, the FARC—EP was well aware of the risk that in the future, either another president, or the Colombian Congress, or the high courts could neglect or even reverse the peace agreements. After having negotiated for over four years, the FARC—EP realized that the peace accords could simply vanish due to the democratic procedures inherent to a check and balances system.

In order to ensure that the peace accords would be implemented and that their implementation would not be jeopardized in the future, the government and the FARC—EP agreed on a special procedure by which the peace accords would initially be approved by Congress (without undergoing modifications), then revised by the Colombian Constitutional Court, and finally considered as a special treaty of the Geneva Conventions and incorporated into the Constitution. This convoluted formula basically implied giving a non-modifiable, almost supra-constitutional status to the peace accords, which caused great deal of controversy. However, during the renegotiation of the accords, this procedure was virtually discarded. Eventually the Colombian

Congress was put in charge of introducing changes in the laws and the Constitution, in accordance with the peace accords, and following a 'fast-track'[5] procedure. That is, the FARC—EP had to rely on the government's majority in Congress for the introduction of normative changes that would allow the implementation of the accords.

Finally, concerning the DDR process, the FARC—EP agreed to gradually hand in all its weapons to the United Nations and temporarily concentrate its combatants in different locations across Colombia, in order to facilitate its transition from a guerrilla organization to a legal political party (see Chapter 8).

The successes of peace and its uncertainties

The Santos government epitomizes rationality under fire. Accordingly, it approached FARC—EP leaders only when the rebel group seemed to have real incentives to seek an end of war. The peace process started through a pre-negotiation scheme that agreed on a roadmap for the peace talks—and a series of reasonable rules for making progress and solving differences at the bargaining table—and that clarified that there would be no 'negotiated revolution' in Colombia. Santos's government formed a negotiation team that included trustworthy, competent negotiators. After four years of a continuous and difficult negotiation process, the government and the FARC—EP signed a peace accord.

Unlike all previous Colombian presidents and governments, President Santos was able not only to negotiate productively with the FARC—EP, but also to arrive at definitive, well-crafted peace accords. Structure preceded rhetoric and guided the negotiations towards achievable objectives. Whereas most people expected that Colombia would finally turn the page of war after five decades of suffering, an unexpected turn of events provoked a severe crisis. The spoiling efforts of former President Uribe and opponents to the agreements apparently paid off when most Colombians rejected the accords in October 2016.

While the peace accords entailed a few and relative modest (albeit important) political and economic transformations, Uribe and his followers (as well as other conservative groups) convinced many people that, rather than bringing a sustainable peace, the peace accords were tantamount to disaster and the surrender to terrorism, as they would transform Colombia into a communist nightmare: 'another Cuba or Venezuela'.

Against all odds, the Santos government was able to sign new accords in such a way that many concerns of the opposition were taken into account. While overcoming this hurdle, implementing the peace accords will be no easy matter, and will constitute the final test for peace for the Colombian state. Politicians such as Uribe will keep riding on the discontent with the government, spreading fear and polarizing the country around peace. Trust in the current government has been successfully eroded, and, with every future election, the question remains whether the newly elected officials will help implement these agreements successfully. Peace is itself a prisoner to politics and the passions of a country trying to envision a future without warfare and violence.

Notes

1 Plan Colombia was originally intended to be a counter-narcotics (not a counter-insurgency) programme. However, as the FARC—EP became involved in drug trafficking, and after the '9/11' attacks in the USA, it became easy for the US and Colombian Governments to taunt the rebels with being a drug-trafficking organization and devote most of Plan Colombia's resources to attacking the rebels.
2 A civil war that involved Liberals and Conservatives fighting for state power.
3 The seat of the major of Bogotá is Colombia's second most important political position, behind that of President.
4 Corresponding to 3.73% of the total amount of seats in the Colombian Congress.
5 The 'fast track' procedure reduces from eight to three the number of debates that are necessary in order to introduce (or modify) laws in Congress, and also limits the possibility of making substantial changes in the text of the laws in which the government and the FARC have reached an agreement (El Espectador, 2016).

References

BBC Mundo, 2016. *Colombia: el Congreso aprueba el nuevo acuerdo de paz con las FARC y las divisiones se trasladan a las presidenciales de 2018*. [Online] Available at: www.bbc.com/mundo/noticias-america-latina-38165978 [Last accessed 30 June 2017].

Bejarano, J. A., 1995. *Una agenda para la paz: Aproximaciones desde la teoría de la resolución de conflictos*. Bogotá: TM Editores.

Congreso de la República de Colombia, 2011. *Ley de Víctimas y Restitucion de Tierras— Ley 1448 de 2011* [Online] Available at: www.centrodememoriahistorica.gov.co/descargas/ley_victimas/ley_victimas_completa_web.pdf [Last accessed 3 June 2017].

Corporación Observatorio para la Paz, 2009. *Guerras inútiles. Una historia de las FARC*. Bogotá: Intermedio.

Dudley, S., 2008. *Armas y urnas: historia de un genocidio político*. Bogotá: Planeta Colombiana.

El Colombiano, 2016. Los principales cambios que trae el nuevo acuerdo. [Online] Available at: www.elcolombiano.com/colombia/acuerdos-de-gobierno-y-farc/lo-que-se-sabe-del-acuerdo-definitivo-con-las-farc-DF5362126 [Last accessed 23 May 2017].

El Espectador, 2015. FARC—EP no aceptarán acuerdo que contemple cárcel por ejercer derecho a rebelión. [Online] Available at: www.elespectador.com/noticias/paz/farc-no-aceptaran-acuerdo-contemple-carcel-ejercer-dere-articulo-547196 [Last accessed 30 June 2017].

El Espectador, 2016. ¿Qué es el 'fast track'? [Online] Available at: www.semana.com/nacion/articulo/fast-track-que-es-y-por-que-es-importante/509302 [Last accessed 30 June 2017].

El Heraldo, 2014. Zuluaga pide al Gobierno suspender diálogo con las Farc. [Online] Available at: www.elheraldo.co/politica/zuluaga-pide-al-gobierno-suspender-dialogo-con-las-farc-146666 [Last accessed 30 June 2017].

El Tiempo, 2010. Las Farc dicen que quieren hablar con gobierno de Santos, 'pero sin condicionamientos'. [Online] Available at: www.eltiempo.com/archivo/documento/CMS-7951020 [Last accessed 30 June 2017].

Ferro, J. G. & Uribe, G., 2002. *El Orden de la Guerra—Las FARC—EP-EP, entre la organización y la política*. Bogotá: CEJA.

FundaciónIdeaspara la Paz, 2013. *La guerra en las coyunturas de negociación: Tlaxcala, Caguán, La Habana*. Bogotá: Fundación Ideas para la Paz.

García Durán, M., 1992. *De la Uribe a Tlaxcala: Procesos de paz*. Bogotá: Cinep.

Goebertus Estrada, J., 2016. *Una reflexión para quienes votaron 'No' en el plebiscito*. [Online] Available at: www.ifit-transitions.org/fondo-de-capital-humano/articulos/una-reflexion-para-quienes-votaron-no-en-el-plebiscito-el-tiempo [Last accessed 30 June 2017].

Granada, S., Restrepo, J. & Vargas, A., 2009. Guerra y violencias en Colombia: herramientas e interpretaciones. In: S. Granada, J. Restrepo & A. Vargas, eds. *El agotamiento de la política de seguridad: evolución y transformaciones recientes en el conflicto armado colombiano*. Bogotá: Pontificia Universidad Javeriana, pp. 27–124.

Human Rights Watch, 2013. *El riesgo de volver a casa: violencia y amenazas contra desplazados que reclaman restitución de sus tierras en Colombia*. [Online] Available at: www.hrw.org/sites/default/files/reports/colombia0913spwebwcover.pdf [Last accessed 30 June 2017].

Human Rights Watch, 2015. *El rol de los altos mandos en falsos positivos: Evidencias de responsabilidad de generales y coroneles del Ejército colombiano por ejecuciones de civiles*. [Online] Available at: www.hrw.org/es/report/2015/06/23/el-rol-de-los-altos-mandos-en-falsos-positivos/evidencias-de-responsabilidad-de [Last accessed 22 June 2017].

Isacson, A., 2010. *Don't Call It a Model. On Plan Colombia's Tenth Anniversary, Claims of 'Success' Don't Stand Up to Scrutiny*. [Online] Available at:www.wola.org/publications/colombia_dont_call_it_a_model [Last accessed 30 June 2017].

La Silla Vacia, 2016. *Compare fácil el nuevo Acuerdo de paz y el anterior*. [Online] Available at: http://lasillavacia.com/silla-llena/red-de-la-paz/historia/compare-facil-el-nuevo-acuerdo-de-paz-y-el-anterior-58734 [Last accessed 3 July 2017].

Machado, A., 2009. *Ensayos para la historia de la política de tierras en Colombia. De la colonia a la creación del Frente Nacional*. Bogotá: Universidad Nacional de Colombia.

Nasi, C., 2009. Colombia: Building peace in a time of war. In V. Bouvier, ed. *Colombia's peace processes, 1982–2002: Conditions, strategies, and outcomes*. Bogotá: United States Institute of Peace, pp. 39–64.

Nieto, R., 2001. Economia y Violencia. In *Colombia: conflicto armado, perspectivas de paz y democracia*. Miami: Latin American and Caribbean Center.

Oficinadel Alto Comisionado para la Paz, 2012. *Acuerdo General para la Terminación del Conflicto y la Construcción de una Paz Estable y Duradera*. [Online] Available at: http://peacemaker.un.org/colombia-generalaccordendconflict2012 [Last accessed 30 June 2017].

Oficinadel Alto Comisionado para la Paz, 2016. *Acuerdo Final Para La Terminacíon del conflicto y la Contruccíon De Una Paz Estable y Duradera*. [Online] Available at: www.altocomisionadoparalapaz.gov.co/procesos-y-conversaciones/Documentos%20compartidos/24-11-2016NuevoAcuerdoFinal.pdf [Last accessed 5 June 2017].

Palacios, M., 2012. *Violencia pública en Colombia: 1958–2010*. Bogotá: Fondo de cultura económica.

Pardo, R., 2004. *La historia de las guerras*. Bogotá: Editorial B de Colombia.

Pizarro Leongómez, E., 2011. *Las Farc (1949–2011): de guerrilla campesina a máquina de guerra*. Bogotá: Grupo Editorial Norma.

Pizarro Leongómez, E. & Valencia, L., 2009. *Ley de justicia y paz*. Bogotá: Grupo Editorial Norma.

Ramirez, W., 1991. Las nuevas ceremonias de la paz. *Analisis Politico*, Issue 14, pp. 8–33.

Rettberg, A., 2013. Victims of the Colombian armed conflict: The birth of a political actor. In B. Bagley & J. Rosen, eds. *Colombia's Political Economy at the Outset of the 21st Century: From Uribe to Santos and Beyond*. s.l.: Lexington Books, p. 111–139.

Revista Semana, 2016a. 'El Congreso sí puede refrendar nuevo acuerdo de paz': Consejo de Estado. [Online] Available at: www.semana.com/nacion/articulo/consejo-de-estado-dice-que-el-congreso-si-puede-refrendar-acuerdo-de-paz/507377 [Last accessed 30 June 2017].

Revista Semana, 2016b. 'Las mentiras" de las campañas del No, según el Consejo de Estado. [Online] Available at: www.semana.com/nacion/articulo/el-consejo-de-estado-dice-que-se-le-mintio-al-electorado-en-campanas-del-no/510040 [Last accessed 30 June 2017].

Romero, M., 2003. *Paramilitares y autodefensas: 1982–2003. Vol. 13*. Bogotá: Temas de Hoy.

Sánchez, G., Meertens, D. & Hobsbawn, E. J., 1984. *Bandoleros, gamonales y campesinos: el caso de la violencia en Colombia*. Bogotá: El Ancora.

Santos Calderón, E., 2014. *Así empezó todo: el primer cara a cara secreto entre el gobierno y las FARC—EP en La Habana*. Bogotá: Intermedio Editores.

4 The emergence and consolidation of transitional justice within the realm of Colombian peacebuilding

Marco Alberto Velásquez Ruiz

Introduction

This chapter gives an account of how transitional justice has emerged and has consolidated within the realm of peacebuilding processes in Colombia. In particular, the chapter describes the progressive inclusion of a transitional justice legal framework as part of the peace negotiations that have taken place in the country, from the decade of 1980 until the formulation of The Victims and Land Restitution Law (hereinafter VLRL) and its supplementary regulations.[1]

The chapter's main statement is that the emergence and adoption of a transitional justice framework in Colombia is aligned with the conducting of peace negotiations with diverse actors of the country's armed conflict. The advancement of these initiatives was the outcome of a favourable political scenario for the inclusion of a transitional justice framework as part of the national peacebuilding agenda. On the other hand, transitional justice—both its normative foundation and institutional structure—has progressively acquired a crucial role in the shaping of the content and extent of the corresponding negotiations. Therefore, it is argued that the processes of consolidation of transitional justice frameworks here considered are the direct precursors of the current Colombian peacebuilding initiative, which incorporates a vital transitional justice component. Thus, the current agreements are a new stage of the peace infrastructure that has been under construction in Colombia since the 1980s.

The chapter is organized as follows: firstly, it presents the legal antecedents to the adoption of a transitional justice framework within the context of Colombian peacebuilding. Herein, particular focus is given to a series of domestic laws that, during the decades of the 1980s and 1990s, embedded alternative criminal justice incentives into the process towards the effective disarmament, demobilization, and reintegration of the members of different insurgent armed groups. Next, the study focuses on Law 418 of 1997, which is considered to be the earliest attempt to introduce certain transitional justice elements into the political context of a peace negotiation between the Colombian Government and the insurgency. Thirdly, Law 975 of 2005, or the

Justice and Peace Law[2] (JPL), is depicted as a law that, for the first time, recognized the need to incorporate a proper transitional justice project in the country in order to achieve durable peace. Finally, the chapter presents the main aspects of the VLRL, which was a fundamental instrument for the peace agreements with the FARC—EP, and was the existing jurisprudence before the implementation of the currently applicable transitional justice framework.

Antecedents: peace through alternative criminal justice

Nowadays it is widely accepted by both academics and practitioners that addressing the legacies of past violence and human rights abuses is necessary for fostering sustainable peace. In this regard, it is argued that the implementation of transitional justice mechanisms—both as a preliminary requisite and as a subsequent measure—may lead to the success of peace negotiations and the sustainability of what is accorded. However, at the outset of the 1980s, transitional justice and peacebuilding were on separate paths. The former was an emerging field that devoted its attention to addressing transitions from dictatorships to democracies in the western hemisphere. As a result, the negotiated settlement of internal armed conflicts had the formulation of disarmament, demobilization, and reintegration (DDR) strategies as its main focus. Further actions linked to the correction of the structural causes that gave rise to the conflict to reduce the risks of that conflict relapsing. The structural conditions fuelling violence were not directly considered at the time.

Colombia had a long history of political violence that, by the 1980s, was increasingly affecting the country's stability. Public authorities were dealing with the strengthening of the guerrilla groups that emerged in the 1960s (see Chapter 2). Likewise, the occasional association between the radical political right, certain landlords, and the drug cartels, resulted in the consolidation of paramilitary structures that contested the power of the state. From being originally a matter of public order, mainly located at the fringes of the state (in

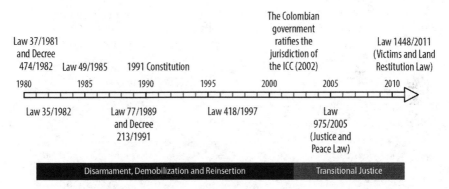

Figure 4.1 Legal Evolution of Transitional Justice in Colombia
Source: Own elaboration.

rural Colombia), the confrontations and the challenges to the state's authority turned into a serious concern for authorities across the country. Under such strains, the achievement of peace became a central aim for the state and society, and thus it became an attractive political platform for politicians.

Several governmental initiatives to facilitate the cessation of hostilities between the parties of the conflict, promote the demobilization and reincorporation of rebel soldiers, and encourage the further establishment of peace dialogues, took place with variable results (Boudon, 1996). Between 1981 and 1993, a series of norms were enacted to offer amnesty or pardon for political crimes (sedition, rebellion, and riot) and other connected conducts to members of the insurgent armed actors who decided to leave the arms and reincorporate to civilian life.

The government of President Julio César Turbay Ayala (1978–1982) inaugurated the passing of these types of norms with Law 37 of 1981 and its supplement, Decree 474 of 1982. These legal instruments provided for amnesty on political and connected crimes—except for kidnapping, extortion, and homicides not related to clashes and combats—to promote the end of conflict. Yet, this legal framework contrasted with the fact that in 1978 a controversial 'security statute' had been enacted to invest both the executive and the military with exceptional mechanisms to counter the activity of the guerrilla groups and other criminal structures associated with the drug cartels. The legal framework facilitated a peace initiative and the possibility of the demobilization of fighters; however, disarmament within an environment of the restriction of freedoms and rights characteristic of the 'security statute' came at odds with the intentions of Law 37. This limited the impact of this framework to support the achievement of peace agreements. The legal framework was in place; however, political willingness was missing at the time.

The arrival of President Belisario Betancur Cuartas to power in 1982 entailed the assumption of a different approach to the insurgency and the alternatives and mechanisms to be used to settle the internal armed conflict. Turbay's 'security statute' had ceased in June of that year, and a peace commission was subsequently created to drive negotiations—under a distinct political environment—with certain armed groups. This move was accompanied by the enactment of new laws concerning the granting of incentives to the members of the guerrillas aimed at encouraging their demobilization and reintegration to civilian life. Law 35 of 1982 was one of them. While it offered the same benefits as its predecessor, it included additional features that could arguably be identified as early manifestations of justice and reparation as part of a jurisdiction for peace. The law recognized the possibility that the victims of the conflict could obtain economic redress from the members of insurgent armed groups, regardless of the granting of amnesties. Likewise, it authorized the government to seek resources to develop social assistance programs in favour of both the expunged and the people located in the regions affected by the conflict.

In 1984, President Betancur's incipient peace negotiation policy became more robust. Preliminary accords with the guerrilla groups Fuerzas Armadas

Revolucionarias de Colombia—Ejército del Pueblo (FARC—EP), Movimiento 19 de Abril (M-19), and Ejército Popular de Liberación (EPL) were promoted in order to start formal negotiations. Within this context, the Colombian Congress passed Law 49 in June 1985, as a way of advancing on the incentives to accelerate peace dialogues. In comparison with its predecessor, which acknowledged the possibility to concede amnesty to the members of the insurgency, this law assumed a different approach. Instead of offering the clearing of criminal records upon demobilization, it authorized the executive to reprieve the members of the armed groups after they were subject to a judgement, which in any case had to be limited to political and connected crimes. Since the infraction was not disregarded, it was possible for the victims to seek truth and reparation from the responsible actor. This can be regarded as an innovative element that resembles a transitional justice framework: a tacit recognition of the existence of a series of entitlements for the affected population, within the context of a peace process. Yet, although they initially appeared to hold enormous potential, the prospective peace processes failed, and the application of the corresponding legal framework did not fulfil the promise of the mandate given by the law (Boudon, 1996).

Be that as it may, by the end of the 1980s, a number of peace negotiations started to have positive results. In particular, the national government and various guerrilla groups including M-19, EPL, Partido Revolucionario de los Trabajadores (PRT), and Movimiento Armado Quintín Lame (MAQL), reached peace agreements between 1990 and 1993 (Palacios, 2012). As with the previous attempts to finalize the internal political violence, these accords were supplemented by a legal base that provided incentives for the massive disarmament, demobilization, and reintegration of guerrilla members. Framed within a comprehensive peace plan entitled the Political Pact for Peace and Democracy[3], Law 77 of 1989 and Decree 213 of 1991 offered both the cessation of criminal procedures and pardons for the insurgency. In turn, these laws acted as a catalyst to the promulgation of other legal instruments that allowed the demobilization of smaller rebel groups in the following years.[4] An overview of these attempts to regulate the context of peace negotiations in Colombia indicates that although they were conceived to respond to the need to finalize conflict and provide stability, they did not directly include the components of justice, truth, and reparation required of modern transitional justice. Moreover, it is evident that these laws had similarities with the DDR programmes developed by the United Nations (UN) in the context of peacekeeping operations (Laplante & Theidon, 2006).

Colombia has pioneered these kind of DDR measures, since the UN Observer Group in Central America (ONUCA)[5] became the first peacekeeping mission mandated to assist in a DDR process in 1990 (United Nations Department of Peacekeeping Operations, 2010). Overall, the main goal of the Colombian Government was to address the concerns associated with the maintenance of public order within the country. In contrast, subsidiary considerations were directed at securing lasting peace beyond the mere

Transitional justice elements within a peacebuilding context: Law 418 of 1997

As the previous section illustrated, the DDR-oriented legal instruments, enacted between 1981 and 1991, produced variable outcomes with respect to the effective achievement of peace agreements with insurgent actors. During the next ten years, while the human rights discourse started to expand within and through several popular and institutional scenarios in Colombia, the country experienced a considerable escalation of the armed conflict's extent and intensity.

In spite of the conflict's upsurge, by 1997 the Colombian Government and FARC—EP initiated a number of humanitarian actions toward the possible establishment of new peace dialogues. In that regard, a portion of the country's rural territory was cleared to facilitate the commencement of negotiations (El Tiempo, 1997).

Within this context, Law 418 was passed by Congress by the end of 1997, in order to offer an alternative to the legal initiatives that had already been proposed and thus to facilitate the formalization of negotiations. In fact, on 14 December 1998, the Pastrana administration and FARC—EP agreed to begin formal peace talks the next year, on 7 January 1999.

Although this law continued to address the country's armed conflict issue as a strict matter of public order, and not as a circumstance that required exceptional measures such as a transitional justice framework, it introduced an alternative perspective to the normative meaning of peace for Colombian society. In that regard, the law's regulatory aim was the provision of effective tools to ensure the validity of the constitutional principle of the *estado social de derecho*, [6] and the effective protection of the rights and fundamental freedoms enshrined by the Constitution and the international treaties to which Colombia subscribed.

Law 418 authorized the government to conduct dialogues and sign peace accords with insurgent armed groups in order to end the armed conflict, ensure the effective implementation of international humanitarian law and human rights, and encourage ceasefire and demobilization. Thus, it established a commission to determine the possibility of negotiating with the guerrillas, and included provisions to consider the importance of other armed groups, such as the right-wing paramilitary groups, and the importance of their existence for the sustainability of peace policies (Laplante & Theidon, 2006, p. 61). Additionally, the law provided for amnesty for political crimes to those members of the outlawed armed groups who chose to participate in an individual or collective demobilization (Center for Justice and Accountability, 2014). In this way, Law 418 shared the scope of the laws previously enacted in Colombia to develop alternative criminal-oriented mechanisms to facilitate the end of conflict (Burbidge, 2008; Kerr, 2005; Ahmad, 2006).

Most importantly, Law 418 recognized the situation of the victims as one of the key factors to be addressed in order to achieve peace and stability in the country. Unlike the legal instruments previously enacted to address the termination of the armed conflict, this law transcended the setting of DDR-oriented measures. It included specific mandates for several national authorities for the assistance of people affected by violence caused by the actors in the internal conflict in Colombia.

In order to determine the constellation of people that should be assisted, the law included a definition of 'victim'. Thus, Law 418 provided the first definition of 'victim' in Colombian legislation. The definition accounts for the civilian population whose life, personal integrity, and property were affected by actions that occurred in the context of the armed conflict. Therefore, the law indicates that the state has the duty to provide humanitarian assistance, education, and healthcare to the victims; create housing programmes directed to meet their specific requirements; and give financial assistance for the replacement of belongings of those people affected by conflict-related violence. Although Law 418 was a legal device that created incentives to facilitate the end of the conflict and confrontations, the incorporation of the victims' assistance component indicates the rise of a concern around the need to balance the attribution of alternative criminal treatment with the requirements of justice in its retributive, restorative, and distributive versions, proper of a transitional justice discourse.

Given its content and extent, the institutional obligations introduced by Law 418 were supported by the application of the social solidarity principle. This principle states that when a person is in a situation of manifest vulnerability due to his economic, physical or mental condition, and assistance cannot be provided by himself or his relatives, an exceptional obligation to assist that person is grounded in head of the state.[7]

Yet, it is important to assert that the social solidarity principle was not yet a formal recognition of the victims' rights to justice, truth, and reparation. Moreover, article 47 of Law 418 established that the assistance given to the victims was by no means an acceptance of any type of responsibility by the state. Hence, the state's scope of action was associated with the above-mentioned social solidarity principle and not to any type of transitional justice duty. The state's responsibility was the principle, rather than the assumption of responsibility towards their citizens. The introduction of Law 418 into the Colombian legal framework contributed to changing the identification of DDR initiatives as isolated strategies to finalize the armed conflict in Colombia. Rather, it included the idea that any institutional scheme to achieve durable peace should consider the situation of the victims of the conflict. Thus, it permeated previous considerations about the role of the state in guaranteeing order and stability within its territory. Moreover, it made visible the obligation to assist people affected by the violence produced in the context of internal war, even if such duty arose from considerations of social solidarity. While Law 418 includes no express reference to transitional justice, it certainly incorporated a number of discursive and normative elements that resemble the field.

The Justice and Peace Law (JPL): the recognition of the need for a transitional justice project in Colombia (TJ 1.0)

Whilst Law 418 is recognized for the incorporation of the victims' rights discourse within the Colombian legal framework and its relation to conflict resolution and peace, the JPL (Law 975 of 2005) introduced transitional justice's rationality and structure to the Colombian legal regime and jurisdiction. However, such novelty did not come without controversy. On the one hand, some critics identified this legal instrument as a strategy to decree amnesties regarding serious crimes and human rights violations to paramilitary groups. On the other hand, although the JPL consecrated the victims' rights to justice, truth, and reparation in the context of the achievement of peace, it lacked operative measures to ensure their effectiveness.

The rise and development of the JPL is directly related to the negotiation process and the attempt at dismantling paramilitary groups that occurred under the mandate of President Álvaro Uribe (2002–2010). In May 2002, Uribe became the president of Colombia after a fierce political campaign that was based on two ideas: the rejection of dialogue with guerrillas after a failed peace negotiation attempt with FARC—EP (Cárdenas, 2002), and the promise of the intensification of military activity against illegal armed groups in order to achieve the end of the conflict (Burbidge, 2008). Surprisingly, in August 2002, the government began negotiations with the paramilitaries' umbrella organization, the Autodefensas Unidas de Colombia (AUC).[8] By July 2003, the parties reached a preliminary agreement in which the establishment of national peace was identified as a primary objective (Arvelo, 2005; Forer & Guerrero Torres, 2010; Pizarro Leongómez & Valencia, 2009).

Although the corresponding demobilization process was initially conducted under the framework of Law 418[9], it soon became clear to the authorities that the nature and magnitude of the crimes committed by paramilitary groups surpassed the possibilities of a legal instrument designed to grant amnesty for political crimes. In August 2003, the Uribe administration submitted a first draft law to Congress, whereby certain crimes associated with serious human rights violations—not pardonable under Law 418—could be subject to alternative punishment (Kerr, 2005; Posnanski, 2005; Pizarro Leongómez & Valencia, 2009)[10]. International governance actors, political actors and Colombian civil society levelled strong critiques at the legal instrument's systematic lack of awareness of the rights of the victims. The proposed legislation coincided with the International Coordination and Cooperation Roundtable for Colombia, held in London in July 2003 and Cartagena in February 2005, in which the Colombian Government and potential donors discussed the suggested DDR process's compatibility with international standards on truth, justice, and reparation (Laplante & Theidon, 2006). Consequently, the

Government introduced a new proposal in which provisions for truth, justice, and reparation were included as part of the strategy to finalize the conflict and achieve peace. In that regard, the Colombian Congress approved the JPL in July 2005 (González Chavarría, 2010; Easterday, 2009).

The JPL's aims to incorporate a transitional justice framework in Colombia faced two major challenges: first, the continuation of hostilities around the country by different armed groups, and second, the systematic denial by the government of the existence of an armed conflict in the country. In this regard, it is worth noting that although the process was compared with other peace and reconciliation projects in 'transitional societies' such as South Africa, Guatemala, and Northern Ireland, Colombia fell short of being a transitional society as different guerrillas were still at war (Burbidge, 2008).

In this context, like its predecessor, the legal instrument embodies a tension between the state's political need to promote DDR and the obligation to respect the rights of the victims of the armed conflict. In that regard, the law seeks to compensate the granting of generous penal benefits to those who committed atrocious crimes—seen as an incentive for demobilization and reinsertion—with the recognition of the rights of the victims (Laplante & Theidon, 2006). However, when compared with Law 418, the JPL brings about important novelties in relation to the role of the state in the achievement of durable peace. Particularly, it includes new elements on the assumption of the state's obligations regarding the situation of people affected by the conflict.

The incorporation of an extended definition of victim reflects a more comprehensive understanding of the context and dynamics of the conflict, and increases the authorities' duty to assist the victims by extending the definition of 'victim' to include relatives of those directly affected by violence. In addition, the provision of assistance to victims does not depend on the identification of the victimizer.

The formal consecration of the victims' rights to justice, truth, and reparation represents the inclusion of a transitional justice framework within the realm of institutional action. In this respect, the expansion of the role of the state not only occurs in terms of the amount of people to be attended, but regarding the nature of the measures that have to be implemented.

Notably, the law establishes a formula to conduct reparations: when it is not possible to undertake actions oriented to place the victim back in the situation prior to his affectation (restitution), authorities must provide monetary compensation for the damages caused. In parallel, the JPL provides for both actions towards the re-establishment of the victim's dignity and guarantees of non-repetition. This formula is supplemented by the development of collective reparations programmes, which are oriented to recover institutional stability at the zones most affected by violence, and where most of the vulnerable communities were originally located (Pizarro Leongómez & Valencia, 2009).

The prescription of restitution as the most adequate way to redress people affected by the conflict raises a very important consideration. In the realm of transitional justice, authorities might have to affect certain private rights and expectations in order to reconstruct the prior situation of the claimant. In a number of cases, compliance with the demands of effective restitution might require the implementation of distribution-oriented measures, which go beyond the provision of humanitarian assistance to the victims or their preferential inclusion in regular social programmes intended for the most vulnerable sectors of the society. The very content and extent of the right to reparation might require the production of exceptional actions, able to transform certain situations related with the access to scarce resources.

Be that as it may, the JPL has fallen short of fulfilling its formal aspirations with regards to integral reparation, and particularly in relation to restitution. Despite the consecration of a sophisticated transitional justice rationality that has an undisputable influence on both the content and extent of the victims' rights and the role of the state in ensuring such entitlements, the mechanisms designed to crystallize the normative pretentions of transitional justice have proved to be either incomplete or inoperative. By January 2013 only 14 sentences had been passed, and although in the process important progress was made with regards to the right to the truth, this legal framework actually led to a de facto amnesty for almost all of those who demobilized (Oficina Internacional de Derechos Humanos Acción Colombia—OIDHACO, 2013). Therefore, in the quest for durable peace, a generous formulation of the reparatory principle contrasts with a precarious institutional design that has severe logistical and procedural problems (Uprimny Yepes, 2005).

Although the victims' right to reparation is thoroughly consecrated, the JPL ends up restricting its scope to the obligation of the insurgent armed actors to provide redress to victims. In that sense, reparation is projected as a mere procedural action in the context of the alternative criminal procedures aimed at facilitating demobilization, and not as an independent component of the transitional justice process in Colombia. Reparation is instrumental for demobilization and reintegration, thus victims become a token of sorts. Within this context, effective redress depends on either the victimizer's confession in an ongoing criminal procedure, or the establishment of a connection between the victim's affectation and the proof of activity of an armed group that is going through a process of demobilization and reinsertion (González Chavarría, 2010). Moreover, reparation—including the restitution of lands and other assets—requires the surrender of goods proceeding from illegal activities by the armed actors, and exceptionally on government resources from the national budget and private donations that are administered by a reparation fund specifically created for that purpose (see Chapters 5 and 6). Finally, whereas the law identifies the return of property as an act of restitution, it does not provide any further regulation on the matter (Burbidge, 2008, p. 574).

The JPL defined the criminal justice system as the sole mechanism by which victims could claim economic redress. This prevented victims from being integrally redressed, and it also restricted many citizens from having the chance to access a formal procedure to claim their rights (Easterday, 2009). In a country with entrenched asymmetries of power between the poor and the wealthy, victims were placed in a condition of marginalization and sociopolitical ostracization, which reduced the possibility of accessing a formal justice system (see Chapters 6 and 7). In addition, the basket of funds and resources to fund reparation initiatives was reduced to goods that proceeded from illicit activities. This disregarded the capacity of paramilitary groups to legalize through legal and illegal means their assets and their illicit origin (Díaz & Marín, 2008).

Moreover, the Uribe administration introduced a series of legislative initiatives that contributed to regularize the illegality of the land appropriation that occurred in the context of the conflict. In addition, the government's denial of the existence of an armed conflict in Colombia minimised the co-responsibility of the state towards the victims. This had the effect of limiting the obligation to pay reparations or implement further measures to address the harm produced both in the context of armed confrontations, and with respect to structural causes limited to the implementation of the law (Laplante, & Theidon, 2006).

The Colombian Constitutional Court addressed some of the JPL's deficiencies. In 2006, the tribunal revised the law's adjustment to the Constitution and clarified several aspects related to the right to reparation, in order to provide 'teeth' to the law's application (Uprimny Yepes, 2005). The tribunal required that all goods coming from demobilizing armed actors—not only those with an illicit origin—should be considered eligible to supplement the funds and resources for restitution or compensation as the law originally established. Although the tribunal rejected limits in the budget as a reason for not complying with the mandate for paying reparations to the victims, the criteria on the exclusion of state liability and the application of the principle of social solidarity were maintained. In this regard, the Court considered that taxpayers were also victims of the conflict, and had not caused any damage from which compensatory duties could be established (Laplante & Theidon, 2006).

The gaps left by Law 418 and the JPL were the object of concern within Colombia's Congress. Thus, in 2007, a number of congressional representatives from different political movements registered a bill that intended to formulate and develop a state policy with respect to the rights of the victims in Colombia. This was informed by the critiques formulated by different societal actors (Proyecto de Ley 157/2007 Cámara de Representantes, and Proyecto de Ley 044/2008 Senado de la República). Such proposals aimed at compiling the dispersed legal instruments with respect to the protection of victims, and included a number of innovative dispositions regarding the effective reparation of people affected by the conflict (Rettberg, 2008).

Whilst the projected bill followed the ethos introduced by the JPL with respect to the victim's right to reparation, it intended to extend such protection to people affected by any of the warring parties of the conflict—including state agents—thus recognizing the complexities of the Colombian conflict. Moreover, the proposal went further with the introduction of specific mechanisms in order to guarantee the centrality of material restitution. The 2007 proposal included a guiding principle to operationalize patrimonial reintegration. According to it, reparation should be driven by the need to reconstitute the victim's economic worth, understood as the set of rights and obligations that can be economically estimated or the universe of assets and liabilities attributed to an individual. Furthermore, the bill had specific references to the state's obligation to adopt measures enabling the effective restitution of goods whose dispossession was a consequence of the conflict, regardless of the nature of those assets, or their legal status, in favour of the victim (this was included because a great deal of dispossession affected peasants who did not have the legal titles of their properties).

However, in spite of the great support that the proposal had among different sectors of Colombian society and other international actors, in July 2009 the legislative project was defeated after two years of discussion. The Government argued that budgetary constraints made it untenable, but the radical reluctance of the Uribe Government to accept the existence of state victims within the Colombian conflict was a central aspect of the rejection of this initiative. This acceptance on the part of the state would have entailed the consequent acceptance of an obligation to repair the situation, not grounded in the principle of the state's duty towards its citizens, but rather as a response to a legal mandate (González Chavarría, 2010).

The Victims and Land Restitution Law: Transitional Justice Redux (TJ 2.0)

An analysis of the previous transitional justice initiatives in Colombia revealed the complexities and the evolution of the jurisdiction behind a state's aim to achieve peace. An account of the early attempts to develop a legal response to the problem of violence (and its consequences) illustrated how the country's national project—the consolidation of the rule of law and a social compact—became gradually intertwined with the specific objectives of transitional justice.

Informed by the spirit of the human rights discourse, the process of creating legal responses to the problem of violence (and its consequences) in Colombia evolved from the plain implementation of DDR strategies—to facilitate the resolution of the conflict and bring stability—to the recognition of the fundamental relevance of the rights of the victims, and finally towards a understanding of peace that included the victims. Transcendental to this shift was the participation of a variety of actors, including different sectors within the polity, civil society, and the international community. They have played a central role in the inclusion of a wider and more comprehensive transitional justice rationality into the legal processes, whereby the victims' rights to justice, truth, and reparation are equipped to become effective entitlements.

Land policies acquired importance in the design and implementation of transitional justice in Colombia as a result of the identification of restitution as central to redressing victims' rights. Yet, the very ambitious objectives incorporated within these legal instruments have lacked effective mechanisms to fulfil such expectations. This is due to the absence of efficient mechanisms to enforce the victim's entitlements and rights. In that sense, transitional justice was a plan that still required the refinement of its components and its operation to achieve its transformative goals.

From a political standpoint, the current Colombian transitional justice project is grounded in a number of events: the election of President Manuel Santos in 2010; the recognition of the existence of an armed conflict within Colombia by the Government; and the start of a peace process with FARC—EP. In September 2010, the Santos Government introduced a new transitional justice initiative to the Colombian Congress, which incorporated some features of the bill that was defeated in 2009.

The new proposal considered both the establishment of a general framework to address the rights of the victims of the conflict, and the creation of an exceptional land restitution regime to conduct reparations. In June 2011, the Congress passed Law 1448—commonly known as the Victims and Land Restitution Law[11] (LVRT). This law was designed as a general framework that recognizes victims as subjects of special protection, and consequently provides provisions for their rights to be appropriately redressed. Land restitution was placed as the primary reparatory component. In turn, the LVRT demanded a number of supplementary norms that could provide institutional support to its mandate, and would allow it to comply with its mandate, in order to align it to the country's constitutional order.

A number of decrees that supplement the LVRT (Decree 4800 of 2011 and Decree 4829 of 2011) formed the first group of supporting norms. They defined operative mechanisms, new institutions, and differential criteria to meet the objectives of the transitional justice project envisioned in Law 1448. In particular, the victims' right to reparation was regulated comprehensively, as these norms addressed the processes required to undertake the process of land restitution, and defined mechanisms in order to protect the property rights of the victims over abandoned and looted lands. In addition, a number of institutions were created to facilitate these processes. These are the Administrative Unit for Victims Reparation,[12] which performs as the co-ordinator of the reparation component, and the Administrative Unit for Land Restitution,[13] which is in charge of the material accomplishment of this task (Decrees 4801, 4802, and 4803 of 2011). Finally, as a result of the inclusion of the human rights discourse in the Colombian constitutional order, specific reparation measures were provided for ethnic groups, including indigenous groups, and Afro-Colombian communities (Decrees 4633, 4634, and 4635 of 2011).

The enactment and implementation of the LVRT in 2011, including its supplementary regulation, was crucial for launching the new version of the Colombian state's transitional justice project. As a result, restorative justice was conceived to address the complex consequences of the conflict, in a manner that went beyond addressing past human rights violations. In this way, the norms and regulations embedded in Law 1448 provide a wider array of answers to the social needs created by the confrontations (Moore, 1973).

For that reason, it can be argued that this law and its associated regulation had a better chance of addressing the rights of the victims, and it is more likely to produce tangible changes in society, including the possibility to distribute—or redistribute—economic entitlements. This due to a massive and systematic land restitution programme, which is expected to facilitate the realization of the victims' right to reparation. Furthermore, this restorative justice initiative is designed to work in tandem with the outcomes of the peace process between the Colombian Government and the FARC—EP. Therefore, the implementation of Law 1448 and its mandate constitutes not only an act of individual reparation intended to reconstitute the situation of the victim, but also a peacebuilding framework.

The land restitution programme included in the Victims' Law is a fundamental part of the transitional justice initiative, since it intends to expeditiously realize and secure the victims' right to reparation by means of the restitution of the lands that were denuded by widespread acts of violence. Not only is it a restorative measure, but it could prove to be a structural driver for post-agreement peacebuilding. Thus, the challenge for the state is to be able to redress the extensive damage suffered by more than half a million rural households, most of which are mired in dire poverty. The success of restitution depended on the design of a system and an institutional infrastructure capable of restoring the usurped rights in an effective way (see Chapter 6).

To achieve this, the system required specific measures for addressing the particularities of plundering. For example, in regular civil law, in disputes between private individuals in which the ownership of property rights is to be determined, ordinary legislation applies, but applying it in post-conflict scenarios fails to understand the challenges of massive land dispossession in a framework where stolen land is legalized (see Chapters 6 and 7). Rather, the land restitution procedures aiming at justice should incorporate an understanding of the impact of the armed conflict on peasantry and their livelihoods (Ibáñez & Velásquez, 2008). For this reason a law incorporating restorative justice was required. The establishment of a special land dispossession fund (see Chapter 6) supported such an intervention. Finally, since violence is a social process that radiates its effects beyond direct victims to affect other persons collaterally, collective reparations are also considered within Law 1448.

Finally, it is important to bear in mind two specific issues around the operative possibilities of victims' reparation brought by Law 1448. First, although social welfare measures are based on the state's general obligation to provide for its citizens and do not intend to substitute reparations, in the case of the victims of the armed conflict these measures are imbued with an intrinsic reparatory effect and should be recognized as such (De Greiff & Duthie, 2009). Second, the authorities must perform in a way that the implementation of the transitional justice scheme will be effective and will not compromise the country's promises for sustainable peace.

Conclusion

This chapter has given an account of how transitional justice emerged and consolidated in Colombia as part of the national project of peacebuilding. The progressive adoption of a transitional justice framework in the country is the product of efforts undertaken by different actors—the national government, the insurgent groups, civil society, international organizations, and diplomatic agents—towards the achievement of peace. The evolution of the frameworks and the consolidation of a legal infrastructure around the national project of peace have permitted the progressive enactment of legal instruments dedicated to address the situation and rights of the victims of the conflict in a more comprehensive way. Likewise, the transitional justice mechanisms that have emerged in the middle of peace negotiations have paved the way to give legal space and legitimacy to the undergoing peace negotiations and brought up important elements to the corresponding discussions.

A series of legal instruments that were enacted during the 1980s and 1990s, which intended to facilitate the disarmament, demobilization, and reinsertion of the insurgency, included certain normative elements that resemble, and in fact, in the Colombian case, built the legal infrastructure that informed a widening understanding of rights and victims within the Colombian transitional justice discourse. Examples of this are the provisions for the victims to obtain economic redress from the insurgency, or that the government should create social assistance programmes in favour of the parties of the conflict. However, it was not until the passing of Law 418 of 1997 that the rights of the victims started to be recognized explicitly by public authorities. This law linked the possibility to achieve peace in the country to international human rights and humanitarian law standards. In 2005 (the limitations and contradictions proper of the political environment of that period notwithstanding) the JPL provided the foundations of the current Colombian transitional justice project. The rights of the victims to justice, truth, and reparation were formally consecrated and developed, even if this initiative lacked efficient mechanisms to make the mandate of the law effective. Finally, the Victims and Land Restitution Law appeared in 2011, and was the natural evolution of a framework that has been drafted in Congress and implemented in practice as the result of different peace initiatives in the country. Thus its vocation—to aim for durable peace by means of the deployment of a responsive system of promotion and protection of the rights of the victims—was not a surprise. Rather it was the outcome of the learning from the experiences, errors, and challenges of the Colombian state attempting to reassert its role as sovereign and guarantor of human rights to its citizens.

Notes

1 *Ley de Víctimas y Restitución de Tierras*, Law 1448/2011.
2 *Ley de Justicia y Paz*.
3 *Pacto Político por la Paz y la Democracia*.

4 A series of decrees provided the legal framework for the demobilization of a series of groups, such as the Decree 1943/1991(for the demobilization of the Ernesto Rojas Movement); the Law 104/1993 (for the demobilization of the Milicias urbanas de Medellín, Frente Francisco Garnica de la Coordinadora Guerrillera Simón Bolívar); and the Law 241/1995 (a framework which allowed the extension of the benefits to non-demobilized members of the latter armed groups).
5 (November 1989 – January 1992.
6 Social and democratic rule of law.
7 This principle has its origin in the Colombian Constitution of 1991.
8 United Self-Defence Forces of Colombia.
9 Extended and amended in regards of that occasion by law 782/2002 and decree 128/2003.
10 Decree 2758/2003.
11 *Ley de Víctimas y Restitución de Tierras.*
12 *Unidad Administrativa para la Reparación de Víctimas.*
13 *Unidad Administrativa para la Restitución de Tierras.*

References

Ahmad, J., 2006. The Colombian Law of Justice and Peace: One Step Further from Peace and One Step Closer to Impunity. *Transnational Law & Contemporary Problems*, Volume 16, pp. 333–372.

Arvelo, J. E., 2005. International Law and Conflict Resolution in Colombia: Balancing Peace and Justice in the Paramilitary Demobilization Process. *Georgetown Journal of International Law*, Issue 37, pp. 411–426.

Boudon, L., 1996. Guerrillas and the state: The role of the state in the Colombian peace process. *Journal of Latin American Studies*, 28(2), pp. 279–297.

Burbidge, P., 2008. Justice and Peace?–The Role of Law in Resolving Colombia's Civil Conflict. *International Criminal Law Review*, 8(3), pp. 557–587.

Cárdenas, M. C., 2002. Colombia's Peace Process: The Continuous Search for Peace. *Florida Journal of International Law*, Issue 15, pp. 273–297.

Center for Justice and Accountability, 2014. *Colombia: The Justice and Peace Law.* [Online] Available at: http://cja.org/where-we-work/colombia/related-resources/colombia-the-justice-and-peace-law/ [Last accessed 3 March 2017].

De Greiff, P. & Duthie, R., 2009. *Transitional Justice and Development: Making Connections.* 1st ed. New York: Social Science Research Council.

Díaz, A. M. & Marín, C. A., 2008. *Colombia: el espejismo de la justicia y la paz: balance sobre la aplicación de la Ley 975 de 2005.* 1st ed. Bogotá: Comision Colombiana de Juristas.

Easterday, J. S., 2009. Deciding the fate of complementarity: A Colombian case study. *Arizona Journal of International & Comparative Law*, Issue 26, pp. 49–111.

El Tiempo, 1997. *Un Año de Paz y Guerra.* [Online] Available at: www.eltiempo.com/archivo/documento/MAM-715447 [Last accessed 3 March 2017].

Forer, A. & Guerrero Torres, A., 2010. La Ley de Justicia y Paz, un ejemplo de justicia transicional en Colombia. *Iberoamericana*, 10(38), pp. 161–168.

González Chavarría, A., 2010. Justicia transicional y reparación a las víctimas en Colombia. *Revista mexicana de sociología*, 4(72), pp. 629–658.

Ibáñez, A. M. & Velásquez, A., 2008. *El impacto del desplazamiento forzoso en Colombia: condiciones socioeconómicas de la población desplazada, vinculación a los mercados laborales y políticas públicas.* 1st ed. Santiago de Chile: Naciones Unidas.

Kerr, K., 2005. Making Peace with Criminals: An Economic Approach to Assessing Punishment Options in the Colombian Peace Process. *The University of Miami Inter-American Law Review*, 37(1), pp. 53–117.

Laplante, L. J. J. & Theidon, K., 2006. Transitional justice in times of conflict: Colombia's Ley de Justicia y Paz. *Michigan Journal of International Law*, Issue 28, pp. 49–106.

Moore, S. F., 1973. Law and social change: the semi-autonomous social field as an appropriate subject of study. *Law & Society Review*, 7(4), pp. 719–746.

Oficina Internacional de Derechos Humanos Acción Colombia (OIDHACO), 2013. *Reforma de la Ley de 'Justicia y Paz'*. [Online] Available at: www.oidhaco.org/uploaded/content/article/571674914.pdf [Last accessed 18 August 2017].

Palacios, M., 2012. *Violencia publica en Colombia, 1958–2010*. 1st ed. Bogotá: Fondo de Cultura Economica.

Pizarro Leongómez, E. & Valencia, L., 2009. *Ley de Justicia y Paz*. 1st ed. Bogotá: Grupo Editorial Norma.

Posnanski, T., 2005. Colombia Weeps but Doesn't Surrender: The Battle for Peace in Colombia's Civil War and the Problematic Solutions of President Álvaro Uribe. *Washington University Global Studies Law Review*, Issue 4, pp. 719–741.

Rettberg, A., 2008. *Reparación en Colombia¿ Qué quieren las víctimas?* 1st ed. Bogotá: Agencia de Cooperación Técnica Alemana, GTZ.

United Nations Department of Peacekeeping Operations, 2010. *DDR in Peace Operations—A retrospective*, New York: United Nations.

Uprimny Yepes, R., 2005. La Ley de 'Justicia y Paz': ¿una garantía de justicia y paz y de no repetición de las atrocidades? *Revista Foro*, Issue 55, pp. 49–62.

5 The Transitional Justice Framework agreed between the Colombian Government and the FARC—EP[1]

*Camila de Gamboa Tapias and
Fabio Andrés Díaz Pabón*

For Katia, a bright shooting star

Introduction

Colombia has experienced a violent conflict for more than five decades. Since the 1980s, successive governments have implemented differing justice frameworks in their efforts to achieve peace (see Chapter 4). The government of President Juan Manuel Santos negotiated a peace agreement with the FARC—EP (Revolutionary Armed Forces of Colombia). Peace talks began officially in November 2012, with the parties reaching an agreement on 24 September 2016. While the Constitution did not oblige the President to subject the agreement to public vote for its approval, President Santos publicly announced at the beginning of negotiations in 2012 that the agreement would be subject to a plebiscite. This was considered important for the political legitimacy of the agreement.

When the Colombian Constitutional Court reviewed the constitutionality of the plebiscite in July 2016 (i.e. prior to it taking place), it ruled that the agreement could be implemented by the President only if the plebiscite resulted in its approval, expressed through a vote of the citizens (Corte Constitucional de Colombia, 2016). In addition, the Colombian Congress had previously approved a constitutional amendment to give extraordinary powers to the Santos administration to implement the institutions and procedures that the agreement called for, and the Congress also had the power to approve these laws using a 'fast track' mechanism.[2] Thus, the implementation of peace agreements depended on the approval of the agreement through the plebiscite (Congreso de Colombia, 2016a).

On 2 October 2016, Colombians voted in a plebiscite and rejected the agreement by a razor-thin margin.[3] Actors in Colombia and overseas were perplexed by the results of the plebiscite; it was expected that the possibility of peace would produce a consensus among Colombian citizens in favour of the agreement. The vote of the plebiscite against the agreements was not only a vote against peace; it reflected opposition to the demobilization incentives given to the FARC—EP in the agreements. Some segments of the Colombian polity feared losing their economic and political advantages (acquired legally or otherwise), and other citizens opposed the agreements because they opposed Santos's policies in general, rather than the peace agreement specifically.

The vote against the agreements can be seen as evidence of a reduction in the state's legitimacy and the outcome of a dangerous polarization in Colombian society fuelled by some political parties, such as the Centro Democrático[4], led by former President Uribe. A discourse of scepticism and fearmongering, coupled with a successful misinformation campaign, framed the proposed peace as a descent into a communist dystopia (La Silla Vacia, 2016) that would erode traditional family values. This proved effective in mobilizing Colombians against the agreement.

The success of the campaign against the agreement was aided by the Santos administration's ineffective communication of the agreement to large sectors of the population, and the failure of some political parties to adequately mobilize their constituents in favour of the agreement (Revista Semana, 2016). The irony of the outcome of the vote is that the agreement was in fact approved in the majority of the regions which are most affected by the violence (Registraduría Nacional del Estado Civil, 2016; Fundación Ideas para la Paz, 2016a). The idea of retributive justice and its 'absence' from the agreement was one of the main arguments made by the advocates of the campaign against the agreements, and one of the most important issues in the political, juridical, and ethical discussions in Colombia and abroad with regard to the transitional justice taking place in the country. An amended agreement was signed and ratified in November 2016 (see Chapter 3).

In this chapter we analyse the transitional justice framework defined by the peace agreements between the FARC—EP and the Colombian Government, as captured in point five of the final agreement signed in Bogotá in November 2016: the '*Sistema integral de verdad, Justicia, Reparación y No Repetición, incluyendo la Jurisdicción Especial para la Paz; y compromiso sobre Derechos Humanos.*'[5] This system is designed to regulate the transitional justice framework agreed upon in the accords. It aims to recognize the rights of victims, impose certain judicial and extra-judicial burdens upon the members of the FARC—EP and other armed actors responsible for violations of human rights, and establishes guarantees of non-repetition through different mechanisms.

In analysing the transitional justice framework, we examine the principles that inspired the agreements on victims and four of the key mechanisms described in it: the Commission for the Clarification of Truth;[6] the Unit for the Search for Missing Persons in the Context and as a Result of the Conflict;[7] measures on Comprehensive Reparation for Peace Building; the Guarantee of non-Repetition; and the Special Jurisdiction for Peace.[8]

The Special Jurisdiction for Peace and its emergence as an iteration of the previous transitional justice frameworks implemented in Colombia is explored in the section which follows. In the final section, we analyse some of the challenges to the implementation of the transitional justice agreements, reflecting on the uncertainties surrounding the implementation of the agreements, and how this may provide legal stability (or instability) for different constituents and for peace in Colombia.

The principles and mechanisms defined by the transitional justice agreement

The agreement on the victims of the conflict starts with the recognition by the government and the FARC—EP that the main aim of this agreement is to compensate victims. In addition, it states that all the measures described in the agreement are intended to be comprehensive. This introductory portion of the agreement recognizes that the armed conflict in Colombia has multiple causes, and has resulted in great harm and suffering for the population. It describes the kinds of harms produced by the violence, including forced displacement, deaths, disappearances, sexual violence, and trauma; and it lists the different population groups affected by these harms, including women, children, and the poorest and most vulnerable population sectors (including minorities, Romani, indigenous groups and Afro-descendants) (Gobierno de Colombia y FARC—EP, 2016).

The recognition of all the victims of the conflict and of the responsibility of different groups—not only the FARC—EP and the state—for the victims' conditions is one of the guiding principles of this agreement. The agreements provide for the participation of victims to assure the satisfaction of their rights, the clarification of the truth, reparation for victims, guarantees for their personal safety, and reconciliation, as well as the guarantee of non-repetition.

A human rights perspective informs the agreements reached and the transitional justice model agreed on by the parties. This rights perspective is a lens through which the harm that the armed conflict has caused victims is acknowledged, and informs the approach through which the Government, the FARC—EP, other groups, and society in general aim to respond to victims' demands and needs.

The transitional justice system agreed in the peace agreement is considered to be holistic. In a holistic approach, transitional justice mechanisms are complementary, in the sense that all efforts to protect the rights of the victims to justice, truth, reparation, and the guarantee of non-repetition are interrelated and not exclusive of each other (de Greiff, 2012).

Therefore, the agreement considers that justice cannot be achieved in the absence of any of the proposed mechanisms or the victims' rights described above—all of which are regarded as necessary for justice. The comprehensive system thus entails different mechanisms such as: The Commission for the Clarification of Truth; The Unit for the Search for Missing Persons in the Context and as a Result of the Conflict; Measures on Comprehensive Reparation for Peace Building; and the Guarantees of Non-Repetition (see Figure 5.1).

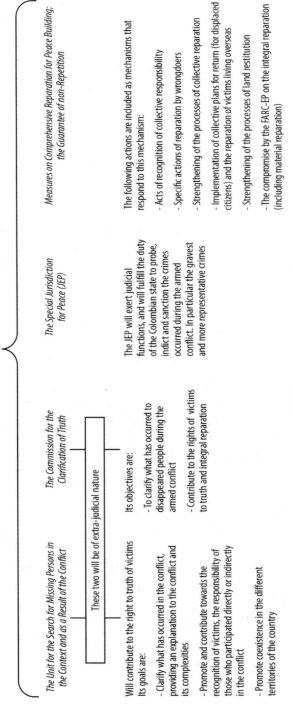

Figure 5.1 Components of the integral system for truth, justice, reparation and guarantee of non-repetition in Colombia
Source: Own elaboration.

The Commission for the Clarification of Truth, Coexistence, and Non-Repetition

The agreement recognizes the clarification of truth, coexistence, and non-repetition as one of the mechanisms that victims' organizations have demanded, thus its inclusion not only responds to best practices in the field but also to the citizen's demands (de Greiff, 2012). The Commission has three goals (Gobierno de Colombia y FARC—EP, 2016):

i   To clarify what happened over the course of the conflict by explaining its complexity and describing the serious human rights violations[9] and breaches of international humanitarian law that occurred in the course of the confrontations, in order to promote a societal understanding of the conflict and make the lesser-known aspects of the conflict visible.
ii To acknowledge victims as: agents whose rights 'were infringed' by society and as political agents who can contribute to the country's transformation. To recognize the responsibility of all the institutions and individuals who have participated directly or indirectly in the conflict.
iii To promote coexistence in the territories where the conflict primarily took place through the peaceful resolution of conflicts and the construction of a democratic culture that promotes tolerance, co-operation and solidarity.

All these goals are based on the premise that truth-building is essential for peacebuilding and reconciliation. The goals and mandates of the Commission for the Clarification of Truth, Coexistence, and Non-Repetition must be understood in conjunction with the other points of the agreement, such as rural development; mechanisms for the prevention of the production and trafficking of illicit drugs; and demobilization, disarmament and reintegration (DDR). This means that in order to build sustainable peace, it is necessary to undertake the task of a truth commission, but the successful implementation of the other elements of the agreements by the state are also necessary (see Chapter 3). Ascribing the whole project of peace and reconciliation to a truth commission might be overambitious, and can hamper its efficiency and effectiveness (de Greiff, 2012).

One of the main aspects of the truth-telling mechanisms included in the agreement between the FARC—EP and the Government is the principle that both actors have a moral and political commitment to respect the rights of victims by contributing to the clarification of the truth and acknowledging their responsibilities. It is important to mention that the Commission is not a judicial body: 'its activities will not be of a judicial nature and cannot imply any criminal accusation against any of those who appear before the Commission [...] and the information [collected] cannot be transferred by it to judicial authorities' (Gobierno de Colombia y FARC—EP, 2016). This serves in principle to maximize the number of involved actors that can contribute towards the work of the Commission. This includes illegal actors, individuals or institutions that suffered directly or indirectly from the conflict or participated in it, and are willing to testify or confess to crimes that they would not be willing to talk about under other circumstances.

Truth commissions are one of the most commonly used mechanisms to bring the history and the memory of past human right violations into the public space in countries transitioning from repressive regimes, civil wars, or internal conflicts. Truth commissions have had different purposes and focuses, emerging in some cases as substitutes for criminal prosecutions, as part of processes of democratization away from dictatorship, or as part of transitions away from civil conflict. In other cases (in Peru, for example), truth commissions were created prior to the initiation of criminal prosecutions, and their results were used as inputs in criminal prosecutions.

Currently, truth commissions are understood as an official, yet extrajudicial mechanism that is not meant to replace criminal prosecutions, but rather to complement the juridical truth with a wider historical account of the political, economic, and social conditions that gave origin to human rights violations, so that the actors involved in the violence recognize their actions, and victims have a space where their histories can be heard (Uprimny Yepes & Saffon Sanín, 2006).

The Colombian Truth Commission's period of study is the entirety of the Colombian armed conflict, but given that the conflict has lasted over 50 years, the Commission has the authority to establish priorities for its research. The Commission has a working period of three years to produce a final report (Gobierno de Colombia y FARC—EP, 2016). To clarify the diverse and complex causes of the conflict, the Commission can analyse previous historical events, and its work can be supported by other previous reports and research,[10] such as the work of the Historical Commission on the Conflict and its Victims[11] and other initiatives.

The Search Unit for Missing Persons in the Context and as a Result of the Conflict

The agreement explicitly addresses forced disappearances, given that it is one of the main crimes of the Colombian armed conflict.[12] The transitional justice agreement recognizes that many people have been 'disappeared' due to actions by state agents, the FARC—EP and other armed groups in Colombia. Some victims' organizations focusing on disappeared persons expressed their satisfaction with the establishment and objectives of this unit (Fundación Ideas para la Paz, 2016b). The goal of the Unit for the Search for Disappeared Persons in the Context and as a Result of the Conflict is to contribute to satisfying victims' rights to truth and reparation. The unit is transitory, and has a non-judicial, humanitarian character. It has three main functions (Gobierno de Colombia y FARC—EP, 2016):

i To account for the universe of disappeared citizens within the armed conflict and identify those still alive.
ii To identify the remains of the deceased.
iii To co-ordinate and promote the processes of 'searching, identifying, locating, and the dignified return of remains'.

These activities must be co-ordinated with other state institutions such as the National Institute of Legal Medicine and Forensic Science, the Truth Commission, and the Special Jurisdiction for Peace, among others, in order to report the unit's actions and provide information, and to allow for the active participation of victims and their organizations, and international organizations such as the International Committee of the Red Cross and the International Commission on Missing Persons.

Reparation: Measures for Comprehensive Reparation for Peacebuilding

Another important aspect of the system of justice agreed upon is its complex conception of reparation, which includes early measures for the acknowledgment of collective responsibilities.[13] Mechanisms to implement this include a national plan for collective reparations and territorial plans for collective reparations, individual and collective psychosocial rehabilitation, collective processes of return for displaced persons, and the reparation of victims living abroad, as well as measures for land restitution.

The agreement expressly states that all groups and individuals who have caused harm during the conflict must contribute to repairing the injuries they caused and that this contribution 'will be taken into the account in order [for them] to receive any special treatment in matters of justice' (Gobierno de Colombia y FARC—EP, 2016, p. 146). This recognizes that there were several groups other than the state and illegal armed groups that participated directly or indirectly in the conflict and benefited in some way from it.[14] The mechanisms outlined in the paragraph above provide avenues for this reparation.

In addition, the agreement states that in its reincorporation into civilian life, the FARC—EP must carry out actions that contribute to reparation. For example, they will undertake reparatory actions by participating in the reconstruction of infrastructure, particularly in territories affected by the conflict; and in programmes to remove anti-personnel mines, by participating in programmes for the substitution of illicit crops; and by contributing to the search, location, identification and recovery of remains of persons reported missing or dead.

The agreement expressly affirms that the FARC—EP, as an insurgent organization, 'commits to contributing to material reparations for victims and in general to their comprehensive reparation, on the basis of the events identified by the Special Jurisdiction for Peace' (Gobierno de Colombia y FARC—EP, 2016, p. 186).[15] The inclusion of this provision is in fact is one of the interesting outcomes of the amendment process which followed the initial rejection of the agreements. The explicit obligation of the FARC—EP to redress victims with their own resources was included in the amended and adopted agreement. As the FARC—EP participated in drug production and trade activities, extortion, and kidnapping, it is likely that they have resources to make this contribution.

It is important to understand that the model of transitional justice proposed for Colombia benefits from Colombia's long experience with reparations, and the establishment of an institutional capacity for this (see Chapter 4). The agreement on victims has the potential to articulate and strengthen procedures for reparation within the context of existing legislation and institutions.

Guarantees of non-repetition

Achieving peace whilst avoiding a relapse into violence is an important goal: however, its attainment depends on the extent of the actual and effective implementation of the provisions in the agreement, including the mechanisms regarding victims. Besides the measures on victims, the accord also creates a unit for persecuting criminals and dismantling criminal organizations. As was shown by the experience of the demobilization and reinsertion of former members of the Autodefensas Unidas de Colombia (AUC)[16] as part of the peace process with the paramilitaries, such measures are necessary to address the risk that criminal structures will continue operating (Centro Nacional de Memoria Histórica, 2015).

Even in the case of a full demobilization and reintegration into civilian life by the totality of the FARC—EP, a series of armed groups that operate in different parts of the country (paramilitaries or other guerrilla groups) will remain. Their existence presents a looming risk to the agreements and their implementation, as these groups may attempt to profit from the power vacuum generated by the demobilization of FARC—EP units. There is also a high risk of retaliations against former combatants and demobilized cadres[17] (MAPP/OEA, 2017). In the case of Colombia, the possibility of non-repetition depends on the dismantlement of other insurgent and criminal organizations across the country. This in turn depends on the consolidation of other peace processes, ensuring the monopoly of violence by the state, and the establishment of mechanisms that could demobilize these groups—which is something to bear in mind as regards the current peace process with the Ejército de Liberación Nacional (ELN)[18].

The Special Jurisdiction for Peace

To analyse the structure of the Special Jurisdiction for Peace, it is important to consider the Justice and Peace Law (JPL),[19] and how the experience in implementing it informs the current framework. It can be argued that the current transitional justice setting was in fact incepted by the lessons learned in enacting the JPL.

The lessons from the Justice and Peace Law

During the first peace process with the paramilitary forces undertaken by the Colombian Government, the Uribe administration created a legal framework for facilitating the demobilization of the AUC. The draft legislation was very generous in protecting the rights of the victims in its declaration of principles, but did not establish legal instruments to implement these rights. The draft bill sought a formula for peace that did not meet the demands for justice for the victims of the crimes committed by the AUC (Uprimny Yepes & Saffon Sanín, 2006). This legislation became the Justice and Peace Law, Law 975 (Congreso de Colombia, 2005).[20]

After this law was approved by Congress, the Constitutional Court of Colombia reviewed the legislation, considering the challenges brought against it by organizations and citizens who claimed that Law 975 did not guarantee victims' rights (Corte Constitucional de Colombia, 2016). The rulings by the Constitutional Court and the modifications this court made to Law 975 sought to provide legal instruments that, while offering generous reductions of penalties to the armed actors, would also seek to guarantee the victims' rights to truth and reparation (Uprimny Yepes & Saffon Sanín, 2006).

Despite the modifications of the Constitutional Court, additional problems were associated with the implementation of the JPL. These related to the institutional weaknesses of the judicial system in Colombia and the lack of appropriate legal instruments to ensure that the mandate of the law was achieved (Uprimny Yepes, et al., 2006). The JPL appeared not to have taken into account the context of institutional weakness inherent in the Colombian criminal justice system, and in this sense failed to consider and establish mechanisms and procedures to respond to these challenges. The JPL, as approved by Congress, was a law created to respond to an extraordinary situation, enacted with ordinary tools (de Gamboa, 2010).

The emergence of challenges facing the implementation of the law was thus no surprise. These included: the low capacity of the criminal justice system; insufficient co-operation between the different state agencies involved in the process; difficulties in effectively monitoring the demobilization and reinsertion of the members of the armed groups; a lack of clarity regarding which governmental entity was responsible for the process of DDR; problems of coordination among state institutions in managing and using information related to the JPL process; the absence of resources to protect ex-combatants, witnesses, victims, prosecutors, and judges; and the creation of institutions with several duties but without the clear legal mandate or enough resources to fulfil them (International Crisis Group, 2006).

Significant power and economic asymmetries between the demobilized AUC members and the victims were also not addressed by the law (see

Chapters 6 and 7). Therefore the guarantees of victims' rights depended almost entirely on the capacity of the state and its institutions to guarantee the legitimate defence of the victims' rights in a context where demobilized AUC members were better positioned to command effective legal representation (de Gamboa, 2010).

The negotiations with the FARC—EP regarding the victims and their rights thus departed from the Santos Government's recognition that previous transitional justice norms, such as the JPL, did not fully assure victims' rights, the promotion of peace, or the strengthening of the rule of law. The previous peace process with the paramilitaries produced just thirty-five sentences from the pool of 4,643 cadres that had been identified to be charged. The process with the paramilitaries appeared to operate as a de facto amnesty, and demonstrated the challenges of implementing a transitional justice framework in Colombia (Verdad Abierta, 2015).

The Government also acknowledged other failures from the peace process with the paramilitaries. The truth mechanisms implemented were recognized as very limited, since they depended on what the paramilitaries chose to admit in the judicial proceedings. In addition, the negotiation team recognized the tensions between a maximalist tradition (the obligation of the state to prosecute all grave violations of human rights) and an approach valuing peace and non-repetition; and the challenge of finding a normative pathway balancing concerns for justice, peace, and non-repetition in a context with strongly held claims, often without available supporting evidence (Orozco Abad, 2012).

The negotiators adopted a hybrid approach, able to meet international standards whilst responding to the particularities of the Colombian context.

The Justice Component of the Agreement on Victims

When the FARC—EP entered into a negotiation process with the Colombian Government, they did not entertain the possibility of embracing a transitional justice framework. They considered this system to be created by their opponent (the Colombian state), and they argued their actions in rebelling against the state should not make them punishable (El Espectador, 2015). However, by the end of the peace process, the FARC—EP had committed themselves to a transitional justice framework that complied with international standards and to a comprehensive agreement on victims' rights.

The agreement on victims supports the creation of a Special Jurisdiction for Peace. This agreement managed to address concerns about the sovereignty and self-determination of the state whilst complying with the principles of international human rights law. The jurisdiction will consider serious human rights violations and breaches of international humanitarian law committed in the course of the conflict between the FARC—EP and the state.

The jurisdiction applies to all those who participated directly or indirectly in the armed conflict. This includes members of the FARC—EP, representatives from the state,[21] and other individuals or groups who were not combatants but who engaged in the financing of or collaboration with paramilitary groups, without having been coerced to do so (Gobierno de Colombia y FARC—EP, 2016).[22]

The agreements defined a jurisdiction that is not solely focused on the dyad of the government and the FARC—EP. In that sense, the agreements and the jurisdiction set in place can promote a wider reconciliation that transcends the process with the FARC—EP. As it stands now, all groups and individuals can recognize their responsibilities in the armed conflict, and all have the same opportunity to take advantage of certain legal benefits in order to establish the truth about their responsibility and assure the reparation of victims. As such, the agreements speak to a wider notion of peace beyond the agreements with the FARC—EP. In addition, they establish the possibility of creating a framework that can be easily implemented should other groups decide to negotiate their demobilization with the state.

The jurisdiction established by the agreements aims to investigate crimes against humanity. The agreement recognizes that according to the Rome Statute of the International Criminal Court (ICC), those who commit these crimes are not eligible for amnesties or pardons. Although judges can prioritize those ultimately responsible and focus on certain serious crimes, they must investigate all the grave crimes enumerated without restrictions.[23] Second, the jurisdiction establishes a series of incentives for those who committed grave crimes to submit to justice voluntarily (in return for some benefits) and disincentives to those electing not to submit to this voluntarily (they will face more severe sanctions). In all cases, offenders must also submit themselves to the other components of the comprehensive system contained in the agreement on victims (truth, reparation, and non-repetition).

Guerrillas that submit themselves to the Special Jurisdiction for Peace will not have their political rights affected. This implies that former FARC—EP cadres are still eligible for public posts and can run for election at a local, regional or national level. This has been strongly criticized by the opposition to the peace agreements, who argue that those citizens who committed crimes should not be eligible to participate in politics at all. A series of conditions has been decided by the Constitutional Court of Colombia in order to clarify the ambiguity with regards to the tension between justice and political participation for guerrillas brought by the Special Jurisdiction for Peace (Corte Constitucional de Colombia, 2017). For guerrillas to maintain the benefits of the special jurisdiction, they will have to comply with all the requirements of the special justice court for truth and reparation of the victims, as well as a not being involved in any criminal activity after 1 December 2016. Otherwise they will lose all the benefits of the transitional justice framework.

The agreement also acknowledges the existence of political crimes. Therefore it gives the state space to operate within international humanitarian law and the Colombian Constitution, allowing the state to grant amnesty exclusively to FARC—EP rebels. The amnesty law approved by the Colombian Congress establishes the criteria and enumerates the different political crimes

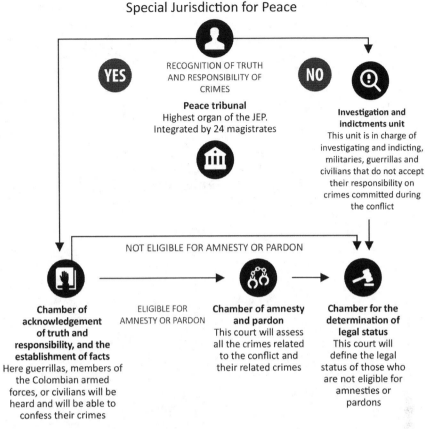

Figure 5.2 How does the special jurisdiction for peace in Colombia work?
Source: Own elaboration.

that will be eligible for amnesty. These include rebellion, sedition, military uprising, and assassination in combat compatible with international humanitarian law. It also links drug trafficking to political offences if the purpose of this activity (drug trafficking) was linked to the financing of rebellion, not for the purpose of personal enrichment.

A series of provisions was tabled with regard to the members of the security forces. In 2016, Congress established a similar arrangement resembling the amnesty and pardons given to the FARC—EP[24] in Law 1820. As with the Special Jurisdiction for Peace, amnesties or pardons for crimes against humanity are not granted under this Law. In addition, these benefits will not apply in the case where offences constitute a threat to the morale, discipline, interests and honour of the armed forces, in accordance with the military penal code. In addition, these benefits are conditional on state agents' fulfilment of their obligation to make reparations to victims and contribute towards the truth (Congreso de Colombia, 2016b).

The Special Jurisdiction for Peace is composed of several bodies (see Figure 5.2). These comprise: the Chamber for the Acknowledgment of Truth, Responsibility, and the Establishment of Facts; the Peace Tribunal; the Chamber for Amnesty and Pardon; the Chamber for the Definition of Legal Situations; and the Investigation and Indictments Unit.

The peace agreements achieved between the FARC—EP and the Colombian Government envision a holistic transitional justice model. In line with this vision, the agreements proclaim the connection and synergy between the rights of victims to truth, reparation, and guarantees of non-repetition. The content of the agreements on victims create a series of institutions that aim to redress and guarantee the rights of the victims. These institutions have been shaped to respond to the needs and particularities of the Colombian context, and appear to fulfil the requirements of international human rights standards. If this system manages to fulfil its mandate in practice, it will constitute a textbook example of a hybrid model of transitional justice (Sriram, 2010).

However, in spite of the achievement of the agreements, it is important to reflect on the challenges facing their implementation.

The long road to justice and peace: From text to institutions, justice and statehood

In order to analyse the challenges with regard to the implementation of the transitional justice framework agreed between the FARC—EP and the Colombian Government, it is important to understand the political context in which the implementation of the agreements takes place and the challenges that some provisions within the transitional justice agreements may create, as well as the structures and the inter-institutional co-ordination required for effective implementation.

Since the agreements process began, the political landscape has become dangerously re-polarized in Colombia. This polarization resembles the split between political actors that preceded the bipartisan violence of the 1940s and 1950s from which the FARC—EP emerged. This polarization was illustrated in the results of the plebiscite on the peace agreement and the related debates in the Colombian Congress. The Santos Government had the majority in the Congress, which allowed the translation of the agreements into normative and operative laws, such as the Amnesty Law (Congreso de Colombia, 2016a), and the law that regulates the transitional justice system (Congreso de Colombia, 2017). These advances can be rolled back if opponents to the agreements decide to reform the peace agreements (El País, 2017). Thus, if a political party that opposes the agreements filibusters the implementation of the peace agreement or wins the next elections, they can stifle or reverse the implementation of the transitional justice agreements. If this occurs, the stalled or stunted implementation of the agreements would fall short of the commitments signed in the agreements, leading to a default on peace agreements produced by selective negligence.

Within the provisions of the agreements, there is great concern in relation to the provisions related to the crimes committed by members of the Colombian armed forces (Revista Semana, 2017). A provision regarding command responsibility establishes that a military commander must answer for the crimes committed by his subalterns. In this case, a superior must be accountable for the actions of the soldiers under his command, even in the case when he has not taken any active role in these actions, but through negligence or apathy did not take appropriate corrective or preventive measures (Uprimny Yepes, 2017). This provision can be interpreted to apply to civilians as well.

International human rights practice establishes that the proof of knowledge by a superior of the crimes committed by his subalterns can be based upon effective or inferred knowledge.[25] It also states that hierarchical responsibility is ascribed on a case-by-case basis; it thus allows inquiries into cases where control and leadership is exerted de facto. However, in the legislation that regulates the agreements, only explicit and effective knowledge is considered as proof. The Special Jurisdiction for Peace would thus not be able to investigate and inquire into cases where military commanders were negligent. There is therefore the risk of the provision of half-truths in the cases where members of the armed forces committed human rights violations. In addition, the laws and regulations tabled in Congress will limit the understanding of the command responsibility; with the effect of limiting the scope of investigations and interventions by the ICC. This may mean that in some cases the actions of military commanders will not be prosecuted at all. The decision by the Colombian constitutional court with regards to the Special Jurisdiction for Peace did not elaborate on this, keeping alive the risk that the framework implemented in Colombia might not fulfil international standards of transitional justice (Corte Constitucional de Colombia, 2017).

In addition, questions remain with regard to the incentives for civilians involved in the conflict (for example as sponsors of armed groups) to participate in the transitional justice process as witnesses or subjects of legal inquiry. While they may not have criminal responsibility (e.g. an industrial agent who was extorted and funded a particular group, or a cattle grower who funded counter-insurgency paramilitary groups), they could have information and knowledge of the actions in the conflict that are vital to establishing the full truth and to enabling state institutions to understand the organizations and agents that were linked to war and violence. The decision by the Constitutional Court declared that third parties such as civilians involved in the conflict cannot be obliged to participate in this jurisdiction. However, this does not absolve them (civilians) from their legal or penal responsibility. Therefore civilians should be judged by the existing judicial institutions and courts. Thus, it would be expected that those civilians who want to benefit from the legal framework for peace could present themselves voluntarily to the Special Jurisdiction for Peace (Corte Constitucional de Colombia, 2017).

Although the implementation of the transitional justice agreements is necessary for peace, transitional justice by itself it is not sufficient. Inter-institutional coordination, commitment, and political consistency are required from the state, so that the other elements of the agreement (relating to political participation, rural reform, demobilization, illicit crops and drug production) are implemented. These additional elements of the agreements point to other structural issues that define the Colombian conflict. Without solid institutions in place, the road for peace will be bumpy; however, peace-making always departs from a point of state weakness, rather than strength and efficiency.[26] This is the departure point for Colombia, as the state aims to consolidate its institutions and navigate towards peace and a new social covenant.

It is in this context that the agreed-upon transitional justice system will take its place. The ambitious aims and objectives of the transitional justice agreements require efficiency, synergies, and a holistic operation from state institutions to ensure that victims' rights are redressed and the structural conditions that gave rise to the conflict can be dealt with. However, there is still ambiguity regarding how the agreements will be enacted, as laws regulating the provisions of the agreements conform to the text of the agreements verbatim. The agreements have defined the goals for the state, but not the processes of how to reach these goals. The repetition of objectives will not realize them, and may risk creating a hollow mythology of justice and peace that can in fact erode the legitimacy of the state in the long term.

While the laws, norms and principles tabled in Congress aim to achieve peace, the practice of implementing the peace agreement is still uncertain.[27] It is vital to develop a clear series of guidelines and principles that operationalize the agreements and the processes associated with them. Explicitly articulating the way these synergies must take place will reduce the risk of tensions, misunderstandings and delays that can compromise the approach to peace for Colombia.

Notes

1 This text is part of the research project, 'Public Policies against the Armed Conflict in Colombia and Transitional Justice'. It is also framed within the research project, 'The Residues of Evil in Post-Totalitarian Societies: Responses from the Perspective of Democratic Politics', reference FFI2012–31635, financed by the Spanish Ministry of Finance and Competitiveness.
2 The 'fast-track' mechanism allows the shortening of the processes that laws usually have to go through in Colombia, reducing the number of debates in the Senate and the Chamber in Congress.
3 The outcome of the vote was: 50.21% of voters voted opposing the agreements and 49.79% voted in favour of the agreements (6,431,376 votes to 6,377,482 votes). The abstention rate was 63% of eligible voters (21,833,898).
4 Democratic Centre.
5 Agreement on Victims of the Armed Conflict: A Comprehensive System of Truth, Justice, Reparation, and Non-Repetition, including the Special Jurisdiction for Peace; and the Commitment to Human Rights.
6 *La Comisión para el Esclarecimiento de la Verdad, la Convivencia y la No repetición.*
7 *Unidad especial para la búsqueda de personas dadas por desaparecidas en el contexto y en razón del conflicto armado.*

The Transitional Justice Framework 81

8 *Jurisdicción especial para la paz.*
9 According to a former Colombian Government official, 'serious violations' are those committed in accordance with a plan or policy.
10 Such as the reports from the *Grupo de Memoria Histórica* (Historical Memory Group), created by the Peace and Justice Law (Law 975). Nowadays, this group has become the *Centro Nacional de Memoria Histórica* (Center for Historical Memory), a national public entity.
11 The *Comisión Histórica del Conflicto y sus Víctimas* (Historical Commission on the Conflict and its Victims) was established as part of the negotiation process. The final report comprises different narratives on the description and explanation of the Colombian conflict (Comisión Histórica del Conflicto y sus Víctimas, 2014).
12 According to the *Unidad de Víctimas* (Victims Unit), 45,646 Colombians have been 'disappeared' since 1985.
13 This form of collective responsibility for wrongs committed, as described in the final agreement, is more akin to political apology than to acts of forgiveness. Although the agreement refers to forgiveness, in the public discourse of Colombian groups, in the Justice and Peace Law (Law 975), and in the agreement between the FARC—EP and the Colombian Government, there is a tendency to describe collective acts acknowledging responsibility as acts of interpersonal forgiveness. However, interpersonal forgiveness is a private and a volitional act between offenders and offended. In political apologies, a person who publicly represents an institution, organization or other group, recognizes the wrongs committed by such groups, and does so in their name (Griswold, 2007; de Greiff, 2008; de Gamboa & Herrera, In Press).
14 It is not clear if those who benefited from the violence have to contribute towards reparations.
15 In principle, if the FARC—EP has any material goods, they must report them. Otherwise they would not be 'contributing comprehensively' to reparations, which could negatively affect the legal benefits that they enjoy as a party to the agreement.
16 United Self-Defence Forces of Colombia.
17 These retaliations could occur because some guerrillas retaliate against the FARC-EP because they agreed to peace, or take place in order to provoke violence to ensure the conflict continues.
18 National Liberation Army.
19 *Ley de Justicia y Paz.*
20 *Ley 975 de 2005.*
21 The Agreement establishes different conditions that apply to the judgment of agents of the state.
22 The Constitutional Court of Colombia decided that the Special Jurisdiction of Peace could not oblige civilians to subject to the special jurisdiction. Thus, the involvement of civilians in the JEP will be only take place when civilians present themselves voluntarily to it.
23 In fact, the prosecutor of the International Criminal Court, Fatou Bensouda, stated that the justice system outlined in the agreement complies with the Rome Statute (El Tiempo, 2016).
24 Opposition from retired members from the Armed Forces rejected the possibility of them to be judged under the same system as the FARC—EP.
25 This can be proved when with the information available to superiors could allow leaders to infer the possibility of atrocities.
26 Some Colombian analysts equate this process to trying to sail a ship on rough seas while attempting to fix it (Pizarro Leongómez & Valencia, 2009).
27 Examples of this are the norms that regulate the Special Jurisdiction for Peace and the Commission for the Clarification of Truth, which do not explain or provide

guidance on how institutions can co-operate and share information with regards to judicial and extra-judicial inquest.

References

Centro Nacional de Memoria Histórica, 2015. *Rearmados y Reintegrados: Panorama posacuerdos con las AUC*. [Online] Available at: www.centrodememoriahistorica. gov.co/descargas/informes2015/desmovilizacionDesarmeReintegracion/rearma dos-y-reintegrados-panorama-postacuerdos-auc.pdf [Last accessed 17 July 2017].
ComisiónHistórica del Conflicto y sus Víctimas, 2014. *Comisión Histórica del Conflicto y sus Víctimas*. [Online] Available at: http://equipopazgobierno.presidencia. gov.co/especiales/resumen-informe-comision-historica-conflicto-victimas/index.html [Last accessed 15 June 2017].
Congreso de Colombia, 2005. *Ley 975 de 2005*. [Online] Available at: www.cejil.org/ sites/default/files/ley_975_de_2005_0.pdf [Last accessed 18 July 2017].
Congreso de Colombia, 2016a. *Por medio del cual se establecen instrumentos jurídicos para facilitar y asegurar la implementación y el desarrollo normativo del Acuerdo Final para la terminación del conflicto y la construcción de una paz estable y duradera*. [Online] Available at: http://es.presidencia.gov.co/normativa/normativa/ACTO%20LEG ISLATIVO%2001%20DEL%207%20DE%20JULIO%20DE%202016.pdf [Last accessed 14 June 2017].
Congreso de Colombia, 2016b. *Ley 1820 de 2016*. [Online] Available at: http://es.pre sidencia.gov.co/normativa/normativa/LEY%201820%20DEL%2030%20DE%20DICIE MBRE%20DE%202016.pdf [Last accessed 18 July 2017].
Congreso de Colombia, 2017. *Acto Legislativo 01 de 2017*. [Online] Available at: http://es.presidencia.gov.co/normativa/normativa/ACTO%20LEGISLATIVO%20N %C2%B0%2001%20DE%204%20DE%20ABRIL%20DE%202017.pdf [Last accessed 17 July 2017].
Corte Constitucionalde Colombia, 2016. *Sentencia C-379- de 2016*. [Online] Available at: www.corteconstitucional.gov.co/relatoria/2016/c-379-16.htm [Last accessed 14 June 2017].
Corte Constitucional de Colombia, 2017. *No. 55 comunicado 14 de noviembre de 2017—Corte Constitucional*. [Online] Available at: www.corteconstitucional.gov.co/ comunicados/No.%2055%20comunicado%2014%20de%20noviembre%20de%20201 7.pdf. [Last accessed 1 December 2017].
de Gamboa, C. & Herrera, W., In press. Las disculpas políticas y su propósito en la justicia transicional. In *Cartografías del Mal*. Bogotá: Siglo del Hombre.
de Gamboa, C., 2010. The Colombian Government's Formulas for Peace with the AUC: An Interpretation from the Perspective of Political Realism. In *Contested Transitions. Dilemmas of Transitional Justice in Colombia and Comparative Experience*. Bogotá: International Center for Transitional Justice, pp. 61–86.
Last accessedDe Greiff, P., 2008. The role of apologies in national reconciliation processes: On making trustworthy institutions trusted. In*The age of apology: Facing up to the past*. Philadelphia, PA: United Nations University, pp. 120–134.
De Greiff, P., 2012. *Informe del Relator Especial sobre la promoción de la verdad, la justicia, la reparación y las garantías de no repetición, Pablo de Greiff*. [Online] Available at: www.ohchr.org/Documents/HRBodies/HRCouncil/RegularSession/Ses sion21/A-HRC-21-46_sp.pdf [Last accessed 15 March 2017].

El Espectador, 2015. *Farc rechazan que se les aplique justicia diseñada para 'bandas criminales'*. [Online] Available at: www.elespectador.com/noticias/paz/farc-rechaza n-se-les-aplique-justicia-disenada-bandas-c-articulo-554244 [Last accessed 18 July 2017].
El País, 2017. *¿Habrá alianza de la derecha para las elecciones presidenciales del 2018?*. [Online] Available at: www.elpais.com.co/colombia/habra-alianza-de-la-derecha-pa ra-las-elecciones-presidenciales-del-2018.html [Last accessed 17 July 2017].
El Tiempo, 2016. *CPI dice que acuerdo con Farc es 'un logro histórico para Colombia'*. [Online] Available at: www.eltiempo.com/politica/proceso-de-paz/la-corte-pena l-internacional-apoya-el-proceso-de-paz-31007 [Last accessed 17 July 2017].
FundaciónIdeas para la Paz, 2016a. *El país que develó la ventaja del No*. [Online] Available at: http://www.ideaspaz.org/publications/posts/1411 [Last accessed 9 October 2016].
Fundación Ideas para la Paz, 2016b. *Especial: Los debates sobre Justicia Trancisional*. [Online] Available at: www.ideaspaz.org/especiales/justicia-transicional/farc/descarga s/plantillaGuion2.pdf [Last accessed 18 July 2017].
Gobierno de Colombia y FARC—EP, 2016. *Final Agreement to End the Armed Conflict and Build a Stable and Lasting Peace*. [Online] Available at: www.altocomisiona doparalapaz.gov.co/Prensa/Documentos%20compartidos/Colombian-Peace-Agreem ent-English-Translation.pdf [Last accessed 28 December 2016].
Griswold, C., 2007. *Forgiveness: A philosophical exploration*. Cambridge: Cambridge University Press.
International Crisis Group, 2006. *Colombia: Towards Peace and Justice?* [Online] Available at: www.crisisgroup.org/latin-america-caribbean/andes/colombia/colombia -towards-peace-and-justice [Last accessed 18 July 2017].
La Silla Vacia, 2016. *Detector de mentiras a Uribe sobre el acuerdo final*. [Online] Available at: http://lasillavacia.com/historia/detector-de-mentiras-uribe-sobre-el-a cuerdo-final-57734 [Last accessed 15 October 2016].
MAPP/OEA, 2017. *El Tiempo: Así está la seguridad en las regiones del país, según la OEA*. [Online] Available at: www.mapp-oea.org/noticias/el-tiempo-asi-esta-la-segur idad-en-las-regiones-del-pais-segun-la-oea/[Last accessed 18 July 2017].
Orozco Abad, I., 2012. *Lineamientos de política para la paz negociada y la justicia post-conflicto*. [Online] Available at: http://archive.ideaspaz.org/images/ivanorozcop oliticadepaz.pdf [Last accessed 17 July 2017].
Pizarro Leongómez, E. & Valencia, L., 2009. *Ley de justicia y paz*. Bogotá: Norma.
RegistraduríaNacionaldelEstado Civil, 2016. *Colombianos habilitados para votar en el Plebiscito 2016*. [Online] Available at: www.registraduria.gov.co/?page=plebiscito_ 2016 [Last accessed 14 July 2017].
Revista Semana, 2016. *¿Y ahora qué?* [Online] Available at: www.semana.com/nacion/a rticulo/gana-el-no-en-el-plebiscito-y-ahora-que/496635 [Last accessed 18 July 2017].
Revista Semana, 2017. *El acuerdo de paz de Colombia demanda respeto, pero también responsabilidad*. [Online] Available at: www.semana.com/nacion/articulo/deseo-corte-penal-internacional-justicia-transicional-en-colombia/512820 [Last accessed 14 June 2017].
Sriram, C. L., 2010. Resolving Conflicts and Pursuing Accountability: Beyond Justice Versus Peace. In O. Richmond, ed. *Palgrave Advances in Peacebuilding*. s.l.: Palgrave Macmillan, pp. 279–293.

Uprimny Yepes, R., 2017. *Responsabilidad de mando y JEP: un debate complejo y polarizado*. [Online] Available at: http://lasillavacia.com/blogs/responsabilidad-del-mando-y-jep-un-debate-complejo-y-polarizado-59906 [Last accessed 15 June 2017].

Uprimny Yepes, R., Rodriguez Garavito, C. & Garcia Villegas, M., 2006. Las cifras de la justicia. In *¿Justicia para todos? Sistema judicial, Derechos y Democracia en Colombia*. Bogotá: Norma, pp. 319–399.

Uprimny Yepes, R. & Saffon Sanín, M. P., 2006. ¿ Al fin, ley de justicia y paz? La ley 975 de 2006 tras el fallo de la Corte Constitucional. In *¿Justicia transicional sin transición?* Bogotá: Dejusticia, pp. 199–230.

Verdad Abierta, 2015. *¿Qué nos dejan 10 años de justicia y paz?*. [Online] Available at: www.verdadabierta.com/especiales-v/2015/justicia-paz-10/ [Last accessed 17 July 2017].

Part II
The Challenges

6 From transitional justice to post-agreement rural reform: many obstacles and a long way to go[1]

Rocío del Pilar Peña Huertas

Introduction

In the 19th century, Colombia failed to develop central state capacity to collect taxes and extract rents (Tilly, 1990). Colombia's government revenues were based on the production of commodities, customs duties, and the sale of vacant lands (LeGrand, 1984). As a result, Colombia has still not fully developed its capacity to define, organize, and guide its agricultural frontier. This institutional vacuum has left the door open for private parties to define and organize land in the countryside (Molano, 1989; Bejarano, 1985; Parsons, 1949; Villegas, 1978).

This indifference by the state to its own role in managing land has led to the persistence of legal procedures through which large businesses, rural élites and others have been able to acquire land, dispossessing peasants and settlers (LeGrand, 1984). This neglect by the state has limited public knowledge around how much land is available in the country, or what it is useful for (Sánchez & Villaveces, 2015; Céspedes-Báez, et al., 2015). As a result, it seems as if Colombia has a land governance regime based on the indirect administration of land tenure. This indifference to organizing the land is in fact a structural cause of disputes over land rights, which have been at the heart of the conflict and violence suffered by Colombians over the last 70 years.

Large land owners and agricultural businesses have appropriated large tracts of land since the 19th century and have dispossessed settlers and peasants in Colombia through usurpation or violence, all of which was de facto permitted by the Colombian legal regime (Peña Huertas, et al., 2017). In fact, one of the particularities of the Colombian armed conflict is that it has involved the massive accumulation and appropriation of rural assets by rural élites and armed groups across the country (Gutiérrez Sanín, 2014).

However, the exclusion of peasants from the system and the failure of the state to organize and regulate rural assets do not fully explain the existence of the Colombian armed conflict itself (Gutiérrez Sanín, 2014). This exclusion of the peasantry and incompetence of the state has been pervasive since the emergence of the Colombian state. The exclusion of peasants from public policy has been a problem since the inception of the Colombian state, and it persists even today in the design and execution of public policies aimed at rural development. For example, the 1991 Constitution did not recognize peasants as political subjects who required special protection from the state (Peña Huertas, et al., 2014a). This failure has recently been ameliorated through the public recognition of the differential effects of the armed conflict in rural areas and rural populations, leading to the enactment of policies, institutions and laws, such as Law 1448 of 2011 (The Victims and Land Restitution Law), which contains measures to protect rural populations.

The violence in Colombia has caused an irreparable damage to its victims, including the systematic forced dispossession of lands from peasants. This dispossession has been estimated at between two and ten million hectares (ACNUR, 2012). The Monitoring Committee on Public Policy on Forced Displacement[2] estimates the dispossession to total 6.6m.ha (the size of Ireland),equivalent to 15% of the country's agricultural surface (Garay, 2011). Interestingly enough, there are no official figures available on this topic by the Colombian State (see Table 6.1).

Within this context, the objectives of the Victims and Land Restitution Law are laudable in seeking to restitute land to the victims of the conflict, while looking to achieve a reparations scheme that enables citizens to regain their land and their rights.

Law 1448 of 2011 (The Victims and Land Restitution Law) is the second attempt by the Colombian state to introduce justice mechanisms in Colombia that could be seen as part of a transitional justice framework before the implementation of the agreements between the Fuerzas Armadas

Table 6.1 Estimations of dispossessed land in Colombia

Study	Figures and estimates of dispossessed and abandoned hectares (in millions of hectares)
Garay Salamanca (dir.) (2011)	6.6
Garay Salamanca (dir.) (2009)	5.5
Ibáñez, A. M., Moya, A. and Velásquez, A. M. (2006)	1.2
Movimiento de Víctimas de Crímenes de Estado (2007)	10
Contraloría General de la República (CGR)	2.9
Programa Mundial de Alimentos (PMA) (2001)	4
Sindicato de Trabajadores del Instituto Colombiano de Reforma Agraria -INCORA-(SINTRADIN).	4.4
Codhes	4.8
Acción SocialPPTP (2005)	6.8
Commission to follow up and monitor the Victims and Land Restitution Law (CSML) (2015)	7

Source: Ruiz-González, 2014.

Revolucionarias de Colombia—Ejército del Pueblo (FARC—EP) and the Colombian Government. The first initiative was Law 975 of 2005, the Justice and Peace Law, which had a very limited scope, and whose results continue to be questioned today (see Chapters 4 and 5). Law 1448 acknowledged the phenomenon of massive dispossession and forced abandonment that took place in the country from the 1980s until the first decade of this century. As such, it represented an opportunity for the Colombian state to belatedly adopt a public policy that acknowledged land dispossession, and positioned the state to correct this historic trend, starting with the restitution of the properties taken away from peasants in recent decades.

This chapter reflects on the challenges facing the implementation of land restitution mechanisms in Colombia in a post-agreement scenario with the FARC—EP. In such a complex scenario, where rural property dispossession and concentration of land ownership and rural assets is high and institutions are frail, the implementation of transitional justice mechanisms from this agreement is likely to be restricted. Therefore, in order to fulfil the mandate of transitional justice mechanisms, the state requires additional mechanisms that can address the damages caused to the victims of mass dispossession, as well as to ensure the explicit inclusion of peasant victims in the transitional justice process.

For this reason, the chapter discusses the issue of the dispossession and concentration of rural assets, and how this is connected to violence and the failure/absence of state institutions. The chapter undertakes a critical reading of a specific transitional justice mechanism that has been implemented in Colombia (the Victims and Land Restitution Law) and the limitations it faces. Finally the chapter presents some lessons from the Victims and Land Restitution Law that might be useful to consider in the implementation of transitional justice agreements between the FARC—EP and the Colombian Government.

Inequality, violence, and land

The Colombian state's capacity to regulate private property rights in the countryside is precarious: some of the indicators of this are the low rates of tax collection on land (Sanchez Torres & España, 2013), the informality of rights over rural assets, the intricate and complex regulations on the nation's vacant lands, outdated or non-existent rural cadastres, the lack of co-ordination between the institutions that regulate lands, and the absence of a land market[3]. Colombia could be described as a weak state in terms of its structural capacities (Mann, 2004). This weakness is particularly evident in the countryside, where the state has been unable to take a leading role in policy development and its implementation, but instead tends to react to the independent actions of illegal or private actors. Several significant pillars of socio-economic development are mostly absent in Colombia. These include: the capacity to establish inclusive political and economic institutions, to involve large numbers of its citizens (in particular peasants) in the governance process; the capacity to establish inclusive institutions that extend legal and economic rights to the greatest number of its citizens; the establishment of mechanisms for the implementation of public policies independent from pressures from local élites; and the construction of a bureaucracy that levies taxes (Bardhan, 2016).

The weak state capacity, and the inequality associated to the dispossession of land caused by the conflict in Colombia (Gutiérrez Sanín, 2014) is an impediment to the state's performance of its duties, as it prevents the application of public policies that aim to correct the problems caused by inequality. Inequality transcends the economic realm, and defines also the legal and the political access of rights of peasants, so that access to opportunities, resources, and arbitration by the state in contentious issues is limited (Bowles, 2012). Therefore, in societies as unequal as Colombia, only the wealthy and the powerful have access to state's protection, justice and resources. For poor peasants and dispossessed peasants, access to justice and protection by the state is limited, if not non-existent. When this is considered in conjunction with the restricted access to credit and insurance it not only reduces their welfare, but also makes them more vulnerable to violence from illegal actors (Bowles, 2012). Poor peasants in conflict-ridden areas thus face a cocktail of structural violence from the state and physical violence from illegal actors.

This inequality of access partially explains why land dispossession has been so widespread and has gone so unnoticed by the state and its institutions. Even though the armed conflict has been a catalyst for dispossession and concentration, the very institutional design for the assignment and management of rural assets contains mechanisms that allow and/or facilitate further dispossession (Gutiérrez Sanín, 2014). Inequality does not only affect land ownership; it limits access to the state and its institutions in favour of those who have knowledge of the system, have access to information, and contacts with the national and local authorities and the legal operators that manage institutions, resources and networks. Thus, although both low-intensity and high-intensity conflict have led to the accumulation of land and have increased land inequality in Colombia (Peña Huertas, et. al., 2017), social, political, and economic structures catalysed these processes due to the weakness of the state in fulfilling its social contract.

The initial regulation efforts to regulate land ownership date from the 19th century, and had essentially two objectives: to raise resources for the state to pay off its obligations, and to promote investment in territories where the state was not present. In practice this meant that the Colombian state delegated the colonization of territories to private parties, disregarding the role of the state as a provider of justice, law, and order. In the 20th and 21st centuries, land regulations focused on providing land to landless peasants and settlers in an attempt to reassert the state's role as a sovereign in its territory. However, despite the state's efforts, its capacity to reassert its missing authority was limited, and the impact has been insubstantial (Sánchez & Villaveces, 2015). In recent decades, there has been a disjunction between the state's intentions (to reassert its authority and the rights of the peasants) and the reality, with millions of hectares of land being forcefully dispossessed or abandoned in the countryside because of the conflict (Ibáñez, et al., 2006).

Therefore, despite the fact that Colombian civil law considers property (ownership rights) a natural and subjective right (Rengifo, 2011), a right which one has and can assert through state institutions appealing to the existing regulations, in practice rights to and the acquisition of land ownership shows that citizens are not equal before the law. The equality before the law touted by civil law is only formal; only those knowledgeable about the law or with resources to access power structures in the country have real access to it. Such 'equality' renders settlers, indigenous persons, Afro-descendants, and peasants, who for the most part cannot access these power structures and much less often understand the legal precepts contained in the code, in an unequal,[4] often defenceless, position in relation to landlords, drug traffickers and power structures that have been consolidated in Colombia for more than a century. This can partially explain why institutions established in the civil code to regulate land ownership in Colombia have only undergone slight changes since the 19th century, making them insufficient to govern rural property law, and feeding tensions with the rules of administrative law for the assignment of vacant lands (Peña-Huertas, et al., 2014b).

What is evident in Colombia is the challenge of the operationalization of practices in the context of state fragility and even a lawlessness of sorts. As Fitzpatrick (2006) points out, ideal models of private property do not account for the failures in developing countries' regulatory systems. These systems are weak; the administrative and coercive capacity and the capacity to regulate land ownership are limited and, where these institutions are in place, it is likely that they have been captured by interest groups. In addition, peasants and victims of land dispossession typically lack the resources, the knowledge, and the access to networks within state institutions to make use of the state as a mediator, driving them instead to support informal or illegal mechanisms that seem to have more legitimacy (or are more accessible) than the state in several regions of the country.

In the case of Colombia, this inequality in the provision of rights and land is a consequence of the design of the system that regulates property rights in the country (LeGrand, 1984). For example, when the national government was responsible for awarding the vacant lands in the 19th century, the Congress of Colombia established procedures that left the frontier lands outside the state's domain, and limited the extent to which citizens could claim land. Thus, when programmes planned to provide land to settlers took place, they included provisions that limited the access of settlers to these programmes. Programmes and projects offering free awards to settlers were established, but they contained hidden provisions. For example, the fees that had to be paid to surveyors (who had to measure and map out the properties), were set by the law, but as small farmers were unable to afford these fees, they were de facto excluded from the possibility of acquiring ownership titles on the land.

Numerous agents opportunistically exploited these regulatory distortions during the periods of high-intensity violence and conflict. Those able to exert violence had access to networks of power, and in some cases they had the capacity to define the formal and informal rules of the game. Thus, in the first half of the 20th century in Colombia, the élites involved in land conflicts were also the same ones who established the rules in Congress to regulate vacant land awards, and they appointed the agents who made the decisions (mayors, notaries, etc.), which put them in a privileged position of control and access (Gutiérrez Sanín, 2014). The violence in Colombia co-created the agents capable of combining the use of violence and law, thanks to their political resources. This created the institutional conditions required for the drop-by-drop dispossession that took place during democracy to become a torrent of expropriation of peasants (Gutiérrez Sanín, 2014).

Violence was historically used for the dispossession of land by leaders of the Conservative and Liberal parties at national and regional level. However, in recent decades, the legal instruments of dispossession have been also used by paramilitary groups and drug traffickers. Paramilitary dispossession involved links with the élites and regulatory institutions through explicit agreements, joint collective action processes, the large presence of members of the élite among their leadership, and participation by trade association leaders in decision-making, among others (Gutierrez Sanín & Vargas Reina, 2016). Other groups involved in the violence in the country have learned the repertoire used by politicians in the 19th century and the beginning of the 20th century. That is why the dispossession has not only been exerted through violence, but also through legal means, adding to the fear of violence the fear of law as an instrument of dispossession (Peña Huertas, et al., 2017).

Even though the dispossession of peasants and settlers in Colombia is a practice that dates back to the 19th century, in the last decades of the 20th century and the first decade of the 21st century forceful dispossession and abandonment reached levels unheard of (or perhaps previously not documented). However, the state still lacks accurate data on the extent of this dispossession (Ibáñez, et al., 2006). This absence of information on the magnitude of dispossession prevents a clear understanding of whom was dispossessed of land, how, and why such dispossession took place, making the design and implementation of successful public policies in this regard more difficult.

Despite the precariousness in the information available, the Colombian Government launched an ambitious public policy for land restitution that became Law 1448 of 2011. The bill, which was later merged with the law on victims, recognizes explicitly that land dispossession was massive, that it affected large numbers of peasants and that it had significant effects on society. The dispossession took several forms, from forced purchases at fire-sale prices to forced exile, physical usurpation of the property and the destruction of houses and fences that delimited the properties. Such land dispossessions were often legalized, through forced transfers, with the participation of notaries and registration offices, and the tracks of the dispossessors were erased through the use of front men and multiple transfers between third parties, apparently in good faith (Congreso de la República de Colombia, 2011). The law is intended to provide reparations to over 7m. victims of the conflict and to make a transition towards a more inclusive democracy. However, it is important to note the context of the law's implementation—the Colombian state, its practices, and its paradoxes. In the provinces where land dispossession is the greatest and the law must be implemented, violence is being exerted and the state is being contested.

Law 1448 of 2011: the intersection of transitional justice, constitutional justice, and public policy in Colombia

According to Uprimny, transitional justice has four basic premises: first, transitional measures for pacification must respect a minimum degree of justice; second, these measures of justice are defined by international law, especially by the rights of the victims; third, transitional justice admits the flexibility of these standards; and finally, there must be a political transition (Uprimny, et al., 2015). In this sense, transitional justice is envisioned as a useful tool for recognizing the harm done to victims in armed conflicts. However, its practice in Colombia has faced challenges in reversing cases of extreme inequality such as land ownership (León Sánchez, 2016). Public policies' justice frameworks must enact and implement structural changes so that the rights of the citizens, especially vulnerable ones, can be recognized and restituted (Ferrajoli, 2004).

Public policies regarding rural development in the first decade of the 21st century in Colombia were based on the premise that there was no armed conflict, but rather a terrorist threat that put all citizens at risk of becoming victims. Thus, these policies failed to recognize the abnormalities in the use of land and its property within the country. However, in 2004 the Constitutional Court, by means of ruling T-025 (Corte Constitucional de Colombia, 2004), ordered the Colombian state to design and implement a public policy to resolve the situation of the displaced and dispossessed population in Colombia which, according to the Unified Victims Registry, amounted to over 7m. displaced persons as at May 2016 (Unidad para la Atención y Reparación Integral a las Víctimas, 2016).

After this ruling, some victim assistance programmes were created by a state agency named Acción Social, but it was only in 2011, with the enactment of Law 1448, that the classification and clear criteria for the victims of forced displacement were unified. Following this, a more coherent policy and institutional framework was devised in an effort to treat the problem in an integral manner. During this period, Law 975 of 2005[5] was issued with the objective of generating a transitional justice mechanism for the demobilization of armed groups, mostly paramilitaries (see Chapters 4 and 5). Although this law has transitional justice elements, it was not focused on the victims, but on ensuring that the perpetrators would contribute to the pursuit of truth in exchange for judicial benefits, including a reduction in prison sentences. In addition, the mechanisms of reparation contemplated in Law 975 were insufficient to cover the universe of the victims of the armed groups.

In 2011, Law 1448 was envisioned as a tool that focused on the victims and their processes of reparation. This law created a transitional jurisdiction and a legal framework in order to restitute the land that was dispossessed or abandoned by citizens in relation to the armed confrontations. The idea of a transitional framework like the one proposed in this bill was to create exceptional mechanisms in order to provide reparations and assist the victims of massive and systematic violations of human rights (Congreso de la República de Colombia, 2011; Unidad para la Atención y Reparación Integral a las Víctimas, 2016).

However, the implementation of this law was not free from challenges, some of which will also affect the implementation of the agreements between the FARC—EP and the Colombian Government. Law 1448 of 2011 represents an enormous step by the Colombian Government to defend the victims and their rights, as it acknowledges that land inequality and the inequalities in the provision of public services by the state are related to the origin and persistence of the armed conflict (Comisión Histórica del Conflicto y sus Víctimas, 2014). Land restitution is perhaps one of the most important objectives of this law, as it sought to establish specific standards and procedures for the restitution of the properties of persons who were displaced or forced into exile during times of repression or armed conflict in Colombia, in accordance to the Pinheiro Principles[6].

Questions around the success of Law 1448, its theoretical viability, and its political convenience have been raised with regards to the focus on land restitution as part of the transitional justice measures in Colombia. There is an existing debate on whether transitional justice has the potential to transform institutions and structures that enable land inequality. This raises deeper questions around government institutions, their construction, and the consolidation of a state apparatus given the structural weaknesses inherent to a transitional context such as the Colombian example.

The institutional design of Law 1448 and a preliminary evaluation of its results (Observatorio de Tierras, 2015) show that the mechanisms that were created for transitional justice can facilitate the distribution of land and provision of public goods. An example of this is the fact that some land restitution judges transcended the recognition of property rights as the only right to be restituted. There is a trend in restitution judgments in which some of the judges issued orders to the local and national authorities to provide public goods such as roads or health centres in addition to the restitution of the land. This shows that there is the potential for an integral understanding of the access to the land and its restitution. That is, one which recognizes that the mere access to a title to property is insufficient if it is not accompanied by public investments that allow the development of long-term sustainable living projects, that will inform a holistic understanding of restitution (Peña Huertas, et al., 2017), i.e. a fully developmental programme. However, in spite of these legal decisions, the success of these initiatives can be questioned. Often they involve considerable public spending that, on many occasions, local governments are not in a position to assume. In addition, there are a number of challenges around the implementation of these mandates that make of these decisions interesting, yet harder to account for and evaluate.

The land restitution limitations observed by the Observatorio de Tierras (2015)[7] suggest that in many cases the victims of forced dispossession and abandonment in Colombia lived in extreme poverty prior to displacement, and in all cases they experienced high levels of vulnerability. Consequently, returning to the conditions prior to dispossession may actually be meaningless in terms of their dignity, as these citizens were already on the fringes in terms of the recognition of their legal and human rights by the state. As most of the victims of dispossession had only informal claims on the land, with the status of occupants rather than owners, it is common to observe that many of the victims of forced displacement held no deeds on their properties, or a deed had been issued but was lost, and/or the deed was not registered at the Public Instrument Registration Office. Such widespread informality, linked to the weaknesses in the country's ownership registration mechanisms, may have facilitated the dynamics of dispossession (Gutiérrez Sanín, et al., 2014).

In addition, it has been argued that the institutional design of Law 1448 imposes a series of barriers for the integral reparation of the victims within the existing deadlines set by the law (the mandate holds for 10 years, until 2021). In addition, some of the processes imply the establishment of mechanisms, but can face severe challenges with regards to their implementation. One salient example is the process of microfocalization, a procedure that enables restitution in territories according to the prioritization of cases. This selection of areas requires a security clearance for intervention by the Ministry of Defence. Thus, as several armed groups still operate in several rural areas, authorizations and processes such as this become roadblocks and impose delays on the process for accessing land restitution. Another example of the challenges in practice is the possibility of secondary occupants who currently live in the estates that are a matter of restitution, and are not related with the dispossession or forced abandonment of land, in a similar extent to the cases of Bosnia and Herzegovina. Thus, challenges remain with regards to the interpretation and the implementation of the mandate of the law and the possible obstacles it might face (Observatorio de Tierras, 2015).

The problem of dispossession and land inequality in Colombia is not explained merely by the use of violence within the context of the Colombian armed conflict. An institutional setting favoured dispossession (by action or omission). This raises questions regarding the adequacy and feasibility of a transitional mechanism, and whether a law will be implemented easily in a context of practices that are embedded in the history and the political economy of institutions in a context of conflict, corruption, and state weakness. Therefore, it is necessary to see beyond transitional justice and its reach through legal, formal, and institutional mechanisms, towards mechanisms that cope with some of the structural elements that facilitate inequality in the rural areas of Colombia, and address the material access to land.

Despite the limitations and the challenges of Law 1448 as a transitional justice mechanism, it is fair to say that it represented significant progress in the design and implementation of public policies aimed at recognizing some of the impact of the conflict that affect the lives of the victims of violence. In addition the law acknowledged the role of land in the Colombian conflict, the right of victims, and the role of the state as a guarantor of the victims' rights. Additionally, the law facilitated the establishment of a series of institutions devoted to implementing land restitution policies, and defined a supporting legal and institutional framework that included the establishment of judges specialized in land restitution, and a government unit devoted to support restitution processes: the Land Restitution Unit.[8] The example of Law 1448 illustrates that the creation and establishment of state institutions might have some inconsistencies and challenges, but have the potential to foster state capacity and the human rights of Colombian citizens.

In addition, a special jurisdiction has been set in place for restitution, where the state has been assigned the responsibility to represent and defend the rights of the dispossessed in the restitution proceedings. This process offers substantially more guarantees to the peasants in terms of access to the administration of justice, as well as post-ruling orders issued by judges for the provision of public goods. The characteristics of the land restitution procedure created for the restitution jurisdiction has demonstrated that it has positive effects in attaining the formalization of and the access to property rights for the peasant population.

There are a series of practices and actions that have managed to successfully reverse dispossession. These are important to support a future institution for peace as framed by the agreements on transitional justice signed between the FARC—EP and the Colombian Government. These can facilitate the possession, registry, and ownership of land in the country (Quinche Ramírez, et al, 2015). Some of the most promising land restitution practices developed under Law 1448 are captured below. If these practices are captured in the new programmes for peace, they can be a step in the right direction in terms of the construction of statehood.

Through the representation of the victims in the restitution proceedings by the state and the provision of assistance during the return process following the ruling by courts, the land restitution process intends to break down the structural barriers that have prevented communities from obtaining effective recognition of their rights (Rengifo, 2011). To a degree, Law 1448 overcomes previous barriers that acted against victims in seeking out and reaching institutional mechanisms to defend their rights such as the cost of the proceedings (in terms of time and money), and access to information and specific knowledge (which creates asymmetries that favour powerful landlords and armed groups entrenched in regional politics). The formalization of this process also reduces the incentives that promote informality in transactions involving rural assets, and counterbalances the prevalence of privatized protocols of specifying rural property rights (Peña Huertas, et al., 2014b).

Furthermore, the creation of a new set of institutions devoted to implement the land restitution policy is a very positive aspect of Law 1448, of which the existence of judges specialized in land restitution constitutes a vital advance. In addition, the national government created the National Lands Agency,[9] which is now the highest land authority of the nation, i.e., an entity that manages, recovers, awards, and defends vacant lands, which by definition are to be awarded to landless peasants. This fills a gap in terms of institutional capacity that has been present in the life of the Colombian state, since the 19th century (LeGrand, 1984; Gutiérrez Sanín, 2014). The way in which land tenure is organized and the legal security of property rights are two of the principal issues addressed by this new agency. Although, the results remain to be seen, taking into account that this entity was created in December 2015, this mandate is promising.

The post-agreement scenario represents a major challenge for these incipient but promising institutions that are conceived to defend the rights of peasants, the dispossessed, and the victims of recent decades of armed conflict and violence. The challenge remains to design public policies aimed to a redistribution of rural assets, breaking with the tradition of excluding peasant communities from public policies that exclusively favour large entrepreneurs (Peña Huertas, et al., 2014b; Uribe López, 2013). In this context, the agreement has major significance because of its promise for changing the structure of state agencies and the way land has been managed (e.g. the absence of a cadastre) and the design of institutions that promote rural development for small and large landholders and producers alike.

Reflections on the post-agreement scenario and its practice

While land inequality was a pre-existing condition in the Colombian conflict, this inequality is at the heart of the armed conflict in Colombia. Therefore, dealing with the land issue is an opportunity to address some of the historic causes of the conflict. Having said this, the agreement on transitional justice is simply not enough to fully reach the objectives outlined in the victims' component of the agreement with regards to land restitution. It is therefore important that the victims' agreement is coherent and is synergetic with the agreement on agrarian matters. Although land restitution constitutes an important mechanism for the state to address vulnerable groups (peasants, women, rural women, ethnic groups, etc.) and handle their claims (secure their rights), as a transitional justice mechanism by itself it is not able to guarantee an complete reparation or, more importantly, a transformation of the structural conditions that enabled the dispossession of land and land inequality in the first place.

For this reason, a more holistic approach, which supports and is supported by the other elements stated by the agreement (e.g. agricultural reform) and their implementation, has the potential to address some of the structural elements that have made land tenure frail in Colombia in a more coherent way.

The absence of public policies, government institutions, and legal mechanisms has favoured the emergence of groups that have preyed on the weaknesses of the state in the exercise of its role as a sovereign. Land, its possession or absence, cannot solely explain the existence of the conflict; there are other factors that unchained the violence and set it in place as a political economy system (Pizarro, 2015; Uribe López, 2013; Duncan, 2015). To address this, the consolidation of public policies in regards to land, titling, and its registry are vital. These require institutions at a national level that can title, formalize and define the use of land.

It should be noted that the transitional justice agreements, in conjunction with the agrarian reform agreement—and other elements of the peace agreement—could provide land to landless peasants and public goods that enable the comprehensive development of the countryside. As such, these elements of the general agreement can be seen as an attempt at rural reform. However, the government commitment to promote co-operative arrangements between small, mid-sized and large growers leaves many open questions about its implementation.

The post-agreement scenario can be seen as a junction, filled with uncertainties about its practice and implementation, not only with regards to the challenges it will face in light of a transitioning political context and state weakness, but also because the agreements are being operationalized by institutions that might have clashed against the ultimate goals of the agreement. The agreement provides a promise and a call for the state to be fulfilled, but it risks its implementation on institutions that are weak, and in some cases non-existent.

This is a context where political entrepreneurs, warlords, and the networks that have profited from war and violent dispossession, can profit from and implement measures that favour the entrenchment of structural inequalities and marginalize de facto victims and their rights. An example of one of these attempts was the debate that arose because of the presentation of a draft of a law to modify the entire agrarian regime (access to property and other rural assets) that was aimed at favouring the interests of large entrepreneurs, leaving the system of unequal access to rural assets by the peasantry intact (Medina, 2017; Peña Huertas, et al., 2017). Actions such as these will provide not only a dissonance between the promise of justice and its practice, but will also undermine the legitimacy of the state. However, these challenges are to be expected: the parallel institutions that have profited from dispossession will not relinquish their benefits so easily.

One of the lessons from the land restitution process implemented with Law 1448 was that it provided mechanisms for previously excluded peasants to gain effective access to land, plans and programmes. It gave peasants and victims an avenue through which to engage with the state, replacing the role of warlords and other armed groups as mediators. This is vital, as the legal jurisdiction that is foreseen in the agreement, as well as the government institutions that were created for land governance in Colombia, have the potential to deepen this process of state consolidation and legitimisation.

Finally, transitional justice is a valuable tool for post-conflict situations. In post-agreement scenarios, such as the one in Colombia, transitional justice constitutes a window of opportunity for the implementation of structural public policies aimed at land distribution, the recognition of the rights of historically excluded groups, and a roadmap for the development of marginalized communities, for example landless peasants. Law 1448, its lessons and its institutions, are thus a valuable starting point for the development of such policies that aim to consolidate state capacity.

Notes

1 This investigation was developed within the programme Observatorio de Restitución y Regulación de Derechos de Propiedad Agraria (Observatory for the restitution and regulation of agrarian land rights), funded by Colciencias. See www.observatoriodetierras.org/. The author thanks María Mónica Parada for her comments and assistance in the paper.
2 Comisión de Seguimiento a la Política Pública sobre el Desplazamiento Forzado.
3 Understood as the ability to carry out, in a free and autonomous way, different transactions, in accordance to the norms and regulations set by the state.
4 The illiteracy rate in the rural areas of Colombia stands around 12%.
5 The Justice and Peace Law, or *Ley de Justicia y Paz*.
6 The Pinheiro Principles on housing and property restitution for refugees and displaced persons are a series of principles adopted by the United Nations on the promotion and protection of human rights for displaced persons.
7 The Observatorio de Restitución y Regulación de Derechos de Propiedad Agraria (Observatory for land restitution and regulation of agrarian rights). See www.observatoriodetierras.org/observatorio-quienes-somos/.
8 Unidad de Restitución de Tierras.
9 Agencia Nacional de Tierras.

References

ACNUR, 2012. *Proyecto de protección de tierras de Acción Social y Comisión de seguimiento a la política pública. Las tierras de la población desplazada.* [Online] Available at: www.acnur.org/t3/fileadmin/Documentos/RefugiadosAmericas/Colombia/2012/Situacion_Colombia_Tierras_-_2012.pdf?view=1. [Last accessed 30 January 2016].

Bardhan, P. 2016. State and development: the need for a reappraisal of the Current Literature. *Journal of Economic Literature*, 54(3), pp. 862–892.

Bejarano, J. A., 1985. Campesinado, Luchas Agrarias e Historia Social en Colombia : notas para un balance historiográfico. In *Historia Política de los Campesinos Latinoamericanos*. México: Siglo XXI.

Bowles, S., 2012. *The new economics of inequality and redistribution*. 1st ed. Cambridge: Cambridge University Press.

Céspedes-Báez, L. M., Peña-Huertas, R. d. P., Cabana González, D. S. & Zuleta-Ríos, S., 2015. Who Owns the Land? Litigants, Justices, Colonos, and Titleholders'

Struggle to Define the Origins of Private Property in Colombia. *Global Jurist*, 15(3), pp. 329–459.

Comisión Histórica del Conflicto y sus Víctimas, 2014. *Comisión Histórica del Conflicto y sus Víctimas*. [Online] Available at: http://equipopazgobierno.presidencia. gov.co/especiales/resumen-informe-comision-historica-conflicto-victimas/index.html [Last accessed 15 June 2017].

Congreso de la República de Colombia, 2011. *Ley 1448 de 2011*. [Online] Available at: www.dps.gov.co/Documentos%20compartidos/Ley%201448%20de%202011.pdf [Last accessed July 2015].

Corte Constitucional de Colombia, 2004. *Condiciones para que las asociaciones de desplazados interpongan la acción*. [Online] Available at: www.corteconstitucional. gov.co/relatoria/2004/t-025-04.htm [Last accessed 25 July 2017].

Duncan, G., 2015. *Exclusión, insurrección y crimen*. La Habana: Comisión de Historia del Conflicto y sus Víctimas.

Ferrajoli, L., 2004. *Derechos y garantías. La ley del más débil*. Madrid: Trotta.

Fitzpatrick, D., 2006. Evolution and Chaos in property rights systems. The third world tragedy of contested access. *The Yale Law Journal*, 115(5), pp. 996–1048.

Garay, L. J., 2011. *Cuantificación y valoración de las tierras y los bienes abandonados o despojados a la población desplazada en Colombia*. Bogotá: Comisión de seguimiento a la política pública sobre el desplazamiento forzado.

Gutiérrez Sanín, F., 2014. *El Orangutan con sacoleva*. 1st ed. Bogotá: Penguin Random House Grupo Editorial.

Gutierrez Sanín, F. & Vargas Reina, J., 2016. *El despojo paramilitar y su variación: quiénes, cómo y por qué*. 1st ed. Bogotá: Editorial Universidad del Rosario.

Gutiérrez Sanín, F., García Reyes, P., & Argoty, C., 2014. *La Restitución y Sus Problemas Según Sus Potenciales Beneficiario*, Bogotá: Observatorio de Ratitución y regulación de Derechos de Propiedad Agraria.

Ibáñez, A. M., Moya, A. & Velásquez, A., 2006. *Hacia Una Política Proactiva Para La Población Desplazada*. Bogotá: Universidad de los Andes.

Ibáñez, A. M. & Muñoz, J. C., 2012. La persistencia de la concentración de la tierra en Colombia:¿ qué pasó entre 2000 y 2009?. In M. Bergsmo, C. A. Rodríguez Garavito, P. Kalmanovitz & M. P. Saffon, eds. *Justicia Distributiva en Sociedades en Transición*. Oslo: Torkel Opsahl Academic EPublisher.

LeGrand, C., 1984. De la tierra publica a las propiedades privadas: acaparamiento de tierras y conflictos agrarios en Colombia, 1870–1936. *Lecturas de Economía*, Enero–Abril 1984(13), pp. 13–50.

León Sánchez, N. C., 2016. *Tierra en transición: Justicia transicional, restitución de tierras y política agraria en Colombia*. Bogotá: Universidad Nacional de Colombia.

Mann, M., 2004. La crisis del Estado-nación en América Latina. *Desarrollo económico*, 44(174), pp. 179–198.

Medina, M. A., 2017. *Proyecto de decreto ley pone la tierra en debate*. [Online] Available at: www.elespectador.com/economia/proyecto-de-decreto-ley-pone-la-tierra-en-debate-articulo-692131 [Last accessed 23 June 2017].

Molano, Alfredo, 1989. *La colonización de la reserva la Macarena: yo le digo una de las cosas*. Bogotá: Fondo FEN; Corporación Araracuara.

Observatorio de Tierras, 2015. *Impacto de la Restitución en Montes de María*, Bogotá: Observatorio de Restitución y Regulación de Derechos de Propiedad Agraria.

Parsons, J. J., 1949. *Antioqueño Colonization in western Colombia*. Berkeley: University of California Press.

Peña Huertas, R., Ruiz, L. E., Parada, M. M., Zuleta, S. and Álvarez, R., 2017. Legal dispossession and civil war in Colombia. *Journal of Agrarian Change*, 17(4), pp. 759–769.
Peña Huertas, R. d. P., Parada Hernández, M. M. & Zuleta Ríos, S., 2014a. La regulación agraria en Colombia o el eterno deja vu hacia la concentración y el despojo: un análisis de las normas jurídicas colombianas sobre el agro (1991–2010). *Estudios Socio Jurídicos*, 1(16), pp. 123–166.
Peña Huertas, R., Zuleta Ríos, S. & Loaiza, M. I., 2014b. *The role of the rural property rights system in dispossession, land concentration and war: an explanation based on case studies*, Bogotá: s.n.
Pizarro, E., 2015. *Una lectura múltiple y pluralista de la historia*, La Habana: Comisión de Historia del Conflicto y sus Víctim.
Quinche Ramírez, M., Peña Huertas, R., Parada Hernández, M. M., Ruiz González, L. E., & Álvarez Morales, R., 2015. *El amparo de tierras: el juez, el proceso y la acicón de restitución*. Bogotá: Universidad del Rosario.
Rengifo, M., 2011. *Teoría general de la propiedad*. Bogotá: Universidad de los Andes.
Ruiz González, L. E., 2014. *Observatorio de Tierras*. [Online] Available at: www.observatoriodetierras.org/portfolio/estamos-tirando-la-toalla-con-la-restitucion-de-tierras/ [Last accessed 31 October 2016].
Sanchez Torres, F. & España, I., 2013. *Estructura, Potencial y Desafíos del Impuesto Predial en Colombia*. Bogotá: Universidad de los Andes.
Tilly, C., 1990. *Coercion, capital and European States*. London: Basil Blackwell.
Unidad para la Atención y Reparación Integral a las Víctimas, 2016. *Registro único de Víctimas. Red Nacional de Información*. [Online] Available at: https://rni.unidadvictimas.gov.co/RUV [Last accessed 24 November 2016].
Uprimny, R., Sánchez, N. C. & Lozano, L., 2015. *Introducción al concepto de justicia transicional y al modelo de transición colombiano. Módulo de Formación Judicial*, Bogotá: Escuela judicial Rodrigo Lara Bonilla.
Uribe López, M., 2013. Civil Wars and Violent Peace in Africa and Latin America: A General Outlook. *Africa Peace and Conflict Journal*, 6(3), pp. 50–63.
Sánchez, F. & Villaveces, J., 2015. *Tendencias históricas y regionales de la adjudicación de baldíos en Colombia*, Bogotá: Universidad del Rosario.
Villegas, J., 1978. La Colonización de vertiente del siglo XIX en Colombia. *Estudios Rurales Latinoamericanos*, 1(2).

7 Creole radical feminist transitional justice[1]

An exploration of Colombian feminism in the context of armed conflict

Lina M. Céspedes-Báez

Introduction

The peace negotiations between the Colombian Government and the Fuerzas Armadas Revolucionarias de Colombia—Ejército del Pueblo (FARC—EP)[2] had to deal not only with the political interest of the parties to the negotiation, but also with the mainstream knowledge Colombian society had accrued over the years to explain the causes and consequences of, and solutions to, the internal armed conflict. International law, particularly human rights, and humanitarian and criminal law, has played a crucial role in determining the content of the peace negotiations. The growing importance this body of law gained in the 1990s (Mattei, 2003), coupled with the pre-eminence the Colombian Constitution of 1991 gave to international human rights law, situated it as a mandatory reference to build the basic narrative of the armed conflict. The content of this narrative has been the implicit point of departure for the negotiators, and has been open to challenge, reinterpretation, or consolidation during the negotiation.

The mainstreaming of international law as a key language to articulate the vicissitudes of the Colombian conflict also entailed the arrival and domestication of its particular feminist framework. International law brought to the Colombian setting a radical feminist reading of women's experiences in conflict that an important sector of the Colombian women's movement appropriated to genderize the internal conflict and advance their feminist claims (Céspedes-Báez, 2017).[3] This feminism, the theoretical point of departure of which places the origins of the subordination of women in men's sexual domination over them, had already proved its ability to include women as distinct victims in the Bosnian and Rwandan conflicts (Halley, 2008). Creole radical feminism emerged in the 2000s from the Colombian women's rights movement's deployment of radical feminism through their strategic use of international law and its appropriation by the Colombian Constitutional Court. This interface between the women's movement and the Constitutional Court placed gender, as a synonym for women, as a germane category to understand the internal war and the design of the transitional justice setting needed to structure a way out of it (Céspedes-Báez, 2017).

Creole radical feminism has shaped a legal subjectivity for women in the Colombian conflict mirroring the influence international law's radical feminism has had on the gender-based interpretation of other wars (Halley, 2008). This has meant the creation of a paradigmatic woman victim, mainly exposed to sexual violence, to allocate specific genderized rights and remedies. It has also entailed the implementation of a particular methodology to build this subject: consciousness-raising through documentation and litigation (MacKinnon, 1991). The inclusion of a gender dimension to the negotiations in Havana, Cuba, entailed bringing this legal subject and methodology to the table, either to strengthen or challenge them. Two years of negotiations between the Colombian Government and the FARC—EP were not able to modify this one-dimensional representation of women's predicament in armed conflict, demonstrating the pervasiveness and wide acceptance of this rendition of womanhood in the context of conflict. Moreover, the role the issue of gender had in the backlash against the agreement in the plebiscite[4] only bolstered a traditional depiction of women as mainly victims of a heterosexual gender order (Céspedes-Báez, 2017). Some opposition groups took advantage of the fact that the notion of gender in the version of the agreement that was voted on the plebiscite (the first version of the agreement, dated 24 August 2016) also included diverse sexual orientation and gender identity to awaken fears within some conservative religious factions. The maintenance of gender as a relevant category in the second version of the agreement (24 November 2016) came at the price of narrowing it down again to the radical feminist version of women (Céspedes-Báez, 2016).

In this article I want to explore the implications of the radical feminist methodology transplanted and translated to Colombia once the domestic women's rights movement embraced international law to advance women's cause in the context of conflict. I further want to explore its influence in configuring a particular legal subjectivity for women, and the implications it had in the peace negotiations with the FARC—EP. To do so, I divide this paper into four sections. In the first section, I lay out the connections between the radical feminist methodology, transitional justice, and the production of specific international law to eradicate sexual violence and discrimination against women. In the second section, I unpack the genderization of the Colombian armed conflict following the radical feminist script and methodology, the emergence of a Creole version of that feminist trend, and its implications in creating a narrow vision of women in this setting. In the third section, I explore how the knowledge built around Creole radical feminism operated in the Havana peace negotiations with FARC—EP regarding the issue of women and land. In the last section, I offer some conclusions and issues to explore further.

Radical feminist methodology and transitional justice

Radical feminism gained traction internationally at almost the same time transitional justice was emerging and consolidating itself as the legal and legitimate model to help countries entrenched in dictatorships and/or conflicts to move towards democracy and peace (Weinstein, et al., 2010). The fall of the Berlin Wall in late 1989 enabled the rise and hegemony of international human rights and criminal law, solidified the international community, and subdued the debates around social and economic rights. Thus, the 1990s were a fertile ground for strengthening feminist enterprises that reinterpreted the conflict/non-conflict dyad as loci to implement an internationalized version of peace, security, and the rule of law (Fassin, 2008; Rincón Covelli, 2012). Radical feminism and transitional justice became ethical manifestos whose programmes and political agendas were camouflaged under the narrative of human rights and protection of victims (Eckel, 2013; Meister, 2011).

Radical feminism is rooted in an understanding of patriarchy as a system that creates and continuously reproduces sex/gender as hierarchies in which men dominate women (Céspedes-Báez, 2014b). Sexuality and sexual violence are central to its explanation of discrimination and violence against women, since gender not only generates the sexes, but also organizes sexuality and society. Law is central to this process, since the state inevitably reflects and breeds this order, and does so using legal regulation (MacKinnon, 1991). Thus, gender as sex is the primary site in which the domination of women takes place and it is enforced through the obligation of women to have sexual intercourse with men. Therefore, sexual violence in the context of warfare is the device to maintain patriarchy and the epitome of gender-based harm (MacKinnon, 1983; MacKinnon, 1991).

Radical feminism offers a structural and standardized explanation of male domination that does not take into account political or socio-economic contexts. Radical feminism constitutes a hegemonic model of womanhood and drafts a linear history that applies to all women in the world. Its theory is universalistic, and aims to explain every harm women endure anywhere (Halley, 2006).

Even though the structural nature of women's subordination seems unchangeable, radical feminism outlines a methodology to research, comprehend, and upset this sexual arrangement (Halley, 2002). Law is the main device through which patriarchy imposes its reasoning and renders women's subordination invisible. Hence, strategic and localized interventions in the legal realm pave the way to undermine patriarchy and its epistemology. To do so, radical feminism determines law's role in reinforcing and diminishing women's role in society, thus designing legal tactics, such as legal reform and litigation, to undermine this order from within (MacKinnon, 1991).

Radical feminism proposes a one-sided epistemology in which only women can talk and create knowledge about women and their relation to men. Its methodology is focused on collecting evidence of their sexual domination, since its conception of gender revolves around the production of sex, sexuality, and mandatory heterosexuality. Its findings place an emphasis on the impossibility of consent in sexual intercourse between men and women, and on the dispensability of force and/or violent rejection as a marker of rape and sexual violence in general (MacKinnon, 1983).

One of the first examples of the consolidation of radical feminism in the international arena can be seen in the 1990s interpretation of the Convention on the Elimination of All Forms of Discrimination against Women (CEDAW) (Céspedes-Báez, 2017). This 1970s instrument of international law was the emblem of the encounter between feminists from the Communist bloc and the west. CEDAW initially focused on discrimination and excluded any rhetoric on violence (Donert, 2014). However, in 1992, after the Berlin Wall had fallen, CEDAW's Committee issued General Recommendation No. 19. In it, an authoritative and expansive reading of the term 'discrimination' to include violence against women was offered. To this end, the Committee stated that discrimination encompasses violence, either the one 'that is directed against a woman because she is a woman or that affects women *disproportionately*' (emphasis added) (Committee on the Elimination of Discrimination against Women, 1992). This recommendation foreshadowed the traction sexual violence would gain in international law, side-lining economic and social issues such as women's land tenure.

Building on the successful introduction of violence against women as an essential topic in international law, radical feminists were able to defy the traditional views on rape and sexual violence in international law that positioned them either as a side effect or as crime against honour (Ni Aolain, 2012). Radical feminists documented cases of sexual violence in the most visible armed conflicts of the 1990s and, after intense lobbying and activism, brought them before the international ad-hoc tribunals for Rwanda and the former Yugoslavia. There, radical feminists began to structure relevant international case law that placed sexual violence at the centre of women's experience in conflict (Halley, 2008).

Based on the knowledge radical feminists had accrued, they organized around the Rome Conference (1998), the body that was going to discuss the International Criminal Court (ICC) statute, with the objective of consolidating the centrality of sexual violence against women as an international crime and to dispute the role of force and consent in its configuration. Although radical feminists did not achieve a complete victory, since force and consent did not entirely disappear from international criminal law (Halley, 2008), they were able to turn sexual violence into the paradigmatic gender-based crime in international law. In this line, sexual violence was placed at the epicentre of international law efforts to achieve peace and security from a gender perspective. Thus, it was turned into an integral part of transitional justice.

In 2000, the United Nations Security Council fortified this connection, approving Resolution 1325 on women, peace, and security. In it, the Security Council underscored the necessity of engaging women in peacebuilding processes and conflict resolution initiatives. Although the resolution's wording strove to underscore women's agency, its depiction of the crimes that affect them the most in contexts of armed conflict reinforced understandings of gender rooted in notions of women's sexual vulnerability. Therefore, sexual violence was placed at the centre of the resolution as the paradigmatic gender-based crime, and highlighted that ending impunity and forbidding amnesties for sexual-related crimes were crucial steps to protect women (United Nations Security Council, 2000). This understanding was further narrowed by Resolution 1820 of 2008, which left aside almost any reference to women's agency and focused on women as victims of sexual violence and the use of this crime as a tactic of war (United Nations Security Council, 2008; Otto, 2010). Resolution 1888 of 2009 called for the appointment of a Special Representative of the Secretary General on Sexual Violence and Armed Conflict (United Nations Security Council, 2009). In 2013, in London, the foreign ministers of the Group of Eight major industrialized nations (G8) signed the Declaration on Preventing Sexual Violence in Conflict, and resolutions 2106 and 2122 of the same year reiterated the urgency of prosecuting this type of violence (Foreign and Commonwealth Office; G8 UK, 2013; United Nations Security Council, 2013a; United Nations Security Council, 2013b).

Several reasons could explain why international law was receptive to radical feminism: (i) it was formulated in English by the Global North; (ii) it presented a totalistic interpretation of women's experiences that was easily extrapolated to every part of the world; (iii) it allowed an understanding of discrimination and violence against women that did not challenge the existing economic and political order; and (iv) it was coherent with the emphasis placed by both transitional justice and international criminal law on prosecution to achieve peace and security (Céspedes-Báez, 2014b).

Creole feminist transitional justice

The genderization of the Colombian armed conflict was the outcome of a process that started in the 1990s. It followed the radical feminist script and adapted it to the particular conditions of the Colombian setting. An élite within the Colombian women's movement focused on consciousness-raising, legal advocacy, and litigation to make their presence and their agenda relevant in the Colombian context. They became Creole radical feminists (Céspedes-Báez, 2014a). The momentum radical feminism had gained in international law and transitional justice made this development almost inevitable. However, embracing this approach to situate women in conflict has impeded an in-depth analysis of the socio-economic damages inflicted upon Colombian women.

The 1990s was a decade of escalation for the Colombian armed conflict. The fight for territorial control drove the escalation of attacks and produced an increase of human rights violations against civilians. Millions of Colombians had to flee their homes to escape from massacres, selective killings, combats, forced disappearances, and torture, among others (Pecaut, 2004). The influx of internally displaced persons (IDPs) to the cities and nearby towns attracted the attention of the government and the international community (Céspedes-Báez, 2014b).

The Colombian state responded to the increase in forced displacement by passing legal regulations to provide remedies for its victims. The Colombian

Congress passed Law 387 of 1997 to define who qualified as an IDP, created a national system to attend this population, and provided guidelines to design public policies to support their transition out of that status.

The prevalence of armed conflict and forced displacement narratives in public opinion influenced the feminist movement in Colombia to leave aside their historical fights for equality in the family, work, and public life, and turn their attention to the situation of women in war in their own country (Wills Obregon, 2007). To do so, and in order to genderize the analysis of IDPs' situation in Colombia, the Colombian feminist movement employed a twofold strategy. On the one hand, they appropriated and deployed international law to build a solid theoretical framework in which women's rights were at the centre, coupled with the narrative of their particular vulnerability. On the other hand, they replicated radical feminist methodology and collected testimonies of women in conflict to give substance to their legal arguments. Their main goal was to have a robust argument to pressure the Colombian Government, shame it before the international community, and litigate against it before national and international courts. They embraced law in its ambivalent nature as the instrument of patriarchy, but also as the means to dislocate male domination.

The Creole radical feminist's theoretical approach was grounded on the CEDAW Committee General Recommendation No. 19 and on a radical feminist approach. This entailed positioning sexual violence at the centre of women's experiences in peace and in conflict. For women, their argument goes, peace and war take place in the context of patriarchy, thus violence against them does not vary substantively, only in proportion. Even though forced displacement did not target women nor men particularly, situating women in conflict first and foremost as victims of sexual violence allowed the linking of gender with forced displacement (Rueda, 2001; Mesa de Trabajo, Mujer y Conflicto Armado, 2003). In this sense, sexual violence paved the way to claim that forced displacement was impacting women disproportionately, because women IDPs were exposed to the intensified incidence of sexual domination that occurs in the context of conflict (Céspedes-Báez, 2017).

In the Creole radical feminist reading of forced displacement, women were fleeing from their home towns to escape from the increased occurrence or threat of sexual violence. This move permitted the genderization of forced displacement and the Colombian conflict. Although Creole radical feminists did not have reliable data on the incidence of sexual violence against women in the context of conflict at the time, this approach dispensed the use of precise figures to support the Creole radical feminists' claim (Roth, et al., 2011).[5]

Consciousness-raising was vital to make radical feminism operative in the Colombian context. Creole radical feminists needed not only to prove the link they had established between forced displacement and sexual violence, but also to underline that the experience of one woman who had been victimized represented all women in conflict. Testimony-gathering and case documentation served that purpose. Both promoted the standpoint of the victim and contributed to her and the readers' consciousness and knowledge of patriarchy.

Underscoring the commonalities across different women's accounts, they illuminated the ubiquity and oppressiveness of patriarchy, and constituted material for litigation and advocacy (Rueda, 2001).

As early as 2001, Colombian women's rights non-governmental organizations (NGOs) and feminist coalitions were collecting testimonies, documenting cases, and publishing reports on women and armed conflict (Mesa de Trabajo, Mujer y Conflicto Armado, 2001). Over the years they put together a methodology and guidelines that gradually gave more prominence to the documentation and litigation of sexual violence in Colombia (Rueda, 2001; Mesa de Trabajo, Mujer y Conflicto Armado, 2006; Corporación Humanas Colombia, 2009). Although at the beginning they tried to document other human rights violations, such as obstacles related to access to health, work, and education, their scope of research and findings were narrowed by methodological, theoretical, and strategic reasons that gave pre-eminence to sexual violence and the genderization of the internal armed conflict along the lines of radical feminism. That contraction did not entail eliminating other abuses from their reports, but implied linking sexual violence or the threat of sexual violence as the primary cause or underlying meaningful experience of any other armed conflict-related harm. In this way, they kept theoretical coherence, built a strong advocacy campaign centred on just one crime, and successfully genderized every other aspect of the internal conflict.

In the late 1990s and early 2000s, land dispossession had been secondary to forced displacement in the Colombian Government's responses to the internal conflict. The Government's priorities were localized in attending IDPs at host towns and cities. Land was turned into a matter of its own when the Colombian state embarked on its first transitional justice effort to demobilize paramilitary groups through tailored prosecutions (see Chapters 4 and 6). To do so, Congress approved Law 975 of 2005, commonly known as the Peace and Justice Law. The discussions this law sparked around victims' rights and reparations paved the way for exploring what had happened to the land IDPs lost in their flight and offered women's rights NGOs and activists the opportunity to litigate through a procedure specifically established to try armed conflict crimes (Comisión Nacional de Reparación y Reconciliación—Grupo de Memoria Histórica, 2010). In this context, the Peace and Justice Law constituted an opportunity to strengthen the narrative of sexual violence against women in conflict and tie it to land seizure and abandonment.

The deployment of the Creole radical feminist theoretical framework and methodology to participate actively in the space of litigation and advocacy brought by Law 975 enriched the account of women's ordeals in the internal conflict, and at the same time reinforced their depiction as victims of sexual violence. Even though Creole radical feminists and their NGOs began to investigate the impact of forced displacement on women's land tenure, they did so mainly to link it to sexual domination. Their theoretical commitments, drawn in the early 2000s did not give them a lot of room for manoeuvre. Sexual violence was at the heart of their account of masculine privilege, and their genderization of the conflict depended on it. Predictably, their methodology replicated the world vision they had decided to endorse to make women stand out as a group that was bearing a differentiated and disproportionate impact in the context of conflict.

In 2006, after several years of presenting the problem of women and land tenure in the context of conflict just as a peripheral issue, Colombian Creole radical feminists began to hammer out the connections between forced displacement, sexual violence, and land loss. They held the state accountable for not protecting IDPs' real rights over land, and highlighted that women usually face more hurdles in defending their property since male kin usually mediate their ownership over it. For this reason, they alleged that frequently women do not know with certainty what kind of right they have to the land, whether the deeds were in their and/or their partner's name, and the area and boundaries of the lot (Mesa de Trabajo, Mujer y Conflicto Armado, 2007). Creole radical feminists built the association with forced displacement and sexual violence using a particular interpretation of the findings of a survey conducted in 2007 by the Ombudsman's Office of Colombia among IDPs and other vulnerable populations (Defensoría del Pueblo, 2008). Although the study included a small percentage of men and the questions regarding sexual violence were not formulated to capture exclusively women as victims, feminist NGOs read the study findings as evidence exclusively pertaining to women IDPs, and turned it into the definitive ground to support the ideological centrality of sexual domination in the incidence of forced displacement and land loss (Defensoría del Pueblo, 2008; Mesa de Trabajo, Mujer y Conflicto Armado, 2008; Céspedes-Báez, 2017). The Colombian Constitutional Court applied this mode of argumentation to protect the rights of women IDPs from the State's lack of enforcement. It placed sexual violence as the paradigmatic gender-based crime and described other damages women endure in the internal conflict without giving them the same pre-eminence (Corte Constitucional de Colombia, 2008).

After the 2008 survey by the Ombudsman's Office, Colombian feminist NGOs devoted more energy to documenting the relationship between sexual violence and land loss, to expand their knowledge on female sexual domination in the context of conflict (Céspedes-Báez, 2017). Land loss thus became another type of evidence of the pervasiveness of sexual violence and of its use as a weapon of war. In 2009, Corporación Sisma Mujer[6] reported that the evidence it gathered through a victims' support group suggested that there was a strong relationship between forced displacement and land abandonment, paving the way to make the connection between land loss and sexual violence (Mesa de Trabajo, Mujer y Conflicto Armado, 2009). That same year, Corporación Humanas[7] published a guide to litigating cases of sexual violence in the context of the armed conflict. Drawing on the experience of the international ad-hoc tribunals and the regulations of the Rome Statute of the ICC, this guide aimed to advance an interpretation of sexual violence in the Colombian conflict as torture, and as an international crime, and at fighting impunity through an effective prosecution in domestic tribunals. The guide established that sexual violence has been used as a strategy to seize land in conflict (Corporación Humanas Colombia, 2009).

In doing so, the NGO reinforced the idea that this crime is conscientiously deployed to obtain a military gain, and that sexual violence is the primordial weapon against women through which other harms are imposed. In this sense, if sexual violence is eradicated, women's subjugated position would be upset and the correlated harms to which this crime contributes would disappear. The three *amicus curiae*[8] Corporación Humanas filed to participate in the prosecution of paramilitaries under Law 975 of 2005 supported this conclusion. Land loss was only made a relevant issue when it was possible to link it to sexual violence (Corporación Humanas Colombia, 2013).

The terms of the genderization of the internal armed conflict and its impact on the understanding of the issue of women and land tenure were thus informed by these interventions when the Colombian Congress discussed the bill that led to Law 1448 of 2011. The particular knowledge the deployment of radical feminism, and its method, had created to genderize the understanding of the conflict demonstrated its strengths and shortcomings when it was time to debate and approve that ambitious transitional justice scheme. Deliberations in Congress underlined the importance of providing special consideration to sexual violence, while its considerations on women and land loss were scarce (Congreso de la República de Colombia, 2010; Congreso de la República de Colombia, 2011)

Feminist advocacy before Congress placed an emphasis on tightening the link between sexual violence and land loss. To do so, feminist organizations proposed the introduction of a presumption in which women victims of sexual violence would not have to prove their status as victims for land restitution purposes (Corporación Sisma Mujer et al., n.d.). Whereas the definitive regulation paid particular attention to the prosecution of sexual violence as a remedy, the issue of women and land was tackled in cursory terms. The only operative provision for women in the matter of land restitution was the reiteration of the obligation of joint titling, a victory rural women had obtained in the late 1980s (Sañudo Pazos, 2015).

The discussion and approval of Law 1448 of 2011 was a lost opportunity to effectively promote women's land tenure through a transitional justice mechanism. Creole radical feminist knowledge was not able to offer a strong case for the issue of women and land in Colombia, and its interaction with armed violence. For that reason, their proposals were not able to grasp what was needed to effectively promote women's acquisition, control, and recovery of real rights. Their interest in mastering the discourse of international law and transitional justice to make visible sexual violence against women led them to leave aside the study of national property law. When the time came to debate the Victims and Land Restitution Law, they were experts in international human rights and criminal law, but did not have the needed expertise on the specialized mechanics of property regulation. Even though Colombian feminist activists and NGOs advocated for the recognition of women's legal relationship to real estate while Law 1448 was being discussed, they were not able to provide clear evidence on how a country that recognized full legal capacity for women since 1932 was still having problems promoting and guaranteeing women's economic and property rights (Corporación Sisma Mujer et al., n.d.).

While Creole radical feminists demonstrated their expertise on sexual violence, they did not explore in depth whether the social separation of reproductive and productive work was having any influence on the regulation of property to women's disadvantage. Also, recommending only that Law 1448 should presume that women claiming land restitution were possessors, occupants, and good faith tenants, missed that the land restitution process was not going to reproduce the heterosexual order having exclusively women as plaintiffs and men as defendants, but that it was likely going to be a judicial forum in which women would have to confront other women.

At the time of writing, Colombian feminist NGOs continue to produce mostly reports and materials on sexual violence in conflict, while they have not published any significant assessment on how women have fared in the Law 1448's land restitution process (Casa de la Mujer, n.d.). Their fixation on the radical feminist version of violence and discrimination against women has impeded their capacity to systematically approach the study of women in property-related litigation; however it might be feasible that this is due to the lack of information (in a country in which reliable data has been always evasive and land tenure records defective), or of expertise on researching on these topics. Whereas they have devoted a significant number of analyses to the litigation of sexual violence in peace and war, their examination of the instances in which women litigate property is almost non-existent.

Women and land in Havana

In 2012, when the peace talks with FARC—EP started in Havana, Creole radical feminists had consolidated a well-recognized expertise on gender and conflict centred on sexual violence against women. Since the main negotiation agenda to which the guerrillas and the government had agreed did not incorporate gender as a specific item for discussion, feminists exerted pressure to have this topic recognized and included as an indispensable aspect of the discussions (Gobierno de la República de Colombia and Fuerzas Armadas Revolucionarias de Colombia FARC, 2012). For that purpose, in 2014 the Government and FARC—EP created a commission for the analysis of gender within the peace process. The mandate of this advisory body was to produce recommendations and inputs to effectively introduce gender in the dialogues (Mesa de Conversaciones Gobierno Nacional—FARC—EP, 2014).

On 24 August 2016, the Government and FARC—EP signed an agreement that was rejected in a plebiscite on 2 October. This outcome led to its revision and the publication of an amended version on 24 November 2016. The combination of these two documents revealed how Colombian society had reached some shared understandings of the conflict and of the strategies which were needed to resolve its structural causes, and in which areas that consensus had not been reached or was under challenge. Gender became one of the main weapons the detractors of the agreement wielded against it. The essence of their argument was that the agreement was subverting traditional heterosexual values (Céspedes-Báez, 2016).

While the agreement of 24 August 2016 deployed a wider understanding of gender (not limited to women), its use of this category was complex and confusing. In most cases, the term 'gender' was used in the agreement to identify women and the gender binary, and sometimes to refer to sexual orientation and diverse gender identities (Céspedes-Báez, 2016). Even though it was difficult to grasp the precise meaning of gender in the 24 August accord, the inclusion of a more fluid rendition of gender constituted an opportunity for the lesbian, gay, bisexual, and transgender (LGBT) communities to have a more visible place and role in the transitional justice setting.

In this fashion, the first version of the agreement incorporated the Creole radical feminist knowledge, but also opened the door for more inclusive understandings of gender and its role in the internal armed conflict. While it mostly deployed sexual violence to genderize different issues of the agreement, it also ordered government measures to promote the constitutional rights of LGBT persons.

The agreement was amended to narrow the meaning of gender in order to incorporate the voice of the sectors that argued that its gender components were subverting traditional mores in Colombia. The references to sexual orientation and gender diversity were erased, gender was watered down to the heterosexual interrelation between men and women, and the link between sexual violence and women was strengthened (Céspedes-Báez, 2017).

Two main ideas that illustrate the pervasiveness of the trope of women and sexual violence remained in the adjusted agreement. The first was the approach to sexual violence in the transitional justice jurisdiction to try armed conflict-related crimes. The peace agreement pledged not to grant amnesties to those who committed these crimes, and created a special investigation group to guarantee its investigation and prosecution before the transitional justice apparatus, as well as defining a series of psychosocial rehabilitation measures for sexual violence survivors.

The second idea was the issue of women and land tenure that replicated or drew on interventions of the past, such as (i) an inclusive language aimed at making sure that every policy, action, and plan takes women into account; (ii) explicit references to the importance of outlining affirmative actions in the implementation phase to guarantee women's empowerment in areas related to the strengthening of their organizations; and (iii) the inclusion of sex as a relevant category in the establishment and update of the rural cadaster, among others (Sañudo Pazos, 2015). Although all of these will make women more visible in the agrarian world, facilitate the enforcement of their rights through the availability of specific inclusive wording, and contribute to establishing a baseline regarding their ownership of real estate, they fatally mirror approaches that have failed before because the basic association between women and reproduction has not been systematically addressed in agrarian policy and legal regulation.

The agreement reflects the recent history of Creole radical feminism and the strategies it has employed to guarantee the genderization of the peace negotiations with the FARC—EP. While Creole radical feminists conducted an intense campaign to make the negotiators aware of the seriousness and high incidence of sexual violence against women, they fell short in offering them insights regarding the subject of women and land tenure. Their advocacy campaign *Cinco Claves*[9], which focused on the necessity of including sexual violence against women as a specific transitional justice topic, did not have an analogous intervention to demonstrate the importance of offering real remedies to women's situation regarding access, control, and recovery of real rights over land to the negotiation parties (Red Nacional de Mujeres; Corporación Sisma Mujer; No es Hora de Callar; Corporación Humanas Colombia, n.d.). Their exclusive focus on the study of sexual violence impeded them from outlining an accurate diagnosis on the subject of women and land that would have contributed to reaching a more robust and adequate approach to solve this issue in the context of the negotiations between the Colombian Government and the FARC—EP.

Although some women's rights activists considered the subject of women and land tenure key to the negotiations and advocated for its inclusion, their input was not able to challenge the pervasiveness of the Creole radical feminist narrative of women and sexual violence that has dominated the interpretation of gender in the management of conflict and transitional justice in Colombia since the 2000s (Cumbre Nacional de Mujeres por la Paz, 2013).

The peace agreement has become an instrument of the reinstitution and enhancement of the severance between production and reproduction in as far as it states that women have two roles—reproductive and productive—and remains silent regarding men's involvement in the former. Failing to address this ignores the hurdles women face in securing land tenure in the allocation of land in the rural world in patriarchal societies. A methodical examination of the particular manifestations of these assumptions would be a good place to start in constructing an understanding of how public policy and legal regulation helps to maintain them, and thus creates specific hurdles to women's access, control, and recovery of land tenure. If there is not an accurate understanding of the mechanisms that support and legitimate this divide, women's land ownership and control will remain exceptional, insecure, and, sometimes, unattainable.

Although the parties to the accord agreed to recover inappropriately occupied wastelands, massively formalize land tenure, and establish an agrarian jurisdiction to expeditiously resolve land-related conflicts, amongst other commitments (see Chapter 3), the current structure of the agreement can pose additional dangers to rural women on the matter of land tenure. If land restitution programmes are not paired with particular knowledge on how women fare in litigation and the structural hurdles they face, women will still encounter the same problems they have had before in presenting evidence to support their relationship to property, thus restricting and impeding their acquisition, control, and recovery thereof (Comisión Nacional de Reparación y Reconciliación— Grupo de Memoria Histórica, 2010; Osorio Perez & Villegas Caballero, 2010).

A possible response to this challenge would be to take some distance from radical feminism and its methodology to make room for other theoretical frameworks and methods that investigate the validity of displacing the source of discrimination against women from sexual domination to the divorce between production and reproduction (Comisión Nacional de Reparación y Reconciliación—Grupo de Memoria Histórica, 2010; Villegas Caballero, 2010).

Conclusion: radical women are mainly victims, yet not owners

A systematic reading of the agreements of 24 August and 24 November 2016 indicates how radical feminism has become embedded in the narrative of the internal armed conflict, the extent to which its methodology has sought and found the evidence to sustain its foundations, and the blind spots it creates in its deployment. It also demonstrates that this feminist understanding of violence and discrimination against women is incapable, in some cases, of offering a full appreciation of, and strategy to respond to, the economic impacts of conflict on women. Centring radical feminist strategies to improve women's lives in conflict and peacebuilding through the foregrounding of sexual violence and its prosecution overlooks the complexities of their experience, and ingrains a conception of women as primarily bodies, psyches, and sexual objects.

An analysis of conflict that tackles the relationship between production and reproduction is necessary to determine the conflict's impact on property-related litigation, land restitution plans, and important dimensions of women's experiences of the conflict. Eradicating discrimination and violence against women entails more than putting sexual violence offenders behind bars. It also requires acknowledging women's entrepreneurship, work, and contribution to development, and creating economic opportunities to grant their autonomy.

The bias of Creole radical feminism became evident not only through the agreement, but also through the interpretation the FARC—EP has presented around women in conflict as well. Although this guerrilla organization seems to have initially endorsed the Creole radical feminist agenda, it has left a point of entry to develop its own version of it in the future. It has challenged the radical feminist tone of the agreement underscoring that patriarchy was deeply entrenched in the logic of capitalist domination. Although the FARC—EP did not develop this idea further, it certainly forecast the possible impact its integration in civilian life would have in the interpretation of the situation of women in conflict and peace. Perhaps its feminism will force Creole radical feminists to consider other dimensions and explanations of discrimination against women (Fuerzas Armadas Revolucionarias de Colombia—Ejército del Pueblo, 2016).

Notes

1 This article draws on my previous work about feminism and armed conflict in Colombia. In 2014, I coined the term "creole radical feminism" to refer to a group of Colombian feminists that has strategically used international law and radical feminism to genderize the reading of the internal conflict and position themselves as experts on the situation of women in this context (Céspedes-Báez, 2014a).
2 Revolutionary Armed Forces of Colombia.
3 According to research I have conducted, the entirety of the women's movement did not subscribe to and/or appropriate the radical feminist discourse to introduce women as a relevant category in the understanding of the internal conflict in Colombia. Some women's rights activist organizations localized in Bogotá, who already had connections with the Government and the NGO movement, and the international community, embraced it to genderize the conflict and become relevant actors in the national public sphere.
4 In Colombia, the plebiscite is a constitutional public participation mechanism (article 103 of the Colombian constitution). According to Law 134 of 1994, the President can call for a plebiscite to ask the polity whether they approve certain executive decisions. President Juan Manuel Santos called on Colombians to vote against or in favour of the peace agreement with the FARC—EP on 2 October 2016. A narrow majority rejected the agreement, thus the negotiators had to revise it to adjust it to the demands of the opposition. The revised version of the agreement, or its second version, was approved by the negotiators on 24 November 2016. This agreement was not subjected to a plebiscite and was ratified by Congress.
5 This situation has changed with the Consolidated Registry of Victims (Registro Único de Víctimas) established in Law 1448 of 2011.
6 One of the most important Colombian Creole radical feminist NGOs in Colombia, devoted to advocacy and litigation.
7 Another well-known Colombian Creole radical feminist NGO.
8 An impartial advice offered to a court of law in a particular case.
9 Five Points.

References

Casa de la Mujer. *Restitución de Tierras para las Mujeres en el Marco de la Ley 1448 de 2011. Revisión desde la Perspectiva del Derecho Sustantivo Privado.* [Online] Available at: http://www.casmujer.com/wp-content/uploads/2017/10/ff58cd_95e2f366d9784cccbeef414be3391b6b.pdf [Last accessed 24 February 2018].

Céspedes-Báez, L. M., 2014a. Conflicto armado colombiano y feminismo radical criollo: una aproximación preliminar a las lecciones aprendidas. *Aristas del Conflicto Colombiano*, September, pp. 125–146.

Céspedes-Báez, L. M., 2014b. Far Beyond What Is Measured: Governance Feminism and Indicators in Colombia. *International Law—Revista Colombiana de Derecho Internacional*, 25(1), pp. 311–374.

Céspedes-Báez, L. M., 2016. Gender Panic and the Failure of a Peace Agreement. *AJIL Unbound*, Volume 110, pp. 183–187.

Céspedes-Báez, L. M., 2017. En los confines de lo posible: inclusión del enfoque de género en el Acuerdo de la Habana. In Céspedes-Báez, L. M. & E. Prieto-Rios, eds. *Utopía u Oportunidad Fallida. Análisis Crítico del Acuerdo de Paz.* Bogotá: Universidad del Rosario, pp. 295–326.

Comisión Nacional de Reparación y Reconciliación—Grupo de Memoria Histórica, 2010. *La Tierra en Disputa. Memorias del Despojo y Resistencias Campesinas en la Costa Caribe 1960–2010.* Bogotá: Editorial Taurus.

Committee on the Elimination of Discrimination against Women, 1992. *CEDAW General recom. 19, A/47/38. (General Comments).* [Online] Available at: www.nichibenren.or.jp/library/ja/kokusai/humanrights_library/treaty/data/CEDAW_GC_19e.pdf [Last accessed 21 May 2017].

Congreso de la República de Colombia, 2010. *Gaceta del Congreso No. 865*, noviembre 4 de 2010. Bogotá: Imprenta Nacional.

Congreso de la República de Colombia, 2011. *Gaceta del Congreso No. 116*, marzo 23 de 2011. Bogotá: Imprenta Nacional.

Corporación Humanas Colombia, 2009. *Guía para Llevar Casos de Violencia Sexual*, Bogotá: Ediciones Ántropos.

Corporación Humanas Colombia, 2013. *La Violencia Sexual una Estrategia Paramilitar en Colombia. Argumentos para Imputarle Responsabilidad Penal a Salvatore Mancuso, Hernán Giraldo y Rodrigo Tovar.* Bogotá: Ediciones Ántropos.

Corporación Sisma Mujer et al., s.d. *Propuesta Conjunta de Organizaciones Sociales y de Mujeres Apoyadas por Parte de la Bancada de Mujeres del Congreso de la República con Relación a los Derechos de las Mujeres en el P.L. 107/10 Cámara—213/10 Senado.* s.l.: s.n.

Corte Constitucional de Colombia, 2008. *Auto 092 (2008).*

Cumbre Nacional de Mujeres por la Paz, 2013. *Cumbre Nacional de Mujeres y Paz. Octuber 23 al 25 de 2013.* [Online] Available at: www.humanas.org.co/archivos/Sistematizacumbre_mujeres_y_paz.pdf [Last accessed 23 May 2017].

Defensoría del Pueblo, 2008. *Promoción y Monitoreo de los Derechos Sexuales y Reproductivos de Mujeres Víctimas de Desplazamiento Forzado con Énfasis en Violencias Intrafamiliar y Sexual*, Bogotá: Defensoría del Pueblo.

Donert, C., 2014. Whose Utopia? Gender, Ideology, and Humand Rights at the 1975 World Congress of Women in East Berlin. In J. Eckel & S. Moyn, eds. *The Breakthrough: Human Rights in the 1970s.* Philadelphia: University of Pennsylvania Press, pp. 68–87.

Eckel, J., 2013. The Rebirth of Politics from the Spirit of Morality: Explaining the Human Rights Revolution of the 1970s. In J. Eckel & S. Moyn, eds. *The Breakthrough: Human Rights in the 1970s.* Philadelphia: University of Pennsylvania Press, pp. 226–259.

Fassin, D., 2008. The Humanitarian Politics of Testimony: Subjectification through Trauma in the Israeli-Palestinian Conflict. *Cultural Anthropology*, 23(3), pp. 531–558.

Foreign and Commonwealth Office; G8 UK, 2013. *Declaration on Preventing Sexual Violence in Conflict.* [Online] Available at: www.un.org/ruleoflaw/files/G8%20Declaration%20Sexual%20Violence%20in%20Conflict%20-%20April%202013.pdf [Last accessed 21 May 2017].

Fuerzas Armadas Revolucionarias de Colombia—Ejército del Pueblo, 2016. *X Conferencia—Tesis para la la Discusión.* [Online] Available at: www.ipc.org.co/agenciadeprensa/wp-content/uploads/2016/09/X-CONFERENCIA.pdf [Last accessed 24 May 2017].

Gobierno de la República de Colombia andFuerzas Armadas Revolucionarias de Colombia FARC, 2012. *Acuerdo General para la Terminación del Conflicto y la Construcción de una Paz Estable y Duradera.* [Online] Available at: www.altocomisionadoparalapaz.gov.co/procesos-y-conversaciones/acuerdo-general/Documentos%20compartidos/Acuerdo_General_para_la_terminacion_del_conflicto.pdf [Last accessed 23 May 2017].

Halley, J., 2002. Sexuality Harassment. In W. Brown & J. Halley, eds. *Left Legalism/ Left Critique*. Durham: Duke University Press, pp. 80–104.

Halley, J., 2006. *Split Decisions. How and Why to Take a Break from Feminism*. Princeton, NJ: Princeton University Press.

Halley, J., 2008. Rape at Rome: Feminist Interventions in the Criminalization of Sex-Related Violence in Positive International Criminal Law. *Michigan Journal of International Law*, 30(1), pp. 1–123.

MacKinnon, C. A., 1983. Feminism, Marxism, Method, and the State: Toward Feminist Jurisprudence. *Signs*, 8(4), pp. 635–658.

MacKinnon, C. A., 1991. *Toward a Feminist Theory of the State*. Cambridge, MA: Harvard University Press.

Mattei, U., 2003. A Theory of Imperial Law: A Study on U.S. Hegemony and the Latin Resistance. *Indiana Journal of Global Legal Studies*, 10(1), pp. 383–448.

Meister, R., 2011. *After evil: a politics of human rights*. New York: Columbia University Press.

Mesa de Conversaciones Gobierno Nacional—FARC—EP, 2014. *Comunicado Conjunto La Habana, 11 de Septiembre de 2014*. [Online] Available at: www.mesa deconversaciones.com.co/sites/default/files/Comunicado%20Conjunto%2C%20La% 20Habana%2C%2011%20septiembre%202014-Versi_n%20Espa_ol.pdf [Last accessed 16 November 2016].

Mesa de Trabajo, Mujer y Conflicto Armado, 2001. *Informe sobre Violencia Sociopolítica contra Mujeres y Niñas en Colombia*. Segundo Avance, Bogotá: Ediciones Ántropos.

Mesa de Trabajo, Mujer y Conflicto Armado, 2003. *III Informe sobre Violencia Sociopolítica contra Mujeres, Jóvenes y Niñas en Colombia*, Bogotá: Ediciones Ántropos.

Mesa de Trabajo, Mujer y Conflicto Armado, 2006. *VI Informe sobre Violencia Sociopolítica contra Mujeres, Jóvenes y Niñas en Colombia*, Bogotá: Ediciones Ántropos.

Mesa de Trabajo, Mujer y Conflicto Armado, 2007. *VII Informe sobre Violencia Sociopolítica contra Mujeres, Jóvenes y Niñas en Colombia*, Bogotá: Ediciones Ántropos.

Mesa de Trabajo, Mujer y Conflicto Armado, 2008. *VIII Informe sobre Violencia Sociopolítica contra Mujeres, Jóvenes y Niñas en Colombia*, Bogotá: Ediciones Ántropos.

Mesa de Trabajo, Mujer y Conflicto Armado, 2009. *IX Informe sobre Violencia Sociopolítica contra Mujeres, Jóvenes y Niñas en Colombia*, Bogotá: Ediciones Ántropos.

Moran, M., 2003. *Rethinking the Reasonable Person: An Egalitarian Reconstruction of the Objective Standard*. Oxford: Oxford University Press.

Ni Aolain, F., 2012. Advancing Feminist Positioning in the Field of Transitional Justice. *The International Journal of Transitional Justice*, 6(2), pp. 205–228.

Osorio Perez, F. E. & Villegas Caballero, H., 2010. *Uno en el campo tiene esperanza. Mujeres rurales y recomposición en el acceso, tenencia y uso de la tierra*, Bogotá: CINEP.

Otto, D., 2010. Power and Danger: Feminist Engagement with International Law Through the UN Security Council. *The Australian Feminist Law Journal*, Volume 32, pp. 97–121.

Pecaut, D., 2004. Guerra, Proceso de Paz y Polarización Política. In G. Sanchez & E. Lair, eds. *Violencia y Estrategias Colectivas en la Región Andina. Bolivia, Colombia, Ecuador, Perú y Venezuela*. Bogotá: Editorial Norma, pp. 73–102.

Red Nacional de Mujeres; Corporación Sisma Mujer; No es Hora de Callar; Corporación Humanas Colombia, n.d. *Cinco Claves para un Tratamiento Diferencial de la Violencia Sexual en los Acuerdos sobre Juscticial Transicional en el Proceso de Paz*. [Online] Available at: www.humanas.org.co/archivos/Cinco_claves_de_la_vio

lencia_sexual_en_los_acuerdos_sobre_justicia_transicional-completo.pdf [Last accessed 12 November 2016].

Rincón Covelli, T., 2012. La Justicia Transicional: una concepción de la justicia que se hace cargo de atrocidades del pasado. InT. Rincón Covelli & J. Rodríguez Zepeda, eds. *La Justicia y las Atrocidades del Pasado. Teoría y análisis de la justicia*. México, D.F.: Universidad Autónoma Metropolitana y Miguel Ángel Porrúa, pp. 59–121.

Roth, F., Gubereck, T. & Green, A. H., 2011. *Using Quantitative Data to Assess Conflict-Related Sexual Violence in Colombia: Challenges and opportunities*. Bogotá: Opciones Gráficas Editores Ltda.

Rueda, P., 2001. *Documento Marco Conceptual*. [Online] Available at: http://pmayobre.webs.uvigo.es/textos/cecilia/documento_marco_conceptual.pdf [Last accessed 3 November 2016].

Sañudo Pazos, M. F., 2015. *Tierra y Género. Dilemas y obstáculos en los procesos de negociación de la política de tierras en Colombia*. Bogotá: Pontifica Universidad Javeriana.

United Nations Security Council, 2000. *Resolution 1325 (2000) S/RES/1325 (2000)*. [Online] Available at: https://documents-dds-ny.un.org/doc/UNDOC/GEN/N00/720/18/PDF/N0072018.pdf?OpenElement [Last accessed 21 May 2017].

United Nations Security Council, 2008. *Resolution 1820 (2008) S/RES/1820 (2008)*. [Online] Available at: www.securitycouncilreport.org/atf/cf/%7B65BFCF9B-6D27-4E9C-8CD3-CF6E4FF96FF9%7D/CAC%20S%20RES%201820.pdf [Last accessed 21 May 2017].

United Nations Security Council, 2009. *Resolution 1888 (2009) S/RES/1888 (2009)*. [Online] Available at: www.securitycouncilreport.org/atf/cf/%7B65BFCF9B-6D27-4E9C-8CD3-CF6E4FF96FF9%7D/WPS%20SRES%201888.pdf [Last accessed 21 May 2017].

United Nations Security Council, 2013a. *Resolution 2106 (2013) S/RES/2106 (2013)*. [Online] Available at: www.securitycouncilreport.org/atf/cf/%7B65BFCF9B-6D27-4E9C-8CD3-CF6E4FF96FF9%7D/s_res_2106.pdf [Last accessed 21 May 2017].

United Nations Security Council, 2013b. *Resolution 2122 (2013) S/RES/2122 (2013)*. [Online] Available at: https://undocs.org/en/S/RES/2122(2013) [Last accessed 21 May 2017].

Weinstein, H. M., Fletcher, L. E., Vinck, P. & Pham, P. N., 2010. Stay the Hand of Justice. Whose Priorities Take Priority? In R. Shaw, L. Waldorf & P. Hazan, eds. *Localizing Transitional Justice. Interventions and Priorities After Mass Violence*. Stanford, CA: Stanford University Press, pp. 27–48.

Wills Obregon, M. E., 2007. *Inclusión sin Representación. La irrupción política de las mujeres en Colombia 1970–2000*. Bogotá: Grupo Editorial Norma.

8 From combatants' boots

Reincorporation and reconciliation[1]

Diana Acosta-Navas and Carlos Felipe Reyes

Introduction

Peacebuilding efforts encompass diverse and often conflicting elements. Processes of disarmament, demobilization and reintegration (DDR) often require offering incentives to ex-combatants, which may be at odds with the goals of truth, accountability, and reparation pursued by institutions of transitional justice. However, transitional justice and DDR need not be antagonists transitional justice mechanisms can actually contribute to prevent large-scale recidivism by enabling local, community-based processes of reconciliation. Hereinafter we examine a potential alliance between DDR and transitional justice in the implementation of the peace accord between the Colombian Government and the Fuerzas Armadas Revolucionarias de Colombia-Ejército del Pueblo (FARC–EP)[2].

Efforts at DDR in Colombia currently face several challenges: threats to FARC members, murders of social leaders, persistence of illegal armed groups and drug-trafficking networks, and the desertion of ex-combatants. These realities leave little room for DDR institutions to maneuver. Transitional justice mechanisms can contribute to the prevention of large-scale recidivism by enabling local, community-based processes of reconciliation. We argue that insofar as the peace accord creates an institutional apparatus designed for the reconstruction of social fabric, it has the potential to discourage former combatants from re-engaging in criminality. However, while the mechanisms for state-led reconciliation are well delineated in the accord, their local counterparts have not been as clearly devised. And whereas this allows grassroots initiatives to take control over local processes of reconciliation, it also opens the door to corruption and co-option by a variety of political operators.

Recent DDR experiences and challenges in Colombia

For the past three decades Colombia has implemented DDR programmes to facilitate several waves of demobilization. Between 1989 and 2007, nine different armed groups demobilized,[3] accounting for 36,362 fighters (López, 2016). Between 2003 and 2016, 58,765 combatants demobilized;[4] 58% of whom did so as part of collective processes, and 42% as individual demobilizations (ACR, 2017).

In the midst of the peace process with the Autodefensas Unidas de Colombia (AUC) between 2003 and 2006, the administration of the erstwhile President Álvaro Uribe established a new institutional architecture for demobilization processes, naming it the Alta Consejería para la Reintegración (ACR).[5] The entity's mandate was twofold: to facilitate former combatants' re-entry into civilian life and to motivate further demobilizations. Of the guerrillas and paramilitaries who have demobilized since then, 85% have been through the DDR process established by the ACR, and 24% have successfully completed it (ACR, 2017).

Among the results of previous DDR efforts in Colombia, three indicators shed light on the risks and challenges that lie ahead. Homicide rates reveal the risks associated with the return to civilian life. Between 2003 and 2016, 2,830 demobilized combatants were killed. These constitute over 5% of the entire population registered in the ACR programme during this period (ACR, 2017)[6]. High homicide rates of former combatants occurred in departments with high levels of urban and rural crime. At the top of the list are the departments of Nariño and La Guajira, where murder rates of the demobilized population are above 13%; Arauca, Córdoba, Valle del Cauca, Chocó, Norte de Santander, and Antioquia have rates greater than 8% (ACR, 2017). In some departments, homicide rates of ex-combatants are as high as six percentage points above the annual average in the departmental population.

Unemployment reveals ex-combatants' difficulty to be assimilated into the economic life of host communities. Rates vary greatly across regions. In Bogotá, Casanare, Antioquia, and Cundinamarca unemployment rates for ex-combatants are below 10%, following the national average. In other departments, such as Sucre, Guaviare, and Vaupés, unemployment rates for former combatants are 24.8%, 30.6% and 33.3%, respectively (ACR, 2017), whereas unemployment in these departments' capitals is 10% (Sincelejo), 13.2% (San José del Guaviare) and 9.2% (Mitú) (DANE, 2017).

The third and perhaps the greatest challenge is the prevention of recidivism. The Centro Nacional de Memoria Histórica (2015) estimates that by 2009 some 15.5% of the entire demobilized population, including guerrillas and paramilitaries, had returned to criminal activities.[7] In 2014, the Fundación Ideas para la Paz[8] calculated the average recidivism rate across the country to be around 24% (Zukerman Daly, 2014). A former FARC–EP combatant reports being regarded as 'high-skilled labour for criminal organizations'.[9] The demobilization of paramilitaries in the early 2000s left a clear sign of caution against large-scale recidivism (Centro de Memoria Histórica, 2012 and 2015). By 2007, the Organization of American States reported the discovery of 22 criminal networks with participation, command, and control structures attributed to former AUC combatants (Ribetti, 2009). An estimated 25% of the demobilized combatants captured for criminal activities in the period between 2005 and 2009 were associated with emerging criminal gangs (*bandas criminales*, or BACRIM). Scholars refer to the DDR process as one of recycling and re-engineering existing structures under new franchises rather than dismantlement (Theidon & Laplante, 2006; Buitrago, 2006).

Research on the causes of recidivism yields heterogeneous results. Some of the relevant factors include: the welfare, status and ties that fighters had in armed groups, and whether they were subjected to abuse during their participation in the group (Humphreys & Weinstein, 2007). Structural elements, such as poverty, lack of economic opportunities, and unemployment, also increase the likelihood of returning to war (Hill, Taylor, & Temin, 2008).

In the case of Colombia, recidivism rates are explained by the interaction of driving and restraining factors (Kaplan & Nussio, 2016). Driving factors, which increase the probability of recidivism, include personality traits and the presence of criminal or armed groups in the territory where the cadre is residing. Restraining factors, which decrease the likelihood of recidivism, include strong family ties, and educational attainment.

It has been noted that recidivism in Colombia is significantly higher among former paramilitaries than among former guerrillas. In fact, former paramilitaries are almost 50% more likely than former guerrillas to return to criminal activity (Ribetti, 2009; Kaplan & Nussio, 2016). Before 2016, most ex-guerrillas who demobilized did so out of an individual choice to abandon their groups, incurring substantial risks in the process. By contrast, the great majority of paramilitaries, on the other hand, merely followed orders to demobilize.

Another contributing factor, is the persistence of ties between cadres and warlords, which facilitates re-engagement in war and criminality, and exposes former combatants and their families to threats and violence (Godos, 2013). Hence, severing the links between combatants and their former groups could, in theory, facilitate the demobilization process, and improve the success rate of DDR processes (Themner, 2011; Zyck, 2009).

From a different perspective, the experiences of former cadres in the reintegration process have been found to be more accurate predictors of direct recidivism than external factors, and this experience is deteriorated by the erasure of their identity as member of an armed group (Zukerman Daly, 2014). Studies by the ACR claim that 80% of the ex-combatants that completed the ACR route express satisfaction with their lives after demobilization (Mitrotti, 2016). Independent studies, however, reveal their discontent with paternalistic aspects of the ACR route (Gómez, 2014). Of particular concern is the institutionally-based rejection of ex-combatants' past: 'the government projects an image of reintegration as a "rebirth" that denies the past of former combatants [… Reintegration] routes are based on alleged social, emotional and production defects of former combatants favouring individual interventions, neglecting the context in which they live, their differences, postponing the integration of their family and social networks' (Fattal & Hoyos, 2013, p. 8; see also Hoyos, 2011; Cárdenas, 2005).

A process that disregards the beliefs, past experiences, and group identities of former fighters renders the process of reintegration more likely to produce dissatisfaction. This highlights the need for DDR policies to be attuned to the specific reasons of individuals who joined illegal armed groups (O'Neill, 2015). Such tailoring requires sensitivity to the psychological and emotional characteristics of individuals who have been affiliated with a guerrilla organization. These include: loyalty, solidarity and the perceived primacy of the organization over individuals (Castro, 1997); identification with a political project (Henao, 1997); and pervasive models of masculinity (Theidon, 2007; Theidon, 2009). The structure, cohesion, and collective identity of FARC—EP may thus serve to tailor a reintegration policy that successfully prevents the dispersion and atomization of ex-combatants (ICG 2014).

Successful DDR will also turn on communities' disposition to assimilate the presence of ex-combatants, and their ability to come to terms with their past. Although a recent study reveals that a large number of Colombians have positive attitudes towards reconciliation, considerable obstacles remain. In conflict-afflicted areas, 41% of community members view ex-combatants with fear, and 82% perceive them as being less trustworthy than non-ex-combatants (Rettberg, 2014). Cadres are well aware of this, as one of them relates: 'You end up stigmatized as if you were the scum of the earth, a plague or something, like that [sic] demobilized people are bad people' (Kaplan & Nussio, 2015).

Given these conditions, current DDR efforts will need to counteract the various factors driving recidivism. Educational attainment and job opportunities may not be sufficient. Strengthening social participation in the wider community is also a crucial step in allowing former combatants to be successfully reincorporated (Kaplan & Nussio, 2015). Special attention should be payed to the acknowledgment and recognition of former combatants' identity, past experiences, their sense of belonging and agency, and the acceptance of former fighters as members of the community. Both will require the promotion of social reconciliation.

Because the current DDR process is part and parcel of a wider peacebuilding effort that includes transitional justice initiatives, it may be seen as particularly well adapted for the promotion of social reconciliation. However, the joint action of transitional justice and DDR does not straightforwardly lead to reconciliation and successful reintegration. Furthermore, the goals of DDR and transitional justice tend to conflict and to hamper processes of reconciliation. The next section will revisit, and address, some arguments against the use of transitional justice institutions for facilitating DDR.

DDR and transitional justice: friends and foes?

This section argues that local institutions of transitional justice can operate in tandem with DDR to promote social reconciliation, and that the Colombian case could be a fertile ground for such a collaborative approach. For the purposes of this chapter, we will adopt a minimalist conception of reconciliation, as the re-establishment of constructive and productive political relationships that leverage and sustain other political and economic changes (Rettberg, 2014). Reconciliation, in this sense, does not require agreement, but the possibility of peaceful public debate and collective deliberation. It does not require forgiveness, but the reparation of large-scale political relationships (Murphy, 2010). The reconstruction of political relationships requires forging the conditions for mutual trust, which ought to be based on interpersonal accountability, as it is enforced by the power of the state. Hence, the restitution of trust in the rule of law plays an important role in this process.

At a first glance, DDR policies run contrary to regular forms of accountability, and may sow mistrust among citizens. The presence of ex-combatants in communities may be perceived as compromising security and the rule of law. Moreover, the amnesties and monetary incentives provided to incentivize demobilization may be regarded as rewards for criminality (Sriram & Herman, 2009). This perception of unfairness and lack of accountability is likely to erode the broader community's trust, and create resentment.

The role of creating accountability and promoting reconciliation in post-conflict scenarios is normally attributed to institutions of transitional justice. Someone could argue, however, that such institutions are unnecessary or even harmful to the prospect of achieving reconciliation. International bodies, including the World Bank, the Office of the United Nations (UN) High Commissioner for Human Rights and the UN itself, advocate the use of 'dual-targeting strategies'. These are designed to reduce apprehension towards ex-combatants' benefits, by providing proportional assistance to former combatants and members of conflict-afflicted communities. (Pfeiffer, 2014; Verzat, 2014; Lundy & McGovern, 2008; Mani, 2000; Pugh, 2000; United Nations Inter-Agency Working Group on Disarmament, 2014). These strategies can be implemented with the aid of 'peace infrastructures' meant to empower members of society, from grassroots organizations to national-level agencies, to take ownership over peacebuilding processes (Pfeiffer, 2014; Verzat, 2014).

The proper implementation of these strategies might suffice to counteract resentment in the community and create a more welcoming environment for ex-combatants. If that were the case, transitional justice mechanisms might seem superfluous. However, isolated from transitional justice, dual-targeting strategies cannot secure reconciliation, as they are purely forward-looking mechanisms that fail to address past human rights violations. If trust is based on forms of mutual accountability that are sanctioned and enforced by an authoritative body (either the state or the community), it requires a warranted expectation that citizens will be backed in their claims against others who harm them. Allowing these harms to go unaddressed and unacknowledged sabotages the accountability upon which trust could be built.

Furthermore, simply offering economic incentives to community members in exchange for their acceptance of ex-combatants may be negatively perceived as a way of purchasing their acquiescence. Such a perception, in addition to the silent, or passive, denial of abuses, is more likely to erode than to bolster trust.

An official attempt at confronting and acknowledging past abuses could lie the grounds of accountability and trust that drive political reconciliation (Quinn, 2010). Transitional justice institutions are meant to seek the truth about past harms and acknowledge them as the basis of a social renewal project (Du Toit, 2000).

Nevertheless, it is far from clear that they can drive society towards reconciliation. Although some see these institutions as means of 'settling accounts with the past' (Minow, 1998; Hayner, 2001), sceptics believe that, at best, truth seeking institutions could enable 'contentious coexistence' in post-conflict societies (Payne, 2008). Perpetrators' accounts in truth commissions are transgressive. They may cause social instability, unrest, and resentment, thus undermining relations of mutual trust.

Moreover, nationally-led transitional justice institutions may appear alien and distant from the actual stakeholders, namely, victims, combatants and members of host communities (see Chapter 14 for the case of Bosnia and Herzegovina). And even though these mechanisms can serve the creation of a national narrative of reconciliation, they may also instill the fear 'that it is all a "façade"—the state in its theatrical register, orchestrating a transition that does not reach beyond the flat shiny surface of the television screen" (Theidon, 2007, p. 88; see also Payne, 2008).

While these objections are fair, they are based on a particular picture of transitional justice institutions, and a prevalent model of violence. The model takes the paradigmatic case of violence to be exercised by a powerful perpetrator, usually embodied in a state, on a powerless victim. This form of 'vertical violence' is essentially asymmetrical. It is opposed to 'horizontal violence', which is characterized by the absence of power imbalances, and the fact that a large percentage of agents can simultaneously be identified as victims and perpetrators (Orozco, 2005).

Although we do not argue for this view, there are several reasons to think that Colombia's conflict is horizontal (Orozco, 2005; Molano, 2015; Comisión Histórica del Conflicto y sus Víctimas, 2015). For instance, it has been reported that around 50% of FARC—EP members were victims of child recruitment (Semana.com, 2014). Further, several illegal armed structures participating in the conflict had their origins as self-defence movements. Many combatants in Colombia enlisted in illegal armed groups seeking either security or revenge (Orozco, 2005). Thus, cadres in armed groups 'find themselves in the tension of having to represent themselves through the different categories that include them: ex-combatants, perpetrators, non-beneficiaries of the war, beneficiaries of the state, victims of the groups that recruited them, structural victims of the conditions that led them to enlist' (Hoyos, 2011, p. 14).

The traditional discourse on human rights that informs transitional justice framers ignores these overlaps (Orozco, 2010). Blindness to this fact may impair the reconciliatory powers of such institutions. A truth commission designed to address instances of state violence is unlikely to ease the reincorporation of fighters into—mostly rural and vulnerable—host communities, which necessitates that cadres are integrated in the networks of reciprocal accountability and trust that bond community members *qua* community members. This entails that they hold themselves accountable to the community, and vice versa. A truth commission designed to address instances of state-led violence, through nationwide broadcast of a confession, and a state-sanctioned amnesty, cannot re-establish this reciprocity, and hence cannot create the conditions for reconciliation.

The South African Truth and Reconciliation Commission (TRC) is a useful illustration of such 'top-down' transitional justice. Although the TRC may have been successful at promoting political reconciliation at the national level (Minow, 1998; Gutman & Thompson, 2000; Kiss, 2000), it prevented the direct confrontation of victims and perpetrators, which gave victims the idea that white South Africans were entirely disengaged from the process (see Chapter 12). Hence, their punitive and revengeful impulses were intact (Wilson, 2001), and the local-level conflict dynamics were unaddressed (Van Der Merwe, 2008).

In the words of the former Mayor of Bogotá, 'different forms of barbarism require different transitions' (Mockus, 2005, p. x). In cases of horizontal violence, reconciliation requires the recognition of 'the presence and meaning of the gray zones; of figures that are simultaneously victims and perpetrators'. (Orozco, 2005, p. 256; Theidon, 2006; Theidon, 2012). In recognizing this dual status, there is an acknowledgment of both the harms done to the ex-combatant, and the harms they did to the community. This mutual acknowledgement lays the foundations for accountability. This requires, in turn, an exercise of empathy (Orozco, 2005). The performance of this empathetic act may lead to a shift in the way that we perceive ex-combatants, re-humanizing them, restoring our perception of them as individuals as opposed to anonymous members of a stereotyped group (Halpern & Weinstein, 2004). This shift could potentially contribute to remove the obstacles for the forging of mutual trust.

There are known cases of post-conflict societies that have appealed to local peacebuilding strategies, framed with the rhetoric of transitional justice, as mechanisms for the pursuit of accountability and reconciliation (Sharp, 2013). These include the Gacaca Courts in Rwanda (Fierens, 2005; Kirby, 2006; Schabas, 2005); the Ardoyne Commemoration Project in Northern Ireland (Lundy & McGovern, 2008); communal justice practices in Peru (Theidon, 2012); and unofficial truth projects, in Guatemala, Brazil and Uruguay (Bickford, 2007), among others. These processes were led by the communities themselves, and not imposed by central governments. (Theidon, 2006). These 'bottom-up', participatory approaches to peacebuilding bring communities much closer to properly addressing the essential detail of conflict dynamics (Lundy & McGovern, 2008). In fact, some community-led approaches to transitional justice are described as reversing the dehumanization process that took place during the conflict, and fostering the reintegration of combatants in society (Theidon, 2006).

These initiatives carry their own set of drawbacks. Given that local communities are not accountable to state-wide institutions, they risk having little to no legitimacy, and becoming a simple means for the entrenchment of existing power imbalances. In Rwanda, for instance, the Gacaca Courts prohibited legal counsel for defendants and compelled them to answer the Court's questions, leading to a grave disregard for due process, and large numbers of false convictions (Schabas, 2005; Kirby, 2006; Fierens, 2005). The Ardoyne Commemoration Project ran afoul of exclusiveness, establishing a one-sided version of history (Lundy & McGovern, 2008). Thus, overly romanticized ideas of community and empowerment can become a cover for marginalization and exclusion, and a recipe against reconciliation. In the case of Colombia, these risks are particularly salient. Unhealthy power dynamics in local communities may be further entrenched if these bottom-up approaches to justice remain unchecked and unaccountable.

This brings us to the last objection we will consider in this section, namely that the recent attempt at DDR and transitional justice in Colombia resulted in large-scale recidivism and not much reconciliation. In fact, the transitional justice institutions implemented during the paramilitary demobilization were criticized for legitimizing existing criminal structures and power imbalances (Hurtado, 2010; Tapias, 2010), forcing reconciliation on victims and afflicted communities (Castro, 2010), and devaluing victims' rights (Tapias, 2010). So why should we expect the current process to be any different?

The current peace accord is significantly different from the one reached in the early 2000s. During the implementation of Law 975 of 2005, the discourse adopted by the Government and the heads of paramilitary organizations stood in stark opposition to bottom-up and grassroots narratives of that peace process (Diaz, 2008; Arias, 2010). Victims' voices did not have the platform they were given during the negotiation of the current accord. Furthermore, the truth commission that was implemented then was limited to perpetrators' *versiones libres*[10] (Lecombe, 2010). This resulted from a partial importing of the South African model (Lecombe, 2010), which failed to fully incorporate transitional justice measures to the reintegration process. That attempt was essentially a top-down mechanism, which excluded victims' and afflicted communities' voices, and deprived them of agency in the process of peacebuilding. While it created truth-telling institutions, these did not promote direct engagement between ex-combatants and communities.[11]

The institutional structure created by the current peace accord has the potential to grant decision-making power to, and foster the participation of, community-based, ex-combatants' and victims' organizations, while preserving bonds of accountability to nationwide institutions. These institutions seem better suited to the task of creating community-wide accountability promoting reconciliation, and preventing recidivism of ex-combatants. While this may not be sufficient to guarantee the overall success of the process, it may contribute to creating a different perception of reconciliation, and thus creating a more favourable social environment for reintegration.

DDR and transitional justice in the framework of the Peace Accord

This section explains the conditions for the reintegration of former combatants after the period when they will be located at Temporary Rural Areas of Normalization (ZVTN).[12] Section 3 of the peace accord sets the conditions for the economic, social, and political reincorporation of FARC—EP members over the age of 18 years[13] (Gobierno Nacional de Colombia and FARC—EP, 2016). The accord creates several lines of support through which ex-combatants will be assisted in their reintegration process, and may voluntarily continue to interact with other former FARC—EP members.

Several institutions will assist in the process of reintegration. The National Council for Reincorporation[14] (CNR) establishes activities, timetables, and monitoring mechanisms (Gobierno Nacional de Colombia and FARC—EP, 2016). The process will use the existing infrastructure of the reintegration agency, the ACR. The CNR council will contribute to tailoring some of the policies to the specific needs of FARC—EP cadres.

For the political reincorporation of former guerrillas, a new political party has been created. The FARC[15] enjoys legal status, economic and technical support, access to media outlets, and security conditions. The party constitutes a venue from which former cadres can pursue lawfully their political project (Gobierno Nacional de Colombia and FARC—EP, 2016).

A series of economic aids are given to each demobilized FARC—EP member (Gobierno Nacional de Colombia and FARC—EP, 2016): First, a basic income corresponding to 90% of the country's minimum wage (around US $253 per month in 2017), which they receive for 24 months after the end of ZVTN. Second, unemployed cadres can receive social security for a period of 24 months. Third, a sum of 2m. Colombian pesos (US $688), to be used for relocation. Fourth, a lump sum of 8m. Colombian pesos (approximately US $2,750) for the implementation of productive projects, which can be executed individually or through the Economías Sociales del Común (ECOMUN)[16]. The latter is a solidarity-based economic organization aimed at promoting productive initiatives and supporting reincorporation through income-generating activities (Gobierno Nacional de Colombia and FARC—EP, 2016).

The aforementioned economic benefits grant cadres a large degree of independence in the realization of their personal projects and in the process of reincorporation. They are not conditional on the maintenance of links with other ex-combatants or the FARC political party. These measures respect ex-combatants' autonomy to decide what bonds with the organization they want to preserve, and which they rather prescind.

In addition, the peace accord contemplates the design and implementation of social programmes for the demobilized population, which include formal education, job and skills training, as well as psychological support. These programmes will be designed by the CNR and implemented by the Colombian Government through the ACR.

Guidelines for the interaction of FARC—EP members with host communities are established as part of reparations programmes. Participation in concrete actions of reparation is voluntary, but can be taken into account for judicial benefits in the context of criminal prosecution (Gobierno Nacional de Colombia and FARC—EP, 2016). These are not tailored to FARC—EP members but to all the parties involved in the conflict, including state agents.

FARC—EP is collectively committed to carrying out reparative activities, such as: working on infrastructure reconstruction in the most affected territories; cleaning and decontaminating programmes in territories of anti-personnel mines, improvised explosive devices, unexploded ammunition or explosive remnants of war; participating in illegal crop substitution programmes; contributing to the search, location, identification and recovery of remains of persons killed or missing in connection with the conflict; and supporting reforestation programmes and other environmental projects (Gobierno Nacional de Colombia and FARC—EP, 2016).

National plans for collective reparation of victims are also embedded in the Rural Development Plan[17]. Finally, the national government will develop programmes for the reconstruction of the social fabric in territories afflicted by violence (Gobierno Nacional de Colombia and FARC—EP, 2016). While this constitutes an ambitious agenda for reparative and reconciliatory activities, it should be noted that none of them are mandatory. Further, the conditions for the encounter of FARC—EP members with receiving communities are not explicitly stated by the document, and will be determined by the CNR.

The challenges ahead for DDR and transitional justice in Colombia

Over the past decades the Colombian Government has created a peace infrastructure as part of its various attempts to end the conflict (Pfeiffer, 2014). However, some DDR programmes were executed by the central government without a clear articulation and co-operation with regional and local authorities. The programme for the mass demobilization of former AUC combatants, for instance, imposed reintegration programmes while failing to provide local authorities the appropriate resources and incentives to participate in the process (Jaramillo, et al., 2009). It has been argued, on the other hand, that the 'lack of reconciliation [after this peace process] is partly due to the fact that initiatives aimed at ensuring truth, justice and reparations did not accompany the DDR process' (Jaramillo, et al., 2009, p. 5).

The current peace accord lays the institutional groundwork for a collaborative interaction between DDR and transitional justice while incorporating some lessons from those past efforts. The juridical framework creates transitional justice mechanisms to hold the perpetrators of serious human rights violations accountable. The Jurisdicción Especial para la Paz (JEP—Special Jurisdiction for Peace)[18] grants amnesties to combatants that did not commit human rights abuses. The accord also creates opportunities to articulate DDR and transitional justice in ways that redress past harms. The measures for reparation that the FARC—EP has committed to undertaking as an organization can contribute to creating venues for reconciliation and collaborative work with communities.

The burden falls mostly on the CNR, as it is in charge of planning and monitoring the political, economic, psychological, and social reincorporation of former combatants, and is responsible for carrying out pedagogical activities for peace and reconciliation. The institutional architecture of the CNR lends itself to address the horizontal aspects of reconciliation. Although it is a central governmental agency, one of its tasks is to create 'territorial councils', and seek alliances with local and regional governments. Territorial councils open a potential space for local and community initiatives, giving a voice to the main stakeholders of the process. In this sense, the CNR is part of a peace infrastructure, which makes use of the existing architecture of the ARN[19] (Pfeiffer, 2014; Verzat, 2014). Since FARC—EP members are part of the board of this institution, there is a higher likelihood that initiatives will be more responsive to the voice and needs of former combatants. Thus, the CNR harbors the potential to foster ex-combatants' constructive participation in their receiving communities, without denying their past and identity. The accord applies a horizontal model of reconciliation to address a horizontal conflict.

There are, however, serious risks in the process of implementing these policies. First, improvisation is one of the greatest detractors for the effectiveness and the legitimacy of peace infrastructures (Verzat, 2014). Improvisation is part of what undermined previous DDR processes in Colombia (Jaramillo, et al., 2009; Ribetti, 2009), and has created serious downfalls for the current one, as has been made clear from the preliminary reports on the situation of the ZVTN.[20]

Second, the fact that the Government has not committed resources to the CNR means that it must seek funds from international non-governmental organizations (NGOs) and donors. The donor-based architecture allows international organizations to determine the agenda of peacebuilding efforts, thereby imposing their own values, interests, and agendas (Pugh, 2000; Mani, 2000; Lundy & McGovern, 2008), instead of bolstering the work of grassroots organizations that represent the real interests of the community (Pfeiffer, 2014; Lundy & McGovern, 2008). Thus, the ideal of community empowerment may be eroded, as the local actors are deprived of agency.

These institutions also run the risk of being co-opted by criminal organizations. In the early 2000s, a number of high-profile cases took place, including the co-option of DDR resources by an AUC front (Ribetti, 2009), and the Corporación Democracia.[21] This was an agency founded by the local government in Medellín to assist the process of AUC reintegration, and was designed to implement community-based projects, involving former combatants. A few years after its creation, it was found to be co-operating with the so-called Envigado Office[22]. The agency had essentially become a façade to capture public resources while carrying out illegal activities (ICG, 2014; Verdad Abierta, 2011).

In addition to the challenges inherent to process of reincorporation, the broader picture should be kept in mind. Any DDR policy will be vain if the violence against social leaders and ex-combatants continues, or if their lack of confidence in the process leads them to desertion. Likewise, the presence of other illegal armed groups and their influence across the national territory could undercut any attempt at reconciliation. The possibility of linking transitional justice with DDR is an interesting point of entry to prevent the return of cadres into warfare and to promote reconciliation at the level of communities. While it may be the case that the values guiding the processes of DDR and transitional justice are at odds with each other, the implementation of the current peace accord with the FARC—EP can provide a fertile ground for productive interactions between them.

Notes

1 The authors would like to express their gratitude towards all the people who contributed to the development of this work. In particular, we want to thank Germán Escovar Álvarez, for his contribution to the first section of the paper and his tireless support throughout the process; Cristina García Navas, for collaborating in the organization of the 'Empathy and Reconciliation' workshop at the IV Harvard-MIT-BU-Tufts Colombian Conference (Cambridge, MA, April 2016), which prompted us to write on demobilization and reintegration; Fidelis Magalhaes and Joshua Mitrotti, for their interventions at this workshop; and to Regis Ortiz, for sharing with us his story, which gave us the inspiration and motivation to write this piece.
2 Revolutionary Armed Forces of Colombia—People's Army.
3 The Ejército Popular de Liberación (EPL), Movimiento 19 de Abril (M-19), Partido Revolucionario de los Trabajadores (PRT), Movimiento Armado Quintín Lame (MAQL), Comandos Ernesto Rojas (CER), Corriente de Renovación Socialista, El Frente Francisco Garnica, El Movimiento Independiente Revolucionario Comandos Armados (MIR—COAR) and the Autodefensas Unidas de Colombia (AUC).
4 From different guerrilla and paramilitary groups
5 In 2017 the Agencia Colombiana para la Reintegración (ACR), a Colombian agency for the reintegration of people and armed groups, changed its name to the Agencia para la Reincorporación y la Normalización (ARN—Agency for Reincorporation and Normalization.
6 Official estimates show that the proportion of deceased within the demobilized population that has not joined the ACR programme is three times higher (Mitrotti, 2016).
7 These calculations are based on captures and homicides related to delinquency: however, it is argued that impunity—and under-reporting—might in fact imply that this rate could in fact be much higher (Centro Nacional de Memoria Histórica, 2015).
8 Foundation Ideas for Peace.
9 Quoted from a conversation with ex-FARC combatant, Regis Ortiz, in the context of the IV Harvard-MIT-BU-Tufts Colombian Conference. Cambridge MA, April, 2016.

10 Voluntary declarations. These are the voluntary statements from actors involved in a particular legal process, in which the involved actors can present their account of particular events.
11 There are exceptional cases of locally-based institutions that fostered these encounters and sought to do justice to the horizontal nature of the conflict, including the Victims Project and the mental health programmes sponsored by AMOR (Asociación de Mujeres del Oriente Antioqueño), Conciudadanía, and the Peace Programme of the Jesuit Community, all grassroots organizations based in Antioquia. (See Diaz, 2008)
12 Zonas Veredales Transitorias de Normalización.
13 FARC—EP combatants under the age of eighteen will be given the same legal treatment awarded to victims of the conflict, and special conditions for their reintegration will be set by the CNR.
14 Consejo Nacional de Reincorporación.
15 Fuerza Alternativa Revolucionaria del Común.
16 A co-operative company created by FARC members that aims to undertake productive projects with former guerrillas in their transit to civil life.
17 Programas de Desarrollo con Enfoque Territorial (PDET). They will be the state's main instrument to implement development projects in the municipalities most affected by the armed conflict.
18 The framework that defines the Transitional justice setting in Colombia. For an explanation on the mechanisms and institutions taking place in the JEP, see Chapter 5.
19 Agencia para la Reincorporación y la Normalización (ARN). Formerly known as the ACR, see footnote 5.
20 Press articles have denounced the absence of appropriate infrastructure, the breaking-down of community bonds among former FARC—EP members, and the high rates at which they are joining other illegal armed groups in their areas. (See Prieto, Ardila, Velez, & Arenas, 2017; Ardila, 2017)
21 Democracy Corporation.
22 The '*Oficina de Envigado*' is a powerful criminal gang based in the Medellín area. It was led by the paramilitary leader Don Berna until his extradition to the USA in 2008. Despite the death or capture of many of its leaders, the Envigado Office remains active today.

References

Agencia Colombiana para la Reintegración (ACR), 2017. *La Desmovilización en Cifras*. [Online] Available at:www.reintegracion.gov.co/es/la-reintegracion/Paginas/cifras.aspx [Last accessed 1 March 2017].

Ardila, L., 2017. *La incertidumbre de Gallo a La Fortuna*. [Online] Available at: http://lasillavacia.com/silla-caribe/la-incertidumbre-de-gallo-la-fortuna-62862 [Last accessed 10 October 2017].

Arias, G. , 2010. Civil Society in the Colombian Transitional Justice Framework. In A. N. Lyons, *Contested transitions: Dilemmas of transitional justice in Colombia and comparative experience*. 1st edn. Bogotá: International Center for Transitional Justice.

Bickford, L., 2007. Unofficial Truth Projects. *Human Rights Quarterly*, 29, pp. 994–1035.

Buitrago, F., 2006. La política de seguridad democrática: 2002–2005. *Análisis Político*, Volume 57.

Cárdenas, J. A., 2005. *Los Parias de la Guerra*. Bogotá: Ediciones Aurora.

Castro, I. C., 2010. A Model of Justice for Democracy. In A. N. Lyons, *Contested transitions: Dilemmas of transitional justice in Colombia and comparative experience*. 1st edn. Bogotá: International Center for Transitional Justice.

Castro, M. C., 1997. Introducción. In C. L. María Clemencia Castro, ed., *Guerrilla, reinserción y lazo social*. Bogotá: Almudena editores.

Centro Nacional de Memoria Histórica, 2012. *Justicia y Paz: ¿Verdad Judicial o Verdad Histórica?* Bogotá: Publicaciones Semana.

Centro Nacional de Memoria Histórica, 2015. *Rearmados y Reintegrados: Panorama Postacuerdos con las AUC*. Bogotá: CNMH.

Colombia2020, 2016. *Las Cifras Sobre los Niños y la Guerra*. [Online] Available at: http://colombia2020.elespectador.com/pais/las-cifras-sobre-los-ninos-y-la-guerra [Last accessed 30 July 2016]

Comisión Histórica del Conflicto y sus Víctimas, 2015. *Contribución al entendimiento del conflicto armado en Colombia* . Centro de Memoria Histórica, Bogotá.

Departamento Nacional de Estadística (DANE), 2017. *Gran Encuesta Integrada de Hogares -GEIH- Mercado Laboral*. [Online] Available at:www.dane.gov.co/index.php/estadisticas-por-tema/mercado-laboral/empleo-y-desempleo [Last accessed 25 October 2017].

Diaz, C., 2008. Challenging Impunity from Below. In K. McEvoy and L. McGregor, eds, *Transitional justice from below: Grassroots activism and the struggle for change (Human rights law in perspective; vol. 14)*. Portland, OR and Oxford: Hart Publishing.

Du Toit, A., 2000. The Moral Foundations of the South-African TRC: Truth as Acknowledgment and Justice as Recognition. In R. I. Rotberg & D. Thompson, eds, *Truth v. Justice: The morality of truth commissions*. Princeton: Princeton University Press.

Fattal, A., and Hoyos, A., 2013. *Hacia una reforma del DDR para la paz: Propuestas desde la academia y las experiencias actuales de desmovilización*. [Online] Available at:www.academia.edu/7090339/Hacia_una_reforma_del_DDR_para_la_paz_Propuestas_desde_la_academia_y_las_experiencias_actuales_de_desmovilizaci%C3%B3n [Last accessed 4 July 2016].

Fierens, J., 2005. Gacaca Courts: Between Fantasy and Reality. *Journal of International Criminal Justice*, 3, pp. 896–919.

Gobierno Nacional de Colombia and FARC—EP, 2016. *Acuerdo Final para la Terminación del Conflicto y la Construcción de una Paz Estable y Duradera*. [Online] Available at: www.mesadeconversaciones.com.co/sites/default/files/24-1480106030.11-1480106030.2016nuevoacuerdofinal-1480106030.pdf [Last accessed 24 October 2017].

Godos, J. G., 2013. Colombia: Accountability and DDR in the pursuit of peace? In C. L. Sriram, J. García-Godos, J. Herman & O. Martin-Ortega, eds, *Transitional justice and peacebuilding on the ground: Victims and ex-combatants*. New York: Routledge.

Gómez, L. F., 2014. *La reintegración social y económica de los grupos armados ilegales en colombia: reflexiones a partir de la trayectoria de nueve excombatientes*. [Online] Available at:www.reintegracion.gov.co/es/la-reintegracion/centro-de-documentacion/Documentos/La%20Reintegraci%C3%B3n%20social%20y%20econ%C3%B3mica%20de%20los%20grupos%20armados%20ilegales%20en%20Colombia.pdf [Last accessed 4 July 2016].

Gutman, A., & Thompson, D., 2000. The Moral Foundations of Truth Commissions. In R. I. Rotberg & D. Thompson, eds, *Truth v. Justice: The morality of truth commissions*. Princeton, NJ: Princeton University Press.
Halpern, J., & Weinstein, H., 2004. Rehumanizing the Other: Empathy and Reconciliation. *Human Rights Quarterly*, 26(3), pp. 561–583.
Hayner, P., 2001. *Unspeakable Truths.* New York: Routledge.
Henao, I., 1997. Reconstrucción del imaginario de proyecto de vida en la reincorporación social del guerrillero: el poder de lo simbólico. In C. L. María Clemencia Castro, ed., *Guerrilla, reinserción y lazo social*. Bogotá: Almudena editores.
Hill, R., Taylor, G., & Temin, J., 2008. *Would You Fight Again? Understanding Liberian Ex-Combatant Reintegration*. Washington, DC: United States Institute of Peace.
Hoyos, J. F., 2011. *Capitales para la Guerra y el Testimonio en un Contexto Transicional*. Bogotá: Universidad Nacional de Colombia.
Humphreys, M., & Weinstein, J. M., 2007. Demobilization and Reintegration. *Journal of Conflict Resolution*, 51(4), pp. 531–567.
Hurtado, M. R., 2010. Transitional Justice Under Fire. In A. N. Lyons, *Contested transitions: Dilemmas of transitional justice in Colombia and comparative experience*. 1st edn. Bogotá: International Center for Transitional Justice.
International Crisis Group (ICG), 2014. *The Day after Tomorrow: Colombia's FARC and the End of the Conflict (Latin America Report)*. Brussels: International Crisis Group.
Jaramillo, S., Giha, Y., & Torres, P., 2009. *Transitional Justice and DDR: The Case of Colombia*. New York: International Center for Transitional Justice.
Kaplan, O., & Nussio, E., 2015. Community Counts: The Social Reintegration of Ex-Combatants in Colombia, *Conflict Management and Peace Science*, pp. 1–22.
Kaplan, O., & Nussio, E., 2016. Explining Recidivism of Ex-Combatants in Colombia, *Journal of Conflict Resolution*, 62 (1), pp. 1–30.
Kirby, C., 2006. Rwanda's Gacaca Courts: A Preliminary Critique. *Journal of African Law*, 50(2).
Kiss, E., 2000. Moral Ambition Within and Beyond Political Constraints. In R. I. Rotberg & D. Thompson, eds, *Truth v. Justice: The morality of truth commissions*. Princeton, NJ: Princeton University Press.
Lecombe, D., 2010. A Conflicted Peace. In A. N. Lyons, *Contested transitions: Dilemmas of transitional justice in Colombia and comparative experience*. 1st edn. Bogotá: International Center for Transitional Justice.
Lundy, P., & McGovern, M., 2008. Whose Justice? Rethinking Transitional Justice From the Bottom Up. *Journal of Law and Society*, 35(2), pp. 265–292.
López, C., 2016. *Adiós a las FARC ?Y ahora que?*Bogota: Debate.
Mani, R., 2000. The Rule of Law or the Rule of Might? In M. Pugh, *Regeneration of War-Torn Societies*. New York: Macmillan Press.
Minow, M., 1998. *Between Vengeance and Forgiveness*. Boston, MA: Beacon Press.
Mitrotti, J., 2016. *Reintegration Strategy:. IV Colombian Conference* (pp. 1–10). Cambridge, MA: Harvard University.
Mockus, A., 2005. Del 'Fueron' al 'Fue'. In I. Orozco, *Sobre los Límites de la Conciencia Humanitaria*. Bogotá: Temis.
Molano, A., 2015. *50 Años de Conflicto Colombiano*. Bogotá: El Espectador.
Murphy, C., 2010. *A Moral Theory of Political Reconciliation*. Cambridge: Cambridge University Press.

O'Neill, J., 2015. *Engaging Women in Disarmament, Demobilization, and Reintegration: Insights for Colombia*. Washington, DC: The Institute for Inclusive Security.

Orozco, I., 2005. *Sobre los Límites de la Conciencia Humanitaria*. Bogotá: Temis.

Orozco, I., 2010. La Barbarie Horizontal: Un Desafío al Movimiento de Derechos Humanos. In A. Rettberg, *Conflicto Armado, Seguridad y Construcción de Paz en Colombia*. Bogotá: Universidad de Los Andes.

Payne, L., 2008. *Unsettling Accounts: Neither Truth nor Reconciliation in Confessions of State Violence*. Durham, NC: Duke University Press.

Pfeiffer, S., 2014. *Peace Infrastructure in Colombia*. Berlin: Berghof Foundation.

Prieto, J., Ardila, L., Velez, J., & Arenas, N., 2017. *El duro aterrizaje de las Farc a la realidad*. [Online] Available at: http://lasillavacia.com/el-duro-aterrizaje-de-las-farc-la-realidad-62692 [Last accessed 25 September 2017]

Pugh, M., 2000. The Social-Civil Dimension. In M. Pugh, *Regeneration of War-Torn Societies*. New York: Macmillan Press.

Quinn, J., 2010. *The politics of acknowledgement: Truth commissions in Uganda and Haiti. Law and society series (Vancouver, BC)*. Vancouver: University of British Columbia Press.

Rettberg, A., 2014. Encuentro con los otros: perspectivas para la reconciliación en Colombia. In D. M. Ana María Ibañez, ed., *Costos económicos y sociales del conflicto en Colombia: ¿Cómo construir un posconflicto sostenible?* Bogotá: Ediciones Uniandes.

Ribetti, M., 2009. Disengagement and Beyond: A Case Study of Demobilization in Colombia. In T. Bjorgo & J. Horgan, *Leaving Terrorism Behind* (pp. 152–169). New York: Routledge.

Schabas, W., 2005. Genocide Trials and Gacaca Courts. *Journal of International Criminal Justice*, 3, pp. 879–895.

Semana.com, 2014. *El 47% de los Integrantes de las Farc fueron Reclutados en la Niñez*. [Online] Available at:www.semana.com/nacion/articulo/el-47-de-los-integrantes-de-las-farc-fueron-reclutados-siendo-ninos/407422-3 [Last accessed 24 October 2017].

Sharp., D., 2013. Interrogating the Peripheries: The Preoccupations of Fourth Generation Transitional Justice. *Harvard Human Rights Journal*, 26.

Sriram, C. L., & Herman, J., 2009. DDR and transitional justice: bridging the divide? *Conflict, Security & Development*, 9(4), pp. 455–474.

Tapias, C. d. G., , 2010. The Colombian Government's Formulas for Peace with the AUC. In A. N. Lyons, *Contested transitions: Dilemmas of transitional justice in Colombia and comparative experience*. (1st edn). Bogotá: International Center for Transitional Justice.

Theidon, K., & Laplante, L. J., 2006. Transitional Justice in Times of Conflict: Colombia's Ley de Justicia y Paz. *Michigan Journal of International Law*, 28(1), p. 49.

Theidon, K., 2006. Justice in Transition: The Micropolitics of Reconciliation in Postwar Peru. *The Journal of Conflict Resolution*, 50(3), pp. 433–457.

Theidon, K., 2007. Transitional Subjects: The Disarmament, Demobilization and Reintegration of Former Combatants in Colombia. *The International Journal of Transitional Justice*, 1, pp. 66–90.

Theidon, K., 2009. Reconstructing Masculinities: The Disarmament, Demobilization, and Reintegration of Former Combatants in Colombia. *Human Rights Quarterly*, 31, pp. 1–34.

Theidon, K., 2012. *Intimate Enemies*. Philadelphia: University of Pennsylvania Press.

Themner, A., 2011. *Violence in Post-conflict Societies: Remarginalization, Remobilizers and Relationships.* London: Routledge.
United Nations Inter-Agency Working Group on Disarmament, Demobilization and Reintegration, 2014. *Integrated DDR Standards (IDDRS).* [Online] Available at: http://unddr.org/iddrs.aspx [Last accessed 24 September 2017].
Van Der Merwe, H., 2008. *Truth and reconciliation in South Africa: did the TRC deliver?* Philadelphia: University of Pennsylvania Press.
Verdad Abierta, 2011. *Verdad Abierta.* [Online] Available at: http://verdadabierta.com/component/content/article/50-rearmados/3107-el-ocaso-de-la-corporacion-democracia [Last accessed 1 July 2016].
Verzat, V., 2014. *Infrastructures for Peace.* Berlin: Berghof Foundation.
Wilson, R. A., 2001. *The Politics of Truth and Reconciliation in South Africa.* Cambridge: Cambridge University Press.
Zukerman Daly, S. P., 2014. *Retorno a la legalidad o reincidencia de excombatientes en Colombia: dimensión del fenómeno y factores de riesgo.* Bogotá: Fundación Ideas para la Paz.
Zyck, S., 2009. Former Combatant Reintegration and Fragmentation in Contemporary Afghanistan Analysis. *Conflict, Security and Development*, 9(1), pp. 111–131.

9 Historical memory as symbolic reparation

Limitations and opportunities of peace infrastructures as institutional designs

Eliana Jimeno

Introduction

Memorialization processes implemented in deeply divided societies in the wake of mass violence have the potential to repair social relations, dignify the survivors, and reestablish relations between victims and the state. When implemented appropriately, efforts to memorialize a conflict can be an important part of a government's symbolic reparation programs. However, this is not always the case. In Colombia, a lack of victims' ownership over symbolic reparation processes resulted in memorialization processes that had negative repercussions on communities rebuilding after violence. Examining the institutional design of Colombia's mechanism for victims' participation within the National Reparations Program demonstrates how these can become a barrier to victims proper involvement. To analyse this situation, the chapter discusses the concept of peace infrastructures.

Colombia has implemented transitional justice mechanisms to redress victims since the 1997 *Ley de Atención a Población Desplazada*[1] (Internal Displaced Population Law), which aimed to address the consequences of internal displacement in the country. However, in 2005 a fully-fledged transitional justice framework was implemented with the enactment of the *Ley de Justicia y Paz* [2] (Justice and Peace Law—JPL) (see Chapter 4).

Previous work has criticized the Justice and Peace Law (JPL) for its perpetrator-oriented approach and its lack of results (Stone, 2011; Cepeda, 2011). The process was deemed to be largely ineffective and the judiciary instruments to vindicate victims' rights proved insufficient (International Crisis Group, 2013). The exception was the symbolic reparation mechanisms, which found reasonable success despite the ongoing violence (OACDH, Oficina del Alto Comisionado de las Naciones Unidas para los Derechos Humanos, 2009; Ruiz, 2015).

In 2011, the government of President Juan Manuel Santos incorporated lessons from the JPL to pass a new law: the *Ley de Víctimas y Restitución de Tierras*[3], a framework oriented towards victims' recognition and integral reparation. The law created the *Plan Nacional de Atención y Reparación Integral a las Víctimas*[4] which comprised measures for reparation to be provided at the individual and collective level through material and symbolic means.[5]

The inclusion of satisfaction measures facilitated the development of a broader understanding of symbolic reparations to support peacebuilding in Colombia, and facilitated the recognition of the state's duty towards remembrance, through measures such as memory reconstruction, commemorations, and official apologies. These measures revised and modified of the mechanisms for victims' participation in symbolic reparations that had been established by the JPL, therefore affecting the frameworks that were under operation. However, this created a transitory uncertainty for victims around how to access to the new procedures.

This chapter uses the concept of peace infrastructures to analyze the institutional design of victims' participation in symbolic reparation measures within Colombia's transitional justice framework. The findings offer key lessons and recommendations for implementing new mechanisms for victims' participation in the symbolic reparation measures considered in the recent peace agreements with the Fuerzas Armadas Revolucionarias de Colombia—Ejército del Pueblo (FARC—EP).[6] Importantly, I argue that a constantly changing institutional framework can have negative consequences on the social dynamics of victims' mobilization and on their ability to effectively partake in the processes of symbolic reparation and memory reconstruction.

Symbolic reparations in transitional justice: finding the balance between top-down and bottom-up approaches to historical memory

When mass violations of human rights during periods of conflict, dictatorship or political repression are dealt with in accordance to international law, give rise to transitional justice processes which include judicial mechanisms such as prosecutions, trials, and vetting, and non-judicial mechanisms such as truth seeking, institutional reform, and reparations (Teitel, 2003; Sriram, 2007; Sisson, 2010). Although both mechanisms are equally relevant in a society's attempt to come to terms with the past, a greater deal of attention has been paid on the tools to prosecute human rights violators than to those oriented to satisfy the needs of victims by way of reparations (De Greiff, 2006).

Reparations are considered an integral part of any transitional justice initiative, even though neither the meaning nor the goals of reparations have been settled either in theory or in practice (Richards, 2007). Under international law the most common forms of reparations comprise restitution, compensation, rehabilitation, satisfaction, and guarantees of non-recurrence[7] (De Greiff, 2006; United States Institute of Peace, 2008; REDRESS, 2013). National reparations programmes usually adopt a simplified categorization of reparations with benefits conceived of either individually or collectively, and as material or symbolic. Often times in the case of symbolic reparations, the measures related to satisfaction, rehabilitation, and guarantees of non-repetition are, for policy purposes, combined and put under the same category of actions aiming to repair the intangible impacts of the conflict.

The role of symbolic reparations in transitional contexts has increasingly been recognized as equally important as material reparations, due to the potential of the former to promote redress, foster solidarity, reweave a community's social fabric, and restore the dignity of victims and survivors (De Greiff, 2006; REDRESS, 2013; & Lederach, 2014). Even though 'symbolic reparations may not have the media impact of trials and assertive forms of truth recovery' (Brown, 2013, p. 274), they have a powerful ritual and communicational capacity: symbolic reparations function as carriers of meaning. Victims have a key role in deciding what is meaningful. Otherwise, survivors may feel that the "meaning" that the state has created is empty.

Historical memory initiatives are an important example of symbolic reparation activity that aims to realize the individual and collective 'right to truth', to find out what happened during the conflict and to comprehend the circumstances that led to gross human rights violations. Previous work has defined historical memory as a society's central or dominant narrative while it is consistent in can evolve over time, and exists alongside other narratives that are integrated within the community's social and political life. However, while in some cases historical memory can bring individuals together and form an important part of nationalist movements, these narratives can also be polarizing. Hence, the importance of memory reconstruction in transitional contexts lies in the possibility it provides to build a narrative of the future, based upon a thorough revision of the past and the elements and actors that elicited and enacted violence. These initiatives of historical memory open space for the emergence of victims' testimonies, contributing to the creation of a wider account of what happened, in which victims can controvert, validate, and challenge the hegemonic narratives of the conflict.

The scope of memory reconstruction processes within transitional justice endeavours is usually defined 'from above' with mechanisms designed by the actors who negotiate the peace, and implemented by national governments and institutions or by international non-governmental organizations through different procedures that seek to ascertain the truth and achieve accountability according to minimum international human rights standards (Mani, 2002; Minow, 1998; Gómez Isa, 2012). However, memorialization practices are not exclusive to the state, international parties, or negotiating groups. In fact, societies and communities that have endured long periods of conflict develop mechanisms that seek to preserve testimonies and other accounts of the conflict in the hope that in a transition period those narratives can emerge. These informal practices of memory reconstruction may take the form of localized memory initiatives and make use of non-institutional vehicles such as murals, poetry, music, and storytelling among others (Centro Nacional de Memoria Histórica, 2013).

This recognition of the value of historical memory 'from below,' builds on the participation of a wider constituency beyond the state and seeks to be context-sensitive, allowing the local to inform the instruments of memory reconstruction (Uprimny & Saffon, 2008). The process then rests more meaningfully on citizens as key stakeholders and agents of change, on their knowledge of the root causes of the conflict they experienced, and on their experience of the socio-political environment, as opposed to externally imposed assessments of their realities and needs (Lederach, 1997; Doyle & Sambanis, 2000).

Exclusively 'top-down' processes of memory reconstruction find their weakness in the lack of victims' effective participation. This hinders the potential for memory processes to effectively transform a society as they fail to integrate social sectors that have been historically disenfranchised, and therefore reproduce schemes and structures of segregation and power. This effect is amplified when the institutions that implement the reparations programme are the same or mimic the practices of those that committed human rights abuses during the conflict. Likewise, historical memory processes, when driven by predefined understandings of justice and operationalized as 'one-size-fits-all' programmes, fail to recognize and respond to the multi-faceted complexities and dimensions of a conflict, leaving the needs of victims ill-addressed (Mani, 2002; Heyzer, 2004; McEvoy & Eriksson, 2006).

Exclusively bottom-up historical memory processes also have their own limitations. In the first place, the term 'bottom-up' implies that the information must come from the 'bottom' and the responses should also be 'localized'. However, the meaning of 'local' is often not clear, since local is defined *in relation to* places, levels, and networks (Hirblinger, 2017). Therefore, 'localized' memory initiatives mean different things to different people. Secondly, there often is an assumption, when using the term 'local', that there is a community attached to it. However, multiple group identities can exist within a single community; and some even have opposing beliefs, norms and values. Therefore, romanticizing the local can fall into the trap of failing to recognize complexities such as the existence of different identities, the presence of 'good' and 'bad' locals (peacebuilders and peace spoilers), as well as the unequal power relations that occur at the grassroots level (Mac Ginty & Polanska, 2015; Hirblinger, 2017).

Likewise, 'bottom-up' historical memory initiatives are not *per se* context sensitive nor empowering to the most affected and silenced victims of a community. There is the risk of assuming that all locally-led historical memory process will represent victims' needs, when in reality local memory initiatives can also reinforce existing power structures and narratives and leave victims' needs unaddressed (Mac Ginty & Polanska, 2015).

Both top-down and bottom-up memory reconstruction approaches are nonetheless based on the great potential of memory to reconstruct a nation's narrative, re-establish community life, provide symbolic closure and cathartic healing, foster reconciliation, and transform social relationships (see Chapter 12). However, designing a symbolic reparation programmes as part of national transitional justice processes requires a thoughtful consideration of how to strike balance between the political interests and goals of the state in awarding reparations and the victims' need to break their silence, share their testimonies, find and have their suffering acknowledged, and have their dignity restored. After all, public memory is a contested space where different narratives of the past dispute their place in a nation's future identity. Therefore, the institutional design of symbolic reparations programmes is a key aspect for bridging the gap between bottom-up and top-down approaches to historical memory.

Institutional Design of Victims' Participation Mechanisms in Colombia: An Evolving Framework?

Colombia has been implementing national reparation programs within transitional justice frameworks for many years (see Chapter 4). The Internally Displaced Population Law (IDPs Law, 1997) set a precedent for the mechanisms for victims' participation within reparation processes, as it established procedures to allow Internally Displaced Populations (IDPs) to partake in the design, implementation, and monitoring of reparations-like programmes at the local and national level. The IDPs Law was established to address the consequences of forced internal displacement in the country. While the law was not originally designed as part of a transitional justice framework, it has had an important impact on subsequent transitional justice initiatives.

The law created two mechanisms that considered victims' participation: 1) The *Plan Integral Único* (PIU),[8] a planning instrument that compiled the programmes and projects for IDPs territorial attention, and 2) the *Comités Territoriales de Atención a Población Desplazada*[9] as councils for the discussion of the design of the IDP regional strategy. Despite their existence, the mechanisms were left unimplemented until 2005 when the Constitutional Court of Colombia ordered the Colombian state to guarantee the effective participation of IDPs in the implementation of the law (López Pedraza & Restrepo, 2009). In response, the state activated the aforementioned mechanisms and created eight new mechanisms: four permanent 'National Boards', one for each stage of the IDP policy—prevention and protection, emergency humanitarian assistance, socioeconomic development, and organization strengthening—and four equivalent 'Territorial Roundtables.'

On the surface, it appeared that this would ensure victims were more involved in the process, however the implementation of these participation mechanisms had multiple flaws. First, they presumed victims' organizations had a type and level of organizational structure, as they demanded all local organizations to be articulated with national ones in order to have access to the established participation scenarios. Second, no clear operational rules and procedures for the participation of victims' representatives were defined. Third, the institutional design disregarded any informal forms of victims' organizations that did not fit into the parameters established by the law. Fourth, the absence of clarity in the distribution of responsibilities made it difficult to guarantee their effective implementation; and finally, the lack of funding for the newly constituted participation bodies translated into the stifling of these participation scenarios (Vargas Reina, 2014)

As a result – despite having formally opened a space – integrating victims' participation in the implementation of reparation-like frameworks, few victims actually participated. As one scholar describes, the institutional design of the IDPs Law did not consider the 'formal and informal procedures, routines, norms and conventions that are embedded in the organizational structure of the political community' (Uribe-López, 2015, p. 9). Therefore, the law transferred the responsibilities to local authorities that did not have the required technical capacity and created participation scenarios without considering the nature of the organizational processes of the IDPs, falling into the trap of assuming 'the success of peacebuilding depends on the design of 'right' institutions, without taking into account the plurality of situations related to the various relationships between formal and informal rules' (Uribe-López, 2015, p. 10).

In 2005, a second precedent for mechanisms of victims' participation was established through the JPL, a transitional justice framework issued to achieve the demobilization, disarmament, and reintegration of illegal armed groups, mainly former members of the Autodefensas Unidas de Colombia (AUC).[10] The law also aimed to recognize and enforce the rights of the victims to truth, justice, and reparation, and to conduct criminal proceedings against the leaders of these groups that were responsible for the commission of serious crimes (International Criminal Court, 2010).

In writing, the JPL adopted the standard reparations mechanisms recommended in international law, including restitution, compensation, rehabilitation, satisfaction, and guarantees of non-recurrence. Moreover, to implement the provisions specifically related to measures of satisfaction, guarantees of non-repetition and memory preservation, the Comisión Nacional de Reparación y Reconciliación (CNRR)[11] was created in 2005. The CNRR adopted the concept of 'integral reparation' in the execution of its mandate. This implied, on the one hand, that reparations must coherently advance justice, truth and reparations, and on the other, that reparations should not be limited to their material dimension but should also include the symbolic dimension for individual and collective victims (Comisión Nacional de Reparación y Reconciliación, 2006).

The CNRR conceived mechanisms for victims' participation within the National Program of Reparations in four types of processes: (1) the process of psychosocial recovery and attention to special needs, (2) the judicial investigation process of judgement of the person responsible, (3) the administrative process of collective reparation to communities or groups affected by acts of systematic violence, and (4) the process of social construction of truth and memory (Comisión Nacional de Reparación y Reconciliación, 2006). However, due to the CNRR's institutional design, planned as a centralized institution with restricted articulation to the country's municipalities and departments and with insufficient regional presence,[12] victims had limited access to the aforementioned participation mechanisms (Comisión Interamericana de Derechos Humanos, 2013).

The Grupo de Memoria Histórica (GMH)[13] was the office within the CNRR in charge of advancing the memory reconstruction process as part of symbolic reparations. The GMH's objective was to construct and disseminate a comprehensive narrative of the Colombian conflict that could serve as a platform for dialogue between the diverse conflict actors and issue a final report on the origin and evolution of the illegal armed groups (Congreso de la República de Colombia, 2005). Two important aspects made the GMH's memory reconstruction process distinctive. First, its non-legally binding character, meaning that no testimony collected by the GMH could serve as evidence to support judicial cases; second, its academic-oriented approach was thought of as a shield to protect the GMH's memorialization work from the national political dissension and social discomfort potentially caused by the exercise of memory reconstruction in the midst of conflict.

The absence of clear mechanisms for victims' participation within the GMH's symbolic reparation process was not well received by victims and victims' organizations. In a country where locally led memorialization initiatives had existed since the late 1980s, the proposed top-down, centralist approach did not take root. As a result, the GMH adjusted its discourse and framed historical memory reconstruction as a participative process where the testimony of the victims should be at the centre of the historical account of the country's violence. As a former GHM researcher put it:

> The GMH opted to redefine the interpretation of the law's mandate by incorporating four principles about the role memory reconstruction should play in a society in transition as follows: First, to contribute to clarify human rights violations and acts of violence from the victims' perspective; second, to dignify and serve as a platform to provide the victims with a space in which to voice their suffering; third, to make visible the damage caused by conflict; and fourth, to effectively repair victims.
> (GMH Researcher #1, 2013)

By adopting this discourse and incorporating the demands of victims for an open process, the GMH was able to dissipate the initial doubts victims, victims' organizations, and human rights defenders had about the authenticity of the GMH's historical memory reconstruction project. The GMH was then able to guarantee the inclusion and participation of, at least, those victims who took part in the memorialization processes—also known as 'memory reports'—that the GMH completed during its mandate.[14] Nevertheless, not all victims had the opportunity to participate in this memory reconstruction process.

The failure to include all victims' voices was an outcome of the centralized institutional design of the JPL, which allocated limited budgetary and human resources to its implementing institutions. The GHM only had one office in Bogotá, and no regional presence. This structure made it difficult for victims to have an effective level of participation in the process of memory reconstruction within the spaces provided by the GMH. The process for including the voices of victims lacked a standard process or mechanism for victims' participation. As a result the form and scope of including victims in this process varied depending on the methodological decisions by the lead researcher of each memory report.[15]

Moreover, this centralized institutional design, was further limited by an ongoing and active conflict in Colombia. The dynamics of this conflict imposed physical barriers to the process of memory reconstruction within the JPL. This precluded the inclusion and participation of multiple victims and victims' organizations, since only those victims or organizations located in the regions with adequate security and favorable political conditions were subject to the GMH intervention. As a result, 'the memory report became a privilege among disenfranchised communities' (GMH Researcher #2, 2013). This had the unintended consequence of creating status differences among victims and victims' organizations (Missionary Sister #1, 2013).

Some progress was made during the third and most recent transitional justice framework, the *Ley de Víctimas y Restitución de Tierras*[16] (known as The Victims' Law—see Chapter 4). This is the first piece of legislation by the Colombian state to officially recognize the existence of an internal armed conflict in the country. The law aims to provide a set of measures for victims' integral reparation, including humanitarian assistance, rehabilitation, economic compensation, land restitution, and satisfaction measures. Furthermore, the law establishes a legal victimhood status for any person who suffered grave violations of human rights or international humanitarian law as a result of the conflict since 1985 (Congreso de la República de Colombia, 2011), meaning that access to reparations is also granted to victims of crimes other than forced internal displacement.

With regards to symbolic reparations, the Victims' Law strengthened the pre-existing institutional framework, focusing on memory reconstruction through the creation of the Centro Nacional de Memoria Histórica (CNMH)[17], which assumed the role of the GMH. With CNMH, the Colombian government gave a strong political backing of the role of memory reconstruction as a tool for reparation and peacebuilding. The law's provisions also designed mechanisms for victims' participation in all reparation measures, including the process of memory reconstruction. This was done via the reactivation and adjustment of the aforementioned mechanisms created under the IDPs Law, as well as through the establishment of a Participation Protocol to regulate the effective and active participation of victims.

The enactment of this protocol embodies the institutional recognition of the failures and limitations of previous initiatives by the Colombian state. The Victims' Law sought to guarantee that all victims would have the right to participate in memory initiatives. It implied a change in the participation rules by means of regulating the requisites for the period of, election by, functions of, prohibitions of, and incentives for the participation of victims' representatives in the boards and institutions that execute the Victims' Law (Vargas Reina, 2014). Likewise, in comparison to the participation framework stated in the IDPs Law, the protocol 'promotes the inclusion of people affected by different victimizing facts, creates mechanisms for articulation between the different levels of government, establishes open dialogue sessions in the territorial councils and assemblies, and offers incentives for participation' (Vargas Reina, 2014, p. 186).

The intention of this institutional design was to decentralize the implementation of all the main components of the Victims' Law.[18] With regards to those components pertaining to memory as symbolic reparation, the goal was to give victims a higher degree of influence in the framing and decision-making over the institutionally-led memory processes, to recognize the diversity of the country's memory landscape, to strengthen local memory initiatives, and to further expand the state's duty to remember to local authorities. However, as can be seen in Table 1, the number of formal mechanisms created specifically for memory reconstruction, even when put into effect in all of the country's 1,122 municipalities and 32 departments (DANE, 2016), are insufficient to effectively guarantee the right of more than 8.5m. victims to participate in symbolic reparations (UARIV, Unidad para la Atención y Reparación Integral a las Víctimas, 2017).

Neither the Victims' Law nor the Participation Protocol addressed the absence of specific mechanisms that could ensure the effective participation of victims effective in the processes led by the CNMH, former GMH. Even the institution that was created to coordinate the implementation of the Victims' Law, the Unidad de Atención y Reparación Integral a las Víctimas (UARIV) was unable to guarantee victims' participation in memory initiatives.[19] Moreover, the two institutions did not have clear procedures to harmonize their memory reconstruction programmes. This has often led to duplication of efforts, ineffective budgetary execution, and further obstruction of victims' participation. This is because the scope of the competencies of each institution at the territorial level is not necessarily clear to victims and victims' organizations. In this sense, the institutional design of the participation mechanisms for memory reconstruction within the Victims' Law inherited both the representation and co-ordination problems of the IDPs Law, and those of the JPL transitional justice framework (Arias & Caballero, 2005).

While these examples highlight the shortfalls of mechanisms for victims' participation in historical memory processes in Colombia, this experience also provides important lessons for improvement, to achieve the goal of guaranteeing and promoting the effective participation of victims and victims' organizations in the institutionally-led national, regional, and local processes of historical memory. In the following section, I discuss the concept of peace infrastructures to analyse the Colombian institutional design for the participation of victims in symbolic reparation programmes. Building from this idea, I argue that the social dynamics of victims' mobilization needs to be

Table 9.1 Mechanisms of Victims' Participation in Colombia

Function	IPD Law Law 387 of 1997	Victims' Law Law 1448 of 2011	Number of victims that participate
Co-ordination mechanisms			
Co-ordination of the system	National Comprehensive Care System for the Displaced Population (SNAIPD)	National System of Victims' Support and Reparations (SNARIV)	2 representatives
Executive body	National Council for the Comprehensive Care of Displaced Population (CNAIPD)	Executive Committee of Victims' Support and Reparations (CARIV)	2 representatives
Planning Instrument	Unique Integral Plan (PIU)	Territorial Action Plan (PAT)	DNA
Participation mechanisms			
Participation body – national level	National Boards for the Comprehensive Care of Displaced Population	National Victims' Participation Roundtable	2 representatives
Participation body– territorial level		Departmental and Municipal Roundta- bles for Victims' Participation	Up to 24 representa- tives (municipality) or up to 26 representatives (department)
Territorial executive body	Territorial Committees for the Comprehensive Care of Displaced Population	Territorial Committees for Transitional Justice	2 representatives at territorial level
Participation mechanisms for memory related symbolic reparations within the Victims' Law			
National level	Board of Directors of the CNMH		2 representatives
	Board of Directors of the UARIV		2 representatives
Territorial level	Departmental and Municipal Roundta- bles for Victims' Participation	Thematic working group on memory *(optional and non-permanent)*	Up to 6 representa- tives at the municipal and department level

Source: Own elaboration.

considered when designing victims' participation mechanisms if the goal of victims' inclusion in symbolic reparation processes to be realized.

Symbolic Reparations as Peace Infrastructures

The concept of peace infrastructures is part of the turn to the contested local in peacebuilding studies and peacebuilding practice (Richmond, 2013). Peace infrastructures are a 'dynamic network of interdependent structures, mechanisms, resources, values, and skills which [...] contribute to conflict [transformation] and peacebuilding in a society' (Kumar, 2011, p. 385). These peace infrastructures have, as the name suggests, a structured and systematic character that 'distinguishes them from the 'naturally evolved' peace constituencies found at different levels of society. [...] They have a high level of government involvement and intra-governmental coherence that emphasizes the commitment of the regime to support peace efforts' (Hopp-Nishanka, 2013a, p. 4), as well as a domestic foundation, meaning the performance aspect of the network depends on the capacities of the socio-political structures and the stakeholders that comprise those networks.

The concept of peace infrastructures can enrich studies on how victims' participation mechanisms are designed and implemented and the ways in which existing institutions can support the reparation process. First, the idea of peace infrastructures suggests an interdependent network of structures or values, acknowledges the complexity of any peacebuilding endeavour. This accounts for the different levels of decision-making that need to be involved, (the social, cultural, political and economic factors that need to be accounted for) and the meanings (values) attached to the mechanism. Second, the structured character of peace infrastructures speaks to a holistic understanding of peacebuilding, where different parts of the process need to be articulated in a complementary manner. Third, the systematic quality of peace infrastructures articulates an effort that needs to be sustained in time. Finally, this concept highlights the need for a domestic foundation or ownership of the structure at its level of implementation implies that these infrastructures rely on societal participation, and are as affected by informal rules as they are by formal ones.

Based on these elements, I argue that symbolic reparations should be established as a peace infrastructure, as a 'system' involving not only the sum of different types of symbolic measures (memory reconstruction, archives, apologies, commemorations, museums) but also the set of societal levels (top, middle, and grassroots), administrative units (local, district, regional, and national), actors (institutions, organizations, and individuals), frameworks (councils, roundtables, boards, and committees), processes (validation, election, and participation) and outcomes (alliances, platforms, projects, and initiatives) which are involved in the design, implementation, sustainability, and appropriation of this form of reparation (Hopp-Nishanka, 2013a).

A peace infrastructure approach could address the deficiencies in the design of mechanisms for victims' participation in memory reconstruction processes in Colombia as the concept highlights the extent to which a careful consideration of the synergies between the different aspects involved in implementing symbolic reparations have been absent. Peace infrastructures emphasizes the importance of considering the interdependent interaction between the type of symbolic measure, the societal level at which is implemented, the administrative unit responsible for the implementation, the actors involved in the process, and the outcome expected has in the design and implementation of mechanisms for victims' participation in symbolic reparations.

The analysis of the participatory components of historical memory processes as symbolic reparations in Colombia shows that the aforementioned aspects are either disregarded or not fully considered in the institutional design of the mechanisms. This is precisely because they are not being conceived as a system, but rather seen as independent processes. Hence the disconnection between the reparation goals and the impact of those reparations at the local level is made evident in practice—a disconnection that the institutional design is not able to, or does not intend to, address (Paladini Adell, 2013).

This is not to say that all the already constituted councils, committees, roundtables, and other mechanisms for victims' participation created by the three transitional justice frameworks analysed do not create a network. In the laws, the connections between these frameworks exists: they are part of the institutional framework for victims' participation. However, in the context of their performance as a mechanism that guarantees effective victims' participation, and in their functioning as a structure in interaction with other institutions of the transitional framework, these participation mechanisms have failed to deliver in their role as transitional institutions for symbolic reparation. Their physical and material presence is irrefutable, but so is their limited scope and impact as they have, in many municipalities, 'remained empty shells, risking being captured and instrumentalized for partisan interests' (Hopp-Nishanka, 2013b, p. 58).

In this context, framing symbolic reparations as a peace infrastructure for institutional design purposes directs policy makers to carefully consider how the interaction of all components of the system, and victims' inclusion, can work in order to have a positive impact in the moment of practical implementation of the reparation (Moon, 2012; Paffenholz, 2015). It also prompts policy makers to consider all of the interactions between the institutions and actors, facilitating reparations and bringing into the light the lessons from previous initiatives. Two decades of attempts at reparation cannot be discarded by decree.

Thus, the effective inclusion of a systemic lens and a lessons-learning perspective that informs this peace infrastructure in reparation programmes calls for the active participation of a broad number of actors (such as local authorities, local leaders, victims' representatives and other grassroots and middle-level actors and organizations) not only as beneficiaries, but also as key contributors to the decision-making around the establishment of the frameworks to implement effective victims' participation in symbolic reparations.

To address this disconnect in the implementation of symbolic reparations (including historical memory processes), giving monitoring competencies to other sub-national actors who have been supporting peacebuilding in Colombia for years could provide a venue for bringing lessons and reflection on what works and does not work in this system. For example, institutions such as the Programas de Desarrollo y Paz del Magdalena Medio[20] and the Comunidades de Paz[21] de San José de Apartadó, Samaniego, Mogotes and Tarso, as well as structures such as the Consejo Nacional de Paz[22] or the Comisión Nacional de Conciliación[23], *inter alia*, can serve as guarantors, not only of the effective participation of victims, but also of the adequate interlocution and interaction of the different components of the system of symbolic reparations as a peace infrastructure, with enough recognition to bring legitimacy to these discussions and enough institutional capacity to serve as holders of the lessons of past initiatives.

As a new set of victims' participation mechanisms for symbolic reparation measures are considered as part of the peace agreement between the Colombian government and the FARC-EP, this chapter offers four recommendations. First, future efforts should make use of the country's polycentric territorial organization, which involves the existence of multiple decision centres such as municipalities, departments, provinces, sub-regions, and regions, as guarantors of the implementation of the symbolic reparations mechanisms included in the final accord and for the participation of victims (Uribe-López, 2015). Second, these efforts should promote the self-transformative aspect of peace infrastructures in symbolic reparation processes by creating awareness at the decision-making level about the flaws and limitations of the current mechanisms for victims' participation in symbolic reparation processes so that current mistakes become lessons for policy makers (Hopp-Nishanka, 2013b; Powers & Proctor, 2015). Third, new processes of symbolic reparations should be linked to long-term agendas for change such as the ones that several victims' organizations have already created as part of their 'Collective Reparation Plans' (Paladini Adell, 2013). Fourth, these initiatives should design participation mechanisms that connect the identity, history, traditions, and forms of organizations of victims and victims' organizations, for the proposed mechanisms of symbolic reparations. After all, only by bringing sub-national issues and ideas to the national level, and contextualizing and rooting the participation mechanisms in local realities, aspirations, and agendas, can the symbolic reparation measures contemplated in the peace agreement be turned into an effective infrastructure to build sustainable peace in the long run in Colombia (Paladini Adell, 2013).

The lens offered by the concept of peace infrastructures helps us think of the institutional settings and the ways in which organizations and their capacities can prove or fail to provide reparation. It also allows for the recognition of the different actors, structures, and issues that are part of a complex system that shape peacebuilding infrastructures, and the ways in which they coalesce and dissociate not according to fixed norms, but in response to the incentives and deterrents the context offers (Mac Ginty & Polanska, 2015).

This implies the norms, the institutions, and the peacebuilding activities developed by local and national actors are constantly reshaped by means of the everyday interactions among them (Richmond & Mitchell, 2012). As a result, tactics ranging from total acceptance, negotiation and co-optation, to counter organization, resistance and open rejection become visible. These bring to the forefront the processes of negotiation, adjustment, and accommodation that take place at different implementation levels, among a broad range of actors, over local, national and international peace goals such as symbolic reparations and victims' participation.

The utility of adopting the concept of peace infrastructures lies in the possibilities it opens to grasp historical memory reconstruction at the local level for what it is: a complex, living social process where memory entrepreneurs at the local, national, and international level are constantly interacting and adapting their behaviour according to the emerging changes in the context. Likewise, this approach to memory reconstruction brings to light the social, political, and economic factors that can influence the participation of victims and victims' organizations, such as: their form of organization, level of strength, degree of knowledge about memory and reparations. It also highlights contextual aspects such as institutional designs, security conditions, political will, and the availability of economic resources for the implementation of the symbolic reparation.

In the case of Colombia, the value attributed to the bureaucratic design and procedural details necessary for establishing symbolic reparations tends to overshadow the emblematic meaning and operational procedures for the reparation itself. This is true even when it is that symbolism that plays a crucial role in reconstructing the social fabric, and healing collective and individual social wounds (Lykes & Mersky, 2006). This leaves little to no room for victims to have a say in neither the design of the main objectives, or the mechanisms through which memory is being implemented. Too often these decisions have been made at a governmental level, without the effective participation of victims. This creates tensions in local memorialization practices, especially when the language, symbols, and metaphors in which communities frame their narratives are not integrated or considered in the institutional symbolic reparation endeavour.

As the Colombian government begins establishing mechanisms to implement the transitional justice agreement with the FARC-EP, there is a critical need to bridge local and national goals through memory reconstruction as symbolic reparation. It is important to create effective participation scenarios where negotiation over the interests, needs, meanings, and goals related to memory reconstruction can take place, peace infrastructures is a useful concept for improving the design of victims' participation mechanisms during memory reconstruction in the country, as it directs policy makers towards an approach that is more flexible and responsive to the complex realities and diverse expectations of a transitional period. This can help ensure that processes of memory reconstruction are relevant to the collective and to the individual, by both speaking to the institutional needs of the state and achieving the goals of symbolic reparations for victims.

Notes

1. Law 387 of 1997.
2. Law 975 of 2005.
3. Victims and Land Restitution Law, Law 1448 of 2011.
4. National Plan for the Attention and Integral Reparation of Victims (PNARIV).
5. Compensation, satisfaction, rehabilitation, restitution, and guarantees of non-repetition.
6. Acuerdo Final para la Terminación del Conflicto y la Construcción de una Paz Estable y Duradera.
7. *Restitution* seeks to restore the victim to the situation that would have existed had the crime not happened. *Compensation* refers to the quantification of the harm suffered and the measures to make up for it. *Rehabilitation* refers to social, medical and psychological care. *Satisfaction* includes apologies, commemorations, public disclosure of the truth, searches for the disappeared, and the restoration of the dignity of victims through remembrance. *Guarantees of non-recurrence* include cessation of violations, administrative and judicial sanctions, and institutional reform.
8. Unique Integral Plan.
9. Territorial Committees for the Comprehensive Care of Internally Displaced Population.
10. United Self-Defence Forces of Colombia.
11. National Commission of Reparation and Reconciliation.
12. The CNRR only had five regional offices, in Antioquia, Bucaramanga, Sincelejo, Barranquilla and Bogotá; and a non-permanent presence in seven cities: Valledupar, Cartagena, Quibdó, Cali, Pasto, Mocoa and Villavicencio. These are 12 offices, in just 12 out of 1,122 municipalities.
13. Historical Memory Group.
14. Under the GMH mandate, 13 processes of historical memory reconstruction were conducted. During this time, the GMH also initiated the research phase of the General Report published in 2013, *Basta Ya! Colombia: Memorias de Guerra y Dignidad*.
15. The methodology applied by the GMH to advance the memory reconstruction process was based on 'emblematic cases' that could portray the different modalities of violence in the Colombian conflict and exemplify its impact on transversal issues such as gender, ethnicity, and justice, among others.
16. Victims and Land Restitution Law, Law 1448 of 2011.
17. National Center for Historical Memory.
18. i) Comprehensive care and assistance; ii) integral reparation; iii) prevention and protection; iv) truth and justice; and v) complementary measures (such as judicial and psychological support).
19. Unit for Attention and Integral Reparation of Victims.
20. The Programs of Development and Peace of the Magdalena Medio.
21. Peace Communities.
22. National Peace Council.
23. The National Conciliation Commission.

References

Arias, X. C. & Caballero, G., 2005. Instituciones, Costos de Transacción y Políticas Públicas: Un Panorama. *Revista de Economía Institucional*, Junio, 5(8), pp. 117–146.

Brown, K., 2013. Commemoration as Symbolic Reparation: New Narratives or Spaces of Conflict. *Human Rights Review*, 14(3), pp. 273–289.

Centro Nacional de Memoria Histórica, 2013. *Recordar y Narrar el Conflicto: Herramientas para Reconstruir Memoria Histórica*. 1st edn. Bogotá: Imprenta Nacional.

Cepeda, I., 2011. *Debate Falsas Desmovilizaciones AUC*. [Online] Available at: www.youtube.com/watch?v=VOOJ3VTalIg [Last accessed 6 September 2013].

Cobb, S., 2011. Narratives Matther at ICAR: Center for the Study of Narrative and Conflict Resolution. *ICAR News—George Mason University*, March, 2(5).

Comisión Interamericana de Derechos Humanos, 2013. *Verdad, justicia y reparación: Cuarto informe sobre la situación de derechos humanos en Colombia*, Washington, DC: Organización de Estados Americanos.

Comisión Nacional de Reparación y Reconciliación, 2006. *Fundamentos Filosóficos y Operativos: Definiciones Estratégicas de la Comisión Nacional de Reparación y la Reconciliación*, Bogotá: Comisión Nacional de Reparación y Reconciliación.

Congreso de la República de Colombia, 2005. *Ley 975 de 2005*. 1st edn. Bogotá: Diario Oficial.

Congreso de la República de Colombia, 2011. *Ley 1448 de 2011*. 1st edn. Bogotá: Ministerio del Interior y de Justicia.

DANE, 2016. *Proyecciones de Población Colombia 2017*, Bogotá: DANE.

De Greiff, P., 2006. Repairing the Past: Compensation for Victims of Human Rights Violations. In: P. De Greiff, ed. *The Handbook of Reparations*. 2nd edn. New York: International Center for Transitional Justice, pp. 1–18.

Doyle, M. W. & Sambanis, N., 2000. International Peacebuilding: A Theorethical and Quantitative Analysis. *American Political Science Review*, 94(4), pp. 779–801.

GMH Researcher #1, C., 2013. *Interview CNMH #1* [Interview] (24 June 2013).

GMH Researcher #2, C., 2013. *Interview CNMH #2* [Interview] (25 June 2013).

Gómez Isa, F., 2010. Challenges for transitional justice in contexts of non-transition: the Colombian case. In A. N. Lyons and M. Reed, eds. *Contested Transitions: Dilemmas of Transitional Justice in Colombia and Comparative Experience*. Bogotá and New York: Royal Norwegian Ministry of Foreign Affairs–ICTJ.

Heyzer, N., 2004. *Women, War and Peace: Mobilizing for Security and Justice in the 21st Century*. San Diego, CA: University of San Diego, pp. 27–43.

Hirblinger, A., 2017. *Preventing Violent Conflict through Community-based Indicators*. Caux: Inclusive Peace and Transition Initiative.

Hopp-Nishanka, U., 2013a. Giving Peace an Address? Reflections on the Potential and Challenges of Creating Peace Infrastructures. In B. Unger, S. Lundström, K. Planta & B. Austin, eds. *Peace Infrastructures: Assessing Concept and Practice*. Berlin: Berghof Foundation, pp. 1–20.

Hopp-Nishanka, U., 2013b. Circularity, Transversality and the Usefulness of New Concepts: Reflection on the Response Articles. In B. Unger, S. Lundström, K. Planta & B. Austin, eds. *Peace Infrastructures: Assessing Concept and Practice*. Berlin: Berghof Foundation, pp. 53–58.

International Criminal Court, 2010. *Justice and Peace Law: an experience of truth, justice and reparation*. [Online] Available at: https://asp.icc-cpi.int/iccdocs/asp_docs/RC2010/Stocktaking/RC-ST-PJ-M.1-ENG.pdf [Last accessed 20 July 2017].

International Crisis Group, 2013. *Transitional Justice and Colombia's Peace Talks*. [Online] Available at: www.crisisgroup.org/~/media/Files/latin-america/colombia/049-transitional-justice-and-colombia-s-peace-talks [Last accessed 3 September 2013].

Kumar, C., 2011. UN Assistance for Internally Negotiated Solutions to Violent Conflict. In S. Allen Nan, Z. C. Mampilly & A. Bartoli, eds. *Peacemaking: From Practice to Theory*. New York: Praeger, pp. 384–399.

Lederach, J. P., 1997. *Building Peace: Sustainable Reconciliation in Divided Societies*. Washington, DC: United States Institute for Peace Press.

López Pedraza, B. & Restrepo, D. I., 2009. *Las Entidades Territoriales en la Realización de Derechos de la Población Desplazada. Limitaciones y Posibilidades Frente al Estado de Cosas Inconstitucional*. 1st ed. Bogotá: CODHES.

Lykes, B. & Mersky, M., 2006. Reparations and Mental Health: Psychosocial Interventions Towards Healing, Human Agency and Rethreading Social Realities. In P. De Greiff, ed. *Handbook of Reparations*. 1st ed. New York: International Center for Transitional Justice, pp. 589–622.

Mac Ginty, R. & Polanska, M., 2015. When the Local Meets the International. *Global Trends: Prospects for World Society*, pp. 193–208. [Online] Available at: www.global-trends.info/fileadmin/Globale-Trends/beitraege_kapitel/gt-2015_en.pdf [Last accessed 24 January 2018].

Mani, R., 2002. *Beyond Retribution: Seeking Justice in the Shadows of War*. Cambridge: Polity Press.

McEvoy, K. & Eriksson, A., 2006. Restorative Justice in Transition: Ownership, Leadership and 'Bottom-Up' Human Rights. In D. Sullivan & L. Tifft, eds. *The Handbook of Restorative Justice: A Global Perspective*. New York: Routledge.

Minow, M., 1998. *Between Vengeance and Forgiveness: Facing History After Genocide and Mass Violence*. Boston: Beacon Press.

Missionary Sister #1, H. A. M., 2013. *Interview #1—Missionary Sisters* [Interview] (15 June 2013).

Moon, C., 2012. 'Who'll pay reparation on my soul?' Compensation, Social Control and Social Suffering. *Social & Legal Studies*, 21(2), pp. 187–199.

OACDH, Oficina del Alto Comisionado de las Naciones Unidas para los Derechos Humanos, 2009. *Informe Anual Derechos Humanos en Colombia*. [Online] Available at: www.derechoshumanos.gov.co/Prensa/Comunicados/2009/documents/2009/090306b-aspectospositivos.pdf [Last accessed 13 September 2013].

Paffenholz, T., 2015. *Can Inclusive Peace Processes Work? New Evidence From a Multi-Year Research Project*, Geneva: Inclusive Peace and Transition Initiative.

Paladini Adell, B., 2013. From Peacebuilding and Human Development Coalitions to Peace Infrastructure in Colombia. In B. Unger, S. Lundström, K. Planta & B. Austin, eds. *Peace Infrastructures: Assessing Concept and Practice*. Berlin: Berghof Foundation, pp. 44–52.

Powers, K. L. & Proctor, K., 2017. Victims' Justice in the Aftermath of Political Violence: Why Do Countries Award Reparations? *Foreign Policy Analysis*, 13 (4), 1 October, pp. 787–810.

Foreign Policy Analysis, Volume 13, Issue 4, pp. 787–810.

REDRESS, 2013. *Reaching for Justice: The Right to Reparation in the African Human Rights System*, London: REDRESS Trust.

Richards, M., 2007. *The design and implementation of an optimal reparation: How should limited resources for material reparation be distributed across victims of the Colombian conflict?*, Bogotá: Conflict Analysis Resource Center.

Richmond, O., 2013. Missing Links: Peace Infrastructures and Peace Formation. In B. Unger, S. Lundström, K. Planta & B. Austin, eds. *Peace Infrastructures: Assessing Concept and Practice.* Berlin: Berghof Foundation, pp. 22–28.

Richmond, O. & Mitchell, A., 2012. Towards a Post-Liberal Peace: Exploring Hybridity Via Everyday Forms of Resistance, Agency and Autonomy. In O. Richmond & A. Mitchell, eds. *Hybrid Forms of Peace: From Everyday Agency to Post-Liberalism.* 1st edn. New York: Palgrave Macmillan, pp. 1–38.

Ruiz, M., 2015. *¿Qué Nos Dejan 10 Años de Justicia y Paz?* [Online] Available at: www.verdadabierta.com/especiales-v/2015/justicia-y-paz-10/#myAnchor1 [Last accessed 28 September 2016].

Sisson, J., 2010. A Conceptual Framework for Dealing with the Past. *Politorbis*, 50(3), pp. 11–16.

Sriram, C. L., 2007. Justice as Peace? Liberal Peacebuilding and Strategies of Transitional Justice. *Global Society*, 21(4), pp. 579–591.

Stone, H., 2011. *Fake Colombian Demobilization Stories Explain Rise of BACRIMs.* [Online] Available at: www.insightcrime.org/news-analysis/fake-colombian-desmobilization-stories-explain-rise-of-bacrim [Last accessed 3 September 2013].

Taylor, L. K. & Lederach, J. P., 2014. Practicing Peace: Psychological Roots of Transforming Conflicts. *Global Journal of Peace Research and Praxis*, 1(1), pp. 12–31.

Teitel, R., 2003. Transitional Justice Genealogy. *Harvard Human Rights Journal*, 16 (Spring), pp. 69–95.

UARIV, Unidad para la Atención y Reparación Integral a las Víctimas, 2017. *Unidad para las Víctimas.* [Online] Available at: https://www.unidadvictimas.gov.co/ [Last accessed 15 August 2017].

UARIV, Unidad para la Atención y Reparación Integral a las Víctimas, 2016. *Unidad de Atención y Reparación Integral a las Víctimas.* [Online] Available at: www.rni.unidadvictimas.gov.co/RUV [Last accessed 20 August 2016].

United States Institute of Peace, 2008. *Transitional justice: Information handbook.* [Online] Available at: www.usip.org/sites/default/files/ROL/Transitional_justice_final.pdf [Last accessed 2 August 2017].

Uprimny, R. & Saffon, M. P., 2008. *Usos y Abusos de la Justicia Transicional en Colombia.* Chile: Universidad de Chile.

Uribe-López, M., 2015. *Ordenamiento Territorial como Infraestructura de Paz en Colombia.* Lima: Pontificia Universidad Católica del Perú.

Vargas Reina, J., 2014. Análisis Comparativo de los Diseños Institucionales que Regulan la Participación de las Víctimas en Colombia: Antes y Después de la ley 1448 de 2012. *Estudios Socio-Jurídicos*, April, 16(1), pp. 167–207.

10 Enhancing reconciliation in the Colombian Truth Commission by embracing psychosocial tasks

Natalia Tejada V.

Introduction

Colombia has been at war for more than 50 years, and is now embarking on an ambitious process of reconciliation. What constitutes the practices of reconciliation, the timing to achieve it, whether it is a goal or process, or if it occurs at national or individual levels are a few of the questions that make it difficult to agree on a definition of reconciliation (Gloppen, 2005; Olsen & Reite, 2010; Skaar, 2013). Objectives of reconciliation widely discussed in the literature include: acknowledging the past, restoring relationships, bringing justice, establishing a common narrative, unveiling the truth, and re-establishing trust within a society. These objectives are usually presented in different combinations, sequences, and timing with respect to implementation.

Most authors agree that reconciliation more closely resembles a process rather than a specific outcome, and that this process entails a constant iteration between the micro interpersonal dimension and the macro national/political dimension (Hamber, 2009; Lederach, 1997; Philpott, 2015). Some scholars, however, see reconciliation as both a goal and a process, with the goal of reconciliation being to provide vision or ideal from which the process of transitioning from war can find inspiration and meaning (Bloomfield, 2016). For the purposes of this chapter, it is useful to provide a working definition, which includes common elements from other definitions (Gloppen, 2005; Lederach, 1997; Philpott, 2015; Hayner, 2001):

> Reconciliation can be understood as a multi-level process of restoring broken relationships among individuals or groups of a given society, whereby they find ways to deal with a violent past and envision the goal of building a cohesive society in which their rights are acknowledged and respected.

Reconciliation does not happen in the abstract and cannot be mandated by decree or judicial order. Because it involves individuals and groups discerning ways to decrease tensions, change negative beliefs about others, and heal emotional and social damage, it is clear that reconciliation involves psychosocial[1] tasks. This chapter discusses the psychosocial tasks present in national reconciliation efforts, and identifies opportunities to tackle them in one present-day example of a practice of reconciliation—the forthcoming Colombian truth commission.[2]

Truth commissions—usually with a mandate to contribute to national reconciliation—are a common element of transitional justice frameworks. For example, the goals of the Colombian truth commission highlight the importance of promoting coexistence and guarantees of non-repetition.[3] While a well-implemented truth commission has enormous potential for enhancing national reconciliation in a country, its success in so doing is far from assured. While some authors are critical of the link between transitional justice mechanisms and reconciliation,[4] (Hayner, 2001; Leebaw, 2008; Ignatieff, 1997; Mendeloff, 2009), these critiques often originate from various schools of thought (e.g. juridical, political, etc.), which tend to view reconciliation through their respective methodological lenses.

In this chapter, a psychosocial lens is used to refocus the discussion on the processes and procedures practices of truth-seeking exercises, wherein it is believed that the potential of reconciliation lies.

Provided that complete healing is not possible (Herman, 2015; Minow, 1998), adopting a psychosocial lens in the design and implementation of the Colombian truth commission will help to clarify the complexities and ambivalences that surround the socio-emotional[5] tasks of reconciliation. Specifically, this chapter argues that if the Colombian truth commission looks beyond truth-seeking and truth-telling as the core objectives of the commission, to include enabling practices for reflecting and processing contested collective and social identities and narratives, it will have a greater likelihood of supporting the emotional healing of its participants and promoting the reconstruction of shattered political identities and projects. Therefore, enhancing the potential for reconciliation.

Truth commissions, psychology and reconciliation

Truth commissions and reconciliation

A truth commission is usually a mandated mechanism of inquiry and truth-telling, which is supported by a legal framework. Its procedures, objectives, and results are determined by the context in which it takes place. Three main objectives of truth commissions are: 1) establishing the truth about crimes and events, what persons/groups are responsible for crimes, the causes of abuses, and historical explanations; 2) protecting, recognizing, and restoring the rights of victims; and 3) fostering positive social and political transformations (González & Varney, 2013). As such, truth commissions provide a middle ground between trials and amnesties as they balance political limitations (such as peace agreements) and demands of justice, such as acknowledgment, truth-seeking and truth-telling (Olsen & Reite, 2010). Because truth commissions create a platform where key elements to converge (for example, different narratives, victims and perpetrators, and public accounts), they have the potential to enable the use of specific psychosocial tasks that foster national reconciliation.

However, what holds the potential to be reconciliatory in a truth commission is not entirely clear and some authors have expressed their concern in assuming a causal link between the two (Hayner, 2001; Hamber, 2009; Ignatieff, 1997; Mendeloff, 2009). For instance, one assumption is that hearing and telling truth leads to psychological healing or is in itself reconciliatory. Even though storytelling and testimony can provide a significant form of denunciation of human rights violations and could be used as a ritual with positive psychological effects, the potential to foster healing or reconciliation goes beyond truth by itself. The healing potential lies in the quality of practices, procedures, and methodologies in which that truth is revealed or heard. In other words, assuming simplistically that 'revealing is healing' could even undermine the potential for healing and reconciliation presented in a truth commission (Castro & Gómez, 2013; Hayner, 2001).

Often, the possibilities of achieving synergies between truth commissions and reconciliation are lost when the vast project of a truth commission is reduced to just 'telling the truth' or to an outcome—usually a report. This simplification risks overlooking the significance of the process and its related potential to rebuild trust in the social contract, repair relations, and bring acknowledgement and awareness of what happened during the conflict.

In transitional justice mechanisms, there is a tendency to see psychology and law as contradictory, rather than complementary, disciplines. This creates a lack of reference of psychological knowledge in these mechanisms, such as the case of the South African Truth and Reconciliation Commission (Hamber, 2009; Minow, 1998). This presumed tension between psychological and judicial procedures may reflect a false dichotomy between individual and socio-political processes, or could be based on the belief that psychology is subjective, hence ambiguous and uncontrollable, and that judicial methods are objective, hence easier to measure and control (Estrada Mesa, et al., 2010; Hamber, 2009). However, legal practices such as those enacted in a truth commission (statement-taking, hearings, inquiry, and testimonies) can exert an important influence on the socio-political dimension of the psychological damage inasmuch as they can provide public acknowledgement of this damage by giving voice back to those once silenced, restoring the dignity of victims, and contributing to building a more diverse and inclusive narrative of what happened. As such, commissions should consider developing and articulating psychological and judicial processes—'psycho-judicial' processes—into their work (Falk, 2002).

Psychology and truth commissions

A psychosocial approach to understanding the emotional impacts of the armed conflict in Colombia highlights the relationships between mental health, trauma, coexistence, and the national reconciliation project. Therefore, psychosocial healing and reconciliation are closely related because the experience of violent conflict tears the social fabric, sparks negative emotions, causes emotional suffering, creates rigid beliefs, and weakens human relationships. However, violent conflict and war also ignite resilience and activate personal and collective resources that help people and communities to deal with the consequences of violence. Therefore, a psychosocial approach to reconciliation entails restoring positive human relationships and seeks to reactivate community and cultural resources that contribute to social reconstruction and coexistence, with a focus on agency (PNUD, 2012).

It is likely that we can better grasp the complexities of human experience in conflict, and the psychosocial harms produced by political violence and war, by highlighting the intrinsic interconnection of psychological and social processes. In doing so, we can contribute to the discussion on the complexities of the tasks of reconciliation within truth commissions (Martín-Baró, 1988).

The psychological dimension of reconciliation is often related—and rightly so—with the emotional damage that victims have suffered due to violent conflict. Psychology can make clear that this damage is not exclusively related to individual trauma, nor is it isolated from other social and political factors. These external factors influence and transform the psychosocial manifestation's intensity, and the trajectories of the psychological damage. Therefore, these social and political factors too determine what could be useful or not in helping to heal this damage. When the emotional damage is also placed in collective and political realms, it is more evident how justice, truth, reparations, and non-repetition guarantees can contribute to healing (Martín-Beristain, et al., 2010; Herman, 2015). In line with this, highlighting that the victimization caused by political violence and war does not stop with the individual subject, but that victims are also collective and political projects shattered and silenced in their socio-organizational processes, allows for a wider understanding of the nature of the trauma, and the need for reconciliation (Castro & Gómez, 2013).

The psychological lens also highlights the importance of ethical considerations of the workings of the commission in order to restore dignity, empower citizens, and avoid doing harm to its participants. For example, there is a psychological importance for aiding healing in the storytelling and narrative processes that take place in a truth commission (Hamber, 2009; Castro & Gómez, 2013), an aspect that must not be forgotten or underestimated in lieu of mere fact-checking or truth-seeking practices.

The lens of psychology in reconciliatory practices unveils the task of questioning and renegotiating parts of one's own beliefs and one's own social identity in order to decrease the perception of the other as a 'threat'. Transforming perceptions and social identities is necessary for building a sense of community where justice, truth, and responsibility can take place (Kelman, 2010). Truth commissions, as a space where different narratives and identities converge, provide a valuable opportunity for such interpersonal transformation, which is necessary for reconciliation.

The next section of this chapter identifies three specific psychological tasks for reconciliation that Colombian truth Commission could support in its process of implementation: (1) transforming social identities, (2) healing the psychological damage, and (3) reactivating social action and civic engagement. Although they are presented separately to facilitate the identification of contributions, these tasks in reality are interconnected and inform each other.

Contributions and recommendations

Transformation of social identities

Reconciliation involves the restoration of broken relations between people and social groups in a society divided by violent conflict (Lederach, 1997). The re-establishment of these relations necessarily involves, to some degree, changing negative beliefs, feelings, and stereotypes. The narrow and often rigid categorizations of the 'other'[6] that people create during times of conflict constitute an example of a psychological mechanism of protection of one's social identity (Kelman, 2005). However, these social identities need to be redefined and expanded on some level in order to enhance the prospects of reconciliation.[7]

Social identities work by comparison with other groups. People use characteristics of their own group as a reference and then compare it with other groups in order to establish their own identity. These social categorizations are then used to positively assess one's own identity and negatively assess the other's identity, and to trace boundaries between 'our' and 'their' identities, creating a cognitive bias and becoming a potential source of conflict (Van Knippenberg & Tajfel, 1984). A task of reconciliation is then to create opportunities for negotiating certain elements of one's own identity in order to provide commonality wherein elements of reconciliation—such as justice, truth, and accountability—can take place. For instance, the work of Kelman (2010) in inter-group political conflicts, such as the Palestine-Israel conflict, describes a process of revisiting one's own identity to an extent that allows the acknowledgement, accommodation, and coexistence of the other's identity in an internally coherent narrative. In this process, which includes progressive contact with the other, old conflicting attitudes start to transform through interaction, and, with time, new and more accommodating attitudes replace the old ones.

Thus a truth commission in Colombia whereby different social actors, 'truths', and identities converge in public hearings, and before audiences, represents a significant opportunity for aiding in the transformation of contested social identities. If the Colombian truth commission wants to contribute to reconciliation, the procedures of its implementation should promote conversations and encounters that amplify contested identities and enrich the national narrative about the past in a way that builds conditions for the future. Despite the difficulty of shifting narratives about the conflict that have become anchored in social identities after decades of conflict, this could become more viable if promoted through multiple mechanisms in the transitional justice framework and at multiple levels of Colombian society (Sluzki, 2010). The more opportunities social groups have to reflect on stereotypes, contrasting versions of the conflict, prejudices and beliefs about others, the better the prospects for reconciliation.

From victim to survivor: transforming for empowerment.

A particular transformation of social identity that contributes to reconciliation is the transition from the identity of a 'victim' to the identity of a 'survivor' (Sugiman, et al., 2008). Victims must first realize that they have been subjected to damage so they can make sense of their own experience and realize that their rights were neglected. Identifying themselves as victims is one of the first steps towards recovery (Herman, 2015). However, this realization of victimization should serve as a precondition for regaining a sense of agency; by making sense of their experience, they can create more empowered narratives of themselves as survivors.[8]

The use of testimony by the truth commission in Colombia as part of its inquiry activities can facilitate narratives that support empowerment, by recognizing the psychological importance of storytelling for transitioning from victim to survivor of political violence (Herman, 2015; Becker, et al., 1990). The testimony itself constitutes an important acknowledgement of the victim's story and their recognition as a political subject, but it is the process of preparing and giving testimony that allows people a reshaping of victimizing narratives and restores a sense of dignity and coherence to their identities that can greatly contribute to overcoming victimization (Rebolledo & Rondón, 2010; PNUD, 2012). For the Colombian truth commission, this requires an understanding that its truth-seeking activities are tools of identity building and not mere factual accounts of what happened during conflict.

An example of using testimony for transforming identities comes from the case of Chile, where victims of the political repression in the 1970s and 1980s were supported by therapists and trained advocates to create testimonies useful for their own personal processes, such as speaking their truth, demanding information and accountability from their perpetrators, and claiming their right to reparations (Becker, et al., 1990; Lira, et al., 1995). This constitutes an example of how the psychological and judicial tasks of reconciliation can come together in the context of a truth commission.

Addressing the identity needs of the perpetrator

A central, but often forgotten, aspect for fostering reconciliation via restoring broken relationships is addressing the harms felt also by perpetrators who have inflicted harm onto others or who have participated in the conflict (see Chapter 8). Nadner & Shnabel (2008) depict this in their research on socio-emotional reconciliation between victim and perpetrator. Both parties suffer a negative impact on their identities. The victims suffer an impact in the power dimension of their identities because the pain that the perpetrator has inflicted goes unpunished. The perpetrators suffer an impact in their moral dimension by recognizing that their actions have harmed others. These impacts can be resolved positively by the apology-forgiveness interaction between victim and perpetrator, whereby the latter apologizes and victims are entitled to grant or deny forgiveness, and both parties start to diminish the threats to their identities (Nadler & Shnabel, 2008).

One case depicted as an example of positive changes in the perceptions of victim/perpetrator identities is the Gacaca courts in Rwanda. A study showed a reduction of the negative stereotypes about 'others' and less pronounced in-group categorizations after the declaration of culpability and an apology within a ritualized ceremony. This transformation also contributed to the social cohesion of involved communities (Berinstain, 2000).

Healing the emotional and psychosocial damage

Dealing with the psychosocial trauma[9] of violent conflicts involves both victims and perpetrators working through emotions like pain, grievance, fear, anguish, anger, and guilt (Martín-Baró, 1988). It also implies making meaning of the potentially traumatic experiences and how they can be integrated into their own story and into a collective story of the past (Hamber, 2009). The psychosocial task of making meaning of violence and generating a more empowered narrative can promote reconciliation. The social platform created in a truth commission, where different testimonies and truth can emerge, represents a significant opportunity for supporting victims in dealing with psychosocial damage.

Perhaps the most obvious initiative that the Colombian truth commission can take to help heal the psychosocial damage of victims and perpetrators is the provision of psychological services to manage the stress or suffering that the procedures of the commission may produce in its participants. Indeed, it is of utmost importance to provide culturally sensitive and differential psychological support by well trained and supervised staff with particular attention to victims (PNUD, 2012), while also not forgetting the healing needs of perpetrators. Notwithstanding this central component, the contribution to healing of psychosocial trauma in the Colombian truth commission can go well beyond provision of services. In general terms, it can be summarized in the following four aspects: 1) psychosocially sensitive and dignifying practices and procedures; 2) a better understanding of the interconnection between public testimony, truth and healing (Becker, et al., 1995); 3) an acknowledgement of the limitation of complete healing (Hamber, 2009); and 4) a focus on resources instead of deficiencies to avoid the pathologization[10] of victims (PNUD, 2012; Estrada Mesa, et al., 2010). These aspects are not mutually exclusive and they are all inspired by the ethical and political intention of doing no harm and restoring the dignity of victims as tasks of reconciliation.

The practices and procedures of the truth commission are linked to examination practices like statement-taking and giving or hearing testimonies. The latter are typically marked by fact-based or judicial style processes, as they are mainly for unveiling truths and facts about what happened during the conflict. However, as discussed earlier, truth becomes more meaningful for reconciliation and healing the psychosocial damage when it serves the purpose of weaving together memory and providing meaning to the violence suffered (Castro & Gómez, 2013). In order to do this, these examination practices will greatly benefit from incorporating more psychological and narrative styles, hence choosing dignifying communicative styles, establishing a caring and respectful rapport, posing better questions aimed at protecting the integrity of the victim, and identifying opportunities to highlight resources and coping mechanisms (Montero, 1991; Rebolledo & Rondón, 2010). This also means that the staff involved in such practices could greatly benefit from psychosocial training.

Making the most of truth-telling/seeking practices in the truth commission for enhancing its healing and reconciliation potential entails the use of the public characteristic of testimony. The establishment of a detailed record of the victim's traumatic experience, and the process of creating and contributing with their testimony to the historical memory of the conflict, constitute a form of acknowledgement of the wrongdoings and provide meaning to the past, as well as a regained sense of control over the environment (Herman, 2015). Therefore, truth is not only a report of factual events, but it becomes a form of transformative social action with expected positive psychological effects. The use of testimony provided a significant form of psychosocial support in truth commissions in Central America, and helped some victims restore a sense of connection to the collective as survivors (Herman, 2015), thanks to their participation in the commissions. However, the contrary can also happen, as reliving traumatic stories through testimonies without the appropriate care and support can leave individuals feeling vulnerable and re-traumatized (Martín-Beristain, et al., 2010; Hayner, 2001).

Including a psychosocial lens in the design and implementation of the truth commission in Colombia will assist in understanding the complexities and ambivalences that surround the emotional recovery of victims. There are intrinsic limitations to attaining 'complete healing', since it is not possible to return to a state prior to the harm occurring (a rape or a murder cannot be undone). Additionally, the ambivalence of healing is attached to contextual and wider factors that play a significant role in the process of healing, such as access to justice, reparations, and truth for acknowledgement. Similarly, like reconciliation itself, the trajectories of psychosocial healing in people are not linear, nor do they follow a clear progression, so assumptions about whether the person is a 'victim' or 'survivor' must be avoided, because while some people feel like victims, others might feel like survivors (Hamber, 2009). This fact should shape expectations and different practices of what a commission can and cannot do.

Reactivating personal and collective resources is a better process for promoting psychosocial healing than focusing too much on the trauma and its deficiencies. While it is a moral imperative to acknowledge the suffering of victims, highlighting their personal and collective resources in facing violence should also be an ethical standpoint of the commission (Castro & Gómez, 2013).

Social action and civic engagement

The armed conflict in Colombia had political causes and motivations, and violence has been used to silence alternative political projects and to destroy socio-organizational processes of individuals and groups (Centro Nacional de Memoria Histórica, 2012). These collective forms of violence and trauma erode the social fabric and social capital, constrain narratives about what happened in the past, and weaken people's capacity to mobilize politically, undermining the relationship between citizen and state (de Greiff, 2008). The transitional justice framework in Colombia, including its truth commission, should also address these psychosocial damages embodied in individuals and groups, in order to bring back oppressed voices, promote a plural narrative of the past, and help restore damaged local socio-political projects.

The truth commission can become an important public forum where victims can denounce past abuses, talk about the damages produced and, as such, create more specific demands for reparations. Moreover, through their testimony, victims can show society that the harms they suffered also activated their capacities and sources of resilience and resistance through socio-organizational projects (Castro & Gómez, 2013).

Applying a psychosocial framework to truth commissions helps to unveil an ethical and political dimension of truth-telling, as it recognizes that the testimonies come from victims of an intentional violence that created harms in their personal lives, but also in their political subjectivity. Testimony, as long as it is addressed integrally, becomes one of the most powerful symbolic tools of reparation of the harm and distrust between citizen and state. It provides the opportunity to dignify the victim through active and respectful listening, to acknowledge responsibility for harms of commission or omission, and to incorporate the victim's story into the narrative of the country (Minow, 1998).

Hamber (2009) recognizes that for victims of political violence, social action can be the first opportunity to initiate their psychological recovery. When victims recover the possibility of speaking out and telling their truth via testimony in different transitional justice scenarios, this tends to unchain socio-organizational initiatives that mobilize them for social action in demanding justice, social changes, and reparations (Herman, 2015). As an example, research on truth commissions such as the Truth and Reconciliation

Commission in South Africa, the Guatemalan Truth Commission and the Gacaca courts in Rwanda (Martín-Beristain, et al., 2010) reveals the importance of public testimony for increasing the political efficacy of victims and their self-confidence. This reactivation of civic engagement could be a positive sign of psychosocial healing and empowerment that in turn can also contribute to making progress towards the re-establishment of the social contract and civic trust between citizen and state; thus, advancing in the path of national reconciliation (de Greiff, 2008).

Another layer of the ethical and political dimension that the psychosocial lens contributes to transitional justice practices is the nature of the socio-emotional support most conducive to reactivating social action and civic engagement in a transitional society. This type of support could be defined as psychosocial accompaniment, which is informed by a human rights perspective, is committed to do no harm, and respects the agency and capacities of the victims to deal with their difficulties (Rebolledo & Rondón, 2010; Estrada Mesa, et al., 2010). As might be expected, it takes distance from interventionist and directive approaches in psychology, to avoid overlooking fundamental social and personal resources for recovery and to avoid pathologizing normal psychological reactions to abnormal situations such as political violence (Martín-Baró, 1988; Montero, 1991).

Adopting more empowering methodologies to accompany and support victims and even perpetrators in exercises of truth-telling is not new in Colombia. The country is home to many national, regional, and civil society-led practices of historical memory that have thoughtful psychosocially-informed methodologies, which offer capacities and lessons learned to enrich the design and implementation of an official truth commission.[11]

Conclusion

As Colombia leaves a political conflict behind, it is confronted with the paradox of building a peaceful future from a violent past. This transition requires an adequate and timely balance of justice and peace to facilitate the level of national reconciliation needed to prevent the re-eruption of conflict and political unrest.

This chapter has argued that transitional justice mechanisms have a potential to contribute to national reconciliation, and to coexistence. In particular, a psychosocial lens is thus useful for enhancing the reconciliatory potential of truth commissions. In order to maximize its potential, the Colombian truth commission must not only be a vehicle to unveil factual truths, but principally, it must exploit the richness of the truth-telling process, support the transformation of contested identities, address the psychosocial damage, and enhance the social action and civic engagement of its participants. Should the commission's mandates, strategies, relationships and communicative practices be sensitive to these three aspects, the value of the truth-seeking exercise could be augmented, and so too its effectiveness in fostering national reconciliation and coexistence.

The Colombian truth commission could add value to national reconciliation if it offers opportunities for victims, perpetrators and society in general to safely confront the stereotypes, beliefs, and narratives that positively feed their social identities. A negotiation of parts of those social identities will facilitate the creation of common narratives that positively add to the national social cohesion. For this, it is imperative that victims are supported in their healing process through dignifying practices and the provision of ethical and relevant services, and that participants feel that they are effectively accompanied in the ambivalence of recuperating from the emotional harm caused by others.

The reactivation of social action and civic engagement by assisting in repairing socio-organizational processes damaged by violent conflict is something that can be facilitated by the Colombian truth commission, as it can be a useful space for regaining agency, while it can facilitate the restoration of the relationship between citizens and state.

Ultimately, the contribution of psychology and of a psychosocial approach is re-framing the value of the truth commission in the process; thus, seeing truth as a process may spark important reflections on the types of justice needed for victims and society at large when seeking to create healthier narratives of the past and a future without violence. A transitional justice framework which is aware of the reconciliatory potential that lies in the implementation of its practices will contribute to broaden the perspectives of justice beyond punishment towards the goal of restoring broken relationships, and it will be more attuned to providing the necessary conditions for individuals and groups to live in a more peaceful society.

Notes

1 The term 'psychosocial' is a compound word. Psycho- refers to the psychological dimension of individuals. The term 'social' indicates the social dimension of individuals and communities. Thus, the term 'psychosocial' coins the interrelation of individual, psychological factors of human experience with the cultural, social and political dimensions.
2 *Comisión para el esclarecimiento de la verdad, la convivencia y la no repetición.*
3 The creation of the commission was agreed under point 5 of the Havana peace agreement relating to the victims of the conflict (Gobierno de Colombia y FARC—EP, 2016). See www.acuerdodepaz.gov.co/.
4 In particular as regards tasks related to emotional healing and closure, the creation of a national narrative about the past and the extrapolation of individual and national healing.
5 Socio-emotional and psychosocial are used as interchangeable terms in this chapter.
6 The other is understood here as an abstraction of 'what I am not', or the limit between 'me and other'.
7 This aspect is exemplified in the case of Bosnia and Herzegovina, where ethnic identities became even more polarized after the war and constituted the most important identity marker, creating an obstacle for peaceful coexistence.

8 Colombia has made significant progress in acknowledging the existence of millions of victims of the internal conflict by passing Law 1448 of 2011, which was instrumental in formally starting the process of recognition and reparation of victims and land restitution by the state.
9 Ignacio Martín-Baró coined the term 'psychosocial trauma' when talking about the emotional impacts of war and human rights violations, to refer that this trauma is a phenomenon embedded in the social, political and historic particularities of the context where it happened.
10 Pathologization is the tendency to judge as abnormal, inadequate, or pathological those behaviours of those providing testimonies. This entails the awareness of assuming that all victims are traumatized and require psychological or psychiatric treatment. Avoiding pathologization also acknowledges the possibility of dealing with past experiences with other mechanisms that require more of accompanying processes, so that victims can make sense of their experience in a way that helps them to build their future.
11 For instance, a national women's organization, Ruta Pacífica de las Mujeres, published the report of a national project of truth-telling of Colombian women victims of the armed conflict called *La verdad de las Mujeres*, which helped in recuperating the voice and different experiences of women victims through an innovative methodology of data gathering informed by a psychosocial approach. Another important initiative in truth-seeking and historic memory is the National Center of Historic Memory, which gathers and produces information about human rights violations within the internal armed conflict. Another initiative is The Historic Memory Commission, created in the context of the negotiations in Havana, which provided a comprehensive account of the causes and consequences of the internal conflict. Initiatives like these can provide important contributions that inform the work of the truth commission.

References

Becker, D., Lira, E., Castillo, I. I. & Kovalskys, J., 1995. Therapy with victims of political repression in Chile: The challenge of social reparation. In N. J. Kritz, ed. *Transitional justice: how emerging democracies reckon with former regimes.* Washington, DC: United States Institute of Peace Press.

Becker, D., Lira, E., Castillo, M. I., Gomez, E. & Kovalskys, J., 1990. Therapy with victims of political repression in Chile: The challenge of social reparation. *Journal of Social Issues*, 46(3), pp. 133–149.

Berinstain, C. M., 2000. Justicia y Reconciliación: El papel de la verdad y la justicia en la reconstrucción de sociedades fracturadas por la violencia. *Cuadernos de Trabajo Hegoa*, Volume 27.

Bloomfield, D., 2016. *Rehabilitating Reconciliation.* [Online] Available at: www.c-r.org/downloads/Accord%20Insight%203_reconciliation_WEB_1.pdf [Last accessed 3 March 2017].

Castro, C. & Gómez, O., 2013. Elementos Psicosociales en los Procesos de reconstrucción de la Memoria con Víctimas en Colombia. In C. Avre, ed. *Acción Colectiva y Transformación*. Bogotá: Corporacion Avre, pp. 161–178.

Centro Nacional de Memoria Histórica, 2012. *Basta ya! Memorias de Guerra y Dignidad.* [Online] Available at: www.centrodememoriahistorica.gov.co/micrositios/informeGeneral/ , 2012 [Last accessed 3 March 2017].

De Greiff, P., 2008. *The handbook of reparations*. New York: Oxford University Press.

Estrada Mesa, Á. M., Ripoll Núñez, K. & Rodríguez Charry, D., 2010. Intervención psicosocial con fines de reparación con víctimas y sus familias afectadas por el conflicto armado interno en Colombia: equipos psicosociales en contextos jurídicos. *Revista de estudios sociales*, Volume 36, pp. 103–112.

Falk, E. P., 2002. *South Africa's Truth and Reconciliation Commission: A reckoning of psychology's contribution*. Berkeley: The Wright Institute.

Gloppen, S., 2005. Roads to reconciliation: A conceptual framework. In E. Skaar, S. Gloppen & A. Suhrke, eds. *Roads to reconciliation*. New York: Lexington Books, pp. 17–50.

Gobierno de Colombia & FARC—EP, 2016. *Acuerdo Final para la Terminación del Conflicto y la Construcción de una Paz Estable y Duradera*. [Online] Available at: www.altocomisionadoparalapaz.gov.co/procesos-y-conversaciones/Documentos%20compartidos/24-11-2016NuevoAcuerdoFinal.pdf [Last accessed 30 April 2017].

González, E. & Varney, H., 2013. *En Busca de la verdad: Elementos para la creación de una comisión de la verdad eficaz*. [Online] Available at: www.ictj.org/es/publication/en-busca-de-la-verdad-elementos-para-la-creacion-de-una-comision-de-la-verdad-eficaz [Last accessed 3 March 2017].

Hamber, B., 2009. *Transforming societies after political violence: Truth, reconciliation, and mental health*. New York: Springer Science & Business Media.

Hayner, P. B., 2001. *Unspeakable truths: Confronting state terror and atrocity. Psychology Press*. New York: Routledge.

Herman, J. L., 2015. *Trauma and recovery: The aftermath of violence—from domestic abuse to political terror*. New York: Basic Books.

Ignatieff, M., 1997. The elusive goal of war trials. *Harpers*, 294(1762), pp. 15–18.

Kelman, H. C., 2005. Building trust among enemies: The central challenge for international conflict resolution. *International Journal of Intercultural Relations*, 29(6), pp. 639–650.

Kelman, H. C., 2010. Conflict resolution and reconciliation: A social-psychological perspective on ending violent conflict between identity groups. *Landscapes of Violence*, 1(1), p. 5.

Lederach, J. P., 1997. *Building peace: Sustainable reconciliation in divided societies*. 9th ed. Washington, DC: United States Institute of Peace.

Leebaw, B. A., 2008. The irreconcilable goals of transitional justice. *Human Rights Quarterly*, 30(1), pp. 95–118.

Lira, E. et al., 1995. Therapy with victims of political repression in Chile: The challenge of social reparation. In N. Kritz, ed. *Transitional Justice. Volume I: General considerations*. Washington, DC: United States Institute of Peace Press, pp. 583–592.

Martín-Baró, I., 1988. *Psicología social desde Centroamérica*. 3rd ed. San Salvador: UCA Editores.

Martín-Beristain, C., Páez, D., Rimé, B. & Kanyangara, P., 2010. Psychosocial effects of participation in rituals of transitional justice: A collective-level analysis and review of the literature of the effects of TRCs and trials on human rights violations in Latin America. *Revista de Psicología Social*, 25(1), pp. 47–60.

Mendeloff, D., 2009. Trauma and vengeance: Assessing the psychological and emotional effects of post-conflict justice. *Human Rights Quarterly*, 31(3), pp. 592–623.

Minow, M., 1998. *Between vengeance and forgiveness: Facing history after genocide and mass violence*. Boston, MA: Beacon Press.

Montero, M., 1991. *Acción y discurso: problemas de psicología política en América Latina*. San Isidro: BPR Publishers.

Nadler, A. & Shnabel, N., 2008. Instrumental and socioemotional paths to intergroup reconciliation and the needs-based model of socioemotional reconciliation. In E. Thomas & J. D. Rischer, eds. *The social psychology of intergroup reconciliation*. New York: Oxford University Press, pp. 37–56.

Olsen, T. D. & Reite, A. G., 2010. *Transitional justice in balance: Comparing processes, weighing efficacy*. Washington, DC: United States Institute of Peace.

Philpott, D., 2015. *Just and unjust peace: An ethic of political reconciliation*. Oxford: Oxford University Press.

PNUD, 2012. *Acompañar los procesos con las víctimas: Atención psicosocial en las violaciones de derechos humanos*. [Online] Available at: www.psicosocial.net/grupo-accion-comunitaria/centro-de-documentacion-gac/trabajo-psicosocial-y-comunitario/herramientas-investigacion-accion-participante/833-acompanar-los-procesos-con-las-victimas/file [Last accessed 3 March 2017].

Rebolledo, O. & Rondón, L., 2010. Reflexiones y aproximaciones al trabajo psicosocial con víctimas individuales y colectivas en el marco del proceso de reparación. *Revista de estudios sociales*, Issue 36, pp. 40–50.

Skaar, E., 2013. Reconciliation in a transitional justice perspective. *Transitional Justice Review*, 1(1), p. 10.

Sluzki, C. E., 2010. The pathway between conflict and reconciliation: Coexistence as an evolutionary process. *Transcultural Psychiatry*, 47(1), pp. 55–69.

Sugiman, T., Gergen, K. J., Wagner, W. & Yamada, Y., 2008. *Meaning in action: Constructions, narratives, and representations*. Berlin: Springer.

Van Knippenberg, A. F. & Tajfel, H., 1984. *The social dimension: European developments in social psychology*. Cambridge: Cambridge University Press.

11 Transmission in times of transition
Intergenerational approaches to Colombia's violent past and present

Ariel Sánchez Meertens

War, knowledge and transitional justice

When I recently asked high school students in the town of Gaitania whether they remembered a particular incident of violence in their village—from where, back in 1964, the Fuerzas Armadas Revolucionarias de Colombia—Ejército del Pueblo (FARC—EP) originated—one of them replied: 'Yes, one day we were celebrating Halloween in the town's main square, when suddenly the guerrilla came. One person was killed; it was the clown ... who was a soldier'.[1] This recollection points to the role of testimony in making sense of war.

But testimony is nevertheless only one form, among multiple forms, of knowledge (re)production on war. The production of memories is part of 'a larger process of cultural negotiation' (Macgilchrist, et al., 2015, p. 2) of which, I suggest here, transitional justice should have a critical awareness, for the design of interventions and policies.

The transmission of knowledge in war is deployed through an array of communicative actions, among them the institutionally sanctioned practices in high schools. What meanings surrounding our troubled history are we allowing to remain through time? How do we teach the youth about what happened in Colombia? How can we acknowledge the horrors, offer victims the recognition they deserve, sanction perpetrators, and simultaneously promote reconciliatory attitudes among the younger generation? How do we begin to do all this today, when the rush of reintegration, demobilization, and the other initiatives taking place as part of the peace accord may overshadow the pedagogical imperatives of transitional justice?

As Colombian society steps from the twilight of an armed conflict into a critical political transition, the implications of knowledge production regarding that violent past and present must be scrutinized. Thus, it is vital to study the transmission of knowledge in times of transition.

Even though the definition of transitional justice refers to measures implemented to redress the legacies of crimes under international law (Duthie, 2009), achieving this is not solely dependent on the kind of justice provided in courts, nor are transitional justice instruments limited to legal dispositions. The effects of sustained violence that transitional justice seeks to confront, and the implied societal commitment required to move on, makes transitional justice an effort in rethinking the state. Thus transitional justice is not about a return to the normalcy experienced before the war, but about establishing a new normality in the country (Davies, 2004).

However, instituting this new normalcy is in fact an effort that involves the social construction of knowledge, values, and experiences embodied in the interactions between citizens (Giroux & Searls Giroux, 2004). Therefore, transitional justice is part of an enterprise that requires the consideration of cognitive and emotional interventions. Transitional justice and its link with education is consequently of the utmost importance in order to guarantee the rights of all citizens in the process of transition, to avoid the repetition of violence, and to foster the necessary changes to achieve durable peace. Thus, in order to be able to understand the links between transitional justice and education, the first step is to understand how knowledge about war in Colombia has been produced and reproduced.

As transitional justice recommendations do not generally encourage such a diagnosis before mandating educational and curricular reforms, they risk implementing measures without knowing the departure point from which these reforms should take place. These difficulties are partly symptomatic of the lack of previous diagnoses, and a 'liberal peace' approach, where a 'top-down' policy is imposed, disregarding local expertise on education that responds to particular contexts (Chandler, 2004). This is also informed by an ontology that considers students as subjects of policy reform, never as agents of change.

Although high school students cannot yet vote, they constitute nothing less than the cornerstones of post-war Colombian society and are historical agents and stakeholders of the future: students are old enough to have known the armed conflict, yet are young enough to still have their entire adult life ahead of them. Thus, given their position, it is vital to diagnose and conceptualize high-school students' knowledge of war.

There is a tendency in the academic literature to address separately the spaces of transmission (museum, family), its modalities (testimony, experience, second-hand learning), the vehicles (texts, conversations, expositions), and its agents (teachers, peers, community leaders). This propensity underestimates the critical aspects of the processes that restructure, fuse, and reinvent narratives. In addition, it underestimates their components, the different discursive domains in the production of memories, and more broadly, of knowledge. To avoid such fragmentation, we combined attention to education policy, school textbooks, teachers' and students' voices, but we also identified their source of information allowing us to explore the ways in which diverse data emerging from multiple domains are narratively brought together by single or collective actors.

During 2015 and 2016, my research team and I gathered more a than 1,500 accounts by high school students across Colombia (see Figure 11.1), collecting their knowledge on the armed conflict's history, details on the sources from which they obtained their information, as well as their personal

170 *Intergenerational approaches to violence*

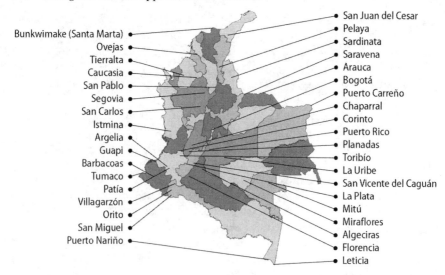

Figure 11.1 Municipalities where data was collected
Source: Own elaboration

experiences with violence and their views of the future. The research focused predominantly on students in grades 10 and 11[2], combining interviews, ethnography, and questionnaires (consisting of 25 questions pertaining to students' media consumption and learning processes, as well as knowledge about the armed conflict and their sources, the responses to which were individual and supervised).

For this, we visited more than 40 schools, in areas directly affected by the armed conflict, but also in regions less hit by its violence. Of the students interviewed, nearly half claimed they or their close family members had been affected by the armed conflict.

The study of knowledge transfer requires special attention in educational spaces. Yet, the focus is less on the institution as such (school), and more on the ways in which multiple forms of knowledge transmission converge and are refashioned within schools.

The school is a space designed to produce and transmit knowledge with the potential to join together other sites of pedagogical efforts. Yet, when the link between education and conflict is made, and schools are the locus of analysis, this institutional space is generally engaged with the education about the conflict as if it is separated from other social fields of knowledge production such a family settings, the media, the church, etc. This chapter aims to bring insights into this gap.

To do this I begin with a brief revision of pertinent educational policy regarding the teaching of a violent history in Colombia; then I explore how course materials, teachers, and schools relate to the armed conflict and their history. Next, I diagnose the current sources of knowledge and transmission among high school students in Colombia. Finally I conclude by presenting a series of recommendations in relation to the centrality of education for a reconciliatory process in Colombia.

Educational policies dealing with contested histories

One of the more salient characteristics of the current political transition in Colombia is the emergence of institutions and practices traditionally associated with post-agreement settings. In Colombia, these institutions are emerging before the actual signing of accords with the different armed groups in Colombia. Policies, practices, and institutions considered to be central to the implementation of peace agreements have appeared in Colombia's public arena before the signing of a political settlement, functioning instead as peacebuilding mechanisms. These institutions created a 'peace infrastructure' (Unger, et al., 2013) that paved the way to a successful negotiation process between the Government and the FARC—EP. Examples of such infrastructure include the Victims Unit[3], the Land Restitution Unit[4] and the National Centre for Historical Memory, as well as the Peace Curriculum Law (*Cátedra de la Paz*), all of which were established before the signing of the Peace Agreement in 2016.

Until the first decade of the 21st century, the history of the Colombian conflict was not systematically included in Colombia's educational agenda, either as a curricular subject or as an object of pedagogical work (Rodríguez Ávila & Herrera Cortés, 2012). Rather than designing content around symbolic violent episodes, the focus of programmes and materials was on ethical and civic postures rejecting violence (González, 2011). However, recently two major pillars of public policy have emerged which provide institutional support for initiatives dealing with the past: the Victims' Law and the Peace Curriculum Law[5].

Within the Victims' Law, the Government established the requirements for a social pedagogy promoting constitutional values, which were understood to lead to reconciliation as a guarantee of non-repetition.[6] This is further developed in the decree that regulates this law[7], which states that such pedagogy must create and cement a culture of knowledge and understanding of Colombia's socio-political history with regard to the armed conflict (Ortega Valencia & Herrera Cortés, 2012). It also establishes that the Ministry of Education shall foment, from a rights-based approach, the development of programmes and projects that promote the restitution and fulfilment of children's rights, and foster reconciliation and guarantees of non-repetition of incidents which threaten children's integrity and rights.[8]

The second pillar, known as the Peace Curriculum Law, is further regulated by Decree 1038 of 2015, which can be read as the further development of the Victims' Law with regards to pedagogy and education. It strives *inter alia* 'to foment the process of knowledge appropriation and competencies related to territory, culture, socioeconomic context, and historical memory; with the aim of recreating the social tissue, promoting prosperity, and guaranteeing the effectiveness of the principles and rights consecrated in the Colombian Constitution' (Article 2, Decree 1038 (2015), author's translation). To achieve this, educational institutions are required to address at least two of the following 12 themes: a) justice and human rights, b) sustainable use of natural resources, c) protection of cultural and natural national treasures, d) peaceful conflict resolution, e) prevention of bullying, f) diversity and plurality, g) political participation, h) historical memory, i) moral dilemmas, j) projects of social impact, k) history of international as well as national peace agreements, and l) life projects and risk prevention. Finally the fifth article of Decree 1038 of 2015 establishes that, from 2016 onward, the National Proficiency Exams in Colombia must evaluate achievements corresponding to this peace curriculum.

Though surely well intended, the Peace Curriculum Law has at least three critical deficiencies. First, there is insufficient familiarity among educators (if any) and only very vague implementation guides. In the majority of schools visited for this research, educators were either ignorant of the details and implications of the peace curriculum or they were upset and annoyed that they were expected to implement it without having been consulted or instructed on how to do this. This has exacerbated certain doubts and insecurities as teachers believe in the importance of teaching about the Colombian conflict, but feel unprepared in terms of training and materials—a similar situation to that found in Guatemala by Michelle Bellino (2014). This information and guidance is not only necessary for teachers but also for parents, as they can object to the contents of the courses (Paulson, 2015), or can be even re-victimized in the process of teaching the curriculum.

Second, the design of the Peace Curriculum Law disregards the rather vast experience of educational institutions across the country in dealing—albeit often informally—with violence in Colombia. Due to the relative autonomy of schools in the country there is an ample variety of approaches concerned with direct or indirect experiences of the armed conflict and with teaching its history. One needs to consider that both educators and students can function as critical partners in—and provide crucial inputs to—the design of a peace curriculum.

A third problem with the Peace Curriculum Law is the vagueness of its content. This poses serious difficulties in both in its implementation and in the evaluation of its impact. The holistic approach to the concept of peace is certainly laudable. So, too, is the associated flexibility afforded by offering 12 thematic foci, of which the schools must choose only two (in practice, this gives 66 possible combinations). But this flexibility creates the problem of several combinations of themes where it is possible to avoid dealing with the Colombian conflict and its history, as it indeed is the case in many of the schools visited. Although the importance of several topics should not be undermined, lacking an explicit and mandatory link to the dynamics of the Colombian war can end up sanitizing the debate and preventing uncomfortable but fundamental conversations about history.

All three deficiencies point to a common gap in Colombia: that is, the presence of sophisticated legislation—much of which is impressive and quite innovative—that faces great challenges in its implementation, given the lack of institutions to fulfil these mandates or clarity on the plans and procedures.

Nevertheless, setting these critical issues aside, we can argue that both the political will and legislative tools are available to establish a strategy by which the violent past could be thoroughly addressed in the classroom. It is also clear that there is a need to adjust several of these instruments, and to develop in more detail the resources, activities, and approaches for these mandates to take place. Nonetheless, as the next segment will show, the lack of policy clarity has not prevented several commercial high school publishers from addressing our conflictual history; initiatives brought about autonomously from the government guidelines seem to be capable of providing more clarity on the practice of educating learners about the Colombian conflict.

Finally, one could also suggest a third pillar to support the design of materials about the armed conflict's history in an educational setting. Materials such as the reports from the Historical Commission of the Conflict and its Victims (CHCV)[9], from the Truth, Clarification, Coexistence, Justice and Non-Repetition Commission[10], as well as the reports of the National Centre of Historical Memory (CNMH)[11], can provide these inputs for all educational institutions, following the examples of Guatemala, Argentina and South Africa.

Textbooks, teachers and schools

The possibility of transcending decades of violence through strategies for the emerging political transition relies, at least partly, on the social representations we make of the Colombian armed conflict. It is no surprise, then, that schools, and school textbooks, constitute a key site for the reproduction of normative imaginaries.

History textbooks are 'mass media for the dissemination of officially approved images of history *and*, at the same time, mirrors of societal controversies surrounding sensitive issues' (Macgilchrist, et al., 2015, p. 4). The market also heavily conditions textbooks, for they are produced for sales, with market distribution and consumer needs in mind (Binnenkade, 2015).

Therefore, both political leaders and corporations can shape students' thoughts, interests, and behaviour through textbooks. They also can trivialize debates to guarantee the broadest market possible with a 'one book fits all' strategy (Hickman & Porfilio, 2012). Despite the above, textbooks can also be what Binnenkade (2015, p. 32) calls 'boundary objects', connecting different kinds of knowledge, regions, communities, thoughts, practices, traditions, and duties. Textbooks embody 'the potential to create coherence across a [diverse] cultural landscape' (Binnenkade, 2015, p. 40); however, coherence is not to be equated with uniformity.

Despite the undeniable growth in the coverage of the conflict's history in high school textbooks in Colombia[12], several shortcomings remain. One of them is that violence is still treated in the abstract, with victims and their stories often reduced to statistics. Massacres, forced disappearances, and forced displacement as features of Colombia's recent history seldom appear in most of the textbooks from the last decade. As González (2011) would put it, what the manuals tended to put forward was either a history without events or a collection of events without history.

In some of the textbooks published since 2010, both the voices of survivors as well as elaborate descriptions of specific events have gained more space, being included either directly in the textbook pages or as additional material and suggested references for activities and discussions. Some textbooks even mention the existing legislation and propose debates on specific events, such as the Bojayá massacre.[13] In this instance, the textbook *Caminos del Saber 10* (2012) asks students, amongst other things, what they consider the actions and responsibilities of the illegal armed actors involved in the massacre should be if they were to decide to take part in a peace process, and whether the students believe the perpetrators should offer reparations to the victims of this massacre.

However, not every attempt at addressing the violent past is a successful one. Another textbook, *Sociales para Pensar 10* (2011, p. 59), poses the following question to students: 'What is a massacre and how many deaths do we need to consider that something must change?' This kind of statement embraces the practice of rhetorical and detached debates on topics that seem abstract and distant, lacking the possibility of fomenting knowledge and reflections on the history of violence in Colombia.

As the fieldwork conducted showed, books by themselves are not enough as tools for reflection. It is also important to explore the development and practice of the activities and debates suggested in some teachers' manuals, to shed light onto the actual usage of a course material. However, the diversity of the regions and their practice showed that none of the schools visited thus far used these textbooks or has implemented the proposed exercises. This was because either schools did not have textbooks, teachers refused to use them, or they had older or simpler editions that avoided the history of the war altogether.

An additional concern is that in the event that such representations and activities are mainstreamed, it is possible to anticipate a backlash, given the highly polarized political climate surrounding the peace negotiations, as was the case in Peru (Paulson, 2010), and the imposition of a guiding narrative to Colombian teachers who are representative of the diversity of the Colombian territory. How is one to link very different, sometimes contradictory ways of 'thinking, feeling, talking, and acting about specific events in the past' as part of a national exercise? (Binnenkade, 2015, p. 32) Teachers are not distant from the conflict (Paulson, 2011), and as a personal interview with a teacher showed us[14], they can also be not only victims or observers, but also former combatants and victimizers.

Schools are also sites of physical and symbolic disputes. As in Sri Lanka and most countries affected by civil war, schools in Colombia have been wanted by militant groups as strategic points for stationing troops, recruiting children, and imparting propaganda. The discourses and behaviour of both pupils and instructors are regulated and monitored in conflict areas in Colombia. As recalled by a teacher in Planadas,[15] armed actors instructed teachers on the accepted teaching guidelines and demanded that teachers presented themselves at their base, where they were held accountable for the ways in which they performed their duties. This was sometimes followed by warnings and sometimes by punishment.

Thus in a way school materials and practices can be a locus of mandated institutional knowledge transfer, and at the same time they can be also a theatre of counter-institutional knowledge. In this fashion the guerrillas and paramilitaries have strategically exploited the spaces for the understanding of war and peace, contesting the state from within.

Students, sources and sensitivity

The repertoires of war knowledge transmission are often presumed, rather than identified. Although scholarly work on education and conflict acknowledges the existence of discursive domains other than the educational institution (Cole, 2007; Bekerman & Zembylas, 2011), these are seldom studied.

Both the presupposition of repertoires and the failure to incorporate sources beyond the school miss the opportunity to understand where students actually learn from about conflict, and how these sources relate to the institutional stream of a school.

Instead of assuming the sources of knowledge, in the fieldwork we asked students what they know and how (from where) they know about the conflict. I asked them what they experienced and what they had learned. We inquired about the ways in which the past was incorporated in their consciousness and the future projected in their desires and imaginaries. This is possible due to the fact that students embody what Binnenkade (2015) calls a discursive node. They are citizens in the making and the offspring of society at the same time, hence expected to absorb and reproduce the officially sanctioned knowledge, whilst simultaneously projecting the commonly diverging memories of their own contexts (Macgilchrist, et al., 2015).

Learning through 'zapping'

Students in Colombia learn about Colombia's past through television (28.1% of the total sources mentioned), mainly through news broadcasts, but also through particular television series (see Figure 11.2). This may not come as a revelation; however, it is worth noting that when I asked the same question in Sri Lanka (where I conducted a similar investigation) media also came out on top, yet it was not television that was cited the most, but newspapers.[16] In Colombia television was mentioned as a source of knowledge regarding the history of the armed conflict almost twice as much as educational institutions and teachers (18.3%). This has clear policy implications, as it could mean that

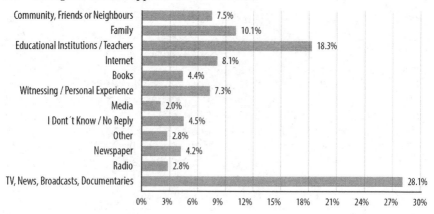

Figure 11.2 Students' Sources of War Knowledge
Source: Own elaboration.

such broadcasts should be used as an input for guiding and accompanying work offered by schools. Educational institutions cannot deny the media as a pedagogical force, but they cannot simply yield to that power either. Perhaps instead of a diluted and ambiguous peace curriculum, a media consumption curriculum might have a bigger impact on memory, identity and knowledge production in general.

Affected, but not learned?

Another interesting point of analysis is that 47.7% of the students claimed to be directly affected by violence, but only 10.7% of the referred sources of conflict knowledge were lived or witnessed experiences. Violence in a civil war can thus be seen as having a 'pedagogical' intention. This difference on the affectation and the sources of knowledge can reveal how testimony and the embodied experiences of violence do not necessarily become structured, appropriated, or 'narratable' knowledge about the conflict. Violence for victims has a clear communicative intent and result, but it is unintelligible on its own.

This makes the case for the production of contexts, and spaces that allow the intertwining of information and experiences beyond a single event, and the fact that both the local and the individual experience can have pedagogical potential that can facilitate learning about the conflict.

Although many students claim not to have been directly affected by the armed conflict, they do remember violent incidents in their communities. Both survivors and 'observers' tend to limit their conception of personal impact to violence inflicted upon the personal or familial body. But having to shelter from bombs, being impeded from attending school or watching your neighbour being shot are not just indirect effects of war upon one's life. Therefore, the fact that violence was so routine for many years has created distortions in people's own definition of victimhood, a distortion that may in fact amount to a mode of trauma that is linked with the capacity and the ability to learn about the conflict.

Many students are able to remember at least one event where violence impacted their lives. These include experiences such as the one that occurred in Gaitania (the assassination of a clown) mentioned at the beginning of this chapter. In addition, in Toribío[17] students (almost all members of the Nasa indigenous community) regularly mentioned the rural bus-bomb[18] that 'destroyed almost half of our town'.[19] Most students in Mitú[20] remembered the town's siege by the FARC—EP. Thus, across the country young citizens build part of their knowledge of the conflict from their memories of specific armed confrontations close to their houses or schools.[21]

However, not all these recollections are lived experiences. Learned recollections also inform the learning of students, such as the case of students in Segovia who recalled the massacre in that town as a memory of their own. Two issues can be highlighted here: first, students referencing this incident were not born at the time; second, students using the same signifier—the Segovia massacre—were actually referencing different incidents taking place in the same location at different times.[22]

Microfoundations of narratives of violence

Studies on violence in civil war have shown how motivations for perpetrating violence at the local level may in fact respond to personal vendettas (Kalyvas, 2006), but are often framed as part of civil war dynamics through deliberate misinformation. These strategies have also been used in Colombia and are part of the narratives and the knowledge transmission mechanisms that were observed. A student in San Miguel[23], mentioned the history of his brother, who was accused and judged by guerrillas for a murder he did not commit.[24] Therefore, the existence of other accounts, in which actions are attributed to different citizens and actors, is part of war dynamics and its transmission.

The latter does not mean that discussing and reflecting on violence, histories, and narratives is an easy task. A youth in Puerto Carreño[25] who, when asked whether he remembered witnessing violent acts, simply but powerfully, replied 'yes [but] I rather keep quiet'.[26] The challenge of having these conversations in a country where violence has not totally stopped and where reprisals are a possibility is something educational interventions must take into account.

The place of violence and conflict

Given the overwhelming presence of violence in the memories and daily lives of the students across the country, one would expect that when asked about places they associated with conflict and violence, their replies would point to their immediate surroundings. Unexpectedly, their answers point to what I call 'War in the Mirror'. Violence is exteriorized. Most of the students surveyed referred to the Cauca region as the place they associate with violence

178 *Intergenerational approaches to violence*

and conflict (see Figure 11.3), with Bogotá, the capital of the country, listed as the second most frequently identified place of violence and conflict (by students from outside the capital). This suggests that often the places associated with war in people's minds are the places of the 'other' and how television imagery can trump one's own experience in consolidating an account. These are conjectures worth exploring further in the future.

What this shows indisputably is the pedagogical impact of the media: if students are bombarded with images of robberies and assaults occurring in Bogotá, to which news outlets dedicate a considerable segment of their broadcasts, then it comes as no surprise that the capital becomes a place

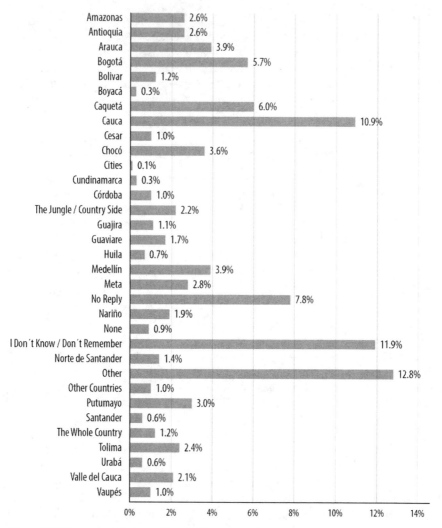

Figure 11.3 Imagined Geographies of Violence—The places associated with war
Source: Own elaboration.

associated with fear and violence. Quite notably, the multiple forms of criminality shown in the media, particularly television, are seen as part of a continuum of violence, thus for students there is no categorical distinction between the robberies seen on television and the armed conflict fought between the Government and the rebel forces.

The origins of conflict in Colombia

I also inquired among students about what they considered was the beginning of the armed conflict, an inquest that—*inter alia*—enables a fruitful discussion on the link between history education and transitional justice. For this, first the conflict and its associated violence must be understood and recognized as a historical process. One-quarter of the students approached (25.5%) had no specific notion of when the war emerged; 9.1% did not answer the question on the origins of the armed conflict; and 6.6% talked about the eternity of war, of the war being something that 'started before Christ'. Even among those that provided some kind of timeframe, several established the origin as 'a long time ago', 'when Christopher Columbus died' or 'since my birth'.[27] Having known no other reality, for many students the existence of armed conflict and violence is a fact of life. Thus, to historicize war is not just a matter of fomenting knowledge on what occurred; it is also a crucial task in denaturalizing violence and thereby generating a sense of agency, and stimulating the reappearance of hope in a better and more peaceful tomorrow.

When students were asked about the causes leading to the armed conflict it was interesting to note there was no dominant answer (see Figure 11.4), though 'ideological differences' did stand out slightly. Such result prompts some important elucidations: first the vagueness of the leading reply suggests little clarity on the issue, which is only reinforced by the second most common answer: 'I don't know'. Moreover, this second most repeated reply suggests both a gap in students' knowledge and insufficient pedagogical intent by institutional as well as informal discourse producers.

Secondly, a war's alleged cause may be considered to differ according to location. The geographical expansion of an armed conflict is hardly the result of the same cause in different places. Instead, local tensions are incorporated into the web of meanings, sustaining and legitimizing violence. This makes it unlikely to find the predominance of one type of justification among a diverse and differentially affected community, as the students' voices indeed substantiate.

Third, the prolonged character of the confrontations contributed to such variations in causal explanations (students also mentioned 'inequality', 'the Spanish conquest,' 'power and territorial disputes' and 'corruption', among others). This also has facilitated the understanding of the conflict having arisen from already existing socio-historical problems, including natural resources and illicit goods. Thus for several students (in particular in regions hit by this phenomenon) drug trafficking is understood to be the originator of armed groups, instead of a later component of war.

180 Intergenerational approaches to violence

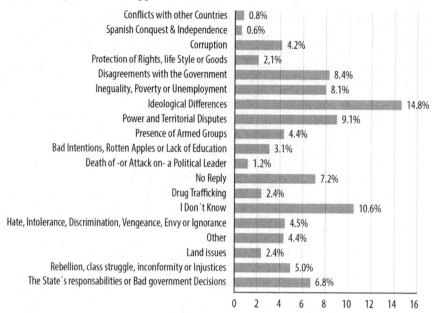

Figure 11.4 Causes of Conflict According to Students
Source: Own elaboration.

The actors of war

Students considered the FARC—EP to be the main actor in Colombia's armed conflict (see Figure 11.5), with the number of mentions doubling any other actor (19%). However, for many students, particularly in the peripheries, the Medellín drugs cartel leader Pablo Escobar, as a symbol of drug trafficking, has the leading role in the conflict (this is partially the result of popular television shows focusing on his life in recent years). It also stands out that in several responses 'the guerrilla' is thought to be an independent and distinguishable actor from the FARC—EP or Ejército de Liberación Nacional (ELN) insurgencies, rather than a generic term.

Peace negotiations and transitional justice

Meanwhile, students' views on the peace agreement between the Colombian Government and the FARC—EP were rather evenly divided (see Figure 11.6). There were those that considered the peace process 'a big step for humanity.'[28] However, when students made explicit their rejection of the dialogues, they often expressed themselves in rather radical terms, notably more so in areas less affected by the dynamics of war. A boy in Leticia[29], for example, said, regarding the negotiations: 'that doesn't work … so are we supposed to let them kill us to achieve peace? It's better to just finish off those bastards.'[30] Another classmate put his pessimism in almost epistemological

Intergenerational approaches to violence 181

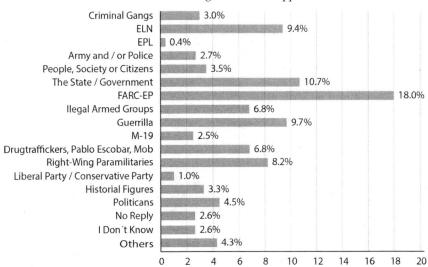

Figure 11.5 Main Actors of Armed Violence in Colombia According to Students
Source: Own elaboration.

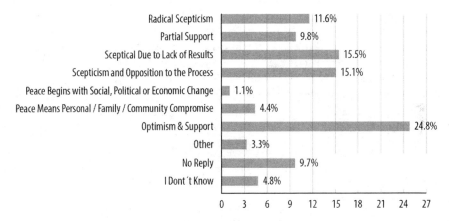

Figure 11.6 Students' Views on the Peace Process
Source: Own elaboration.

terms: '…Why search for peace when man has never had peace, he doesn't know what that is. And if it he doesn't know what it is, how is he to know whether he's reached it or not?'[31] It comes as no surprise then that several of them suggest that the best strategy to end the armed conflict is 'to kill them once and for all'[32], a position shared by others, though at times accompanied by certain doubts. Finally, there are those with a more systemic kind of pessimism: '[the peace process] is a failure because peace is achieved not only with the FARC—EP, there are other groups generating violence death, kidnappings and other sorts of crime. […] [Besides, among the FARC members there are those] who have murdered, kidnapped and aggravated society in general.

They deserve to be in jail, but no, they are free and want to be in government. It doesn't seem a fair process for Colombians.'[33]

There are also those who find it impossible to believe that people who have killed will now somehow find peace, and those that believe the peace agreement to be a farce linking this with the high levels of unemployment in contemporary Colombia. They reason that 'if there's peace what are *they* gonna do? It's going to be worse. [...] It's all bullshit'.[34] Finally, there are those claiming peace is only 'God-given', so the government efforts are misplaced, arrogant or perhaps even insulting to them.

There were nevertheless other types of replies offering alternatives to ending the war, such as 'hiring plenty of psychologists to change people's way of acting and thinking life' or 'making sure combatants demobilize, hand over their weapons while the Government gives them a lot of money for them to be happy and abandon war once and for all'. Lastly there are those who bet on knowledge, education, and memory, and suggest 'giving kids information about this armed conflict so they'll be aware in the future.'[35]

Amongst students there was also a lack of knowledge on the contents of the peace agreements. This indicates the need for pedagogical operations to socialize the details of what was agreed upon as part of the pedagogical dimension of the transitional justice interventions to come. But that alone is not enough. Given the weak understanding about the peace agreements among high school students, it is important to consider how to teach about the peace agreements signed with the FARC—EP. Teaching about the peace agreements will also imply teaching about the history of the armed conflict. As the understanding of future citizens about the role of the transitional justice institutions establishing themselves in the country will be central for the endeavour of peace and reconciliation, education about the agreements and the history of the conflict becomes central for peace.

Twilight transmission: concluding remarks

So what does the above tell us about transmission in times of transition? First, that the knowledge systems sustaining war (Jabri, 1996) are nurtured by historical narratives and emotional memories which are part of a pallet of diversity. Memory is intersectional: what and how things are remembered varies according to region, ethnicity, age, gender, and the experience of violence among other markers of difference. No single narrative is produced, transmitted and shared to maintain a sense of 'the' armed conflict. Instead, both the reproduction of war and its transformations are made possible by a web of semantic alliances.[36] It is by virtue of these semantic alliances that we can conceptualize, imagine, and (intergenerationally as well as translocally) transmit something conceived of as 'the Colombian armed conflict': a single but unstable signifier capturing an array of diverse experiences and meanings.

A key to the transmission of knowledge about the conflict lies less in rigid texts and more in the (re)joining of fragmented knowledge systems, stemming from multiple discursive domains. These can better relate to the experiences of Colombians and give a clearer representation of the diversity of Colombia and its violence.

Students in different parts of Colombia do not share a similarly arranged historical discourse of the decades of armed confrontations. How could they, if they have experienced it differently, their consumption of media varies, and their institutional exposure to specific readings of the past differs? There are, nevertheless, certain images that circulate at a national level, which students seek to connect to local incidents or personal experiences. The pedagogical and educational strategy devised in post-agreement Colombia should not be one in which we settle on a fixed and more or less consensual or institutionally authorized narrative of what happened. The very eclectic, unstructured, associative way in which actual knowledge transfer occurs serves as an important cue for how we can reconfigure our policy on dealing with the past.

Thus, there is great pedagogical value in using students' voices to teach children about the experiences of others in war, to educate through the perspectives of others, and to explore conjointly the imaginaries of the future. The great richness could inform what Jansen and Weldon refer to as post-conflict pedagogies (Jansen and Weldon, 2009). This would entail, not simply including facts in a history programme, but involving 'raw emotions' in the curriculum (Davies, 2004, p. 119).

Students' textbooks and classroom interactions could greatly benefit from having a reservoir of experiences and narratives on conflict and violence from their peers in other parts of the country. Such accounts could serve the purpose of exposing students to occurrences through the eyes of other youngsters much like themselves in other parts of the country. Such exposure may provoke new discussions and the inclusion of their own tales of life and in fact co-produce a diverse historical account.

The choice is often made to postpone addressing the history of the armed conflict in the immediate aftermath of war. I argue instead for the imperative for action in the midst of transition. For this, we should not only focus on creating new curriculums in accordance to the mandate of the Peace Curriculum Law, but as this research shows, how history is in fact taught and learned as well. If education is meant to support a process of reconciliation and cohabitation as part of a transitional justice framework, it is important to pay attention to the future generations of Colombians, what they learn, and how they engage with our history.

The pedagogical dimension of transitional justice I suggested at the beginning of this chapter is more evident now that we have sketched the instructional force of the students' voices. These are voices expressing concerns with the present and future, testimonies of violence and resilience, voices operating as integrating nodes of a nation fragmented by more than half a century of war. Education thus becomes a tool for reconciliation and cohabitation, a space for reflection and debate, a place for democracy.

However, it is important to consider curricular and extracurricular interventions that encourage more critical media consumption by the youth. This is because 'future peace [in Colombia] depends on children being able to resist propaganda' (Davies, 2004, p. 120) and on them recognizing that, despite their visual power, not every 'meme' evokes a truth. From this research the power and impact of television has become evident: therefore, being able to teach students how to reflect on media and their messages becomes central for the process of reconciliation.

This initial approximation to the youth's learning and knowledge paths should be expanded to create a more robust diagnosis of the ways in which teaching and learning about the armed conflict has taken place. Such a diagnosis, hand in hand with truth commission reports, documented reparation strategies, and reconciliation projects, can constitute an important input for any future policy on conflict education as part of a transitional justice strategy in Colombia and its future generations.

Notes

1 Questionnaire PL128, July 15th 2015. From here onward, all quotes are the author's translation.
2 Grades 10 and 11 correspond to the last two years of high school in Colombia.
3 Unidad para la Atención y Reparación Integral a las Víctimas.
4 Unidad de Restitución de Tierras.
5 Law 1732 of 2014.
6 Ordinal (e) of article 149 of the Victim's Law (Law 1448 of 2011).
7 Decree 4800 of 2011.
8 Article 145, paragraph 7, Decree 4800 of 2011.
9 Comisión Histórica del Conflicto y sus Víctimas.
10 Comisión para el esclarecimiento de la verdad, la convivencia y la no repetición.
11 Centro Nacional de Memoria Histórica.
12 For example, the following textbooks: *Caminos del Saber 9* (Santillana, 2013), *Caminos del Saber 10* (Santillana, 2012) *Caminos del Saber 11* (Santillana, 2013), *Hipertexto 9* (Santillana, 2010), *Hipertexto 11* (Santillana, 2010), *Normas Sociales para Pensar 9* (Norma, 2011), *Normas Sociales para Pensar 10* (Norma, 2011), *Normas Sociales para Pensar 11* (Norma, 2011), *Nuevos Horizontes Sociales 9* (Editorial Educativa, 2012), and *Retos Sociales 9* (Carvajal, 2013).
13 In this massacre, 119 civilians were killed while taking refuge in a church while a clash between the FARC—EP and the right-wing paramilitaries was taking place.
14 This teacher admitted proudly to us that he had been part of a right-wing paramilitary force operating in the region, and he had killed a guerrilla member, to be part of the paramilitaries. He also acknowledged he attempted to enter the Colombian Army but had failed the psychological tests. At the time of the interview, he was a school teacher.
15 A municipality in the south of the Tolima Province. It was in this municipality where the FARC—EP emerged in 1964.
16 For more details on my previous research in Sri Lanka see Sánchez Meertens, Ariel. 2013. 'Courses of conflict: transmission of knowledge and war's history in eastern Sri Lanka'. *History and Anthropology.* 24 (2): pp. 253–273.
17 Toribío is a municipality in the Cauca province, one of the most conflict-ridden regions of Colombia.

18 "Chiva-bomba". It was a bus made into a bomb.
19 Questionnaires, 29 September 2015.
20 Capital of the Vaupés province. Mitú was the largest town ever besieged by the FARC—EP.
21 Questionnaires PL112, SR015.
22 The Segovia Massacre generally refers to the killing of 43 people in this mining town (a leader in gold extraction) of the Antioquia Province, which was perpetrated on 11 November 1988 by right-wing paramilitary groups. However, nearly ten years later, on 18 October 1998, the ELN guerrilla group (Ejército de Liberación Nacional) blew up an oil pipe in the outskirts of Segovia (in a hamlet called Machuca). The resulting fire killed 73 civilians. Two years earlier, on 22 April 1996, right-wing paramilitary forces massacred 14 people in two billiards halls in the town, 'El Flay' and 'El Paraíso'.
23 A town and municipality located in the Putumayo province.
24 Questionnaire September 21st, 2015.
25 Capital of the Vichada province.
26 Questionnaire, 24 September 2015.
27 Questionnaires ET046, T019, TO001.
28 Questionnaire LE005.
29 Capital of the Amazon province.
30 This student attends to a school managed by the Colombian Navy. Questionnaire LE003.
31 Questionnarie LE011.
32 Questionnaires LE003, LE010 and LE011.
33 Questionnaire PC026.
34 Questionnaire PL110.
35 Questionnaires LE015, PC026, PL107, PL110 and P126, LE004 and PL108; PL117.
36 See: Sánchez Meertens, 2013.

References

Bekerman, Z. & Zembylas, M., 2011. *Teaching contested narratives: identity, memory, and reconciliation in peace education and beyond.* Cambridge: Cambridge University Press.

Bellino, M., 2014. Whose Past, Whose Present?: Historical Memory mong the 'Postwar' Generation in Guatemala. In J. H. Williams, ed. *(Re)constructing memory: School textbooks and the imagination of the nation.* Rotterdam: Sense Publishers, pp. 131–152.

Binnenkade, A., 2015. Doing Memory. Teaching as a Discursive Mode. *Journal of Educational Media, Memory and Society,* 7(2), pp. 29–43.

Chandler, D., 2004. The responsibility to protect? Imposing the 'liberal peace'. *International peacekeeping,* 11(1), pp. 59–81.

Cole, E., 2007. *Teaching the Violent Past: History Education and Reconciliation.* Lanham: Rowman & Littlefield Publishers.

Davies, L., 2004. *Education and conflict: complexity and chaos.* London: Routledge Falmer.

Duthie, R., 2009. Introduction. In: P. De Greiff & R. Duthie, eds. *Transitional justice and development: making connections.* New York: Social Science Research Council, pp. 17–27.

Giroux, H. & Searls Giroux, S., 2004. *Take Back Higher Education: Race, Youth and the Crisis of Democracy in the Post-civil Rights Era.* New York: Palgrave.

González, M. I. C., 2011. *Textos Escolares Violencia y Memoria*. Bogotá: Colciencias.
Hickman, H. & Porfilio, B. J., 2012. *The new politics of the textbook: problematizing the portrayal of marginalized groups in textbooks*. Rotterdam: Sense Publishers.
Jabri, V., 1996. *Discourses on violence: conflict analysis reconsidered*. Manchester: Manchester University Press.
Jansen, J. D. & Weldon, G., 2009. The pedagogical transaction in post-conflict societies. *Perspectives in Education*, 27(2), pp. 107–108.
Kalyvas, S. N., 2006. *The logic of violence in civil war*. Cambridge: Cambridge University Press.
Macgilchrist, F., Christophe, B. & Binnenkade, A., 2015. Memory Practices and History Education. *Journal of Educational Media, Memory, and Society*, 7(2), pp. 1–9.
Ortega Valencia, P. & Herrera Cortés, M. C., 2012. Memorias de la violencia política y formación ético-política de jóvenes y maestros en Colombia. *Revista Colombiana de Educación*, Issue 62, pp. 89–115.
Paulson, J., 2010. Truth Commissions and National Curricula: The Case of Recordándonos resource in Peru. In: S. Parmar, M. J. Roseman, S. Siegrist & T. Sowa, eds. *Children and Transitional Justice: Truth Telling, Accountability and Reconciliation*. Cambridge: Harvard Law School.
Paulson, J., 2011. *Education and reconciliation: exploring conflict and post-conflict situations*. New York: Continuum International Publishing Group.
Paulson, J., 2015. 'Whether and How?' History Education about Recent and Ongoing Conflict: A Review of Research. *Journal on Education in Emergencies*, 1(1), pp. 14–47.
Presidencia de la República de Colombia, 2015. *La Cátedra de la Paz*. [Online] Available at: http://wp.presidencia.gov.co/sitios/normativa/decretos/2015/Decretos2015/DECRETO%201038%20DEL%2025%20DE%20MAYO%20DE%202015.pdf [Last accessed: 11 August 2017].
Rodríguez Ávila, S. P. & Herrera Cortés, M. C., 2012. Historia, memoria y formación: violencia socio-política y conflicto armado. *Revista Colombiana de Educación*, Issue 62, pp. 12–18.
Sánchez Meertens, A., 2013. Courses of Conflict: Transmission of Knowledge and War's History in Eastern Sri Lanka. *History and Anthropology*, 24(2), pp. 253–273.
Unger, B., Lundström, S., Planta, K. & Austin, B., 2013. *Peace infrastructures assessing concept and practice*. Berlin: Berghof Foundation.

Part III
The Lessons

12 Rethinking the Colombian transition to peace through the South African experience

Jerónimo Delgado Caicedo and Juliana Andrea Guzmán Cárdenas

Introduction

The debate on transitional justice has been defined around the contrast between retributive and restorative justice. While retributive justice focuses on guilt and punishment, restorative justice focuses on responsibility and reparation (McLeod, 2015). In the former, punishment is used to educate the offender; in the latter, the recreation of the bond between the offender and society is prioritized, while truth and justice are a central part of the re-weaving of a social covenant (Armstrong, 2014; Howse & Llewellyn, 1999; Wenzel, et al., 2008; McLeod, 2015).

However, this debate cannot be disconnected from the juridical demands for justice imposed by the international community. Transitional justice processes thus face the challenge of dealing with the tensions between the international legal imperatives of punishment for perpetrators of crimes against humanity, and the need for amnesty in transitional contexts (Gutiérrez Ramírez, 2014; Schabas, 2011). In other words, transitional justice seeks 'to find a politically viable solution that, without giving rise to impunity, does make it possible to achieve lasting peace and reconciliation' (Saffon & Uprimny, 2005, p. 271).

Transitional justice is one of the most difficult mechanisms to implement during the post-conflict period (Duthie & Siels, 2017), where the mismatch between what was agreed upon and the reality of implementation creates tensions (DeRouen, et al., 2010). While most of these agreements are characterized by promises of reform, reconstruction of societies, and the transition to democracy or non-violent contexts, for some, their benefits remain unclear (Sensabaugh & Van der Merwe, 2017).

The Colombian Government reached a peace agreement with the Fuerzas Armadas Revolucionarias de Colombia—Ejército del Pueblo (FARC—EP)[1] on 24 November 2016. The peace agreement's journey forward will most likely not be oblivious to various obstacles and difficulties that usually arise during the processes of national reconciliation and reconstruction of the social foundations of a country after an armed conflict. The reintegration of former combatants and the overall rehumanization of society are amongst the most important hurdles to overcome.

In turn, the history of South Africa and its experience with transitional justice provide a benchmark for reflection about the Colombian case. South Africa is commonly regarded as a successful transitional justice model and experience in recent history (Affa'a-Mindzie, 2015; Gibson, 2009; Mawhinney, 2015; Traniello, 2002; Villa-Vicencio & Verwoerd, 2000): nonetheless, evidence shows that the country's transition was far from perfect. This chapter focuses on the South African transitional justice experience and assesses its successes and failures which, in turn, can inform the policies and practices to be undertaken during the implementation of the Colombian peace agreement.

To do so, the chapter discusses the process of transitional justice in South Africa and the role of the Truth and Reconciliation Commission (TRC) as its main mechanism. Subsequently, an assessment of the main lessons learnt from this process is undertaken, including its main critiques as well as its successes, taking into consideration how pertinent they are for the Colombian process. Finally, several reflections are made on what should be considered for the Colombian case, so that mistakes from other experiences are not repeated and the obstacles can be minimized during the path towards reconciliation.

The South African experience and the TRC

Between 1948 and 1994, the South African government implemented the policy of Apartheid. With the arrival of the National Party to power in 1948, the white government's official policy was based on the term 'apartheid', a system that—at least in theory—intended to generate separate developments for the different races in the country (Delgado, 2016). In reality, however, this regime legalized political, social, and economic discrimination against non-whites (blacks, Indians and coloureds) in order to disempower these communities and make them subservient to the white population in the country.

Apartheid's main characteristic was its policy of 'divide and rule' (Henrard, 2003). During this period, structural violence was present in all spheres of the country (political, economic, and social), which led to a systematic dehumanization of the population based on race and gross human rights violations (Wielenga, 2017).

An institutional framework was designed to enact and reinforce the policy of segregation and discrimination. For example, only English and Afrikaans—languages mainly spoken by whites—were recognized as official languages of the country (Boddy-Evans, 2017). Other examples include the forbidding of marriages between whites and non-whites (Ratuva, 2013), the implementation of residential segregation (Massey, 2013), the separation of public spaces for each racial group (Landis, 1957), and the Bantu Education Act, which established a different education system for whites and non-whites (Christie & Collins, 1982).

In the last years of apartheid, domestic and international factors considerably influenced the need to consider a negotiation agenda (De Klerk,

2002). In the 1980s, mass revolts and mobilizations against the regime increased and spread throughout the country. Also, churches and mainstream media started to play a more active anti-apartheid role which encouraged social mobilization (Maharaj, 2008). Furthermore, the grim prospects for the economy convinced many in the business community that it was necessary to explore other solutions to the conflict (De Klerk, 2002).

In the international arena, with the independence of Angola, Mozambique, and Zimbabwe, the ideological barrier that South Africa had sought to establish began to crumble. Also, Western powers that had supported apartheid, such as the USA, the United Kingdom and France, 'began to come under increasing pressure from their own citizens and within international forums' (Maharaj, 2008, p. 16). Finally, efforts made by the African National Congress (ANC) overseas were successful in pressuring political leadership (De Klerk, 2002; Maharaj, 2008).

The end of apartheid was negotiated between 1990 and 1994 (Barnes & De Klerk, 2002). This negotiation process lasted for a period of about four years, during which, as in Colombia in recent times, destabilizing events and ongoing tensions remained common. In 1994, following that period of negotiation, democratic elections were held, and an interim constitution was passed that legally ended the system of apartheid (Mawhinney, 2015). In 1995, the Mandela Government enacted the Promotion of National Unity and Reconciliation Act[2] which set up the South African TRC. The TRC was undoubtedly the most important transitional justice tool in the country during the transition to democracy, and its objective was 'to promote national unity and reconciliation in a spirit of understanding which transcends the conflicts and divisions of the past' (Parliament of the Republic of South Africa, 1995). This mechanism achieved the most important elements to enable truth and reconciliation during a transition process: legitimacy, neutrality of the commissioners, and a clear mandate (Mawhinney, 2015).

The TRC, using a restorative approach, intended to (i) build a bridge between the past of a deeply divided society and a future founded on peaceful coexistence for all; (ii) prevent a repetition of the past events in the future, through the establishment of truth; (iii) reconcile the people of South Africa and reconstruct the social fabric; and (iv) avoid the proliferation of vengeance by cultivating understanding and reparation (Truth and Reconciliation Commission of South Africa, 2003). According to the Institute for Justice and Reconciliation[3] (IJR), 'it was believed that if the country did not come to terms with its past in a way that initiated a healing process, it would at some point in the future revert to its original cycle of systematic violence' (Govender & Hofmeyr, 2015, p. 3).

The TRC faced many challenges related to its implementation, one of which was related to the scale of injustice this mechanism was commanded to respond to. Even though the number of deaths under the apartheid regime has not been officially established, it is estimated that 18,000 people were killed, 80,000 of the regime's opponents were detained and approximately

6,000 were tortured (Wielenga, 2017). According to Aronson, 'as many as 2,000 people are missing from the Apartheid era in South Africa. Of these, [only] 477 were officially recognized by the TRC' (Aronson, 2011, p. 262). In terms of forced displacement, some 3.5m. black South Africans were forcefully relocated (Abel, 2016). These figures highlight the great challenge the South African Government faced in relation to providing redress to victims, reconciliation, and national unity.

Political support for the TRC was also a challenge, as not all parties involved in the conflict agreed with the implementation of this mechanism (Ladduwahetty, 2011), especially those actors who saw an amnesty as a more desirable alternative for them (Foster, et al., 2017). However, at the time, this was the best alternative that could be achieved, as the adoption of a punitive policy could have had compromised the negotiation process and peace (Buarque de Hollanda, 2013).

The presence of imperfection

Transitional justice initiatives in post-agreement scenarios are far from perfect. In South Africa, after the culmination of the TRC's mandate, a series of critiques have emerged revealing the existence of numerous weaknesses of this process. Different critiques have been raised with regards to the TRC's inability to effectively achieve restorative justice and meet the people's expectations, the construction of selective historical records, and the limited time frame given for fulfilling its mandate, among others (Boshomane, 2016; Buchanan-Clarke, 2015; Cole, 2007; Gibson, 2005; Mawhinney, 2015; Mokgatle, 2016; Valji, 2004; Van der Merwe, 2003).

Four especially salient critiques are explored in this section, as they hold the most relevance for the Colombian process: the granting of amnesties to human rights offenders; the non-binding nature of the TRC recommendations; the institutional weakness of restoration programmes; and the lack of economic reconciliation and transformation.

Amnesty to human right offenders

The issue of amnesty has been one of the main arguments against the South African process and its implementation. According to Mawhinney, 'by offering offenders amnesty in exchange for truth telling, the TRC pursued truth at the expense of restorative dialogue and reconciliation, and thus created a false sense of reconciliation' (Mawhinney, 2015, p. 36). The practice of granting amnesty to perpetrators of crimes regardless of whether they committed massive violations of human rights is still highly controversial.

Amnesty was conceived as an individual prerogative for the interested parties to give a full public disclosure of their crimes, but it was also an opportunity for the victims and the nation to become cognisant of what actually happened during apartheid (McLeod, 2015). The TRC received 7,116 amnesty applications, and ultimately granted amnesty to only 849 applications (Foster, et al., 2017).

Other assessments argue that justice was traded for a truth that was not necessarily complete. This perception of a lack of justice was reinforced by the fact that very few individuals who did not receive amnesty were actually prosecuted (Foster, et al., 2017) as a consequence of the TRC's limited ability to administer justice in terms of prosecutions and reparations, since it could not institute any legal proceedings against perpetrators of crimes (Sensabaugh & Van der Merwe, 2017).

Also, there was a lack of synergy between the perpetrators' and victims' processes due to the fact that they were addressed by different committees. In addition to this, doubts have emerged as to the TRC's capacity to mediate reconciliation between victims and offenders, since there was not real dialogue between them, besides some opportunities the former had to face the latter in an amnesty hearing (Howse & Llewellyn, 1999).

However, one could question the plausibility of a transition from apartheid in the absence of incentives such as amnesties (Mawhinney, 2015). Without them, the transition towards democracy could have failed. Without the offer of amnesty, perpetrators within the apartheid regime could have incentives to spoil the peace process and the transition, or abandon the negotiations, as the continuation of the regime could have been more secure for those perpetrators of crimes (Gibson, 2005). Thus it can be said that the South African model was a pragmatic choice that responded to the necessities of the transition towards a new social order (Hamber, 2013).

In South Africa, in a similar way to Colombia, negotiation emerged as the result of a mutually damaging stalemate (Zartman, 2001). In these cases, the granting of concessions such as amnesties seems to be more natural to a negotiation process, as opposed to a military victory. Amnesty was of great importance to members of the apartheid government, and to ANC members who committed crimes. In fact, most of the applicants for amnesty were individuals who claimed association or membership of the Pan African Congress, the Azanian People's Liberation Army, or the ANC (Foster, et al., 2017).

TRC recommendations were not binding

The TRC was mandated to compile 'a report providing as comprehensive an account as possible of the activities and findings of the commission [...] which contains recommendations of measures to prevent the future violations of human rights' (Parliament of the Republic of South Africa, 1995). The commissioners produced a final report of more than 3,500 pages in seven volumes, published in 2003, which included, among other things, recommendations for redressing past injustices and promoting future justice.

These recommendations, which were supposedly aimed at structural changes, were undermined by the Government's relative inaction in responding to the findings. In fact, the Government's reluctance to follow up on the recommendations, such as lack of prosecution of perpetrators, compensation of victims, and absence of different forms of restitution, is one of the biggest sources of critiques to the process (Govender & Hofmeyr, 2015; Buchanan-Clarke, 2015). Changes implemented by different state bodies following the advice from the TRC would have had a greater impact than the commission itself (Boshomane, 2016), and would have dealt with structural issues such as the widespread inequality that exists in the country (Leibbrandt, et al., 2007).

The South African TRC was only able to make recommendations regarding reparations and had limited resources to assist victims (Sensabaugh & Van der Merwe, 2017). Amongst the main suggestions made to political leaders were: (i) the creation of a reparations fund through corporate contributions, (ii) the restructuring of the foreign debt the apartheid regime incurred to maintain the police state, and (iii) the collection of a one-off tax on the patrimony, from the white population (Truth and Reconciliation Commission of South Africa, 2003).

In April 2003, the South African Government announced its response to these recommendations, which included a small payment to the victims recognized by the TRC[4] and the provision of facilities to those who wanted to make voluntary contributions to the reparations fund (Valji, 2004).

The capacity of the Colombian state to act on the findings and recommendations of its truth commission, the Comisión para el Esclarecimiento de la Verdad, la Convivencia y la no Repetición (CEV),[5] will be critical. Such a commission may call for the establishment of programmes and the implementation of changes that will probably transcend the term of a single government, making reconciliation a state agenda. It is thus imperative to avoid the politicization of truth commissions and ensure that they and their subsequent recommendations form a social commitment that transcends political patronage (Buchanan-Clarke, 2015).

Failure in the implementation of restitution initiatives

Another challenge emerged with regards to the capacity of existing institutions and courts to implement policies the state had created in the post-apartheid period. Land restitution for apartheid's victims is an illustrative example.

Policies implemented by the apartheid governments from the 1950s up to the early 1990s resulted in the fact that 80% of the population lived on 13% of the land (Du Plessis, 2004). This inequality was the consequence of the forced relocation policy implemented during the apartheid regime (Cole, 1993).

The restitution of land by the South African Government has not been as successful as had been intended. After the white minority rule ended, it was a difficult task for the new regime to redistribute the land fairly and efficiently. When apartheid ended, the Government aimed to redistribute 30% of the land from whites to blacks in the first five years of the new government (by 1999); by 2010, only 8% of that 30% had been reallocated (Atuahene & Brophy, 2015).

This is an important warning for Colombia, taking into account that more than 10% of its total population has been forcibly displaced (Díaz & Quiñones,

2015). The Colombian Government has tried to implement land restitution policies before the peace agreement with the FARC—EP[6] (Agencia Presidencial para la Acción Social y la Cooperación Internacional, 2011). The problems that have emerged in this matter are related to the mismatch between the law and the capacity to implement policies by the state, specifically in terms of service delivery (Díaz & Quiñones, 2015).

Economic reconciliation

As the TRC focused on developing a national political reconciliation process, not enough attention was given to the underlying structural socioeconomic conditions created by centuries of institutionalized inequality, colonialism, and racism. The political reconciliation process was not translated into economic redress and restitution (Buchanan-Clarke, 2015).

The historical legacies of apartheid still reinforce old patterns of socialization and prejudice, which have had an impact on inclusive development and growth (Govender & Hofmeyr, 2015). Thus, the current levels of inequality, and high levels of poverty amongst the black population within the country, are in fact connected to the lack of economic reconciliation (Asaf, et al., 2009).

The IJR in South Africa has researched and analyzed public opinion towards national reconciliation, social cohesion, transformation, and democratic governance in South Africa, mainly through the South African Reconciliation Barometer (SARB).[7] They have identified how, for South Africans, income inequality is the main source of social division within the country, and argue that it is impossible to achieve a reconciled society as long as those discriminated under apartheid remain poor (Valji, 2004). In fact, according to the IJR research, over time South Africans have shifted their perception of reconciliation, transcending the forgiveness spectrum to link reconciliation with higher socioeconomic equity (Wielenga, 2017).

Thus although the country 'may have avoided civil war during the transition to democracy two decades ago, this does not mean the country's majority is content with their situation' (Atuahene & Brophy, 2015). Nowadays, the achievements of the South African transition and reconciliation process are hindered by the economic legacy of apartheid and the lack of structural changes in society.

Economic inequality and levels of dissatisfaction related to structural and socioeconomic factors are also salient in Colombia, as the country has a high Gini coefficient (Departamento Administrativo Nacional de Estadística, 2017). Colombia's patterns of violence have been shaped and have shaped stark inequalities. In Colombia, in a similar fashion to South Africa, the use of violence was instrumental for securing economic gains. The legacy of this is entrenched inequalities.

The economic scope of reconciliation will also be important in the case of Colombia for the sustainability of the overall peace process (National Aboriginal

Economic Development Board, 2016). Unchanging inequalities potentially deepen social conflict, affect reconciliation, and present the seeds of future conflicts.

From the good we learn even more

The South African transitional justice process also provides a series of practices and experiences with regards to conflict resolution and reconciliation that provide valuable lessons to consider. Its successes are of key importance for any country beginning a transition, either political or from conflict to peace. While a number of positive aspects can be identified from the South African experience, there are three of special interest to bear in mind for Colombia. These include the construction of historical memory, the achievement of a socio-political reconciliation, and the importance of leadership for reconciliation.

Construction of historical memory

The construction of historical memory is important not only as a reparation and healing mechanism, but also as part of a nation-building project. It implies more than just recording atrocities and facts of the past (Ross, 2006), and includes the creation of a version of the truth about what happened (Gibson, 2005).

Even though it is argued that the truth delivered by the TRC was unbalanced or biased (Sensabaugh & Van der Merwe, 2017), this process offered South Africans, as part of a community, the opportunity to reflect on the past through storytelling, memorialization, and the inclusion of a local perspective. These processes formed the basis for reconciliation, through allowing individual narratives to gain significance and incorporating them into a more general discourse, as well as facilitating discussions and allowing an increased awareness, debate and reflection on the atrocities committed during apartheid (Foster, et al., 2017). Given that the TRC received approximately 22,000 statements from victims and witnesses (Bacler, 2005), the creation of spaces for reconciliation and reflection can constitute a cathartic space for a country.

Although they did not manage to involve all the voices or the narratives, some of the outputs of the TRC, such as the final report and a series of memorials, became a reference point for the events that occurred during the apartheid years (Briceño & Guzmán, 2015). By recording testimonies, the TRC report allowed people to refer to and reflect on the extent of the viciousness of this period. On the other hand, national legacy projects, such as memorialization events and the construction of monuments and memorials, were of key importance in the transformation agenda (Department of Arts & Culture of the Republic of South Africa, 2017).

Socio-political reconciliation

Reconciliation is a complex process that encompasses different domains and requires 'continuous dialogue to better comprehend and address the sources of division that threaten peaceful coexistence' (Du Toit, et al., 2015, p. xii). In this sense, reconciliation processes require a state and a society committed to addressing the structural causes of conflicts, and should be aimed at reconstructing destroyed social structures. These processes do not end with the truth commissions or other transitional justice initiatives (Du Toit, et al., 2015).

For most South Africans, the term reconciliation meant forgiveness of perpetrators, a reduction in violence, a general commitment to peace, and the establishment of the truth about the past. However, it cannot be doubted that the South African society was able to achieve a particular understanding of reconciliation that allowed the emergence of a new politics and the participation of formally marginalized South African in everyday politics (Delgado, 2016). As the 2015 SARB, illustrated, 59.2% of the respondents believed that the country had made progress towards national reconciliation since the end of apartheid. In addition, 69.7% of the respondents believed that the country had to continue to pursue reconciliation as a national objective (Govender & Hofmeyr, 2015).

Despite the fact that the economic consequences of the apartheid regime still loom over South Africa and its future, the country has come a long way towards socio-political reconciliation. The rehumanization of victims and perpetrators alike, the unification of the population around a common national objective, the consolidation of new national symbols, and the creation of a new social covenant are achievements that cannot be denied (Delgado, 2016).

Colombia has significant wounds that will require healing, something that will only be possible with the active participation of the whole society. As in South Africa, there is a need to construct a state of affairs in which the whole population, including perpetrators and victims, can coexist.

Role of leadership

One of the most important lessons that the South African case offers is the role of leadership, demonstrated by figures like Nelson Mandela, Archbishop Desmond Tutu, and Frederik Willem (F. W.) de Klerk. Political will and leadership can define transitions and promote successful spaces for reconciliation and justice (Rognvik & Sánchez, 2012). Without it, South Africa's process could have failed, considering the strong political and social divisions that defined the transition away from apartheid. Leadership does not replace justice, or the structural transformation and reconstruction of social relationships, but it can guide the country in a path where the conditions for justice are possible.

Mandela rejected the exclusion of different groups and dismissed the possibility of revenge. Although in doing so, he placed reconciliation above justice, he nonetheless empowered a unifying vision of the country (Mandela, 1990), that allowed the country to move away from apartheid. This in fact constituted an exercise in nation-building, that 'encourage[d] the blacks and the whites to collaborate because South Africa belonged to them all' (Maanga, 2013, p. 98).

In addition, Mandela's leadership gave unconditional support to the work done by the TRC, affording it the political capital to look for a reconciliation process that was initially seen as valid for the population. This was of great importance, since a truth commission without legitimacy cannot effectively achieve its objectives (Gibson, 2009).

On the other hand, Archbishop Desmond Tutu's role in the TRC as its chairperson was of considerable significance. He firmly believed that South Africa should have a collective catharsis process during the TRC years of work. His leadership was critical on giving the TRC its restorative character (Gibson, 2009).

Finally, F. W. de Klerk was responsible for presiding over the South African transition, representing the minority that had installed apartheid. On 2 February 1990, in his inauguration speech as President, he announced several important reforms to end the apartheid regime and recognized that 'only a negotiated understanding among the representative leaders of the entire population [was] able to ensure lasting peace' (De Klerk, 1990). Without his leadership, there would have been no transition, as he mobilized a sector within the white population to end the regime. This leadership was reasserted in the country's whites-only referendum, where the majority voters (white) agreed on ending the apartheid system and approved the negotiations to end the conflict (South African History Online (SAHO), 1992).

These lessons from South Africa should be kept in mind, especially in processes such as that being pursued in Colombia. The South African transition was led by strong and charismatic political figures that facilitated peace, whereby South Africans came to recognize that more violence would not be the solution. As some political parties and political leaders argue for the rejection of the Colombian peace agreements, the contrast of the South African leadership seems to prove the value of leadership for peace. Although leadership does not replace implementation and institutions, leadership facilitates peace and can mobilize the state towards these goals.

Conclusions

Although the South African experience is regarded as a successful transitional justice model, evidence shows that there were many shortcomings. For South Africa, it has been argued that the absolution of—and absence of legal proceedings against—perpetrators of crimes that contributed to the dehumanization of society, has promoted a culture of impunity and frustration, especially from the victims' perspective. In this aspect, the agreement between the FARC—EP and the Colombian Government aims to address this issue by granting amnesty only for politically-related crimes and not for crimes against humanity. By doing this, the objective is to avoid a general perception of impunity amongst the population and truly contribute to national reconciliation.

Honouring the recommendations delivered by the transitional justice mechanisms such as the TRC is another aspect that should not be overlooked in transition scenarios. After acknowledging the facts that led to a violent context, hearing the victims' and perpetrators' voices and experiences, and promoting forgiveness and coexistence, the transitional justice spaces should inform the state about the necessary steps to guarantee a successful reconciliation in the forthcoming years. Although the CEV will be responsible for providing these recommendations to the Colombian Government, the possibility of structural change transcends reports, and will depend on the government's ability and willingness to implement what is suggested by the CEV in order to enact structural change.

Transitional contexts also demand successful restitution initiatives and proper economic transformation. The incorporation of structural changes that aim to reduce inequalities—not only in terms of income but also, for example, in terms of land ownership—is of outstanding importance in order to facilitate meaningful reconciliation. Allowing past economic legacies caused by violence to prevail might translate into future social conflicts, such as the ones that are currently emerging in South Africa.

The implementation of transitional justice tools should not be considered as the ultimate solution to a conflict. Even though the TRC provided the most important elements towards reconciliation and coexistence, additional initiatives were (and are still) necessary in order to overcome the challenges that have arisen after its implementation. These include significant inequality, poverty and unemployment rates, which create a sense of frustration and discontent in the population.

During a nation-building and social reconstruction project, historical memory is of key importance for the future common understanding on what happened in the past. The construction—not imposition—of truths and memories is an opportunity for a society to redefine its identity, rebuild social bonds, and reconcile. Colombia must avoid a mandated memory or selective amnesia, through encouraging everyone—including members of the FARC—EP—to participate in this process.

The challenge of reconciliation remains for both Colombia and South Africa at different levels. In Colombia, political leadership is required to encourage the participation of the entire population in the construction of a new country. This represents an opportunity for Colombians to be part of the project of shaping a new, peaceful country. South Africa, on the other hand, must continue to address the new challenges that are emerging, such as the importance of equality and opportunities for all South Africans beyond the structural conditions that have defined a legacy of inequality and marginalization.

Leadership, planning and political willingness to overcome the old practices of corruption and *caudillismo* [8] are required in Colombia. Colombian leaders must understand that a country cannot be brought together by decree.

Nobel Prizes can be won, but if the idea of peace is currently meaningless to significant sectors of the population, peace itself is at risk. The Colombian leadership must embrace the task of promoting the idea of reconciliation.

The understanding of reconciliation must be integral, including the social, political and economic spheres. Focusing only on one or two spheres may lead to the emergence of future problems that can considerably undermine the current efforts to achieve peace. Consequently, the approach should not only include forgiveness, coexistence, political inclusion, and rehumanization, but also it must address other structural causes of conflict through reparations and assistance.

After 50 years of conflict, it is time for Colombian society to achieve peace. During the years to come this will be an interesting and instructive process to study and assess, which will provide additional insights on transitional societies and transitional justice. Meanwhile, the South African experience will undoubtedly continue guiding the way in many aspects and, most importantly, will point out the shortcomings, setbacks, and limitations of peacebuilding initiatives in the Global South.

Notes

1 Revolutionary Armed Forces of Colombia—People's Army.
2 Act No 34 of 1995.
3 This institute was founded in 2000 and its objective was to follow up on the TRC work. It aims to ensure that lessons learnt from South Africa's transition were taken into account nationwide and in other countries.
4 Victims of human rights violations received a small, one-off compensation payment of 30,000 rand (about one-quarter of what the TRC recommended) (Sensabaugh & Van der Merwe, 2017, p. 37).
5 Commission for the Clarification of Truth, Coexistence and Non-Repetition
6 Law 1448 from 10 July 2011.
7 It is a survey that has been implemented annually in South Africa since 2003, which measures perceptions regarding progress in reconciliation in the country over time.
8 Caudillo translates to English as leader. Caudillismo refers to a political system, based on the leadership of a strongman or a charismatic figure.

References

Abel, M., 2016. Long-run effects of forced resettlement: evidence from Apartheid South Africa. *Harvard University*, pp. 1–36.

Affa'a-Mindzie, M., 2015. A Comparative Study of Transitional Justice: Learning from the Experiences of African Countries. In B.-S. Baek & R. G. Teitel, eds. *Transitional Justice in Unified Korea*. New York: Palgrave Macmillan, pp. 175–194.

Agencia Presidencial para la Acción Social y la Cooperación Internacional, 2011. *Ley de Víctimas y Restitución de Tierras*. [Online] Available at: www.centrodememoria historica.gov.co/descargas/ley_victimas/ley_victimas_completa_web.pdf [Last accessed 25 July 2017].

Armstrong, J., 2014. Rethinking the restorative-retributive dichotomy: is reconciliation possible? *Contemporary Justice Review*, 14(3), pp. 362–374.

Aronson, J. D., 2011. *The Strengths and Limitations of South Africa's Search for Apartheid-Era Missing Persons.* [Online] Available at: www.ncbi.nlm.nih.gov/pmc/articles/PMC3185365/ [Last accessed 13 July 2017].
Asaf, Z., Cato, N., Jawoko, K. & Rosevear, E., 2009. *Addressing Inequality in Post-Apartheid South Africa.* Toronto: University of Toronto.
Atuahene, B., Brophy, A. L., 2015. *In South Africa, Land Apartheid Lives On.* [Online] Available at: www.nytimes.com/2015/01/16/opinion/south-africas-land-inequity.html?_r=0 [Last accessed 25 February 2017].
Bacler, D., 2005. *Evaluating Transitional Justice in South Africa from a Victim's Perspective.* [Online] Available at: https://quod.lib.umich.edu/j/jii/4750978.0012.207/–evaluating-transitional-justice-in-south-africa?rgn=main;view=fulltext [Last accessed 25 July 2017].
Barnes, C. & De Klerk, E., 2002. South Africa's multi-party constitutional negotiation process. *Accord*, Issue 13, pp. 26–33.
Boddy-Evans, A., 2017. *The Afrikaans Medium Decree.* [Online] Available at: www.thoughtco.com/the-afrikaans-medium-decree-43416 [Last accessed 07 July 2017].
Boshomane, P., 2016. *20 years after the TRC hearings South Africa's pain persists.* [Online] Available at: www.timeslive.co.za/sundaytimes/opinion/2016/04/10/20-years-after-the-TRC-hearings-South-Africas-pain-persists [Last accessed 28 December 2016].
Briceño, D. & Guzmán, J., 2015. Memoria histórica para el posconflicto en Colombia. In A. Molano Rojas, ed. *El Posconflicto en Colombia: reflexiones y propuestas para recorrer la transición.* Bogotá: Instituto de Ciencia Política Hernán Echavarría Olózaga/Fundación Konrad Adenauer Colombia, pp. 95–106.
Buarque de Hollanda, C., 2013. Human rights and political transition in South Africa: the case of the Truth and Reconciliation Commission. *Brazilian Political Science Review*, 7(1), pp. 8–30.
Buchanan-Clarke, S., 2015. *Colombia and the search for truth in Latin America's longest running conflict: lessons from the South African experience.* [Online] Available at: http://africasacountry.com/2015/07/colombia-and-the-search-for-truth-in-latin-americas-longest-running-conflict-lessons-from-the-south-african-experience/ [Last accessed 28 December 2016].
Christie, P. & Collins, C., 1982. Bantu Education: Apartheid Ideology or Labour Reproduction? *Comparative Education*, 18(1), pp. 59–75.
Cole, C. M., 1993. Land Reform from Post-Apartheid South Africa. *Boston College Environmental Affairs Law Review*, 20(4), pp. 699–759.
Cole, C. M., 2007. Performance, Transitional Justice, and the Law: South Africa's Truth and Reconciliation Commission. *Theatre Journal*, 59(2), pp. 167–187.
De Klerk, E., 2002. South Africa's negotiated transition: Context, analysis and evaluation. *Accord*, Issue 12, pp. 14–19.
De Klerk, F., 1990. *F. W. de Klerk's speech at the opening of Parliament 2 February 1990.* [Online] Available at: www.nelsonmandela.org/omalley/index.php/site/q/03lv02039/04lv02103/05lv02104/06lv02105.htm [Last accessed 15 July 2017].
Delgado, J., 2016. *A Colombia le falta un Mandela.* [Online] Available at: http://pacifista.co/a-colombia-le-falta-un-mandela/ [Last accessed 13 January 2017].
Departamento Administrativo Nacional de Estadística, 2017. *Pobreza Monetaria y Multidimensional en Colombia 2016.* [Online] Available at: www.dane.gov.co/index.php/estadisticas-por-tema/pobreza-y-condiciones-de-vida/pobreza-y-desigualdad/pobreza-monetaria-y-multidimensional-en-colombia-2016 [Last accessed 15 July 2017].

Department of Arts & Culture of the Republic of South Africa, 2017. *Statement by the Department of Arts and Culture on National Legacy Projects*. [Online] Available at: www.dac.gov.za/content/statement-department-arts-and-culture-national-legacy-projects [Last accessed 25 July 2017].

DeRouen, K. J. et al., 2010. Civil war peace agreement implementation and state capacity. *Journal of Peace Research*, 47(3), pp. 333–346.

Díaz, F. A. & Quiñones, F., 2015. *The use of managerial tools to support policymaking in a peace process: the case of displaced population in Colombia*. [Online] Available at: www.researchgate.net/publication/277016019_the_use_of_managerial_tools_to_support_the_policymaking_in_a_peace_process_the_case_of_displaced_population_in_colombia [Last accessed 15 July 2017].

Du Plessis, J., 2004. *Land restitution in South Africa*, Bethlehem: BADIL Resource Center.

Du Toit, A., Nyoka, A. & Woolard, I., 2015. *Radical Reconciliation: critical choices for economic justice*, Cape Town: Institute for Justice and Reconciliation.

Duthie, R. & Siels, P., 2017. *Justice Mosaics. How context shapes Transitional Justice in fractured societies*. 1st ed. New York: International Center for Transitional Justice.

Foster, D., Govender, R. & Lefko-Everett, K., 2017. Measuring Social Change in South Africa. In D. Foster, R. Govender & K. Lefko-Everett, eds. *Rethinking reconciliation. Evidence from South Africa*. Braamfontein: HSRC Press, pp. 3–22.

Gibson, J. L., 2005. The Truth About Truth and Reconciliation in South Africa. *International Political Science Review/ Revue internationale de science politique*, 26(4), pp. 341–361.

Gibson, J. L., 2009. On legitimacy theory and the effectiveness of truth commissions. *Law and Contemporary Probelms*, 72(123), pp. 123–141.

Govender, R. & Hofmeyr, J., 2015. *National Reconciliation, Race Relations and Social Inclusion*, Cape Town: Institute for Justice and Reconciliation.

Gutiérrez Ramírez, L. M., 2014. La obligación internacional de investigar, juzgar y sancionar graves violaciones a los derechos humanos en contextos de justicia transicional. *Estudios Socio-Jurídicos*, 2(16), pp. 23–60.

Hamber, B., 2013. *Rights and Reasons: Challenges for Truth Recovery in South Africa and Northern Ireland*. [Online] Available at: http://humanrights.uconn.edu/wp-content/uploads/sites/767/2014/06/RightsReasonsCambridge.pdf [Last accessed 21 July 2017].

Henrard, K., 2003. Post-Apartheid South Africa: Transformation and Reconciliation. *World Affairs*, 166(1), pp. 37–55.

Howse, R. & Llewellyn, J. J., 1999. Institutions for Restorative Justice: The South African Truth and Reconciliation Commission. *The University of Toronto Law Journal*, 49(3), pp. 355–388.

Ladduwahetty, N., 2011. *The forthcoming UNHRC meeting and Darusman Report*. [Online] Available at: www.island.lk/index.php?page_cat=article-details&page=article-details&code_title=32997 [Last accessed 10 July 2017].

Landis, E., 1957. Apartheid Legislation. *Africa Today*, 4(6), pp. 45–48.

Leibbrandt, M., Woolard, C. & Woolard, I., 2007. *Poverty and Inequality Dynamics in South Africa: Post-apartheid Developments in the Light of the Long-Run Legacy*. Cape Town: Southern Africa Labour & Development Research Unit, University of Cape Town.

Maanga, G. S., 2013. The relevance and legacy of Nelson Mandela in the twenty-first century Africa: An historical and theological perspective. *African Journal of History and Culture*, pp. 96–113.

Maharaj, M., 2008. *The ANC and the South Africa's negotiated transition to democracy and peace*. Berlin: Berghof Research Center for Constructive Conflict Management.

Mandela, N., 1990. *Speech. Address by Nelson Mandela, Deputy President of the African National Congress (ANC), at the 26th Assembly of Organisation for African Unity (OAU) Heads of State and Government*. [Online] Available at: www.mandela.gov.za/mandela_speeches/1990/900709_oau.htm [Last accessed 15 July 2017].

Massey, R., 2013. Competing rationalities and informal settlement upgrading in Cape Town, South Africa: a recipe for failure. *Journal of Housing and the Built Environment*, 28(4), pp. 605–613.

Mawhinney, E. B., 2015. Restoring Justice: Lessons from Truth and Reconciliation in South Africa and Rwanda. *Journal of Public Law and Policy*, 36(2), pp. 21–52.

McLeod, L., 2015. *Reconciliation through Restorative Justice: Analyzing South Africa's Truth and Reconciliation Process*. [Online] Available at: www.beyondintractability.org/library/reconciliation-through-restorative-justice-analyzing-south-africas-truth-and-reconciliation [Last accessed 27 December 2016].

Mokgatle, T., 2016. *20 years after the TRC: Are we any the better?* [Online] Available at: https://africlaw.com/2016/08/18/20-years-after-the-trc-are-we-any-the-better/#more-1211 [Last accessed 28 December 2016].

National Aboriginal Economic Development Board, 2016. *Without equal economic opportunities, there can be no reconciliation with Indigenous Canadians*. [Online] Available at: www.naedb-cndea.com/without-equal-economic-opportunities-no-reconciliation/ [Last accessed 25 July 2017].

Parliament of the Republic of South Africa, 1995. *Promotion of National Unity and Reconciliation Act 34 of 1995*. [Online] Available at: www.justice.gov.za/legislation/acts/1995-034.pdf [Last accessed 16 August 2017].

Ratuva, S., 2013. 'Black empowerment' policies: Dilemmas of affirmative action in South Africa. In *Politics of preferential development*. s.l.: ANU Press, pp. 219–240.

Rognvik, S. & Sánchez, E., 2012. *Building Just Societies: Reconciliation in Transitional Settings*. New York: United Nations.

Ross, F., 2006. La elaboración de una Memoria Nacional: la Comisión de Verdad y Reconciliación de Sudáfrica. *Cuadernos de Antropología Social*, Volume 24, pp. 51–68.

Saffon, M. P. & Uprimny, R., 2005. Capítulo 7: Justicia Transicional y Justicia Restaurativa: Tensiones y complementariedades. In *Entre El Perdón Y El Paredón*. Ottawa: International Development Research Centre, pp. 211–232.

Schabas, W., 2011. *Transitional Justice and the Norms of International Law*. [Online] Available at: www.jsil.jp/annual_documents/2011/fall/schabas_trans_just911.pdf [Last accessed 17 July 2017].

Sensabaugh, K. & Van der Merwe, H., 2017. Truth, redress and reconciliation: Evaluating transitional justice from below. In K. Lefko-Everett, R. Govender & D. Foster, eds. *Rethinking reconciliation. Evidence from South Africa*. Braamfontein: HSRC Press, pp. 25–44.

South African History Online (SAHO), 1992. *President F. W. de Klerk announces Whites-only referendum results*. [Online] Available at: www.sahistory.org.za/dated-event/president-fw-de-klerk-announces-whites-only-referendum-results [Last accessed 15 July 2017].

Traniello, M., 2002. Power-sharing: lessons from South Africa and Rwanda. *International Public Policy Review*, 3(2), pp. 28–43.

Truth and Reconciliation Commission of South Africa, 2003. *Final Report*, s.l.: s.n.

Valji, N., 2004. Reconciliación y reparación: un balance. *Vanguardia Dossier*, Issue 12.

Van der Merwe, H., 2003. The Role of the Church in Promoting Reconciliation in Post-TRC South Africa. *Religion and Reconciliation in South Africa*, pp. 269–281.

Villa-Vicencio, C. & Verwoerd, W., 2000. *Looking back, reaching forward*. 1st edn. Cape Town: University of Cape Town Press.

Wenzel, M., Okimoto, T. G., Feather, N. T. & Platow, M. J., 2008. Retributive and restorative justice. *Law and human behavior*, 32(5), pp. 375–389.

Wielenga, C., 2017. A comparison of the reconciliation barometers in South Africa and Rwanda. In K. Lefko-Everett, R. Govender & D. Foster, eds. *Rethinking reconciliation. Evidence from South Africa*. Braamfontein: HSRC Press, pp. 45–61.

Zartman, W., 2001. The Timing of Peace Initiatives: Hurting Stalemates and Ripe Moments. *The Global Review of Ethnopolitics*, 1(1), pp. 8–18.

13 Transitional Justice in Peru
Lessons for Colombia

Jemima García-Godos[1]

Introduction

While the rest of Latin America experienced a 'pink tide' of centre-left politics sweeping across the region from the mid-2000s, Peru and Colombia stood out as the odd cases where this did not happen (Bull, 2014; Yates & Bakker, 2014). Indeed, governments with clear right-wing, or centre-right, orientations have ruled both countries over the past 20 years (1996–2016), some of them even sharing more than a few authoritarian traits in their leadership styles (for example, Alberto Fujimori in Peru and Álvaro Uribe in Colombia, albeit with different approaches to formal democracy). Both countries have experienced internal armed conflict and guerrilla war, waged by leftist guerrillas. However, the scope of the violence experienced in Colombia surpasses that of Peru in terms of the duration of the conflict, the number of victims and actors involved, and most notably, the massive internal displacement and land dispossession characterizing the Colombian armed conflict (see Chapter 6). The countries also have large rural populations, and the profile of the victims is also similar: rural, poor, black or indigenous origin. Yet, in spite of contextual similarities, there are also some significant differences concerning the way the two countries have chosen to deal with human rights violations of the past. Peru underwent two transitions: a transition starting in 1992, following internal armed conflict, and a political transition away from an authoritarian regime in 2000. The achievements recorded by Colombia in terms of applying transitional justice mechanisms, both prior to and after the signing of the peace agreement between the government and the Fuerzas Armadas Revolucionarias de Colombia—Ejército del Pueblo (FARC—EP) guerrillas (see Chapter 3), put the Peruvian experience in perspective, and vice versa.

In this chapter, I aim to explore the Peruvian experience in implementing transitional justice since 2000, adopting a lessons-learned approach in order to highlight those aspects most relevant for the transitional justice mechanisms designed by the Colombian Government. The focus is on the work of the truth commission, the challenges of retributive justice, and the implementation of victim reparation programmes in Peru. I start by discussing the main features of the Peruvian case[2] and conclude the chapter with a discussion of its implications and lessons for the Colombian case.

Characterizing the Peruvian case

The Peruvian transition is characterized as a dual transition: a transition from armed conflict to a post-conflict phase in the mid-1990s, and a political transition from an authoritarian, although formally democratic, regime that could be described as an illiberal democracy (Zakaria, 1997) to a democracy. The end of the armed conflict in Peru is commonly associated with the capture of Abimael Guzmán, the leader of the Maoist Communist Party faction Shining Path (Sendero Luminoso) in September 1992, after 12 years of violence. With Guzmán's capture and trial, the Peruvian state declared both military and political victory over Shining Path, a victory that remains unchallenged in Peruvian society and history and that gave Fujimori (the president at the time) ample political support and popularity. Between 1992 and 2000, however, the Peruvian state and armed forces continued their counter-subversive activity against both real and alleged *senderistas*[3] (Burt, 2006; Burt, 2007). The political transition took place following the collapse of President Fujimori's regime in 2000, while initiating a contested third term in power. The leaking of the infamous 'Vladivideos' showing the presidential advisor and head of the intelligence service Vladimiro Montesinos paying off top leaders of the judiciary, media, and private sector revealed the authoritarian nature of the Fujimori regime.

A second observation concerns the lack of familiarity of the Peruvian society with the term 'transitional justice' and what it entails—in spite of the passage of time and some implementation. The term is seldom used beyond the realm of human rights organizations, not even among victims' organizations. This is at least partly due to the fact that accountability issues and transitional arrangements were never framed in terms of a transitional justice paradigm or framework, in sharp contrast with the Colombian experience. This is even the case after the delivery of the truth commission report, which did address victims' rights. The absence of such a framework limits coherence and a holistic approach to accountability for past human rights violations, although it did not necessarily imply the absence of specific implementation. Thus it is possible to trace the development and implementation of transitional justice mechanisms, including a truth commission, prosecutions, and victim reparations, in Peru since 2001.

In addition, it is important to reflect on the political structures in place and the strength (or weakness) of the judiciary in the country as contextual factors that defined the transitional justice that took place in Peru and the challenges it met. Until recently, the Peruvian political process has been characterized by the near-absence of political parties. This was not always the case, but the economic crisis of the 1980s, combined with the crude violence of the internal armed conflict, resulted in the effective dismantling of the political party system (Tanaka, 1998). State repression weakened labour unions and social movements, suspected of being infiltrated by the guerrillas. As a result, an already fragile system of political representation and interest mediation crumbled. The weakness of political parties and the vulnerability of social movements in the late 1980s left the political scene to be occupied by independent candidates such as Fujimori, who had no previous political experience or party affiliation.

Fujimori rose to the presidency in the 1990s and put an end to the economic crisis with a series of neoliberal market-friendly policies, amid huge social costs. However, his rise to power did not do much to address the crisis of representation or reconstitute the political arena. On the contrary, on 5 April 1992, Fujimori closed the Congress as part of a 'self-coup', allegedly to secure the governability of the country and re-establish the constitutional order by calling for a new constitutional assembly. By 1993 Peru not only had a new constitution, but a reordered political system where the legislative and judiciary were subjected to the interference of the executive, setting the ground for the establishment of an authoritarian regime (Burt, 2007).

Currently, there is a competitive electoral system in Peru, yet congressional representatives still have few incentives to establish constituencies based on collective agendas rather than on individual political ambitions. The latent weakness of a political system characterized by volatile electoral lists rather than solid political parties also affects the relationship between the executive, legislative, and judicial branches of power, as well as the possibility for civil society to influence the political agenda through mechanisms of political representation. Although this threat was most critical during the Fujimori regime, the Peruvian judicial system remains permeable to political influence at all levels.

The weakness of the political and judicial systems is important for the particular case of human rights trials, as advances made by some court decisions are not guaranteed to set jurisprudence. This weakness also reflects the limited political influence held by the Peruvian human rights sector. Advocacy campaigns of victims' organizations typically deal with events that took place a long time ago in remote areas of the country. Their cases are conducted with limited resources, far from the political decision-making scene, and have had limited success in mobilizing popular and political support for accountability issues and in influencing the political agenda. Victims' organizations largely reflect the overall profile of victims of the Peruvian armed conflict in Peru: poor, peasant, indigenous citizens, from rural areas, living at the fringes of the state (García-Godos, 2013).

The Peruvian Truth and Reconciliation Commission

The Peruvian Truth and Reconciliation Commission (Comisión de la Verdad y Reconciliación —CVR) was established in 2001 by the transitional government of President Valentín Paniagua (November 2000—July 2001)[4] and endorsed later by elected President Alejandro Toledo in 2003. The creation of the CVR was not the result of massive popular demand; rather, it reflected the strength gained by the human rights sector at the time the political transition took place. At the broader political level, the transition became a window of opportunity for the political establishment to reconstitute itself and move towards more inclusive and democratic practices. The transitional government was receptive to the issues and demands raised by civil society and non-governmental organizations (NGOs) voicing the demands of victims' groups. The overall idea of the CVR was to initiate a process of accountability for human rights violations committed not only during the armed conflict, but also by the authoritarian Fujimori regime. The period to be investigated was 1980–2000, focusing on violations both by guerrilla groups (Shining Path and the Revolutionary Movement Tupac Amaru—MRTA) and by state agents.

The CVR was composed of 12 commissioners, all of whom were well respected public figures. They included members of academia, the human rights community, the Catholic and Evangelical Churches, and a representative from the military. However, the inclusion of a few commissioners from the left of the political spectrum provoked unnecessary mistrust in the work of the commission, particularly from the political establishment and the armed forces. The CVR's mandate was broad: to investigate the crimes and human rights violations committed in the context of violence by both guerrilla groups[5] as well as state agents, to produce an explanation of the factors that led to violence, to contribute to justice, and to make recommendations for reparations and for institutional reform. The commission had formal authorization to interview victims and others, request information from institutions, and organize public hearings, but could not initiate judicial cases. The CVR was provided with financial and technical resources to carry out its work for an initial period of two years; this was extended to 26 months.

During its time of operations, the CVR effectively collected 17,000 testimonies from victims and organized 12 public hearings with victims in different regions. It investigated a number of cases in an effort to identify perpetrators, demonstrated that the armed actors had committed crimes against humanity, and proposed a legal framework for prosecution of human rights violations. The commission identified 24,000 full names of victims, made a list of 8,000 disappeared persons, and identified the existence of 4,644 burial sites, having collected preliminary evidence in 2,200 of them (Comisión de la Verdad y Reconciliación—CVR, 2003).

On 28 August 2003 the CVR delivered its final report, which included an in-depth account of the events and a well-documented analysis of the armed conflict in Peru, along with a detailed set of recommendations (Comisión de la Verdad y Reconciliación—CVR, 2003). The conclusions of the CVR's Final Report expressed the brutality and discriminatory nature of the conflict:

> Violence fell unequally on different geographical areas and on different social strata in the country. [...] The TRC has established that the tragedy suffered by the populations of rural Peru, the Andean and jungle regions,

Quechua and Ashaninka Peru, the peasant, poor and poorly educated Peru, was neither felt nor taken on as its own by the rest of the country. This reveals, in the TRC's judgment, the veiled racism and scornful attitudes that persist in Peruvian society almost two centuries after its birth as a Republic.[6]

Until the delivery of the CVR's Final Report, Peruvians had come to terms with the official figure of 25,000 fatal victims of the armed conflict. Yet the commission estimated that the total number of dead and disappeared persons exceeded 69,000. This is possibly the most significant finding of the CVR, as the gap between the official (and accepted) death toll and the death toll estimated by the CVR is illustrative and explained by Peruvian society's disregard for the rural peasant and indigenous population which constituted the majority of the victims. Another ground-breaking conclusion of the CVR was that the Shining Path guerrillas were the main perpetrators of violence in the Peruvian armed conflict, accounting for 54% of casualties.

The delivery of the CVR Final Report generated public controversy, particularly from the armed forces and some political parties, but it was generally well received—or at least passively accepted. The recommendations received great attention in political circles, and from human rights organizations and the media, as they addressed measures of retributive justice (including the creation of a specialized prosecutions system), a comprehensive plan of victim reparations (restorative justice), and institutional reform.

Fifteen years after the delivery of the CVR Final Report, there have been some advances in the recommendations concerning justice and reparations, yet institutional reforms have been completely neglected. Recent years have seen a trend toward hostile questioning of the CVR's findings in the public debate, indicating the existence of a struggle for memory in Peru. As observed in the public debate concerning the establishment of the national memory museum, the Lugar de la Memoria (LUM), inaugurated in 2015, the achievements of the Peruvian truth commission and the clarity and vision of its Final Report are yet to be embraced by all political actors. The lack of a broad constituency in support of the CVR findings is possibly the most serious challenge to the legitimacy of the CVR's account.

Criminal accountability after the political transition

The families and relatives of victims of human rights violations have sought justice since the beginning of the armed conflict in the early 1980s. The state of emergency imposed in most of the areas affected by the armed conflict was the main impediment to the independent work of the judiciary in support of victims during the conflict. Military command overran civilian authorities and as a result access to information, habeas corpus, and the right to due process were easy to set aside and ignore. Many cases could not proceed for lack of judicial evidence or simply because the military claimed legal jurisdiction over them—that is, it conducted investigations and cases in military courts. Most of the cases brought in this way were subsequently closed or, if processed, resulted in extremely lenient sentences for those found responsible. A situation of impunity was dominant long before it was institutionalized by the Amnesty Law of 1995,[7] closing all possibilities to pursue criminal prosecutions and accountability for human rights in courts in Peru: civil and military courts alike.

The transition to democracy in 2000 brought about a refreshing impetus concerning criminal accountability for past human rights violations in Peru. In 2001 the Amnesty Law was nullified by the Peruvian congress as a result of the Barrios Altos decision by the Inter-American Court of Human Rights. This decision established the incompatibility of amnesty legislation in Peru with the Inter-American Convention of Human Rights. Following an agreement with the Inter-American Court, Peru identified 159 emblematic cases to be processed and/or reopened to fulfil the effective right to due process.[8] 47 additional cases were presented to the Public Prosecutor's Office following the delivery of the Final Report of the CVR in 2003. The cases were to be monitored by the Peruvian Ombudsman's Office. However, based on data for 194 cases monitored by the Ombudsman's Office since 2001, the results are not very satisfactory.[9] By May 2013, only 32 of the cases had reached a verdict, while 77 had been dismissed (archived). Another 36 were in the preliminary investigation stage, and 32 were in other intermediate stages of the judicial process (Defensoría del Pueblo—Ombudsman, 2013). Of the 35 verdicts issued in the 32 completed cases, 20 were acquittals, 12 were condemnations, and three were mixed sentences (Defensoría del Pueblo—Ombudsman, 2013).

Among institutional changes that promoted criminal accountability in Peru after the transition were: the creation of specialized human rights prosecutorial system operational at national (2002) and regional levels (2003), a specialized chamber for human rights cases in 2004 (Sala Nacional Penal, initially also with regional jurisdictions), and a new criminal code in 2004.[10] The Constitutional Tribunal has also made substantial contributions to criminal accountability in Peru through a significant number of decisions regarding human rights violations, the right to due process, and the unconstitutionality of military jurisdiction for human rights cases and counter-subversive legislation. As a result, judicial processes against guerrilla members conducted by military courts (characterized by 'faceless judges'[11]) during the Fujimori regime were to be started anew after 2001.

A second moment of strength for criminal accountability in Peru occurred during the Fujimori trials, where former president Alberto Fujimori was sentenced to 25 years in prison for two cases of human rights violations on April 7 2009. The verdict marked the end of a 15-month judicial process about the events that took place in La Cantuta–Barrios Altos (1991) and Sótanos SIE (1992), leading to the killing of 25 people by a paramilitary organization called Grupo Colina (Burt, 2009). The prosecuting authorities identified Fujimori as directly responsible for the crimes, referring to a national security policy that allowed the creation of paramilitary groups in order 'to eradicate' guerrilla members. The legal process proved that Fujimori knew about the existence of Grupo Colina, endorsed its methods, and showed little or no willingness to stop its actions in spite of having the powers to do so. Fujimori was convicted as the main culprit responsible for the crimes committed within the framework of a national security policy that allowed systematic human rights violations (Salmón, 2014). Against a grim background of weak judicial independence, Fujimori's conviction was considered a test for the Peruvian judicial system, and has passed into history as the first time a former head of state has been prosecuted for human rights violations in and by his own country.

In spite of the advances made in the first years after the transition and the Fujimori trials in the late 2000s, the path towards criminal accountability for human rights violations in Peru has been uneven, and in some cases even reversed. Structural and institutional changes that weakened the specialized human rights system were accompanied by some serious setbacks concerning political interference in judicial processes during the presidency of Alan García (García-Godos & Reátegui, 2016). In 2005, the judiciary moved towards a centralized institutional design for human rights cases, which meant that all such cases in the provinces would be transferred to courts in Lima for the investigation and trial phases. The argument behind this was that it would improve the effectiveness and quality of investigations. However, the mandate of the specialized units focusing on human rights cases has been expanded since 2006, and now also includes cases of corruption and drug trafficking, illegal mining, money laundering, social unrest, and others (Defensoría del Pueblo—Ombudsman, 2013). Progress has obviously been limited. For the victims, the centralized justice system means that judicial processes take place far from where violations occurred and/or families actually live, in courts overwhelmed with other cases besides those dealing with human rights violations (see Chapter 15 for a similar account in Bosnia and Herzegovina). Additional challenges to accountability include the persistent resistance by the armed forces to providing information about the composition of units deployed during the armed conflict (Defensoría del Pueblo— Ombudsman, 2013); the limited mechanisms of legal support and protection for victims, witnesses and human rights advocates; and the reluctance of members of the Peruvian judicial system to consistently recognize and apply relevant national and regional jurisprudence.

The most serious setback for criminal accountability in Peru came, however, not from the judiciary but from the executive. Indeed, on December 24 2017 former Peruvian president Pedro Pablo Kuczynski granted a humanitarian pardon to the jailed former president Fujimori, on health grounds. Announced only two days after a failed process of presidential impeachment led by the opposition party Fuerza Popular, the pardon has been interpreted as the result of political bargaining and not due to humanitarian considerations. The pardon has been questioned nationally and internationally, producing protests across the country. Human rights organisations representing the victims of La Cantuta-Barrios Altos cases have appealed (once more) to the Inter-American Court of Human Rights, in an attempt to annul the pardon.

Victim reparations in Peru

In Peru the CVR introduced victim reparations as a mechanism of transitional justice, as its mandate included the design of proposals for 'moral and material redress for victims or their relatives' (Comisión de la Verdad y Reconciliación—CVR, 2003, p. 147). The CVR introduced the categories of 'victim of violation' and 'victim reparations' in order to address the needs of the citizens who had experienced human rights violations during the armed conflict and the authoritarian regimes in Peru. Previously the government spoke of 'people in areas affected by violence' or 'support to areas affected by violence'—not of 'victims' and 'reparations' (Garcia-Godos, 2008). Accordingly, the post-conflict reconstruction period of the mid-to-late 1990s involved increased state presence in the 'areas affected by violence' through investment, development projects, public services, employment opportunities, and security and law enforcement—all measures that were necessary for the people living in these areas during and after the end of the armed conflict. The different terminology used before and after the political transition is, however, not merely a matter of linguistic preference. The terms 'victim' and 'reparation' convey a different type of relation between the state and individual citizens, emphasizing that those whose rights have been violated are entitled to remedy offered by the state.

The CVR's Final Report included a comprehensive plan for victim reparations, which guided the reparations programme that was designed two years later. The law creating a national reparations programme (PIR—Programa Integral de Reparaciones) was approved in 2005[12] and regulated in 2006.[13] Interestingly, an administrative unit to design, implement, and monitor victim reparations in Peru was created in 2004, before the law was passed (Multi-Sectoral High Level Commission to follow-up the Truth Commission's Recommendations— CMAN[14]). The law created a National Victims Registry (Registro Único de Víctimas—RUV) to be monitored by a Reparations Council (Consejo de Reparaciones—CR). The CR had an important task to fulfil, involving not only the design and operation of the RUV, but also the development of criteria to determine whether or not a person or groups of people can be characterized as victims (accreditation), and thus be included in the victims' registry and access the benefits granted by the different reparations programmes. While the definitions of 'victim' and 'beneficiaries' in the law and the rules of procedure for the victims' registry are relatively inclusive and broad, including victims of the guerrilla groups and state agents alike, there is an important exclusion from the status of victim, precluding access to reparations: members of guerrilla groups. While military and police personnel as well as peasant patrols (rondas, or self-defence committees) can have the status of victims, the exclusion of guerrilla members (also present in the CVR's Final Report reparations proposal) points to the political character as well as the limits of transitional justice mechanisms in post-conflict societies (Laplante, 2009).

The PIR is a comprehensive reparations programme consisting of six distinct areas or programmes: health, education, housing, civil rights, symbolic reparations, collective reparations and economic compensation to prioritized groups. The Collective Reparations Program (PRC) was the first to be implemented, starting in 2007 on the basis of needs assessments of local communities affected by the armed conflict. The programme was co-ordinated by the CMAN and implemented at the local level by PIR regional offices. The collective reparations programme can be considered mainly as a mechanism of restorative justice. The programme involved financial support to implement smaller development projects in peasant communities, often accompanied by a symbolic act of recognition and commemoration of the victims and survivors. The type of projects most preferred by the communities involved basic infrastructure and productive initiatives, but also included day-care centres, schools or playgrounds. Some human rights organizations have criticized this type of support, as it can be difficult to differentiate collective reparations from development projects (García-Godos & Reátegui, 2016). It is argued that development initiatives are the duty of states under any circumstance, and elude the restorative dimension that reparations are meant to fulfil. The PRC was most active until 2011 and was for long time the only reparations programme in operation. According to the CR, 5,697 communities are registered in the registry of communities affected by the armed conflict, of which 33% have received collective reparations (Defensoría del Pueblo—Ombudsman, 2013).

The National Registry of Victims became operational in 2008, systematizing information on individual and collective victims. By March 2013, the registry included 182,350 individual victims (59% identified as direct victims, 41% as indirect victims) and 5,597 collective victims (Defensoría del Pueblo—Ombudsman, 2013). The registration and accreditation processes have involved a considerable amount of resources, both in terms of technical capacity as well as political commitment. The completion of this registry was considered a precondition for the implementation of programmes focusing on various forms of individual reparations, most notably the Program for Individual Economic Reparation (PREI), which became operational in 2011. While the registry continued to receive applications for accreditation, access to the PREI was closed in 2011[15], a decision contested by victims and human rights groups. Access to the PREI was re-established in 2016.

The economic reparations programme, although welcomed by victim organizations, faced serious criticism due to the unilateral design of the measures provided. Economic compensation was set to a maximum of 10,000 new soles[16] per victim of disappearance, death, sexual violence or permanent or partial disabilities—independently of the number of potential beneficiaries involved. For example, if a victim of disappearance has only one relative-beneficiary entitled to compensation, the full amount will go to that person alone; whereas if for example, the victim left a spouse, children and parents, the same amount will have to be divided among them (50% for the spouse, 50% for the other beneficiaries).

According to the CN, there are 82,710 individual beneficiaries entitled to economic compensation corresponding to 88,559 registered violations (afectaciones). By August 2014, economic compensation had been granted for 62% of these violations. In terms of beneficiaries, 54,856 individual beneficiaries had received compensation, at an average of 3,359 new soles[17] per beneficiary (Defensoría del Pueblo, 2014). Although the programme is currently under implementation, problems have persisted. Other reparations programmes are still at an initial implementation stage.

A number of issues must still be addressed in the majority of victim reparations programmes in Peru, the most important one being that the country does not yet have a coherent and co-ordinated state policy on victim reparations (despite current implementation). For instance, while symbolic reparation initiatives to restore the memory and dignity of victims have been incorporated in the collective reparations programme across the country, these are not the result of a co-ordinated effort to promote symbolic reparations, but rather reflect the sensitization of PRC officers in the field. Institutionally, CMAN lacks the mandate to co-ordinate and execute across sectorial ministries, thus leaving reparations, particularly on education, housing and health, unfulfilled.

Lessons for Colombia

The Peruvian experience with transitional justice mechanisms has been mixed, showing both advances and challenges, and not a few setbacks. What lessons can we extract for the Colombian transitional process with the FARC—EP guerrillas?

To start with truth-finding initiatives and the work of truth commissions, what stands out from the Peruvian experience is that legitimacy is the most crucial aspect in any attempt to establish historical truth. The most competent, trustworthy and technically sound effort to disentangle and explain the many truths left by protracted armed conflict can be let down by the lack of legitimacy and support from at least some political and civil society actors. At the operational level, the CVR is considered a best-practice model due to the effectiveness and scope of the data collection process as well as the quality of the analysis it achieved during the relative limited time it had available. The quality of professional and technical staff available to a truth commission cannot be underestimated. In the Colombian case, the truth commission can build upon the work of the National Centre for Historical Memory, a solid start for a truth-finding initiative.

Concerning civil society engagement, the CVR engaged in outreach activities yet failed in building alliances with actors beyond the NGO and human rights sectors, falling short in communicating and engaging in an effective manner with groups that might be supportive of its findings and proposals, such as students, labour unions, peasant self-defence groups and others. The importance of mobilizing political support for the findings of the truth commission at all levels must not be underestimated if the goal is to consolidate the legacy of its work. Political support is particularly important in relation to the construction of official history/histories for future generations. Given the contentiousness of the peace agreements in Colombia, as shown by the rejection of the agreements in the plebiscite of 2 October 2016, this is a key element to take into account.

Concerning prosecutions and retributive justice, Peru did not establish special judicial jurisdictions or proceedings for the prosecution of perpetrators such as the Justice and Peace courts or the Special Jurisdiction for Peace (the exception being trials against persons accused of terrorism in the mid-1990s during the Fujimori regime, and military trials). Instead, Peru established a specialized human rights system to deal with human rights violations committed during the armed conflict within the existing legal structures. While this was indeed a novel improvement, the success of the specialized jurisdiction has been tempered by the inclusion of other types of crimes in the functions of the courts. The courts' focus on human rights violations has thus been diluted among its many other duties. At the moment, the Special Jurisdiction for Peace to be established in Colombia to investigate and prosecute former FARC—EP guerrillas, members of the military, and other actors involved in the conflict, does not seem susceptible to the danger of a dilution of functions. The challenge will be whether legal action against state agents (police, military, public service) and guerrillas accused of human rights violations will face the same fate as in other countries of the region, including Peru, where constant delays and obstructions to the course of justice have been the norm.

As the trials of key actors of the FARC—EP leadership or high ranking state agents are initiated, the right to due process becomes a key issue. The main lesson from the Fujimori trials in Peru is that paradigmatic trials not only need to be conducted in an impeccable manner; they also need to be presented as such to the media and the general public in order to minimize the risk of future political backlash. Indeed, while for the majority of the country and international observers the proceedings were beyond reproach and the right to due process was strictly observed, for Fujimori's supporters the trials were partial and unjustified, and thus they continue to set doubt about the trials and its key participants.[18] To this day, the Fujimori trials and conviction continue to polarize public debate and the political scene in Peru. The unexpected presidential pardon of December 2017 has increased this polarization even further, dividing the country in those for and those against the pardon. This complex situation shows that the limits to criminal accountability can indeed be at the mercy of political decisions.

Concerning victim reparations, the main lesson from the Peruvian experience is the need for expediency in implementation and the participation of victim groups and beneficiaries in the design of appropriate measures. At the core of these two issues lies the acknowledgement of victims' suffering and agency. Procrastination in the implementation of reparations will negatively affect the prospects of re-establishing trust between the individual victims and the state. Mistrust and disappointment are also likely to be fostered in a context of noticeable expediency in providing support to demobilized ex-combatants relative to victims. Similarly, by offering or imposing measures that decision makers think are appropriate for victims without considering their needs and wishes, reparation programmes will fail to become meaningful vehicles of acknowledgement and recognition, let alone of the loftier objective of reconciliation. The Peruvian experience with collective reparations is illustrative of the mismatch between what some human rights activists, international NGOs and local civil society organizations consider appropriate reparations for victims, and the actual preferences of victims. The Colombian Victims Unit and reparations programmes are well positioned to face this challenge, given the existing dialogue and interaction developed with victim organizations, but this lesson should be continuously reflected upon, as mentioned by Jimeno in Chapter 9.

The main difference between the transitional processes in Colombia and Peru is that while Colombia opted for a negotiated solution to the armed conflict, in Peru the victorious state set the rules of the game. Both during the post-conflict reconstruction period in the 1990s, and the transitional period from the 2000s, the authority of the state has remained unchallenged, in the sense that there is a central state directing more or less the course of the country, not regional power holders keeping the central state out. This is one of the most evident challenges facing Colombian institutions, as in some parts of the country an armed oligopoly still prevails (López, 2016).

Seen from outside, enjoying a partly booming and stable economy, Peru's political scene seems similarly stable. Seen from inside, however, there are far more struggles, mobilizations and contestations than reach the international observer. Yet with ups and downs and some political scandals in between, the state manages to take control over specific situations. The authority of the state remains intact. Social conflicts, sometimes ending in violence, have occurred in Peru since the political transition; yet these seldom invoke human rights of the past. It is other kinds of conflicts that occupy the national agenda, such as socio-environmental conflicts, the provision of welfare services, or the protection of socioeconomic rights. At the same time, the legacy of the armed conflict is so unbearably present. The political scene is currently dominated by a Fujimori-majority in the national congress, and former President Ollanta Humala (2011–16) has been denounced for violations committed during the armed conflict. A case of systematic sexual violence by the military in the 1980s is in the trial phase, and the controversial pardon of former President Fujimori continues to fill the headlines.

Perhaps the most important lesson to be taken from the Peruvian experience for post-agreement Colombia is the need, in spite of all limitations and shortcomings, for an assertive central state that is effectively present and guarantees the rule of law and justice in all corners of the country. Peru did not, and does not, have a coherent, holistic human rights policy to address violations of the past, nor did it publicly and officially endorse a transitional justice approach. Yet the country has made some advances in the path towards accountability. A peace accord or a transitional agreement does not only imply an ending point. It marks the beginning of a transitioning process where the interaction and participation of different social actors in different areas of public life becomes institutionalized and part of the daily life of a democracy in the making (Tarrow, 2011). In my view, Colombia has a good starting point based on the experience the country has already gained from implementing transitional justice before the end of the conflict. The challenge now is how to keep a steady course towards increased accountability, preferably under the leadership of one—and only one—legitimate central state.

Notes

1 I thank Félix Reátegui for initial discussions and inputs in the design of this chapter. The chapter benefits from previous collaborative work (García-Godos & Reátegui, 2016).
2 The present account is obviously not exhaustive for reasons of space. For more detailed discussions of the Peruvian experience, see Villarán de la Puente (2007), Root (2012), Burt (2013) and García-Godos & Reátegui (2016).
3 The term used in Peru to refer to the members of Sendero Luminoso.
4 This transitional government dealt with the political transition after the demise of the Fujimori regime.
5 In Peru, the term commonly used to refer to members of guerrilla groups since the beginning of the armed conflict in 1980 until today is 'terrorists'. Related terms such as 'combatants' or 'guerrillas', used for example in Colombia, are very seldom used by the Peruvian public or officials. I use 'guerrillas' here for the sake of consistency with the rest of the book.
6 From the CVR's official English translation of the report's General Conclusions (paragraphs 8–9), available on the CVR website at www.cverdad.org.pe/ingles/ifinal/conclusiones.php. The nine-volume Informe final (CVR 2003) is available in Spanish in the same website.
7 Law no. 26479, approved on 16 June 1995.
8 *Comunicado de Prensa Conjunto suscrito entre el Estado peruano y la Comisión Interamericana de Derechos Humanos*, Costa Rica, 22 February 2001 (OEA: Comisión Interamericana de Derechos Humanos, 2001).
9 The total number of ongoing human rights cases in Peru is not readily available. As of August 2013, the Peruvian judicial system did not have a single, unified registry or database of human rights cases, according to the Ombudsman report. This situation continues in 2017.
10 Peru's criminal justice system follows a prosecutorial model. The state, represented by the public prosecutor's office, undertakes investigation and presents evidence before a judge or group of judges in public, oral proceedings. The judge(s) reach to a decision based on evidence presented. Victims can participate in the process as a civil party.
11 This is one of the darkest chapters of Peruvian history, when thousands of people were imprisoned and prosecuted on charges of terrorism in military courts in the mid-1990s as part of the counter-subversive strategy. To protect the identity of the

prosecutors and judges from possible revenge, they covered their faces, and were thus known as 'faceless judges' (De la Jara Basombrío, 2001).
12 Law no. 28592, approved on 28th July 2005.
13 Congreso de la República del Perú D.S. N° 015–2006-Jus—Regulations for Law 28592.
14 Comisión Multisectorial de Alto Nivel.
15 Congreso de la República del Perú D.S. N° 051–2011-PCM.
16 About US $3,000 as of 2017.
17 About US $1,000 as of 2017.
18 A similar delegitimizing strategy has already started in Colombia concerning the Special Jurisdiction for Peace. (See for example El País, 2017).

References

Bull, B., 2014. Latin America's Decade of Growth: Progress and Challenges for a Sustainable Development. In A. Hansen & U. Wethal, eds. *Emerging economies and challenges to sustainability: Theories, strategies, local realities*. London: Routledge, pp. 123–134.

Burt, J. M., 2006. 'Quien habla es terrorista': The Political Use of Fear in Fujimori's Peru. *Latin American Research Review*, pp. 32–62.

Burt, J. M., 2007. *Political Violence and the authoritarian state in Peru. Silencing civil society*. New York: Palgrave Macmillan.

Burt, J. M., 2009. Guilty as charged: The trial of former Peruvian president Alberto Fujimori for human rights violations. *International Journal of Transitional Justice*, 3 (3), pp. 384–405.

Burt, J. M., 2013. Justicia transicional en el post-conflicto de Perú: avances y retrocesos en la rendición de cuentas por abusos del pasado. *Aportes DPLF Los retos actuales de la justicia por crímenes del pasado*. pp. 384–405.

Comisión de la Verdad y Reconciliación (CVR), 2003. *Informe Final*. [Online] Available at: www.cverdad.org.pe/ifinal/index.php [Last accessed 6 June 2017].

De la Jara Basombrío, E., 2001. *Memoria y batallas en nombre de los inocentes: Perú 1992–2001*. Lima: Instituto de Defensa Legal.

Defensoría del Pueblo (Ombudsman), 2013. *A diez años de verdad, justicia y reparación. Avances, retrocesos y desafíos de un proceso inconcluso. Serie Informes Defensoriales—Informe N° 162*. Lima: Defensoría del Pueblo.

Defensoría del Pueblo, 2014. *Balance del Nivel de Cumplimiento del Programa de Reparaciones Económicas Individuales (Prei). Informe de Adjuntía N° 008–2014-ADHPD/DP*. Lima: Defensoría del Pueblo.

El País, 2017. *Uribe arremete contra secretario de la JEP y lo acusa de haber trabajado con el Cartel de Cali*. [Online] Available at: www.elpais.com.co/colombia/uribe-arremete-contra-secretario-de-la-jep-y-lo-acusa-de-haber-trabajado-con-el-cartel-de-cali.html [Last accessed 27 September 2017].

García-Godos, J. & Reátegui, F., 2016. Peru: beyond paradigmatic cases. In: E. Skaar, J. García-Godos & C. Collins, eds. *Transitional Justice in Latin America. The Uneven Road from Impunity towards Accountability*. London: Routledge, pp. 227–251.

Garcia-Godos, J., 2008. Victim reparations in the Peruvian Truth Commission and the challenge of historical interpretation. *The International Journal of Transitional Justice*, 2(1), pp. 63–82.

García-Godos, J., 2013. Victims' rights and distributive justice: In search of actors. *Human Rights Review*, 14(3), pp. 241–255.

Laplante, L. J., 2009. The Law of Remedies and the Clean Hands Doctrine: Exclusionary Reparation Policies in Peru's Political Transition. *American University International Law Review*, 23(1), pp. 51–90.

López, C., 2016. *Adiós a las FARC ¿Y ahora qué?: Construir Ciudadanía, Estado y Mercado para Unir a las Tres Colombias*. Bogotá: Debate.

OEA: Comisión Interamericana de Derechos Humanos, 2001. *Comunicado de Prensa Conjuto* [Online] Available at: www.cidh.org/Comunicados/Spanish/2001/PERU.htm [Last accessed 26 September 2017].

Root, R., 2012. *Transitional Justice in Peru*. New York: Palgrave Macmillan.

Salmón, E., 2014. *La condena de Alberto Fujimori y el derecho internacional de los derechos humanos. Un capítulo fundamental de la lucha contra la impunidad en Perú*. Bogotá: Universidad Externado de Colombia.

Tanaka, M., 1998. *Los espejismos de la democracia: El colapso del sistema de partidos en el Perú, 1980–1995, en perspectiva comparada*. Lima: Instituto de Estudios Peruanos.

Tarrow, S. G., 2011. *Power in movement: Social movements and contentious politics*. Cambridge: Cambridge University Press.

Villarán de la Puente, S., 2007. Peru. In: K. Salazar & T. Antkowiak, eds. *Victims unsilenced: the inter-American human rights system and transitional justice in Latin America*. Washington, DC: Due Process of Law Foundation, pp. 95–126.

Yates, J. S. & Bakker, K., 2014. Debating the 'post-neoliberal turn'in Latin America. *Progress in Human Geography*, 38(1), pp. 62–69.

Zakaria, F., 1997. The rise of illiberal democracy. *Foreign affairs*, pp. 22–43.

14 Bosnia and Herzegovina
The challenges and complexities of transitional justice

Louis Francis Monroy-Santander

Introduction

Transitional justice, understood as a way of dealing with past atrocities in the process of transitioning towards peace and democracy, has undergone a significant transformation since its inception. The concept evolved from a focus on war crimes trials to a multilevel process that includes retributive and reparative justice processes, vetting and lustration practices and truth-telling initiatives, as well as processes of remembrance and memorialization; it has adopted an interdisciplinary and comprehensive approach in both theory and practice. This evolution has grown to an understanding of local realities and their political and economic contexts to see how peacebuilding initiatives can address local demands via a wide array of judicial and non-judicial mechanisms.

Transitional justice has gained increased notoriety in post-agreement operations in recent years. Its evolution implied an increase in the scope of transitional justice's aims and activities, making it a complex and contested term for academics and practitioners. Incorporating transitional justice mechanisms into peace agreements has become a method for facilitating peacebuilding that, coupled with state-building measures, is expected to support reconciliation and stability. Transitional justice is assumed to address societal divisions left unaddressed by power agreements seeking the end of conflict (Kostić, 2012).

The evolution of transitional justice can be summarized in three phases (Skaar & Malca, 2015). An initial phase took place between the end of the Second World War and the Cold War. This phase was characterized by interstate co-operation, war crime trials and sanctions via the Nuremberg and Tokyo trials. A second phase emerged in the early post-Cold War years, where mechanisms focused on legal responses, ensuring rule of law and the formalization of transitional justice as a tool for transitioning from dictatorships to democracies. The third (and current) phase is characterized by transitional justice becoming an established component of post-agreement processes, with the presence of non-governmental and non-local actors, and an interest in local and traditional processes for justice and reconciliation, informed by an international jurisprudence and international standards.

The debate around transitional justice has moved from considerations regarding the impact of retributive justice and the rule of law towards discussions about the meaning of truth, justice and reconciliation in post-agreement contexts and the relationships established between these concepts (Skaar & Malca, 2015).

Although the 'peace versus justice' debate continues, there are an increasing number of peace processes inclusive of transitional justice measures, showing not only an international trend towards criminal accountability but also the emergence of different ways in which transitional justice mechanisms can contribute to the implementation of peace accords (García-Godos, 2015).

A comprehensive view of transitional justice is expected to include institutional reforms, the establishment of reparation programmes, and the promotion of reconciliation practices (Van Zyl, 2006). Thus, as transitional justice extends its range of activities, a call for a holistic and comprehensive view has featured in contemporary scholarship. Holistic interpretations focus on the need for accountability, truth recovery, and institution-building: thus, they demand a combination of approaches including both retributive (aimed at punishing perpetrators) as well as restorative practices (symbolic reparation, material compensation that acknowledges victims suffering). Holistic approaches are also inclusive of initiatives for trust and relationship-building that can serve as preconditions for reconciliation (Fischer, 2011). Therefore the combination of options to deal with past atrocities is not a question of either/or, but rather a case where a combination of several choices is possible and desirable (Huyse, 2001). This can be seen as the widening of the mandate of transitional justice processes, and of applying transitional justice practices as an inclusive and comprehensive way of consolidating statehood beyond state-building formulas (Andrieu, 2010).

This approach towards a holistic transitional justice emerges as a response to the failures of previous experiences. Reliance on a 'one size fits all' model often results in a very restrictive and restricted approach for dealing with past human rights atrocities, which does not meet expectations. As the contexts where transitional justice operates are marked by a tradition of non-compliance with norms, devastation of judicial sectors and institutions, and traditions of systematic violations of norms, there is a limit to what a 'standardized' transitional justice programme can achieve by itself. Thus, the holistic approach to transitional justice can be seen as understanding the contexts and their complexities, in order to understand and address how the mechanisms, programmes, and institutions are meant to operate.

Calling for an extended and comprehensive view of transitional justice thus implies recognizing the diversity of tools and mechanisms available, how their choice and implementation relate to the understanding of local realities in conflict areas, and the challenges to post-conflict reconstruction on the ground. Excessive reliance on 'Lego-like' transitional justice mechanisms may be a recipe for failure as they may be insufficient to satisfy specific demands for justice, accountability, truth-seeking, and relationship-building in societies trying to part ways with violence.

This chapter seeks to understand the challenges and failures of transitional justice in Bosnia and Herzegovina after the 1992–1995 war and to show how the overreliance on individual and specific instruments of transitional justice brought a series of unintended consequences that has hindered the processes of reconciliation and state-building. This in fact, can serve as warning for other transitional processes (such as the one taking place in Colombia), with regards to the importance of understanding the need for having a scope of instruments, policies, and approaches that can facilitate inclusion of society within the transitional justice process.

To do this, the document describes how Bosnia's reconstruction incorporated a state-building focus, highlighting the use of ethnic markers as constitutive of the Bosnian political system in the post-accord phase. It also highlights how the international character of the process affected peacebuilding and transitional justice, as it created an internationally legitimate transitional justice process, but undermined the legitimacy of the process locally. Then the chapter presents how the model of state-building and statehood brought by the Dayton Peace Agreements envisioned a particular role for civil society, which, following a Western model, meant to support accountability and statehood. The result is a system that favoured the consolidation of ethnicity as a political marker, in which justice is alien for citizens, and in which civil society is seen as trying to perform a role meant for other geographies. The combination of these three challenges has considerably affected the possibility of reconciliation, justice, and the consolidation of the state.

State-building, the 'ethnic key', and international intervention: peacebuilding in Bosnia and Herzegovina

The focus on state institutions was prioritized in the process of building peace after the Bosnian war. This approach marked a trend in the way peacebuilding interventions were envisioned and developed, and how transitional justice was related to this process. This connection between state-building initiatives had an impact on the process of political, economic, and social reconstruction, and it defined and affected the development and implementation of transitional justice initiatives in Bosnia and Herzegovina.

The Bosnian civil war of 1992–1995 was a violent consequence of the dissolution of Yugoslavia after the end of the Cold War (Šaviha-Valha & Sahić, 2015). Bosnia and Herzegovina was as a test case for thinking about new peacebuilding strategies for a post-socialist state, whose transformation was interrupted by a multi-layered conflict dominated by ethno-national perspectives. Bosnia and Herzegovina reflected a paradigm shift in the way peace was to be conceptualized and treated via the international relations system. The ending of the conflict involved external military intervention and the combination of diplomacy and negotiations.

Peacemaking efforts culminated in the General Framework for Peace, known as the Dayton Peace Agreement (DPA), agreed in November 1995 in

Dayton, Ohio, USA. As the war allowed the emergence of power structures within the three main ethnic groups (Bosniaks, Bosnians-Croats and Bosnians-Serbs) in conflict to emerge, Dayton incorporated their political leadership into the negotiation process. These power structures were represented by three nationalist parties who became the interlocutors during the negotiations: The Bosniak Party of Democratic Action (SDA), led by Alija Izetbegović, the Croatian Democratic Union (HDZ) led by Croatian President Franjo Tuđman, and the Serbian Democratic Party (SDS) led by the Serbian President Slobodan Milosević. All three parties insisted on regional autonomy, control over executive branches and the military, and the management of the economy as their demands during negotiations (Cox, 2001).

Due to the ethno-national interests marking the war and the political views represented in the leadership present in Dayton, the agreement was written up along these 'ethnic' lines and instilled them on the post-war Bosnian political system as a model of consociationalism (Lijphart, 1969).

The Dayton Agreement established a new internal, political and territorial landscape for Bosnia and Herzegovina based exclusively on the register of ethnicity by actors during the war (Šaviha-Valha & Sahić, 2015). Dayton divided Bosnia and Herzegovina into three entities: Republika Srpska (RS), the Croat and Bosniak Federation of Bosnia and Herzegovina, and a third level of government, the national institutions of Bosnia and Herzegovina (Ignatieff, 2003). The establishment of this ethnic distribution within the Bosnian State structure meant a federalization of Bosnia and Herzegovina that established both Republika Srpska and the Federation of Bosnia and Herzegovina as the only constitutionally recognized entities in the country.

This arrangement built consociationalism into all levels of the Bosnian state, turning the country into a confederal union between two political entities (RS and the Federation of Bosnia and Herzegovina) (Bose, 2006). Dayton established an internal territorial division of ethnicities through the creation of entities and cantons whose order was to be guaranteed by an external control mechanism via the United Nations (UN) Office of the High Representative (OHR).[1]

Politically, RS is a centralized entity whereas the Federation is composed of ten cantons: of these, five have absolute Bosniak majority, three have Croat majority, and two cantons are mixed (Institut za društveno-politička istraživanja—IDPI, 2016). This divergence in institutional and political settings builds in complexity for the administration of Bosnia and Herzegovina (Zivanović, 2015). The power-sharing structure brought by the Dayton accord also created a bicameral legislature where the three constituents (Bosniaks, Bosnian Serbs and Bosnian Croats) have representation in parity in the house of peoples and in the collective presidency. In addition, the representatives of each of the three ethnic groups have veto power over any proposed legislation. The executive power distribution was also configured according to an ethnic key, as ministers and deputies are to be chosen in order to comply with the ethnic key present in Bosnia and Herzegovina (Marko, 2005).

The Dayton Peace Agreements defined a nation-building process that wove various international actors into the process of building institutions. For example, the annex on elections required the Organization for Security and Cooperation in Europe to establish an elections programme. The agreement on refugees and displaced persons called for the UN High Commissioner for Human Rights (UNHCR) to develop a repatriation plan for refugee and minority returns. The annex on international police ascribed the task of establishing a police force and a law enforcement agency to the UN. The Dayton Peace Agreements thus seemed to outsource the entire post-conflict state-building and peacebuilding design to international institutions (Sloan, 1998).

Thus, it is no surprise that several critiques of the agreements have emerged. These critiques include: the continuation of ethnic markers created by the war (Bieber, 2006), and the feudalization of the state into two entities, ten federation cantons, 149 municipalities and a special district, Brcko District (Cox, 2001). In addition, the rejection of the existing power structures of the socialist Bosnia and Herzegovina, and the 'airdropping' of a new statehood, created a vacuum as a product of the belief that a state can be built from scratch by an international mandate.

In addition, the diminished sovereignty created by the Dayton Peace Agreements replaced state institutions with international organizations and created a crisis of representation, thus hampering the consolidation of statehood (Chandler, 2000). This, in fact, has made participation by locals more difficult and has affected the sustainability of the new institutions in the long term.

The arrangements about the future of Bosnia and Herzegovina in the Dayton accords resembled a form of protectorate more than a democracy, as a result of the fact that the OHR acquired unlimited powers to impose laws and dismiss public officials through the figure of the 'Bonn Powers' of 1997 (Cox, 2001). The consequence of these actions has been a sharp criticism of the international presence in Bosnia and Herzegovina by the Bosnians. This unexpected consequence has affected the legitimacy and perception of international transitional justice in Bosnia and Herzegovina. Transitional justice thus was not seen as an opportunity for Bosnians to reconcile, but as an imposition from an overlord.

This disconnection between Bosnians and the Dayton Peace Agreements was further stretched by some of the intervening agents. Peace was seen as a problem to be managed and solved through professional managerial structures, vertical subordination, within clear principles and narrow action frameworks corresponding to Western standards (Šaviha-Valha & Sahić, 2015). These practices were informed by the belief that the implantation of democratic practices taking place in Western societies would have the same effects in the target country regardless of different geopolitical, social, and cultural contexts. One in fact could argue that Bosnia and Herzegovina is a perfect example of the liberal peace paradigm (Doyle, 2005).

Thus, for some Bosnians, the Dayton Peace Agreements are a tool of Western ideas and practices, where locals become instrumental, not central to the agenda for peace. This raises serious questions about the role of imposed democratization and marketization in post-conflict societies, and how this compromises the sustainability of peace in the long term (Mac Ginty, 2008). For Bosnians, the Dayton Peace Agreements are a synonym for complex institutions, high unemployment, the imposition of a transitional justice framework, dependency on external aid, the loss of agency and the predominance of ethnic politics (Bieber, 2006).

From the ICTY to the domestic courts: The challenges of transitional justice in Bosnia and Herzegovina

Evaluating transitional justice implies giving attention to how good governance, constitutional, and legal equality can encourage inter-group co-operation; how these mechanisms generate accountability for war crimes; and how an understanding of the past facilitates a conversation about the future of a country (Kostić, 2012). In Bosnia and Herzegovina, transitional justice was based on establishing the International Criminal Tribunal for the Former Yugoslavia (ICTY), rebuilding justice institutions, and fostering a non-governmental organization (NGO) sector for 'bottom-up' reconciliation initiatives. All these mechanisms have faced challenges derived from the imprinting of ethnic keys on the state, and the external influence on the implementation of transitional justice.

The ICTY model of justice is one of retributive justice focused on prosecuting and trying those responsible for the widespread human rights violations, mass killings, systematic detention of civilians, rape, and ethnic cleansing since 1991 (United Nations Security Council, 1993). The ICTY has been leading the prosecution of war crimes and crimes against humanity in the former Yugoslavia (Fischer, 2011).

The ICTY sees as its main achievements (i) holding leaders accountable and dismantling impunity for war crimes in the region, (ii) bringing justice to victims and giving them a voice by holding individuals responsible for crimes, (iii) establishing beyond a reasonable doubt crucial facts related to war crimes committed in the former Yugoslavia, (iv) consistently and systematically developing international humanitarian law, and (v) strengthening the rule of law by influencing the judiciaries in the former Yugoslavia to reform and try perpetrators of war crimes (International Criminal Tribunal for the former Yugoslavia—ICTY, 2017).

The ICTY developed a retributive angle; however, this angle has been the focus of political rejection by several Bosnians. This has been partly due to the disconnection between prosecutions and the rebuilding of social relations. The ICTY narrowly defined its mandate to prosecute war crimes, and thus it either assumed or ignored how the decisions taking place in a court could relate to the society this was intended to help (Eastmond, 2010). The geographical isolation of the court (which is located in The Hague, The Netherlands) geographically removed the courts from Bosnia and Herzegovina's affected citizens and its territory, undermining its capacity to achieve local influence, and making its decisions something abstract and separated from the realities in the country. In addition, the ICTY lacked an outreach strategy (initially) to reach its constituents (the citizens of Bosnia and Herzegovina), making it incapable of linking its decisions with promoting and supporting the reinstatement of the rule of law in Bosnia (Sriram, 2010).

Thus critiques which claimed that the ICTY was ethnically biased against Serb communities, or that it did not put enough effort into the defence of Bosniak and Croat victims, were met with a system located far away, separated from local realities and limited resources, leading to transitional justice being reinterpreted through dominant ethno-political discourses. This negative local perception of the ICTY is the product of its incapacity to reflect the local concerns of Bosnians, and its failure to allow local ownership of the judicial process (Hoogenboom & Vieille, 2010). Trials did not succeed in setting reconciliation as Serbs complained that the ICTY unfairly targeted them and Croats felt excluded from the process.

The ICTY also was not a participatory process for victims. The only way for personal narratives to be present at the ICTY was as witnesses, an outcome of the focus on prosecutions by the court (Garbett, 2004). This might be a consequence of the lack of formal mechanisms that linked the Bosnian judiciary with the ICTY and the society it was supposed to help to reconcile. Disconnecting the court from civil society, and bypassing other spaces for reconciliation outside the judicial sphere, made the ICTY a legal enclave isolated from society (Hoogenboom & Vieille, 2010).

The disconnection between the ICTY and the Bosnian public was not only geographic. The court was conceived within an internationalist ethos, trials were conducted in English and French, and only some parts of the processes were translated into local languages. This facilitated the distortion by local political élites who focused on the 'ethnic bias' of the ICTY (Banjeglav, 2015). These problems were only addressed in 1999 with the establishment of outreach programmes. Despite the development of an outreach programme in 1999, many are still sceptical of the legitimacy of the ICTY in the region. Although ICTY judgments are now available in local languages, these are not necessarily physically accessible by local people, or written in a style to which locals can relate (Banjeglav, 2015).

In addition to this, the politicization of indictments and charges of 'ethnic bias' affected the legitimacy of the courts, and made local institutions highly resistant to co-operation. The compliance with justice and the ICTY in some cases was facilitated to pacify political opposition and show compliance with the international community, rather than to advance democratic accountability. Whilst this allowed the local élites to be more legitimate internationally, it did not develop democratic accountability (Loyle & Davenport, 2016).

These failures of the Bosnia and Herzegovina transitional justice framework were magnified by the lack of results on the delivery of justice in regards to disappeared persons, reparations for victims, and the re-victimization of victims looking for reparations.

Victims' reparations have been unsuccessful and unsystematic in the country. Transitional justice in Bosnia and Herzegovina was focused solely on judicial prosecutions and war crime tribunals (Hronešová, 2016). The ICTY lacked a reparatory notion of justice and left victims with only the national courts as an institutional source for seeking compensation (Garbett, 2004). Thus, reparations have been included as part of the social security and veteran protection systems, which has meant that reparations are being managed by programmes with a different mission (Lai, 2016), and the creation of a hierarchy where veterans who are more politically connected with the state often have better benefits and payments than victims who struggle for their recognition by the state.

Depending where the victim is residing, his or her entitlements vary, and his or her institutional avenues change. For example, female victims of wartime rape have a special status entitling them to compensation at the Federation; however, in the RS, victims of sexual violence need to provide medical evidence of physical disability supported by witness statements.[2]

Thus, in this scenario of institutional inconsistency, it should come as no surprise that victims are unable to enforce their rights to financial compensation in criminal proceedings. For citizens attempting to survive, undertaking the task of facing a complex and diverse system that facilitates patronage and regional patrimonialism is a daunting task.

These challenges place a strong emphasis on the development of the Bosnian judiciary. The state has started to implement a series of measures concerning the challenges mentioned above. In 2005, a section for war crimes was created in the Court of Bosnia and Herzegovina as a state-level organ for dealing with human rights atrocities (Fischer, 2011). Legislation was tabled for supporting this institution together with the establishment of a War Crimes section within the office of the Prosecutor and the Registry, which led to the enactment of the Criminal Code of Bosnia and Herzegovina in 2003. The Bosnian Ministry of Justice has been important in pursuing reforms in the judicial sector since 2003 These have focused on building capacity within the Court and Prosecutor's office in Bosnia and Herzegovina (Grubešic, 2014). Other mechanisms, such as a witness protection programme, were established in 2005. There was also the creation of a National Strategy for the Prosecution of War Crimes (designed in 2008) with the aim of completing highly complex cases by 2015 and other lower level cases by 2023. Also noteworthy is the tabling of the Law on Missing Persons in 2004, a consequence of a consultative process between various national and international institutions (Sarkin, et al., 2014).

Despite advances in legal and political agreements and the establishment of domestic institutions, many processes have been hijacked by local élites. In some cases, politicians have obstructed the extradition of citizens of Bosnia and Herzegovina in war crimes trials, which highlights the need for the repudiation of obstructive ethno-nationalist rhetoric and manipulation. These challenges highlight the need for institutional reforms to ensure and promote non-repetition, education, judicial independence, independent media, and a human rights culture.

Both the international establishment of a retributive instrument for justice (the ICTY) and the domestic process for creating a Bosnian judiciary have been affected by the ethnic dimensions, characteristic of the post-Dayton Peace Agreements state-building model. As political élites co-opted the state structure to pursue their own agendas, they have used ethnic motivations to criticize the ICTY's work, as well as to find strategies to delay and create obstacles for judicial reform.

Importing the Western NGO model: The role of civil society in Bosnia and Herzegovina's transitional justice

A solid and sustainable civil society can be an important complement to the development of state institutions. It can serve as a check on the powers of the government and support social processes for accountability. In the context of transitioning countries, civil society can support restorative justice and creative ways of dealing with the past, greatly supporting transitional justice. Civil society can be a space for fostering political pluralism and for citizens to articulate views and demands to the state, encouraging trust and co-operation between state and society (Hoogenboom & Vieille, 2010). Thus the importance of the work of organizations from civil society in transitional spaces includes documenting past atrocities, giving a voice to victims, and having the ability to increase pressure on governments for accountability towards victims (Austin, et al., 2013).

The Bosnian model for peacebuilding was based on establishing NGOs that would help engage in projects of truth-telling, trauma healing, and other transitional justice strategies. What the international community envisaged for Bosnia was a sector of advocacy organizations that would foster a culture of interaction and political engagement, where local NGOs would present alternatives to the nationalist-ridden political élites (Fagan, 2005). This design was meant to balance the 'top-down' influence of the international community, and bypass the ethnic politics by stimulating local political activity. Thus NGOs have the potential to raise awareness, monitor and advocate around prosecutions, provide psychosocial support and assistance to victims, conduct research and produce publications, promote mediation and interethnic dialogue, and other cultural and artistic activities that can be seen as restorative approaches (Nikolić-Ristanović & Ćopić, 2015).

The end of the war allowed a booming growth of civil society activism through donor-driven NGOs. In the initial years of post-war reconstruction, most NGOs were in fact service providers of humanitarian aid and of internationally planned projects (Monroy-Santander, 2016b).

However, Bosnia and Herzegovina's civil society sector suffered from the artificial implantation of models that were not part of Yugoslav society and that seemed more responsive to Western donor interests than to the local realities of Bosnia and Herzegovina. Bosnian civil society suffered thus an 'NGOization' (Belloni, 2001). This externally driven process, dependent on international resources, affected grassroots-type initiatives that were not necessarily globally connected, ignoring the objective of mobilization of alternative networks for representation and accountability.

The dependency on foreign support by the NGO sector has posed a threat both to the sector's ability to grow and to its sustainability. As Hoogenboom and Vieille (2010) note, Bosnian citizens avoid participating in voluntary organizations as they feel that their needs are not met through the latter, and the prevalence of donor priorities in the country guide the interests of NGOs. This disconnection between the NGO sector and the citizens was evident in the anti-government demonstrations in February 2014 (Lai, 2016). The protests, which brought socioeconomic justice issues to public debate, led to a series of 'plenums' where citizens would state their demands against the state, demanding accountability from local and national politicians. The process was marked by protesters' insistence on keeping NGOs out of the protests.

One of the reasons for this resistance to NGOs derives from the fact that they are internationally incepted and not organic to Bosnian society. The emerging sector of NGO professionals funded by Western donors see their role as essentially technical and apolitical, opposing a nationalist-dominated political arena (Fagan, 2005). However, such separation would result in the inability of NGOs to connect with their communities and to challenge the dominant political discourse within Bosnian society.

The international sources that led to creating Bosnian civil society led to groups that are underdeveloped and unable to exercise power as advocates, government watchdogs, and as forces to set the agenda for political debate, lacking the necessary elements for building social capital in Bosnia and Herzegovina.

The structural disconnection between NGOs and the state is further fuelled by the non-existence of a country strategy for government and civil society co-operation (Sterland, 2006), and NGOs' opposition to engaging in dialogue with political parties, as these are seen as dirty and corrupt (Barnes, et al., 2004). This has created a political vacuum where civil society does not engage with the state.

The political landscape described above is complicated by the emergence of illiberal segments of civil society as obstacles to achieving post-conflict. There are NGOs that operate with nationalist agendas similar to those of political parties. These are generally represented in veteran associations and informal political groups that oppose the acceptance of culpability by the state and processes for political apology.

An example of these challenges is the NGO-led RECOM[3] initiative. RECOM, established in 2004, evolved as a reaction to the shortcomings of retributive justice in Bosnia and Herzegovina, and is concerned with giving a voice to victims and enhancing a debate on how symbolic or material compensation should promote reconciliation (Fischer, 2011). RECOM gathered a network of more than 1,800 NGOs, associations, and individuals to promote the effort of establishing a lasting truth commission (Subotic, 2016). However, RECOM has been met by resistance among certain civil society groups in Bosnia and Herzegovina, where a focus on reconciliation rather than justice was a difficult sell. Other controversies concerning the role of victims versus the role of veterans in these processes became evident. This was due to political discrepancies between victim-focused organizations and veteran groups (known to be closely connected to political parties in Bosnia and Herzegovina).

RECOM's work is also limited by the support and political will of political parties and the leaders of both state and entity structures in order to enact change. Although RECOM has constantly denounced how Bosnia and Herzegovina politicians fail to address reconciliation and have reduced truth-telling to official visits and the signing of documents, without making any bigger steps to involve state action in this process, some of its member organizations have expressed concerns with the many levels of compromise that RECOM has had with politics, which might compromise its own goals and the establishment of the truth (Monroy-Santander, 2016a).

In a similar fashion to the ICTY and the development of reparations within the Bosnian judiciary, RECOM is accused of ignoring ordinary people's voices, particularly due to its lack of public engagement and acknowledgement, including the absence of commoners from the consultations process. RECOM, it is claimed, has become so specialized in its operation and language that it only involves a specific élite of students, victims, and veterans' associations that have been invited to take part in the initiative (Obradovic-Wochnik, 2013). This case shows how the disconnection between the victims and the organizations that claim to represent victims can occur not only at a state or international level, but how even local NGOs can be seen as highly technical and politicized institutions, which can fail to re-weave a social contract.

Concluding remarks

The need for a comprehensive, holistic understanding of transitional justice entails recognizing the interconnectedness of different practices to meet different challenges present in processes for dealing with mass violations of human rights. This requires a conflict-sensitive approach to transitional justice that appreciates diverse local realities and challenges in order to establish the needs and focus covered by different practices that will be part of transitional justice programmes.

In Bosnia and Herzegovina, the process of social reconstruction had a focus on building state institutions for the establishment of democratic and capitalist structures in Bosnia and Herzegovina in accordance to the Dayton Peace Agreements (a 'liberal peace' model). This impacted negatively on the possibilities of transitional justice bringing transformative changes, by imprinting into the agreements an 'ethnic key'. This in turn led to very complex and divided political dynamics, and an administrative system that has allowed the hijacking of state-building and transitional justice by political élites that rely on nationalist ethno-political propaganda. The fact that these processes were externally driven and distant from local processes did not help matters and created a legitimacy gap that would permeate transitional justice.

The process of establishing the ICTY, the rebuilding of justice institutions and the creation of an NGO sector for reconciliation-focused initiatives may have been well intentioned initiatives, but have all been affected by co-option from ethno-political élites of peacebuilding in order to further their nationalist aims. In the case of the ICTY, its geographical and social distance gave way and space to accusations of ethnic bias and illegitimacy by political leaders in Bosnia and Herzegovina. In addition, the initial pre-eminence of the ICTY over the domestic judicial processes led to various deficiencies in the process of implementing judicial reforms, legislative reforms, and the establishment of a fair reparations process.

This pre-eminence of the international vision of Bosnia, rather than the territorial vision of Bosnians, in fact stifled not only the justice system and the transitional justice process but also incepted the NGOs with a series of practices and challenges that affected their possibility of facilitating the transitional justice processes. This was due to the structures and practices imprinted on the sector that have subsequently complicated the consolidation of a sustainable and solid civil society. The case of RECOM is illustrative of these challenges.

The warning that derives from the study of Bosnia and Herzegovina's complex transitional justice history serves as a lesson for Colombia in terms of the need to understand the political, social, and economic realities that derive from a conflict-sensitive view of peace building. A localized view of transitional justice, that visualizes the diversity of the needs and concerns of victims, communities, and collectives, has a greater potential to facilitate institutional reforms and state-building processes that drive post-agreement reconstruction. A disconnection between top-down and bottom-up approaches risks the peril of creating legitimacy gaps and misinterpretations of judicial and non-judicial processes, gravely affecting the prospects for sustainable peace and the efficiency of peacebuilding, which can then be exploited by warlords and political operators. The risk of a legitimacy gap opens the door for transitional justice and peacebuilding to fail.

One important issue that deserves close attention for the Colombian case is the role that reparations have in transitional justice processes and the possible injustices and inequalities, which can be perceived by different sectors. The imbalances between payments to veteran groups or demobilized actors, as opposed to the material and financial reparations for the victims of human rights atrocities, can generate tensions and a new source of conflicts, or can affect the legitimacy of the process of transitional justice. For Colombia, this should serve as a lesson in the need for a clear reparations policy that can reflect an attention to victims' needs, and that avoids any form of discrimination that can later become a barrier to reconciliation.

Equally important is the role of civil society actors in the process of transitional justice and reconciliation. The support that civil society organizations can give to state-based measures can promote accountability and the inclusion of victims and different sectors of society processes of reconciliation, thus giving a voice to citizens. Yet, this process needs to find ways to ascertain legitimacy within local populations and organizations, paying close connection to their needs and demands. In the case of Bosnia, the externally-led and project-driven nature of NGOs became a barrier to their acceptance and legitimacy, both by local populations as well as the political élite. In the case of Colombia, civil society may enjoy a better reputation within local populations, particularly victims' organizations, but it still may suffer the peril of politicization along ideological, donor, and even party lines, which can further affect grassroots-based transitional justice initiatives.

Notes

1 The purpose of the OHR is to oversee the civilian implementation of the Dayton Peace Agreements. The Dayton Peace Agreements created the legal basis for the OHR. Annex 10 provides for the institution of the Office of the High Representative (OHR) in Bosnia and Herzegovina to oversee the civilian implementation of the agreement, representing the countries involved in the Dayton Accords through the Peace Implementation Council. In addition, in 1997 the Peace Implementation Council agreed to grant further substantial powers to the OHR, in order to avoid the implementation of the Dayton agreement being delayed or obstructed by local nationalist politicians.
2 Victims of sexual violence need to prove through medical documentation that they have suffered 60% of bodily harm in order to apply for victim status.
3 RECOM is a regional commission for the establishment of facts about war crimes and other serious violations of human rights committed in the former Yugoslavia from 1 January 1991 until 31 December 2001.

References

Andrieu, K., 2010. Civilizing peacebuilding: Transitional justice, civil society and the liberal paradigm. *Security Dialogue*, 41(5), pp. 537–558.

Austin, A., Fischer, M. & Ropers, N., 2013. *Transforming ethnopolitical conflict: the Berghof handbook*. Berlin: Springer Science & Business Media.

Banjeglav, T., 2015. The micro legacy of the ICTY in Croatiada case study of Vukovar. In M. Fischer & O. Simic, eds. *Transitional Justice and Reconciliation: Lessons from the Balkans*. London: Routledge.

Barnes, C., Mrdja, M., Sijerćič, S. & Popovič, M., 2004. *Civil society assessment in Bosnia and Herzegovina*. Sarajevo: United States Agency for International Development (USAID/Bosnia and Herzegovina).

Belloni, R., 2001. Civil society and peacebuilding in Bosnia and Herzegovina. *Journal of Peace Research*, 38(2), pp. 163–180.

Bieber, F., 2006. After Dayton, Dayton? The evolution of an unpopular peace. *Ethnopolitics*, 5(1), pp. 15–31.

Bose, S., 2006. The Bosnian State a Decade after Dayton. In D. Chandler, ed. *Peace without politics?: ten years of international state-building in Bosnia.* London: Taylor and Francis.
Chandler, D., 2000. *Bosnia: faking democracy after Dayton.* London: Pluto Press.
Cox, M., 2001. *State building and post-conflict reconstruction: Lessons from Bosnia.* Geneva: Centre for Applied Studies in International Negotiations.
Doyle, M. W., 2005. Three pillars of the liberal peace. *American Political Science Review,* 99(3), pp. 463–466.
Eastmond, M., 2010. Introduction: Reconciliation, reconstruction, and everyday life in war-torn societies. *Focaal,* Issue 57, pp. 3–16.
Fagan, A., 2005. Civil society in Bosnia ten years after Dayton. *International Peacekeeping,* 12(3), pp. 406–419.
Fischer, M., 2011. Transitional justice and Reconciliation: Theory and practice. In: B. Austin & M. Fischer, eds. *Advancing Conflict Transformation: The Berghof Handbook II.* Berlin: Barbara Budrich Publishers.
Garbett, C., 2004. Introduction. In E. Stover & H. M. Weinstein, eds. *My neighbor, my enemy: Justice and community in the aftermath of mass atrocity.* Cambridge: Cambridge University Press.
García-Godos, J., 2015. 'It's about trust. Transitional justice and accountability in the search for peace. In C. M. Bailliet & K. M. Larsen, eds. *Promoting peace through international law.* Oxford: Oxford University Press.
Grubešic, N., 2014. The achievements in Bosnia and Herzegovina. In S. Slapšak & N. Kandić, eds. *Transitional Justice and Reconciliation in Post-Yugoslav countries.* Sarajevo: Recom initiative.
Hoogenboom, D. A. & Vieille, S., 2010. Rebuilding social fabric in failed states: Examining transitional justice in Bosnia. *Human Rights Review,* 11(2), pp. 183–198.
Hronešová, J., 2016. Might Makes Right: War-Related Payments in Bosnia and Herzegovina. *Journal of Intervention and Statebuilding,* 10(3), pp. 339–360.
Huyse, L., 2001. Dealing with the past and imagining the future. In: L. Reychler & T. Paffenholz, eds. *Peacebuilding: a field guide.* London: Lynne Rienner Publishers.
Ignatieff, M., 2003. *Empire lite: nation-building in Bosnia, Kosovo and Afghanistan.* London: Viking.
Institut za društveno-politička istraživanja (IDPI), 2016. *Bosnia and Herzegovina and Herzegovina: Federalism, equality and sustainability. A study of Bosnia and Herzegovina redesign to secure institutional equality of constituent peoples.* Mostar: Institute for Social and Political Research.
Kostić, R., 2012. Transitional justice and reconciliation in Bosnia-Herzegovina: Whose memories, whose justice? *Sociologija,* 54(4), pp. 649–666.
Lai, D., 2016. Transitional justice and Its Discontents: Socioeconomic Justice in Bosnia and Herzegovina and the Limits of International Intervention. *Journal of Intervention and Statebuilding,* 10(3), pp. 361–381.
Lijphart, A., 1969. Consociational democracy. *World Politics,* 21(2), pp. 207–225.
Loyle, C. E. & Davenport, C., 2016. Transitional injustice: Subverting justice in transition and postconflict societies. *Journal of Human Rights,* 15(1), pp. 126–149.
Mac Ginty, R., 2008. Indigenous peace-making versus the liberal peace. *Cooperation and conflict,* 43(2), pp. 139–163.
Marko, J., 2005. Post-conflict Reconstruction through State–and Nation–building: The Case of Bosnia and Herzegovina. *European Diversity and Autonomy Papers–EDAP,* Issue 4.

Monroy-Santander, L., 2016a. *Truth-telling in Bosnia-Herzegovina: The RECOM Initiative.* [Online] Available at: www.avangarda.ba/detaljno.php?id=105 [Last accessed 9 January 2017].

Monroy-Santander, L., 2016b. Reconciliation: a critical approach to peacebuilding in Bosnia-Herzegovina. *Peace, Conflict & Development*, Issue 22, pp. 77–116.

Nikolić-Ristanović, V. & Ćopić, S., 2015. Dealing with the past in Serbia—achievements in the past 20 years. In: M. Fischer & O. Simic, eds. *Transitional Justice and Reconciliation: Lessons from the Balkans.* London: Routledge, p. 141.

Obradovic-Wochnik, J., 2013. *Ethnic conflict and war crimes in the Balkans: the narratives of denial in post-conflict Serbia.* London: Tauris.

Sarkin, J., Nettlefield, L., Matthews, M. & Osalka, K., 2014. *Bosnia-Herzegovina: missing persons from the armed conflict of the 1990s: a stocktaking.* Sarajevo: International Commission for Missing Persons.

Šaviha-Valha, N. & Sahić, E., 2015. *Building trans-ethnic space.* Sarajevo: Nansen Dialogue Center.

Skaar, E. & Malca, G. C., 2015. Transitional justice alternatives: claims and counterclaims. In E. Skaar, T. Eide & G. C. Malca, eds. *After violence: Transitional justice, peace, and democracy.* London: Routledge.

Sloan, E. C., 1998. *Bosnia and the new collective security.* Westport: Greenwood Publishing Group.

Sriram, C. L., 2010. Resolving Conflicts and Pursuing Accountability: Beyond 'Justice Versus Peace'. In O. Richmond, ed. *Palgrave advances in peacebuilding: critical developments and approaches.* Berlin: Springer, pp. 279–293.

Sterland, B., 2006. *Civil Society Capacity Building in Post-Conflict Societies: The Experience of Bosnia and Herzegovina and Kosovo.* [Online] Available at: www.intrac.org/wpcms/wp-content/uploads/2016/09/Praxis-Paper-9-Civil-Society-Capacity-Building-in-Post-Conflict-Societies-Bill-Sterland.pdf [Last accessed August 15 2017].

Subotic, J., 2016. Political memory as an obstacle to justice in Serbia, Croatia, and Bosnia-Herzegovina. In M. Fischer & O. Simic, eds. *Transitional Justice and Reconciliation: Lessons from the Balkans.* London: Routledge, p. 121.

The International Criminal Tribunal for the former Yugoslavia (ICTY), 2017. *Achievements.* [Online] Available at: www.icty.org/en/about/tribunal/achievements [Last accessed 12 August 2017].

United Nations Security Council, 1993. *Resolution 827.* [Online] Available at: https://documents-dds-ny.un.org/doc/UNDOC/GEN/N93/306/28/IMG/N9330628.pdf?OpenElement [Last accessed 15 August 2017].

Van Zyl, P., 2006. Promoting transitional justice in post-conflict societies. In: H. Hänggi & A. Bryden, eds. *Security Governance in Post-Conflict Peacebuilding.* Geneva: Geneva Centre for the Democratic Control of Armed Forces.

Zivanović, M., 2015. Discrimination: from construction to deconstruction, an essay on the prospects of reconciliation in Bosnia-Herzegovina 20 years after Dayton. In M. Fischer & O. Simic, eds. *Transitional Justice and Reconciliation: Lessons from the Balkans.* London: Routledge.

15 The quest for justice in post-war Sri Lanka

Shyamika Jayasundara-Smits

Introduction

The history and the causes of the civil war in Sri Lanka (1983–2009) are popularly found to be grounded in the contentious ethnic relations between the Sinhalese majority and the Tamil minority, and the political and economic marginalization of the latter community by the successive majority-backed Sinhalese governments that have come to state power since independence from the British in 1948 (De Silva, 2000; De Votta, 2004). According to a recent literature survey conducted on the state of democracy in Sri Lanka, Uyangoda observed that many scholars had applied cultural and ideological yardsticks to explain the growth and spread of majority and minority ethnic politics within the conventional nation-state framework (Uyangoda, 2009).

In addition to the popular ethnocentric explanations, the aspect of economic marginalization of the minorities in national development planning since independence is identified as another cause for the intensification of tensions between the two main ethnic groups. The economic analysis of the conflict has gained traction in academic and policy studies, particularly since the introduction of liberal economic policy under the J. R. Jayawardene Government in 1977 (Dunham & Jayasuriya, 2001). However, according to Moore, a clear correlation cannot be found between economic liberalization and heightening of ethnic conflict since the late 1980s (op cit., Uyangoda, 2009). To date, although the ethnic aspect of the conflict dominates the mainstream discourses on the conflict, researchers have argued that intra-élite class relations (between the traditional and the new élites in the Sinhalese majority community) conceived during the colonial phase of state capitalist transformation, and their continued struggle for political and state power, having had played a key role in configuring various events that led up to the brutal civil war (Jayawardena, 2003; Jayasundara-Smits, 2013).

While the causes and the manifestations of the ethno-political conflict and the civil war continue to be debated and contested, in May 2009, after almost 27 years of fighting (with brief periods of cessation of hostilities), the civil war ended with a unilateral military victory for the government armed forces. Many in the south of Sri Lanka—the majority of whom were Sinhala-

Buddhists—equated the 'end of war' with 'dawn of peace'. However, this remains hardly the case for many Tamils, especially those who are still living in the parts of war-ravaged north and east of the island (Sarvananthan, 2016).

It is in this context, for the radical Sinhala-Buddhists and for some members in the Tamil diaspora, that the pursuit of peace and justice in the post-war period has become another platform for the continuation of war: a war of words (Jayasundara-Smits, 2011). The civil war that finally ended without a negotiated peace agreement can be seen as establishing a victor's peace[1] (Goodhand, 2010), leaving many blurred boundaries and questions about how to make the transition from war to peace, beyond the military defeat of a particular group. More importantly, it raised a bigger question on how to deal with the issues of past human rights violations and alleged war crimes committed by both warring parties, especially during the last months (January to May 2009) of the war. Particularly, the victor's peace psyche party prevails among the majority Sinhalese community, and stands as a major impediment in envisioning a programme that allows the transition from war to peace and the realization of a 'positive peace'[2] or 'justpeace'[3] agenda in Sri Lanka. As Uyangoda notes, the attempts made by President Maithripala Sirisena and his coalition government towards breaking this adversarial duality of 'victor's peace vs. the Tamil vanquished', have thus far proven to be an enormously difficult task (Uyangoda, 2016). Post-war community relations are also marred by a lack of remorse and empathy towards the direct victims of the war, who largely belong to the Tamil ethnic group. Instead of showing empathy, some radical segments in the majority Sinhala-Buddhist community blame the war victims in the north and east of the country for having supported the Liberation Tigers of Tamil Eelam (LTTE)[4] and the 'terrorists'.

According to the radical Sinhalese Buddhists, war is a 'thing of the past'. Similar to what Van Der Merwe observed in South Africa (Avruch, 2010), also in Sri Lanka, the majority in the Sinhalese community regards granting the alleged perpetrators (in their terms 'war heroes') amnesty from criminal responsibility as a wiser option, and a necessity in order to safeguard the hard-earned peace. Consequently, any attempt made at bringing a justice agenda, particularly the ones that attempt to hold the state or government parties criminally accountable, is perceived as unnecessary and a step backwards. Given these observations, the developments since the end of the civil war in Sri Lanka constitute an incomplete 'transition.'[5] As succinctly summed up by Höglund and Orujela, 'there is no 'transition' in Sri Lanka in the sense of transition from a militarized society to a non-militarized society, nor a transition from an undemocratic to a democratic society' (Höglund & Orujela, 2013, p. 6). Instead, the passage of transition is burdened with haunting memories of recent and past episodes of violence, and a long list of atrocities, committed during and in the post-war period, that has not been addressed[6]. Thus, the end of the civil war is perceived as the closure of one unfortunate episode of violence within the multiple histories of violence of the country (Somasundaram & Sambasivamoorthy, 2013). Therefore, any attempt made at digging in to the legacies of this particular era of violence tends to draw overwhelming attention from the public (across all three main ethnic groups) and add pressure for bringing justice to all the victims of all episodes of violence. Consequently, any piecemeal style of justice process that highlights and privileges one ethnic community's victimhood over others—particularly that of the Tamils over the Sinhalese—finds it difficult to gather support (especially from the Sinhalese majority in the South, who claim victimhood in all past violent episodes.)[7]

Given the above, it is correct to state that politicking of the discourse of justice and accountability has marked the post-war political environment in Sri Lanka.[8] This development has left diminishing space for any moral reflection or conceiving a decent sense of moral accountability towards the victims.[9] Thus, the opportunity presented in post-war Sri Lanka for carrying out a transitional justice process, whether it is led locally, internationally or both in combination, is not welcomed. It is not seen (especially by the radical Sinhalese Buddhists) as a vehicle or a critical moment in achieving the long-due collective political (democratization) and social goals (social justice) that led to a war. As a result, the current debates on post-war transitional justice discourse tend to centre around divisive, politically charged opinions that deny any criminal accountability of the state armed forces and amnesty to the LTTE, and to achieve parochial political interests. Under the above conditions, it is correct to claim that the transition from war to peace only resembles an uncertain peaceful stalemate (Goodhand, 2005). In this context, it remains important to think about how to capitalize on the moments of the peaceful stalemate to inspire and realize a meaningful transitional justice agenda.

The international transitional justice agenda and its domestic muddling effects

Following up on the evidence gathered by a special panel appointed by the United Nations (UN) Secretary-General on war crimes and crimes against humanity, the panel's final report[10] demanded that the Sri Lankan authorities conduct a credible war crime probe into the war and the actions of the warring parties. The evidence of wrongdoing by state forces presented in this report included: shelling on a large scale in three consecutive 'No Fire Zones', where it had encouraged the civilian population to congregate; depriving trapped civilians of humanitarian aid; summarily executing suspected LTTE members; and the torture and harsh interrogation of internally displaced persons in refugee camps (United Nations, 2011). Alongside the evidence against the state armed forces, the report also presented an account of the alleged atrocities committed by the LTTE. These include: forced conscription of children as young as 14 years old; locating military equipment in densely populated areas; and shooting civilians who attempted to escape from certain areas. The report also indicated that, during the last phase of the civil war, as many as 40,000 civilians were killed, mostly as a result of shelling by government forces. According to a recent statement released by the Office of the Missing Persons (OMP)[11] that partially confirms some of these findings, there were about 65,000 disappearances reported in Sri Lanka (Ruki, 2016). Estimates presented by civil society organizations suggest that the number of disappeared citizens and unaccounted deaths is even higher (CPA, 2015).[12]

While the victims and their families continue to struggle to bring a proper closure to their pain and sorrow through the means of cultural and social customs, ritual performances, and/or by official legal and administrative processes,[13] the country's top politico-military élites and some of the surviving members of the LTTE who were in leadership positions continue to enjoy impunity for their actions. The stringent criticisms and increased scrutiny of the international community, spearheaded by the UN, often backed by the USA (under the Obama Administration), the United Kingdom, and the European Union (EU), eventually led to calls for a war crimes probe that have fallen on the deaf ears. As the independent panel appointed by the UN Secretary-General observed, during and even in the aftermath of the civil war, the Sri Lankan authorities and the LTTE have shown a disregard for established international norms (United Nations, 2011).

The disregard for the repeated calls from the UN for the Sri Lankan Government (notably under President Mahinda Rajapaksa) to conduct a credible war crimes investigation was viewed as a serious threat to the entire regime of international law designed to protect individual dignity (Mortimer, n.d.).[14] Although the Rajapaksa regime attempted to present numerous local initiatives of justice—such as the Presidential Commissions of Inquiry, established in 2006, and the Lessons Learnt and Reconciliation Commission (LLRC)[15], appointed in 2016—as sufficient efforts in the pursuit of justice, none of these impressed the West. These local initiatives were seen as politically influenced processes and poor ploys for buying time to avoid responsibility.

The eventual non-implementation of the recommendations of the final LLRC report (issued in November 2011) further proved the duplicity of the local processes as suspected by the international actors. As the UN independent panel also implied, the disappointing outcomes of the local processes of justice demonstrated a lack of political will, on the part of state authorities, to conduct a credible judicial process to hold the perpetrators accountable. Also, the choice to ignore repeated calls made by the UN for the establishment of a credible and independent process by the country's top leadership was seen as a serious assault on international law. As the UN panel put it, 'the entire regime of international law designed to protect individual dignity has been weakened by the Government of Sri Lanka's actions and perceived impunity' (Mortimer, n.d., p. 2). For some critics in the international community, 'the scorched-earth tactics' employed by the Sri Lankan political regime were setting a dangerous trend and were an attempt of legitimizing the breaking of any international rulebook for fighting terrorism (Mortimer, n.d., p. 2). Further, the liberal western coalition for justice also maintained that Sri Lanka's shortcomings in delivering justice and holding the perpetrators accountable for their misdeeds signalled a broader failure of governance and the rule of law (Mytili, 2015). Thus, the subsequent UN resolutions on Sri Lanka put forward even stronger demands for undertaking extensive and meaningful state reforms. In another report issued in 2014 by the UN High Commissioner for Human Rights, Sri Lanka's lack of domestic progress could 'no longer be explained as a function of time or lack of technical capacity rather a question of political will' (Mytili, 2015). In 2016, during a visit to Sri Lanka, the UN Secretary-General, Ban Ki-Moon, accepted the failures of the UN system in protecting the civilians during the last phase of the war while lamenting the lack of progress in bringing justice to the victims and holding the perpetrators accountable for their misdeeds (Deen, 2016).

However, the consistent framing by the former president Mahinda Rajapaksa[16], of the last phase of the civil war as a 'humanitarian war' or 'a war against terrorism', when the war ended with a unilateral military victory for the government armed forces, it also left no room for realizing a political agenda for accountability and justice. Particularly, in his framing of the last phase of war within the international 'war against terrorism', ex-president Rajapaksa hoped to erase any grounds for the need for a special accountability mechanism and a justice agenda that could target the state and government parties to the war. Hence, while the majority Sinhalese took to the streets to celebrate the war victories and the 'defeat of terrorism', the 'top-down' punitive international transitional justice agenda began to make swift inroads into the post-war discourses, and became part of domestic political squabbles.

At the same time, one could also note that the international justice agenda created two levels of division: (i) divisions between the locals that supported the war and those that supported peace (local-local division), and (ii) divisions between the local advocates of war and the international community advocates of justice (local-international division). However, the Rajapaksa regime continued to capitalize on the war victories platform and wasted no time in appropriating the international transitional justice agenda as its main topic in domestic electoral politics, framing it as the main enemy of the 'sovereign local people'. The unexpected defeat of Rajapaksa in the mid-term presidential elections held in 2015 further exacerbated the domestic divisions related to the international justice agenda. Some segments in the southern Sinhalese constituencies framed his electoral defeat as a plot by western governments, aided by some circles in the Colombo-based westernized and liberal intelligentsia, who were targeting the war heroes by advocating for an internationally-oriented transitional justice agenda.

Before the dust settled from the defeat of Rajapaksa, the newly-elected President Sirisena and the coalition government which came to power in early 2015 began to come under pressure from the international community to deliver a credible transitional justice process. The eventual co-sponsoring of a resolution with the UN Human Rights Commission (UNHRC)—Resolution

30/1, adopted in October 2015—with the backing of the USA is one early outcome of this process. It is also the first sign of a new government trying to appease and work around the international agenda. As Bell has observed in her work on the politics of transitional justice, the culmination of a series of developments in post-war Sri Lanka and the bitter fight to control transitional justice mechanisms and their desired direction brought another war: a war of words with regards to justice. As much as the actual physical conduct of the war, the discursive war surrounding the transitional justice agenda in post-war Sri Lanka reflects attempts to tilt the transitional justice process towards an end point that approximates victors' battle field goals (Bell, 2009).

Different agendas of justice: collisions, juxtapositions and marginalization

The literature on the politicization of transitional justice agendas, and their effects on domestic politics in different post-war contexts, is growing in volumes (Van der Merwe, 2009). Following such trends, there is already quite a substantive body of literature dedicated to revealing the different agendas and politics surrounding the transitional justice agendas in Sri Lanka (Uyangoda, 2016; Xavier, 2015; Walton, 2015; Mytili, 2015; Höglund & Orjuela, 2013). These studies advance and advocate for two main agendas for achieving post-war transitional justice, namely (i) a transitional justice agenda that is oriented internationally, and (ii) a transitional justice agenda that is oriented domestically. In addition to these two main agendas, the radical Tamil diaspora's agenda for justice and accountability is widely thought to be intersecting with the internationally oriented justice agenda promoted by the UN and a coalition of western liberal states. As much as the UN-sponsored international agenda for justice and accountability has been criticized, so too has the Tamil diaspora's agenda by the local rivals. Many radical Sinhalese Buddhists believe that the commitment and support extended by the Tamil diaspora, for an internationally handled punitive form of transitional justice and accountability mechanism, is nothing other than playing identity politics and diaspora politics *sans* accountability. These criticisms seem to fall in line with Benedict Anderson's studies on diaspora politics as part of 'long distance nationalism', and 'the guilt of departure' and 'lawfare' (op. cit., Mytili, 2015, p. 1).

As demonstrated above, currently the two main transitional justice agendas are producing clashing effects due to their different framings, purposes, *modus operandi, and modus vivendi*.[17] They often lead to contentions and barriers for bringing justice to the most direct victims of the war. The consistent demands put forward by successive UN High Commissioners for Human Rights, particularly since the end of the war, for establishing a hybrid court with local and international judges remains a major point of contention. Initially, although Sri Lanka agreed to the participation of foreign judges in any war related criminal proceedings, it later backtracked on this agreement by insisting on having purely local courts to investigate the alleged war crimes. The changes in the Government's stances on the international transitional agenda and the cherry-picking of its various components mirrors the domestic political whirlwinds surrounding and going beyond the transitional justice discourse. In a number of respects, the overall situation in Sri Lanka on the question of how to go about post-war justice can be attributed to the legal maxim, 'Justice delayed is justice denied', or, as William Penn echoed, 'to delay justice is injustice'.

The current situation is likely to prevail, and recalls bitter memories of repeatedly failed attempts of international liberal peacebuilding experiments and state-/peacebuilding agendas in the island (Jayasundara-Smits, 2013). To these effects, the promotion of an internationally led transitional justice process in Sri Lanka is undoubtedly a highly controversial and seemingly undesirable measure (Walton, 2015). Domestically, any genuine move towards holding the perpetrators of alleged war crimes accountable, using any process, is like walking in a political minefield. As Uyangoda notes, although some seemingly genuine symbolic gestures and institutionalized initiatives have been pursued by the government of President Sirisena, there are doubts about their seriousness and the Government's ability to manoeuvre the domestic political divisions in constructing a broader political consensus to address issues of justice, accountability, reconciliation, peacebuilding, and state-building (Uyangoda, 2016). As revealed in early 2017 by the then Minister of Foreign Affairs, Mangala Samaraweera (Associated Press, 2017), Sri Lanka's intentions of requesting more time from the UN to conduct the war crimes probes only raises more doubts about the Government's commitment. This further reveals the diminishing political leverage that the Sri Lankan Government has in pursuing a credible justice process in the future. However, it is worth mentioning that, in a similar manner to ex-president Rajapaksa, the President Sirisena also relies on the support of the Sinhala nationalist voter base or 'the victors of the war', for his political survival, thus, facing strong pressures to avoid any restorative measures or retributive justice measures against the state armed forces (Walton, 2015, p. 18).

Any justice process that could potentially frame Rajapaksa and his 'strongmen' as war criminals or perpetrators is likely to have serious negative repercussions on Sirisena's political career, his troubled coalition government, and the overall political environment of Sri Lanka. By all accounts, as Walton sums up, 'Sirisena's [election] victory also reveals the wider constraints facing Sri Lanka's Southern elite in their efforts to build peace' (Walton, 2015, p. 18). As Vinjamuri and Snyder's work suggests, the current situation in Sri Lanka exposes the effects of the creeping of the international justice agenda into the national political context (Vinjamuri & Snyder, 2004). Among which, the political expediency that they render to the divided political élites in the domestic electoral political arena is worrying. Worst of all, they expose the mundane 'politics of denial'[18] of the 'top brass' political élites.

In parallel with the brewing domestic political tensions surrounding the international transitional justice agenda, the tensions within the international community on Sri Lanka's transitional justice process (i.e. the withholding by China and Russia of any support for an international crimes probe) is worth highlighting. The tensions at the international level expose the connection, mutually reinforcing and reproducing effects between the international and local justice agendas, although at the outset they seem constituted as each other's binary opposites. The tensions at the international level surrounding a punitive justice process for Sri Lanka denote 'politics as usual' between the western liberal camp on one side, and China and Russia on the other. It has been argued that the latter were instrumental in allowing Rajapaksa to avoid any internationally oriented justice agenda. They supported Rajapaksa's framing of the situation and his accusations of the West's efforts as threats to the country's sovereignty. They endorsed Rajapakse's claim, the war was a necessary measure, inasmuch as it was a humanitarian war, and it was the duty of the state to exercise its sovereign and legitimate right to protect its citizens, including the innocent Tamils fleeing from LTTE terrorism. Rajapaksa's representation of the conflict in this way exploited and fed into the long-standing tensions within the international community (Höglund & Orjuela, 2013) and, more precisely, fuelled the fight between the 'sovereigntists' and the 'cosmopolitans'. By exploiting these tensions, Rajapaksa attempted to advance his parochial political interests domestically.

Meanwhile, the Rajapakse administration's non-aligned foreign policy, which was increasingly directed towards the East and towards oppressive regimes such as Libya and Myanmar, was judged in some quarters as a serious threat to global peace and justice. Building alliances with these countries to counter war crime charges and human rights abuses using the pretext of a 'war on terror' is considered as a dangerous model and a threat to international peace and security Mortimer, n.d.). The UN's real and perceived failure to address the threats posed by the so-called 'Sri Lankan model' certainly has helped to reproduce the conflict between the 'sovereigntist' and the 'cosmopolitanist' camps in international politics and on the domestic front as well. Although Sri Lanka's trajectory of the pursuit of (or a lack of) a transitional justice agenda shows some uniqueness due to the domestic and international political conditions under which it is being realized. At the same time, it may not be that unique if one considers similar experiences taking place, such as the case of Colombia.

Besides the policing effects of the transitional justice agenda, locally and internationally, the claimed 'successes' of international transitional justice processes (for instance, the trials held in Nuremburg, Tokyo, Croatia, and at the International Criminal Tribunal for the former Yugoslavia), are assumptions that have not been tested rigorously (Vinjamuri & Snyder, 2004). At the same time, as Jacoby noted, we are also running out of ideas about how to address the strong prima facie case or evidence that exists for a moral obligation by the state/society to punish criminals through due process (Jacoby,

2007). Thus, addressing the social repudiation of past human rights violations becomes an important moral obligation for any new government carrying out a transition towards a stable democracy (Verwoerd, 1999). Prosecuting and punishing the perpetrators often brings justice to the victims. Amnesty is the least welcomed element of transitional justice in some sectors. The deep need for retribution to restore a profound sense of moral equilibrium therefore compels one to demand that people pay for the harm they have done to others (Verwoerd, 1999). However, in the current context of post-war Sri Lanka, realizing a societal moral imperative is constrained by the political tug of war between the local and the international justice agendas, and the contentious politics underpinning them.

However, any attempt to bring justice to the victims and hold the perpetrators accountable through the hegemonic popular punitive processes does raise fundamental doubts about whether the 'kind of justice' they generate addresses the full spectrum of justice needs[19] of the most directly affected victims. It is not only that the very process of a punitive approach to transitional justice is met with resistance when it is designed to allocate blame, makes claims about responsibility, and involves criminal punishment. It also often results in more ambiguities about what justice means to individuals and different groups (Bell, 2009). As a result, sometimes justice is framed in multiple ways: as a struggle for human rights, as an international intervention, or as a tool of conflict resolution and state-building (Bell, 2009). To this effect, as recent empirical studies from Nepal have revealed, victims do emphasize the need for the truth about the disappeared, but their immediate priorities are to obtain economic support to help meet basic material needs (Robins, 2011). Such empirical findings call for reassessing the international transitional agenda critically and calling out for a meaningful and contextualized justice process. Scholars and practitioners who have conducted outstanding and extensive ethnographic research with communities in war-torn Sri Lanka have also highlighted the priorities of restoring social capital, strengthening social networks and community ties, and building social organizations as sure ways of addressing the immediate needs of the victims (Human Rights Watch, 2008).

Overall, as opposed to macro-level grand forms of ceremonial political and punitive mechanisms of justice, the empirical findings tend to recommend reforming macro social policies and increasing access to external resources, justice and power, as better ways of satisfying victims' immediate needs of justice and their long-term agendas of social justice[20] (Xavier, 2015). In light of the most recent ethnographic work, one may wonder how any 'top-down' legalist punitive approach to justice in the forms of criminal trials and prosecutions of a few high profile individuals might serve the needs as articulated by the most direct victims of the war. Similar to post-conflict Nepal, in post-war Sri Lanka, the prioritization and early advent of the discourse of individual prosecutions—an agenda pushed by the international community—blatantly reveals the sad truth of ignoring or side-lining the victims' real needs and their agendas (Robins, 2011). These recent case studies also reveal that this approach can marginalize social, economic, and cultural rights in favour of the contentious civil and political rights of the affected people (Villalba, 2011). The narrow view of transitional justice as realized through the mainstream political discourses and their everyday practices fails to address the deep-rooted social stratification of the past; deep inequalities in post-war societies along class, caste, gender and ethnicity lines; and the risks of letting greedy political entrepreneurs exploit them for their parochial benefit.

Concluding Remarks

In general, there are different discourses, agendas, and rationalities that have given rise to various models of justice (Fischer, 2011). All these models continue to grapple with understanding and addressing what justice is, what it looks like, what it feels like, what goals it should entail, who should decide, who should own the process, how it should be done, who its main reference subjects should be, and what the main object of them should be.

In post-war Sri Lanka, so far, for the immediate victims of many episodes of violence, justice largely remains a void promise. Throughout the island's history, 'justice' has been a contested topic and continues to remain so. Post-war (transitional) justice and accountability has become a highly politicized topic. Currently, the various debates surrounding this issue are driven more by the logic of emotions and less by the logic of appropriateness, thus finding it challenging to strike a meaningful balance between the two[21]. As discussed in this chapter, in the post-war context, the two transitional justice agendas (the local and the international) have their proponents and opponents. The clash between these two main agendas veto each other, and prevent the realization of any alternative agenda focus on the needs of the most affected victims of the war. As many analysts and scholars have noted, there is a clash or incompatibility between the two main justice agendas. Together, they have created a situation that blatantly exposes the instrumental use of both these agendas for achieving narrow political objectives (Uyangoda, 2016, Xavier, 2015, Mytili, 2015, Höglund and Orjuela, 2013).

At the same time, Sri Lanka's graduation in 2010 by the International Monetary Fund into lower middle-income country status, just over a year after the end of the war, and the consequent loss of access to traditional development trade concession schemes, has put pressure on global powers to seek new ways to keep their influence in Sri Lanka. This development has brought about tensions within the international community and within their views on transitional justice as a tool to gain a hold in the politics of Sri Lanka. It is in this context, pushing the global templates of the international transitional justice agenda, that the West's strongly embedded punitively-oriented international human rights agenda has become a crucial means of regaining the loss of control and regulatory power over the country. The numerous warnings and threats issued by the international community of western states—that the trade and foreign aid schemes beneficial to Sri Lanka stand to be scrapped unless the country demonstrates good will and compliance with the international human rights agenda—provide evidence of such a relationship. The EU, by initially imposing a total of 58 conditions related to human rights abuses, and linking them to continuation or discontinuation of its Generalized System of Preferences (GSP Plus)[22] provides concrete evidence of the connection between justice and trade[23].

On the part of the local élites, the tensions which were ignited by the international transitional justice agenda gave much-needed breathing space (for both post-war political regimes) to return to politics as usual and continuation in power. For the Rajapaksa regime, against the backdrop of the fading rhetoric of war victories and non-realization of the promised peace dividends, the tensions with the international community helped in buying time for the regime to consolidate its position. For the Sri Lankan state, in turn, opening a new confrontation with the West and the liberal international cosmopolitan élite (joined by some radical Tamil diaspora circles), which continued to press for internationally-oriented punitive transitional justice agenda, became an instrument for building political capital domestically.

In the same vein, for the government of President Sirisena, re-engaging with the transitional justice agenda (subject to limited international orientation) was to be important in the process of regime consolidation. Rather than being a factor of unity, his victory further paved the way for making visible the divergence within the majority Sinhalese-Buddhists, which had been less visible up to that point due to the essentialism of the 'inter-ethnic' aspect assigned to the conflict and the civil war. The overall political atmosphere of post-war Sri Lanka thus continued to be marked by deep divisions between the Troika (the political-military-religious élites). Their divisions became more pronounced when Rajapaksa lost mid-term presidential elections in 2015. Against this backdrop, for Sirisena's coalition Government[24], seeking alliances with the international cosmopolitan élites by re-orienting the international transitional justice agenda with some modifications was to prove a useful strategy, providing Sirisena with a much-needed political safety net domestically and with protection from the international community. In this sense, by all accounts, the Sirisena Government's appeasement towards an international justice agenda, that is adapted and continues to be adjusted to the immediate local political realities, can be regarded as measures undertaken by the national élite in order to recapture the justice agenda.

What has been lost in all these processes is the realization of the victims' agenda of justice and attention to their needs. Similar to the conclusion of Leebaw, we can draw the conclusion that the case of Sri Lanka exposes and continues to unfold the dependent nature of international justice mechanisms on the local élites and the tight interactions, intersections, and reproduction of local and international élites' political agendas (Leebaw, 2008).

Wars only produce and reproduce the power of the powerful. It is often only the promise of justice that is left for the victims. To this effect, it is worth remembering Michael Ignatieff's assertion that truth and reconciliation processes 'only reduce the number of lies that can be circulated unchallenged in public discourse', as the famous Nuremburg and Tokyo trials which only found few guilty left the rest went untouched (*op cit.,* Verwoerd, 1999, p. 121).

However, at this juncture, one may wonder what Colombia and other countries currently emerging out of violent conflicts and civil wars can learn from Sri Lanka's experiences in going about 'thinking and doing justice'? In many respects, at least on paper, the case of Colombia certainly offers more hope for victims in that country than was the case in Sri Lanka. Colombia's main conflict between the state and the Fuerzas Armadas Revolucionarias de Colombia—Ejército del Pueblo (FARC—EP), ending with a negotiated peace agreement, has already taken a positive step in this direction. Furthermore, the current Colombian transitional justice roadmap can be considered as a victim-centred agenda infused with both punitive and restorative measures. However, this is just the beginning of a long, arduous, and painful journey towards healing. In that light, it seems important to think of ways for retaining this current balance of the 'logic of appropriateness', 'logic of consequence' and more importantly the 'logic of emotion' for the sake of the victims (Vinjamuri & Snyder, 2004, p. 345). Since the implementation of the justice agenda takes place over a very long period of time, even decades, there should be practical and institutional measurements to preserve this balance and sustain the current political momentum towards serving the victims' agenda. On both these accounts, saving the transitional justice agenda in both its spirit and its content from un-expected different 'winds of change' in the national and international political arenas is important.

Although at present, the Colombian transitional agenda seems to be largely owned by the Colombians, it is important not to let it be hijacked by the particular local or global economic and political forces, and justice becoming a bargaining chip in the (trans-) national political games of the élites. Implementing justice agendas can be expensive and requires resources. Therefore, generating and mobilizing enough resources (with no strings attached) to prioritize the victims' needs and their agendas is crucial. Last not least, given the root causes of the Colombian conflict (which were similar to those which initiated the violence in Sri Lanka), working on a social justice agenda is vital. To this end, investing in future generations in building a moral-ethical state and a polity that is resilient, empathic and caring is essential.

Notes

1 A 'victor's peace' is understood as a type of peace following a military victory by one warring party on whose terms and conditions the post-war peace is being established. For an elaborated discussion of this concept, refer to (Richmond, 2014)
2 Galtung defines positive peace as not only absence of war and direct violence (negative peace) but also absence of structural forms of violence (Galtung, 1969, p. 183)
3 According to Lederach, 'justpeace' is 'an adaptive process-structure of human relationships characterized by high justice and low violence: an infrastructure of

Post-war Sri Lanka: the quest for justice 247

organization or governance that responds to human conflict through non-violent means as first and last resorts: a view of systems as responsive to the permanency and interdependence of relationships and change' in Preparing for Peace (Lederach, 1995, pp. 3–23).

4 Eelam means 'separate state'.
5 According to Bell, a 'transition' is not the same as a post-conflict scenario. In a context where the conflict settlement is arrived at through negotiation, it creates a set of political and legal institutional structures that enable the same political struggles to take place less violently (Bell, 2009, p. 25).
6 Major periods of violence include; the Janatha Vimukthi Peramuna (JVP) uprising in the late 1980s and early 1990s, the mass expulsion of the northern Muslims by the LTTE in 1993, and the Sinhala-Muslim conflicts in southern Sri Lanka in the more recent past.
7 Vamik Volkan uses the term 'chosen traumas' to explain this particular psychological condition. The chosen trauma functions as a significant marker for the large-group identity and creates a foundation for the society's development of an exaggerated entitlement ideology. It is often subject to political manipulation (Volkan, 2004).
8 Although this chapter primarily focuses on the case of Sri Lanka, the deeper patterns and the underlying structural and international political context seems relevant to other contexts such as Colombia.
9 Among other factors, Uyangoda suggests this is partly a result of the moral community, namely the Buddhist clergy shunning the path of giving leadership to such an agenda, instead following the punitive agenda of justice (Uyangoda, 2016).
10 See United Nations, 2011.
11 Office of Missing Persons (OMP) is the first foundation laid for the proposed four transitional justice mechanisms, which the Sirisena Government has pledged to establish.
12 According to a recent comment made by Prime Minister Ranil Wickramasinghe, many among those reported disappeared could be dead.
13 As anthropologist Sasanka Perera shows in his seminal study, the human body and the absence of a dead human body (which could result from disappearances) makes social practices of mourning incomplete. Besides, under law, the absence of a human body also prevents the state from issuing a death certificate and consequently prevents the closure of the administrative legal process related to a death (Perera, 2008).
14 Edward Mortimer is chair of the Sri Lanka campaign for peace and justice and senior vice-president of the Salzburg Global Seminar. He was chief speechwriter and director of communications for UN Secretary-General Kofi Annan until 2006.
15 A veteran and well-respected former civil servant, Prof. Tissa Vitharana, headed this process.
16 Who was also the commander-in-chief of the armed forces.
17 In Latin these two terms mean, 'a usual way of doing something' and 'a feasible arrangement or practical compromise; especially one that bypasses difficulties' (Merriam-Webster, n.d.).
18 I borrow this term from the works of psychologists Michael A. Milburn and Sheree D. Conrad (1996). The authors argue that the political life of a nation often exhibits shared denial of painful realities. Denial is a common practice for states and nations with histories of atrocities. According to Psychoanalysis, denial functions as a useful defence mechanism to forget or distort the agonizing reality which influences perceptions and attitudes on political issues.
19 As per the practice of restorative justice, information regarding the offence, truth-telling, empowerment, and restitution or vindication are important justice needs demanded by the victims. For more details of these aspects refer to (Zehr, 2002).

20 In the simplest sense, social justice means 'fair and just relation between the individual and society'.
21 Logic of appropriateness stems from legalism and logic of consequences from pragmatism. Logic of emotions recognizes the significance of transitional justice but emphasizes strategies that diverge from the model of legalism (Vinjamuri, and Snyder, 2004, p. 345). The logic of consequences applies a pragmatic approach to justice, weighing the social, political, and institutional outcomes of prosecutions versus amnesties.
22 The Generalized System of Preferences (GSP Plus) is an enhanced EU incentive scheme of which Sri Lanka first became a beneficiary in 2005. It is a scheme whose functioning is based on economic and political conditions. In order to qualify for the GSP+ scheme, a country should comply with 27 international conventions focusing on core human rights, labour rights, the environment, and good governance principles. Presently under this scheme, about 7,200 Sri Lankan products are traded in the EU free of duty (Senewiratne, 2016).
23 After a long 'tug of war' between the EU and the Sri Lankan authorities, on 17 May 2017 Sri Lanka re-entered the GSP Plus scheme following a seven-year suspension. The EU Ambassador to Sri Lanka stated on the occasion of re-entry to the scheme: 'We are satisfied with the Government's progress as well as their commitment.' (Lanka Business Online, 2017)
24 The coalition included the United National Party (UNP), which had a reputation of western liberal orientation.

References

Associated Press, 2017. *Sri Lanka to ask UN for more time to probe war crimes*. s.l.: s.n.

Avruch, K., 2010. Truth and Reconciliation Commissions: Problems in Transitional Justice and the Reconstruction of Identity. *Transcultural Psychiatry*, 47(1), pp. 33–49.

Bell, C., 2009. Transitional Justice, Interdisciplinary and the State of the 'Field' or 'Non-Field'. *The International Journal of Transitional Justice*, Volume 3, pp. 5–27.

CPA, 2015. *Transitional Justice in Sri Lanka and Ways Forward*. Colombo: Centre for Policy Alternatives.

De Silva, K., 2000. *Reaping the Whirlwind: Ethnic Conflict, Ethnic Politics in Sri Lanka*. Kandy: s.n.

De Votta, N., 2004. *Blowback: Linguistic Nationalism, Institutional Decay, and Ethnic Conflict in Sri Lanka*. s.l.: Stanford University Press.

Deen, T., 2016. *UN Chief Non-committal on international judges for war crimes probe here, 28th August 2016*. s.l.: The Sunday Times.

Dunham, D. & Jayasuriya, S., 2001. *Liberalisation and Political Decay: Sri Lanka's Journey from Welfare State to a Brutalised Society*. The Hague: International Institute of Social Studies.

Fischer, M., 2011. Transitional Justice and Reconciliation: Theory and Practice. In: M. F. H. G. B. Austin, ed. *Advancing Conflict Transformation, The Berghof Handbook II*. Opladen/Framington Hills: Barbara Budrich Publishers.

Galtung, J., 1969. Violence, Peace, and Peace Research. *Journal of Peace Research*, 6 (3), pp. 167–191.

Goodhand, J., 2005. Frontiers and Wars: the Opium Economy in Afghanistan. *Journal of Agrarian Change*, 5(2), pp. 191–216.

Goodhand, J., 2010. Stabilising a Victor's Peace? Humanitarian Action and Reconstruction in Eastern Sri Lanka. *Disasters*, 34(s3), pp. S342–S367.

Höglund, K. & Orjuela, C., 2013. Friction and the pursuit of justice in post-war Sri Lanka. *Journal of Peacebuilding*, 1(3), pp. 300–316.
Human Rights Watch, 2008. *Sri Lanka: 'Disappearances' by Security Forces a National Crisis.* [Online] Available at: www.hrw.org/news/2008/03/06/sri-lanka-disappearances-security-forces-national-crisis [Last accessed 13 September 2017].
Jacoby, T., 2007. *Understanding conflict and violence: Theoretical and interdisciplinary approaches.* Abingdon: Routledge.
Jayasundara-Smits, S., 2011. *Conflict, war and peace in Sri Lanka; Politics by other means?* s.l.: EADI/DSA.
Jayasundara-Smits, S., 2013. *In Pursuit of Hegemony: Politics and State Building in Sri Lanka.* The Hague: International Institute of Social Studies-Erasmus University Rotterdam.
Jayawardena, K., 2003. *Nobodies to Somebody: The Rise of the Colonial Bourgeoisie in Sri Lanka.* London: Zed Books Limited.
Lanka Business Online, 2017. *Sri Lanka regains EU's GSP+ tariff benefits this week.* [Online] Available at: www.lankabusinessonline.com/sri-lanka-regains-eus-gsp-tariff-benefits-this-week/ [Last accessed 22 September 2017].
Lederach, J. P., 1995. *Preparing for Peace: Conflict Transformation Across Cultures.* Syracuse, New York: Syracuse University Press.
Leebaw, B., 2008. The Irreconcilable goals of Transitional Justice. *Human Rights Quarterly*, 30(1), pp. 95–118.
Merriam-Webster, n.d. s.l.: s.n.
Milburn, M. A. & Conrad, S. D., 1996. *The Politics of Denial.* Cambridge: MIT Press.
Mortimer, E., n.d. *United Nations Regional Information Centre for Western Europe.* [Online] Available at: www.unric.org/en/sri-lanka/27123-why-sri-lanka-matters [Last accessed 6 September 2016].
Mytili, B., 2015. Transitional Justice in Sri Lanka: Rethinking Post-War Diaspora Advocacy for Accountability. *International Human Rights Law Journal*, 1(1).
Richmond, O.P., 2014. The Victor's Peace in History. In: O. P. Richmond, ed. *Peace: A Very Short Introduction.* s.l.: Oxford University Press, pp. 52–60.
Perera, S., 2008. Societies of Terror: Absence of a Body and Problems of Mourning and Coping. In: J. Uyangoda, ed. *Matters of Violence, reflections on social and politics in perspective.* Colombo: Social Scientists Association.
Robins, S., 2011. Towards Victim-Centred Transitional Justice: Understanding the Needs of Families of the Disappeared in Postconflict Nepal. *The International Journal of Transitional Justice*, Volume 5, pp. 75–98.
Ruki, F., 2016. *Sri Lanka's 65,000 disappeared: will the latest missing persons' office bring answers?.* [Online]. Available at: thewire.in/42687/sri-lankas-disappeared-will-the-latest-missing-persons-office-bring-answers/ [Last accessed 12 September 2017].
Sarvananthan, M., 2016. Elusive economic peace dividend in Sri Lanka: all that glitters is not gold. *GeoJournal*, 81(571).
Senewiratne, H. H., 2016. *GSP Plus concessions by UK to SL seen as being hit with EU exit.* [Online] Available at: www.ips.lk/staff/ed/latest_essays/downloads/gsp_plus.pdf [Last accessed 13 September 2017].
Somasundaram, D. & Sambasivamoorthy, S., 2013. Rebuilding community resilience in a post-war context: developing insight and recommendations-a qualitative study in Northern Sri Lanka. *International journal of mental health systems*, 7(1), pp. 1–24.
United Nations, 2011. *Report of the Secretary-General's Panel of Experts on Accountability in Sri Lanka*, New York: United Nations.

Uyangoda, J., 2009. Sri Lanka: State of Research on Democracy. *PCD Journal*, 1(1 and 2), p. 99.

Uyangoda, J., 2016. *Groundviews*. [Online] Available at: www.groundviews.org [Last accessed 2016].

Van der Merwe, H., 2009. Delivering Justice During Transitions: Challenges for Research. In H. Van der Merwe, V. Baxter & A. R. Chapman, eds. *Assessing the impact of Transitional Justice: Challenges for Empirical Research*. Washington, DC: United States Institute of Peace.

Verwoerd, W., 1999. Individual and/or social justice after Apartheid? The South African truth and reconciliation commission. *The European Journal of Development Research*, 11(2), pp. 115–140.

Villalba, C. S., 2011. *Transitional Justice: Key Concepts, Processes and Challenges*, s.l.: IDRC.

Vinjamuri, L. & Snyder, J., 2004. Advocacy and Scholarship in the Study of International War Crime Tribunals and Transitional Justice, *Annual Review of Political Science*, Volume 7, pp. 345–362.

Volkan, V., 2004. *Blind Trust: Large Groups and leaders in times of crisis and terror*. 1st ed. Virginia: Pitchstone Publishing.

Walton, O., 2015. *Timing and Sequencing of Post-Conflict Reconstruction and Peacebuilding in Sri Lanka*. Bath: University of Bath.

Xavier, S., 2015. Looking for 'Justice' in all the Wrong Places: An International Mechanism or Multidimensional Domestic Strategy for Mass Human Rights Violations in Sri Lanka? In A. Amarasingham. &. D. Bass, ed. *Post-War Sri Lanka: Problems and Prospects*. s.l.: Hurst/Oxford University Press.

Zehr, H., 2002. *Little Book on Restorative Justice*. Intercourse, PA: GoodBooks.

16 A long walk for justice

Fabio Andrés Díaz Pabón

Colombia has been waiting for peace for more than half a century. While waiting, generations of Colombians have had their lives spoilt by war, violence, and tragedy. However, hope is in sight, with the possibility that greater peace will be established and consolidated through the implementation of the peace agreement with the FARC—EP (Revolutionary Armed Forces of Colombia).

The history of Colombia is the history of a country trying to come to terms with itself as a nation. Thus the drive for the consolidation of statehood, incurring numerous setbacks or limitations in this regard, has been central to the country's development in the last seven decades. One could view the current peace process with the FARC—EP as novel, but as Chapter 2 shows, Colombia is a country that has sought peace for more than three decades, with multiple attempts involving different actors, approaches, and negotiation schemes, and with differing degrees of success. Colombia's modern history is one of peace in the making in the middle of war, an example of state-building emerging from the midst of war.

The peace agreement with the FARC—EP emerged in a particular historical and political context. It is the outcome of a series of circumstances and elements that defined why the Government and the FARC—EP opted for a negotiated settlement, including the infrastructure and the capacity of the state to undertake this process and the way the process was structured. This agreement draws on lessons from previous failed peace processes with the FARC—EP and the existing peace infrastructure in Colombia, as shown in Chapter 3.

In the same way that Gabriel García Márquez brought some of the lyricism and rhythm of Latin American narratives to English speakers, the promise of the current peace agreements in Colombia between the FARC—EP and the Colombian Government offers the world a vision of peace crafted by Colombians, which presents a different approach to achieving justice for victims and achieving peace through recognizing local needs, contexts, and visions. As *One Hundred Years of Solitude* was a gift from Colombia to literature, the peace agreements could mark the beginning of the end of more than fifty years of war and can be seen as a gift from Colombia to humanity.

This agreement has been in the making for several decades, and is in fact the outcome of a history of initiatives related to the Colombian state's quest for peace, in part through several peace negotiations. As Chapter 4 illustrated, transitional justice legal frameworks have been progressively included into the peace negotiations that took place in the country from 1980 until the formulation of The Victims and Land Restitution Law in 2011, before the recent agreements reached with the FARC—EP, and this has led to the adoption of transitional justice frameworks in Colombia that have been instrumental for peace negotiations with the diverse actors from the country's armed conflict.

The current transitional justice framework defined by the peace agreement between the FARC—EP and the Colombian Government is the outcome of this historical process. The complex and elaborate system of principles and interlocking institutions that comprise this framework is the outcome of changing needs and of the evolution of understandings as to how to achieve justice and transition away from war over time in Colombia. The institutions of the Truth Commission, the Search Unit for Missing Persons, and the Special Jurisdiction for Peace, as well as the measures for reparation which have been considered and stated guarantees of non-repetition, present a significant promise for peace to take hold in the country. However, these institutions will face uncertainties related to the implementation process: how the peace agreement is implemented and translated from commitments on paper to reality will provide legal stability (or instability) for different constituents and for the peace project in Colombia, as shown in Chapter 5.

A view from the South on peace and justice

Peacebuilding and justice can be exercises of post-colonial thinking. As Mahmood Mamdani recently affirmed at the University of Cape Town (2017), the production of knowledge begins with ordering, and this ordering gives ranking to ideas and initiatives according to a series of different attributes that we use to ascribe them value and meaning.

The colonial project casts knowledge as built using categories, theories and ideas from the Global North, with validation and affirmation harvested in English, French, and German as opposed to isiXhosa or Quechua. The areas of peace and justice are no different, with the North historically used as a primary reference point. In doing so, pre-eminence has been given to the importance of the successes of the Nuremberg war trials: however, less attention has typically been paid to the lessons which could be learned from the failures of humanity with regard to Hiroshima, Nagasaki, Dresden, the gulags, and the colonial enterprises across the world in Indonesia, South Africa, Colombia, the Philippines, Algeria, Congo and many other countries. In many of these contexts, justice and retributive or reparative justice have not been pursued or fully achieved. Inasmuch as the North has been used as a point of reference for justice, we should be honest enough to recognize the lessons offered from its failures as well as its successes. An ideological enthusiasm about the promise of a Western vision of the world obscures productive and critical engagement with the challenges created by its approach and its failures, such as the two World Wars, holocausts and genocides, and the decimation of native populations across the world through missionary and colonial enterprises.

However, even more balanced interpretations of the approaches to peace and justice advanced in the North are unlikely to apply across the South. The realities of the Global South require the assertion of new approaches, that look beyond the imposition of 'universal' models from the North, and that create space for the emergence of ideas that adjust to the needs and the objectives of particular constituents and contexts across the world.

Such an approach should not be seen as an argument in defence of impunity and the deployment of pan-Africanism and pan-Americanism as mediocre excuses for sheltering war criminals. It is rather a plea to reassert and give prevalence to the voice of the victims and civilians in the countries where violence has taken place, so that they have the right to decide the way forward for their futures. Imposing ideal models onto others is another way of imposing one's beliefs onto other human beings—another way of violating their rights. Every society has the right to decide what is better for them, and this reassertion of agency fosters responsibility and maturity for societies. However, the mechanisms for making these decisions may be compromised in contexts emerging from conflict. In these contexts, transitional justice can offer benchmarks for promoting discussions regarding possible interventions or approaches, making visible the tensions between competing options or interests.

In analysing the agreements reached in Colombia we should depart from an understanding that the institutional form that the agreements take is not entirely European or North American, as they are not fully based on Northern representations of the form an agreement should take and what it should include. Although the agreements are informed by international visions of justice, its realization will be only achieved if the text and implementation thereof allows the inclusion of local voices and become an equalizing tool that helps citizens affected by conflict to surpass the existing inequality, and the consequences of violence.

In the case of Colombia, the signing of the agreements with the FARC—EP marks and signifies the beginning of the country's journey towards peace. The achievement of peace will depend on the implementation of the agreements, but also on the role taken by other players in the conflict, such as the paramilitaries and other armed groups, going forward.

Post-agreement, not post-conflict

The text has explicitly avoided the use of the term post-conflict in describing the Colombian context. The term references cases where conflict has ended and implies that peace has been reached. The silencing of the rifles or the signing of a document does not immediately produce a state of peace. A peace agreement does not equate to peace, and failing to make this distinction fails to acknowledge the importance of fulfilling the promises stated in agreements.

Inequality and class in Colombia marginalize millions of Colombians on the basis of their accent or skin colour. To achieve peace it is important to address the inequalities created by a system that sees and treats indigenous groups, Afro-Colombians, Roma and peasants as lesser citizens and makes Colombia the most unequal country on the continent. For peace to take hold, the state and society should be able to deliver services and grant the effective entitlement of rights to all Colombians. The reality in Colombia is that these rights are granted on paper, but not guaranteed in reality; unless changes are made in the direction of reducing inequality, peace will likely not take root. In countries with high inequalities, recruiting the poor and mobilizing the marginalized around different armed movements is relatively easily facilitated. Thus while this peace process removes more than 7,000 cadres from the FARC—EP, each of these were once recruited, and the possibility of further recruitment must be minimized for peace to take hold in the Colombian territory.

If the implementation of these agreements is indeed taken seriously, Colombia then faces a challenge over the coming decades of a post-agreement phase, which will demand consistency, perseverance, and cohesion from the political élites in the country in delivering policies and programmes that can deal with the structural reasons for the emergence and existence of violence and high inequality in Colombia.

The debate between retributive and reparative justice and the idea of peace

This volume recognizes the importance of both retributive and restorative justice practices, but advocates that a more holistic understanding of peace-building should transcend dichotomies between these pre-defined categories. Such a holistic approach would enable countries to draw on both approaches and sets of practices in developing justice models that are responsive to citizens' needs and interests. The justice model agreed upon can thus reflect and respond to the specific needs and social covenant of a country. Country-specific justice models may serve as a key element supporting countries bridging the post-agreement phase towards peace.

While local perspectives and visions of justice should be central, key concepts within the retributive and reparative approaches may prove valuable. The debate between restorative and retributive justice can inform the possibilities and the implementation of initiatives, including via lessons about their usefulness or their weaknesses in supporting processes of reconciliation and state-building. For example, the emphasis on restorative justice can bring to light the importance of supporting the regaining of agency of former victims of the conflict, as well as the possibility of either reconciliation or coexistence/ cohabitation.

Whereas much of the literature dealing with transitional justice depicts a romanticized idea of reconciliation, we need to be aware that imposing a reconciliation perspective might be unfair on victims, as it imposes on them the obligation of having to forgive and, in some cases, embrace their victimizers. Victims have the choice and the right to forgive or not to forgive, and they should be allowed this possibility. A distinction between reconciliation and cohabitation/coexistence should thus be made. The latter allows for the possibility of being able to share the same space with a harm-doer and does not impose onto victims the obligation to forgive. As Chapter 10 argued, the importance of understanding the psychosocial processes of victims allows for the recognition of mechanisms that can assist victims to regain agency.

Retributive justice has a value and an importance for society as well. If for a society the possibility exists of cadres serving time in jail or in alternative punishments that are ways of redressing the harm caused to society, this should be considered. Imposing a reconciliatory framework that is seen as unjust can in fact delegitimize both a peace process and the transitional justice agreements. The receptor of former cadres is society, and society should be willing to accept former fighters. In this sense the search for alternative penalties that serve a restorative and retributive potential have the possibility of improving the reconciliation process and reduce recidivism, as Chapter 8 argued.

Restoring the rights of those who otherwise would be victims if the war continued is as important as retributive and reparative justice for victims of past harms. Saving lives holds a significant restorative potential of the rights of the victims that otherwise would exist in the future. Whereas impunity and the capacity to restore, or retribution should be considered, we should not forget that the continuation of warfare is most likely to create more victims whose rights will need to be restituted and/or restored. Justice thus cannot be presented separately from the idea of peace and a ceasefire. Is justice worth the life of more human beings? Or is the dignity of past victims more valuable than stopping a conflict? These are questions without easy answers, and where accurate forecasts of what will happen are hard to understand. The most we can do regarding this dilemma is to present informed guesses, being mindful of the consequences—the possibility of impunity versus the continuation of war. That is why, instead of a language of assertiveness, the debates around justice should come framed within a language of reflection. A social construct is hard to measure and to understand; its nature is relative and cannot be mandated from other latitudes.

The challenges

The promise of peace and justice brought by the transitional justice agreement is tempered by the challenges that lay ahead. The context in which the agreement is being implemented is that of a country in which drug lords and paramilitaries continue to operate, and in which some sectors within the armed forces and the political élites remain against peace and the possibility of agreement being implemented. The assassination of social leaders after the ratification of the agreements is proof of the serious challenges facing implementation and the hurdles that need to be surpassed to realize the agreement.

The truth is that what has been signed between the FARC—EP and the Colombian Government constitutes the best-case scenario for the implementation of a transitional justice process. Thus, in order to understand what the process will mean in practice necessitates an understanding of how abstract expressions and commitments made in the agreement will be translated into programmes and guidelines that can be implemented at the fringes of the Colombian state, where state capacity is weak, resources are scarce, and challenges are plentiful. These challenges are evident with regard to land; gender; memory; reconciliation; demobilization, disarmament, and reintegration (DDR); and education policies. These multiple and complex challenges highlight the necessity of building sound institutions and policies that can enact change.

To do so it is important to depart from the understanding that the component related to transitional justice in the agreement provides only a limited legal framework for addressing distributive justice issues in contexts of exclusion from access to goods and services. Issues such as the lack of peasants' rights and access to land in Colombia are an important example of this. As Chapter 6 illustrated, a restitution programme has been established through a land restitution law (Law 1448 of 2011) to tackle this lack of rights in the context of the armed conflict and to create a series of legal mechanisms and institutions that have the sole objective of supporting the restitution of land rights for the victims of the conflict in Colombia. This is promising but, again, numerous challenges will need to be addressed for the programme to succeed. Previous land restitution processes in Colombia have had mixed outcomes, and have foregrounded a series of challenges that will require consideration regarding the asymmetries between victims and offenders and their capacity to use the existing institutions and mechanisms, and the need to understand the roles that different institutions play in these processes. However, these previous processes have also generated an institutional framework and a series of state institutions devoted to these goals. This is the departure point for the implementation of the transitional justice agreement between the FARC—EP and the Colombian Government. While challenges with regard to land restitution remain, the institutional capacity to address this has improved.

The importance of adopting a gender lens in understanding the impact of violence on women and minorities is vital; however, a narrow understanding of gender, and of gender harm as primarily related to sexual violence, has led to a missed opportunity to delve into more structural issues that affect women negatively in Colombia. As Chapter 7 showed, a particular interpretation of gender—and what constitutes a war crime, read through a gender lens—has overlooked the particularities of gender and war in the Colombian context, thus embracing a northern epistemology of gender and how it should be understood in relation to transitional justice, obscuring other harms women experience in conflict, such as land loss and dispossession. This presents a dilemma, as the importance of sexual violence should not be undermined, but the fixation on this as the only gendered crime has left aside a large population of women that have been victims of other crimes in Colombia. Chapter 7 further reflected on the challenges women face in the restitution of their rights, as land ownership traditionally follows a patriarchal line, and survivors from war are left to prove their rights in a system where ownership and titling is predominantly attached to males.

The understanding of victims and victimization, however, should also consider the role and the importance of victimizers in a transitional justice process, as cadres who were victimizers may have also been victims. Recognizing this, and taking it into account in DDR, may reduce the risks of recidivism following the conclusion of demobilization processes. Supporting demobilization processes is critical. As Chapter 8 argues, reflecting on the combatants' reintegration into society is central to avoiding recidivism. Recidivism will ultimately affect victims' abilities to exert their rights. Peace will thus rely on synergies between the DDR process and transitional justice institutions and processes. The effectiveness of institutions such as National Council for Reincorporation (CNR), and their capacity to link with transitional justice processes such as the Truth Commission, or the implementation of reparatory measures, will determine the level of support for the reintegration of FARC–EP members into receiving communities and the broader Colombian society. The society that produced war fighters is the same one that will need to embrace them once again as part of society.

However, reconciliation cannot be defined purely in legal terms. It is important to understand its psychological aspect and relation to the societal processes of reconciliation/coexistence/cohabitation. Reconciliation cannot be legislated; it demands an understanding of and reflection on how reconciliation and transitional justice mechanisms can enhance the potential for reconciliation. As Chapter 10 argued, embracing a deeper understanding of reconciliation can facilitate the use of transitional justice mechanisms to support processes through which victims regain their agency, heal psychosocial damage and activate social action and civic engagement within society. Therefore the implementation of transitional justice mechanisms cannot be seen as delinked from psychological and social processes, as the harms caused by human rights violations and violent conflict are experienced by both the individual and the collective. By using a psychosocial lens in truth commissions, it is possible to stress the significance of the processes and procedures for addressing those psychosocial harms in contributing to national reconciliation/coexistence/cohabitation.

These processes of social healing can be aided by memorialization processes, which constitute a form of symbolic reparation. Memorialization processes have the potential to rethread social relations in deeply divided societies, dignify the survivors, and re-establish relations between victims and the state. In Colombia, the institutional programme of symbolic reparations emerged in 2005 with the Peace and Justice Law and was further developed in 2011 through the Victims and Land Restitution Law. However as Chapter 9 discusses, the institutional framework for this programme and its design has, paradoxically, become a barrier to victims' involvement. Although the standardization of these processes—and the number of procedures that victims need to go through and requisites they need to fulfil in order to make the participatory component of each law effective—are well-crafted for accountability, they are not conducive to creating trust for citizens aiming to regain their agency and rebuild their trust in the state institutions. Hyper-bureaucratic approaches can affect victims' ownership of symbolic reparation processes and create mistrust, undermining the role of memory as a transitional justice mechanism. Thus, for victims' participation to be effective, the social dynamics of their participation needs to be considered in the design of such mechanisms. If the goal of victims' inclusion in symbolic reparation processes is to be realized and their participation not treated tokenistically, simply to meet the requirements of a bureaucratic procedure, then the needs of victims should be considered in these processes.

Justice, reconciliation and coexistence require coming to terms with how we learn about war and its history. The pedagogical and educational strategy devised in post-agreement Colombia should not settle on a fixed and institutionally authorized narrative of what happened. Devising an appropriate educational strategy for the post-agreement phase will first require understanding how war and its history have been learned about in the past, and which mechanisms have facilitated reflection upon its history and its nature. In the case of Colombia, it seems that understandings of conflict and war amongst young people have been primarily shaped through television, even in places where the conflict has been viciously active. In addition to this, and as Chapter 11 has argued, there is a great heterogeneity in the conflict and peoples' experiences of it across the Colombian territory. This makes attempting to develop a single mainstreamed version of the Colombian history impossible or artificial. Instead, this heterogeneity demands a series of strategies and pedagogies that will allow future citizens to learn about their country in a way that adjusts to their contexts and allows for reflection on the role of war in their communities. Such an endeavour has the potential to become transformative. Through the mandated peace curriculum, education can become a tool for reconciliation and cohabitation, a space for reflection and debate, a place for democracy.

The lessons: Not reinventing the wheel

The Colombian case is a promising example of a holistic model of justice, responsive to both local needs and international legal restrictions, and incorporating both retributive and reparative elements of transitional justice.

However, the model's innovative design still requires implementation. Lessons from other contexts provide important indications and warnings. As the cases of South Africa, Peru, Bosnia and Herzegovina, and Sri Lanka show, a series of lessons is available to inform transitional justice practices in Colombia as the country seeks to rethread the social compact and promote reconciliation and coexistence.

The case of South Africa points to the importance of political consistency in the implementation of the large and complex changes needed to bring meaningful improvements in the lives of the citizens of a country. In a similar case to South Africa, Colombia will face challenges in effecting the structural improvements that will allow for the real emancipation of its citizens. It will be important to take stock of the suggestions that the Colombian Truth Commission will make, especially related to issues of structural change, and ensure that they inform policy and institutional changes. Failure to do so would leave in place the structural conditions that gave rise to violence in the first instance and sustained it over time unchanged, and result in an incomplete process of reconciliation, as suggested in Chapter 12. As William Ospina, a Colombian poet, argues, wars do not end when the body count is finished but when the reasons for the war cease to exist. Advancing structural change will demand visionary leadership from the political establishment. This type of leadership is not yet evident in Colombia, as élites clash for political posts rather than pursue the project of a nation beyond war.

The case of Peru, as described in Chapter 13, demonstrates the challenges of implementing transitional justice mechanisms as part of political transition. The most vital lesson from the Peruvian case for Colombia is the importance of legitimacy in any attempt to establish historical truth and change. The quality of professional and technical staff available to a truth commission cannot be underestimated in order to achieve this legitimacy; its work should not be left to politicians. Indeed, if trials and processes are seen as partial or biased, then transitional justice processes may be constrained in their ability to contribute to a reconciliation project and may instead contribute to the polarization of the political landscape (something that some Colombian politicians are working towards already). It is further important that alliances are built to connect actors at regional levels with groups that might be supportive of the Truth Commission's findings and proposals, such as students, labour unions, peasant groups and those located at the fringes of the state. This serves to strengthen the bonds between the state and its institutions, and supports the participation of those excluded by the state during the conflict in the consolidation of the Colombian state. The importance of mobilizing political support for the findings of the Truth Commission at all levels must not be underestimated if the goal is to consolidate the legacy of its work. Political support is particularly important in relation to the construction of official history/histories for future generations. Given the contentiousness of the peace agreements in Colombia, as shown by the rejection of the agreements in the plebiscite of 2 October 2016, this is a key element to take into account. Finally, a peace accord or a transitional agreement does not only imply an end point for the conflict. It marks the beginning of a transitioning process in which the interaction and participation of different social actors in different areas of public life becomes institutionalized and part of the daily life of a democracy in the making.

The imposition of transitional justice initiatives that are separated from local contexts, their realities and their representatives poses a great risk. While the transitional justice process will be held in Colombian courts, the distances (geographic, bureaucratic, social) between the provinces and the war affected areas of the country and the centre of the country resembles the distances between Sarajevo and The Hague which problematized the transitional justice process in Bosnia and Herzegovina as described in Chapter 14. The challenges in the transitional process in Bosnia and Herzegovina signal the challenges and pitfalls of how a limited scope in transitional justice can affect its legitimacy within local populations and thus affect the prospects for the sustainability of transitional justice. In a country as diverse as Colombia, it is therefore important to be aware of the local needs and local contexts in the processes of designing and implementing transitional justice initiatives. Without this, there is a risk that the process may be perceived as being alien and imposed, as in the Bosnia and Herzegovina models.

Finally, an additional important element of legitimacy required for the success of transitional justice processes is that the process is regarded by citizens as seriously and meaningfully pursuing its stated objectives, rather than operating as a token policy to generate international standing or legitimacy in accordance with the desires of the international community. Chapter 15 discusses this in relation to the case of Sri Lanka's long-fought civil war between the Government armed forces and the Liberation Tigers of the Tamil Eelam, after which transitional justice was used instrumentally to demonstrate to an international audience the 'liberal' and 'democratic' nature of the country. This put the rights of the victims at risk. If the justice needs of the victims of the civil war and the other multiple episodes of violence that engulf the recent history of countries departing from war are to be addressed, realizing a social justice-centred agenda and investing in building an accountable state is paramount where structural changes must be effected.

The promise of peace

The difference between magical realism and the peace agreement signed in Colombia is that the former was never required to come to life and materialize. However, for peace to take a hold in Colombia it is necessary that the signatories of the agreement and its attendant institutions manifest the promise of the agreement. They need to translate the magical into reality, and this demands the capacity of the state to finally fulfil the promises it has failed to deliver on since its independence. It is not enough that the beautiful and powerful ideas of peace are captured on paper and enchanted with a couple of signatures; this alone cannot overwrite 50 years of violence. If Colombia proves it is capable of implementing these agreements, the country would prove that magic can be transmuted into reality, and peace grafted onto contexts of war.

The challenges are as great as the promises of justice and peace. To achieve this promise, the country needs to overhaul its leadership, its citizenry, and its institutions. In a country that almost closed the office of its High Commissioner for Peace whilst in the middle of the implementation of a peace process (La Silla Vacia, 2017), and in which the promise of peace has been sequestrated by political parties and their interests, it is evident that some sectors of the economic and political élite lack the vision to move the country away from violence. However, the agreements and the transitional justice process constitute an overture and an opportunity that could facilitate these processes of change.

Although the FARC—EP presents itself as the sole victim of this armed conflict and the representative of the victims of the country, they have in fact co-created the victims. The FARC—EP, like the paramilitaries, is a 'Frankenstein's monster' that Colombian society has created, and its existence has helped to conceal corruption, incompetence, and institutional weakness, as well as erode popular belief in the possibility of peace. This distrust is the legacy of the policies of the FARC—EP and its leadership in previous peace processes, where periods of peace and ceasefire were used as opportunities to facilitate warfare. This legacy is as harmful as the void promises of peace made by the state. Now it is the responsibility of both the political establishment and the FARC—EP and its leadership to grant the Colombian citizens the rights they have denied to them for decades: peace and justice.

This transformation will not be immediate. It will demand institutional consistency in the prioritizing and pursuit of peace and the implementation of the peace agreement and the transitional justice agreement, framing this as an objective of the nation, rather than that of a President, a Government, or a political party. Only in this way can the efforts and policies needed to move through the post-agreement phase into peace be ensured for the coming decades. Peace requires consistency, and breaking the back of a political economy of warfare will require plans that are crafted to deliver in the long term, to the middle of the century, to guarantee that the structural issues of inequality, political participation, and access to justice are dealt with.

The case of Colombia and the promise of peace and justice that is now emerging illuminate both the fragility of the contexts in which transitional justice attempts are made, but also the courage of the citizens and Colombian peoples' resilience in the search for justice.

The dignity, and the future, of Colombia as a nation rely on the treatment that it gives to its victims. History is watching.

References

La Silla Vacia, 2017. *Se va el altruista de la paz*. [Online] Available at: http://lasillavacia.com/historia/se-va-el-altruista-de-la-paz-61922 [Last accessed 20 August 2017].

University of Cape Town, 2017. *Mamdani returns*. [Online] Available at: www.news.uct.ac.za/article/-2017-08-24-mamdani-returns [Last accessed 15 September 2017].

Index

Note: Page numbers in *italics* denote references to Figures and page numbers in **bold** indicate Tables.

Acción Social 93
accountability 123, 237
Administrative Unit for Land Restitution 61
Administrative Unit for Victims Reparation 61
agrarian reform 98. *See also* land
Alta Consejería para la Reintegración (ACR) 120
alternative criminal justice, peace through 51–4
amnesty for political crimes 54, 192–3, 236, 242–3. *See also* retributive justice
amnesty law 76–7, 78
Amnesty Law of 1995 (Peru) 210
apartheid 190–1, 193–5, 197
Ardoyne Commemoration Project 126
armed groups in Colombia 15, *17*, 19–22. *See also* Fuerzas Armadas Revolucionarias de Colombia–Ejército del Pueblo (FARC–EP)
Aronson, J.D. 192
Autodefensas Unidas de Colombia (AUC) 24–5, 56, 73–5, 120, 141
Ayala, Julio César Turbay 52

Bantu Education Act 190
Barco, Virgilio 34
Barrios Altos decision 210
Bell, C. 240
Bellino, Michelle 172
Betancur Cuartas, Belisario 21, 34, 42, 52–3
Binnenkade, A. 173
Bonilla, Lara 21
Bonn Powers of 1997 224

Borrero, Misael Pastrana 20
Bosnia and Herzegovina: civil society in 228–30; Dayton Peace Agreement (DPA) 222–4; international vs. territorial vision of 231; NGOization in 228–9; RECOM initiative 229–30; social reconstruction process 230–1; state-building in 222–5; transitional justice challenges in 225–8, 260
Bosniak Party of Democratic Action (SDA) 223
Bosnian Ministry of Justice 227
boundary objects 173

Caminos del Saber 10 (textbook) 174
Cano, Alfonso 36–7
Centro Democrático 67
Centro Nacional de Memoria Histórica 120–1, 143
chosen traumas 247n7
Cinco Claves 113
civil society 228–30, 232
Cobb, Sara 138
collective reparations programmes 57, 72–3, 212–13, 215–16
Colombian Congress: approving extraordinary powers to Santos administration 66; Decree 3398 19–20; Justice and Peace Law (JPL) 56–60, 74, 89; Law 35 of 1982 52; Law 37 of 1981 52; Law 48 of 1968 20; Law 49 of 1985 53; Law 356 of 1994 24; Law 418 of 1997 50, 54–6; Law 975 of 2005 50–1, 89, 93–4, 108; Law 1448 of 2011 88–9, 110; security statute 20–1; Victims and Land Restitution Law

(LVRT) 60–3, 88–9. *See also* public policy
Colombian Constitutional Court 59, 66, 74, 79, 93
Colombian Truth Commission 70
Colombian women's movement 106–7
colonial instruments 4
Comisión de la Verdad y Reconciliación (CVR) 207–9, 212, 214
Comisión Nacional de Reparación y Reconciliación (CNRR) 141
Comisión para el Esclarecimiento de la Verdad 194
Commission for the Clarification of Truth, Coexistence, and Non-Repetition 70–1
compensation 150n7
consociationalism model 223
Constitutional Reform of 1991 42
Convention on the Elimination of All Forms of Discrimination against Women (CEDAW) 104–5, 107
Convivencia y la no Repetición (CEV) 194
Convivir organizations 24
Corporación Democracia 130
Corporación Humanas 109, 110
Corporación Sisma Mujer 109
counter-insurgency self-defence forces 19–20
Creole radical feminism 102, 106–11, 114
crimes against humanity 76, 77
criminal accountability after political transition 209–11
Criminal Code of Bosnia and Herzegovina 227
criminal gangs 44
criminal justice system, defined 58–9
Croatian Democratic Union (HDZ) 223
Cuban Revolution 19

Dayton Peace Agreement (DPA) 222–4, 230–1
DDR. *See* disarmament, demobilization and reintegration (DDR) process
Declaration on Preventing Sexual Violence in Conflict 106
de Klerk, F. W. 198
demilitarized zones 25
demobilization process 56, 73, 119–21, 127–8, 257. *See also* disarmament, demobilization and reintegration (DDR) process
demobilized cadres 23

denial of painful realities 247n18
disarmament, demobilization and reintegration (DDR) process: alliance with transitional justice 119; challenges in 128–30; facilitating demobilization 119–22; implementing 60; improvisation and 129–30; peace agreement focus on 45–6, 51; transitional justice and 123–7; United Nations and 53
dispossession of lands. *See* land
drug trafficking/drug traffickers 19–20, 21, 43–4, 180
dual-targeting strategies 123–4

Echeverri, Rodrigo Londoño 37
Economías Sociales del Común (ECOMUN) 127–8
economic reparations programme 213
education: history textbooks 173–4; Peace Curriculum Law 171–2; schools 174–5; teachers 174; textbooks 173–4, 183; transitional justice linked with 169
educational institutions 171, 172
educational policies 171–3
Ejército Popular de Liberación (EPL) 20
emergent bands 27
Escobar, Pablo 180
ethnic bias 226
ex-combatants 120

falsos positivos (false positives) 28
FARC–EP. *See* Fuerzas Armadas Revolucionarias de Colombia–Ejército del Pueblo (FARC–EP)
fast-track mechanism 46, 47n5, 80n2
Federation of Bosnia and Herzegovina. *See* Bosnia and Herzegovina
feminism. *See* Creole radical feminism
Fitzpatrick, D. 91
forced displacement 107, 109, 192
Frente Nacional (FN). *See* National Front
Fuerzas Armadas Revolucionarias de Colombia–Ejército del Pueblo (FARC–EP): broadening political participation 43; contributing to reparation 72; as an electoral force 23–5; emergence of 16; expansion of 24; military offensive of 24; Pastrana's peace negotiations with 34–5; peace negotiations with 34; peace process with 21–2; Santos negotiations with 34, 35–6, 66; terminating long-

standing insurgency by 41; use of
 demilitarized zones 25
Fujimori, Alberto 210–11
Fujimori regime 206–7
Fujimori trials 210–11
Fundación Ideas para la Paz 121

García, Alan 211
Gaviria, César 34
Gaviria Government 23
gender 104, 256–7. *See also* women
Generalized System of Preferences (GSP
 Plus) 244–5, 248n22
Gómez, Álvaro 19
Gómez, Laureano 18
group demobilizations 121
Grupo Colina 211
Grupo de Memoria Histórica (GMH)
 141–3
guarantees of non-recurrence 150n7
guerillas 19–22, 76, 208
Guzmán, Abimael 206

Hamber, B. 162
Herzegovina. *See* Bosnia and
 Herzegovina
Historical Commission of the Conflict
 and its Victims (CHCV) 173
historical memory 138–40, 147, 196, 199
history textbooks 173–4
Höglund, K. 236
holistic transitional justice 221
Hoogenboom, D. A. 229
horizontal violence 124–5
Humala, Ollanta 216
human rights violations, criminal
 accountability for 209–11
hybrid justice system 4

Ignatieff, Michael 245
Institute for Justice and Reconciliation
 (IJR) 191, 195
institutions. *See* educational institutions
integral reparation 141
Inter-American Convention of Human
 Rights 210
Inter-American Court of Human Rights
 210
internally displaced persons (IDPs) 29,
 106–7, 109, 140
Internally Displaced Population Law
 (IDPs Law) 140–1
International Coordination and Coop-
 eration Roundtable for Colombia 56–7

International Criminal Court (ICC) 76
International Criminal Tribunal for the
 Former Yugoslavia (ICTY) 225–7, 231
international human rights practice 79
international justice agenda 237–40, 241
international law: mainstreaming of 102;
 receptive to radical feminism 106;
 redressing legacies of crimes under
 168–9
International Monetary Fund 244
international transitional justice agenda
 237–40
interpersonal forgiveness 81n13
Izetbegovic, Alija 223

Jacoby, T. 242
Jansen, J.D. 183
Jayawardene, J. R. 235
Jojoy, Mono 36
Jurisdicción especial para la Paz (JEP–
 Special Jurisdiction for Peace) 129
justice, peace vs. 3–4, 221, 252–3
Justice and Peace Law (JPL) 50–1,
 56–60, 73–5, 89, 136, 141
justpeace 236, 246n2

Ki-Moon, Ban 239
knowledge transfer: key to 182–3; sources of war knowledge 168, 175–6, *176*;
 study of 170; through television 175–6

land: appropriation 59; dispossession 88,
 88, 90, 91, 92, 108; ownership regula-
 tion efforts 87, 90–1; policies 61; resti-
 tution 61–2, 94–8, 194–5, 256; tenure
 87, 97–8, 105, 108–14
Land Restitution Unit 96
La Uribe agreements 21–2
La Violencia period 16–18
Law 35 of 1982 52
Law 37 of 1981 52
Law 48 of 1968 20
Law 49 of 1985 53
Law 356 of 1994 24
Law 418 of 1997 50, 54–6
Law 975 of 2005 50–1, 56–60, 74, 89,
 93–4, 108
Law 1448 of 2011 62–3, 88–9, 92–7,
 98–9, 110
Law on Missing Persons 227
left-wing guerrillas. *See* Fuerzas Arma-
 das Revolucionarias de Colombia–
 Ejército del Pueblo (FARC–EP);
 guerillas

266 Index

lesbian, gay, bisexual, transgender, and intersex (LGBTI) minorities 7
Lessons Learnt and Reconciliation Commission (LLRC) 238
Ley de Victimas y Restitución de Tierras (The Victims' Law) 6, 143–5, 171
Liberation Tigers of Tamil Eelam (LTTE) 236, 237
localized memory initiatives 139
Lugar de la Memoria 209

M-19 guerrillas 21
Mamdani, Mahmood 252
Mandela, Nelson 197
Mandela Government 191
material reparations. *See* reparations
material restitution. *See* restitution
Mawhinney, E.B. 192
memorialization processes 136, 257–8
memory reconstruction: bottom-up historical 139–40; bridging local and national goals through 149–50; at local level 149; symbolic reparations and 143–5; top-down processes of 139–40; in transitional contexts 138–40
Michelsen, Alfonso López 20
microfocalization process 95
Milosevic, Slobodan 223
Monitoring Committee on Public Policy on Forced Displacement 88
Montesinos, Vladimiro 206

Nadner, A. 159–60
National Center of Historic Memory 165n11
National Centre of Historical Memory (CNMH) 173
National Constituent Assembly 34
National Council for Reincorporation (CNR) 127–9, 257
National Front 18–19, 42
National Lands Agency 97
national reparations programmes 137, 140
National Strategy for the Prosecution of War Crimes 227
National Victims Registry, Peru 212–13
nation-building 196, 197, 199, 224. *See also* state-building
Nepal 243
NGOization 228–9
non-repetition guarantees 73

Observatorio de Tierras 95
Observer Group in Central America (ONUCA) 53
Office of the High Representative (OHR) 232n1
Office of the Missing Persons (OMP) 238, 247n11
Operation Anorí 20
Organization of American States (OAS) 26–7, 120
Orujela, C. 236
Ospina, William 259

Paniagua, Valentín 208
paramilitaries 24–8, 74, 120–1
paramilitary dispossession 92
Pastrana, Andrés 25, 34, 35
Pastrana Government 27, 37–9, 54
pathologization 160, 165n10
patriarchy, women's subordination and 104
peace agreements: agrarian reform and 41–2; creating land funds 41–2; failure of 67; fast-track procedure 46, 47n5; on illicit drugs 43–4; implementing 41, 171; not equating to peace 253–4; offering world a vision of peace 251; ratification by Congress 40–1; signing of 1, 39; transitional justice formulas 45; transitional justice mechanisms and 220; vote against 66–7. *See also* transitional justice agreement
Peace and Justice Law 50–1, 56–60, 89, 93–4, 108, 258
Peace Curriculum Law 171–2
peace infrastructures 123, 146–50, 171
peace negotiations: citizens' inputs 38; of limited agenda 38–9; limiting public participation in 37–8; partial agreements 38; Pastrana and FARC–EP in 34–5; rule and procedures in 37–9; Santos and FARC–EP in 35–6; transitional justice and 180–2; women and land 111–14
peace/peacebuilding: approaches to 252–3; Bosnian model of 228; bottom-up participatory approach to 126; comprehensive reparation for 72–3; donor-based architecture 130; facilitating 220; justice vs. 3–4, 221; justpeace 236, 246n2; post-colonial thinking of 252; through alternative criminal justice 51–4; top-down

mechanism to 126–7; truth-building for 70–1; victor's peace 236, 246n1
peace process: with FARC-EP 21–2; with guerrillas 21; student's view of 180–2, *181*
Penn, William 241
Pérez, Mariano Ospina 18
perpetrator/victim identities 159–60
Peruvian society: armed conflict analysis in 208–9; Constitutional Tribunal 210; criminal accountability in 209–11; dual transition of 206; economic reparations programme 213–14; national memory museum 209; National Victims Registry 212–13; political process of 206–7; Reparations Council 212; specialized human rights system 215; transitional justice and 206; Truth and Reconciliation Commission 207–9
Pinheiro Principles 99n6
Pinilla, Gustavo Rojas 18
Plan Colombia campaign 27, 35–6, 47n1
plebiscite 39–40, 66, 103, 115n3
political crimes 76–7
Polo Democrático Alternativo 43
post-conflict pedagogies 183
post-war transitional justice 237, 240, 244
Presidential Commissions of Inquiry, Sri Lanka 238
private property 91. *See also* land
privatization of security 24
Program for Individual Economic Reparation (PREI) 213
Promotion of National Unity and Reconciliation Act 191
psychology, truth commissions and 156–8
psychosocial accompaniment 163
psychosocial trauma 160–2, 165n9, 257
public policy: decentralization in 26; exclusion of peasants from 87–8; on land dispossession 89; for land restitution 92–7; women's land tenure and 113. *See also* Colombian Congress; Peace Curriculum Law; Victims and Land Restitution Law (LVRT)

radical feminism methodology 103–6
Rajapaksa regime 238, 239, 242, 245
recidivism 23, 120, 122, 257
RECOM initiative 229–30, 232n3
reconciliation: challenges in 199; defined 154; as a goal 154; horizontal violence and 125; objectives of 154; in post-conflict scenarios 123; psychological approach to 156–7; social 122; social identities and 158; socio-political 196–7; in South African society 196–7; transitional justice romanticizing idea of 255; truth commissions and 155–6
rehabilitation 150n7
reintegration 120, 121, 189
reparations 57–60, 72–3, 137–41, 211–16, 226–7
Reparations Council, Peru 212
Republika Srpska (RS) 223
restitution 57–60, 150n7
restitution jurisdiction 96
restorative justice 6–7, 61–2, 189, 254–5
Restrepo, Carlos Lleras 20
retributive justice 6–7, 189, 225, 243, 254–5. *See also* amnesty for political crimes
Reyes, Raúl 36
Rojas, Victor Julio Suárez 36
Rome Conference 105
Ruta Pacifica de las Mujeres 165n11
Rwanda 126

Samaraweera, Mangala 241
Samper Government 23–4, 25
Santos, Enrique 37
Santos, Juan Manuel 28, 34–7, 66, 115n3, 136
Santos Government 46–7, 78
satisfaction 150n7
Search Unit for Missing Persons in the Context and as a Result of the Conflict 71–2
security privatization 24
security statute 20–1, 52
Segovia Massacre 177, 185n22
segregation and discrimination, South Africa 190
Serbian Democratic Party (SDS) 223
sexual violence against women 105, 107–10, 112, 216, 227, 256
Shining Path (Sendero Luminoso) 206
Shnabel, N. 159–60
Silva, Luis Edgar Devia 36
Sinhala-Buddhists 235–6
Sirisena, Maithripala 245
social action 162–3
social covenant, government's promise of 21–2
Sociales para Pensar 10 (textbook) 174
social healing processes 257–8

social identities 158–60
Socialist Renovation Stream 30n16
social justice 243
social reconciliation 122
social solidarity principle 55
South Africa: Bantu Education Act 190; economic reconciliation 195; forced displacement 192; land restitution 194–5; nation-building project 196; role of leadership 197–8; socio-political reconciliation 196–7; transitional justice and 190–2; Truth and Reconciliation Commission 190. *See also* apartheid
South African Reconciliation Barometer (SARB) 195
South African Truth and Reconciliation Commission (TRC) 125
special jurisdiction for peace 73–8, *77*, 79, 215
Sri Lanka: international transitional justice agenda 237–40; Lessons Learnt and Reconciliation Commission (LLRC) 238; Office of the Missing Persons (OMP) 238; transitional justice agendas in 240–4; UN resolutions on 237–9; war crimes probe 238
state-building 1, 222–5. *See also* nation-building
students: affected by violence 176–7; causes of conflict according to *180*; peace process views of 180–2, *181*
survivors, making sense of war 173–4
sustained violence 168–9. *See also* violence
symbolic reparations: achieving closure through memory 137–40; historical memory processes as 147; implementing 147–8; memory reconstruction and 143–5; as peace infrastructures 146–50

Tamil diaspora 236, 240
teachers 174
television, as source of knowledge 175–6
Temporary Rural Areas of Normalization (ZVTN) 127
territorial councils 129
testimony, in making sense of war 168
textbooks 173–4, 183
Timochenko 37
Toledo, Alejandro 208
transitional justice: DDR processes and 119; defined 2, 168–9; evolution of 220; holistic approach to 221; implementing 5, 256; in international context 6–7; in intra-state conflicts 2; legal evolution of *51*; local vs. international 4; objectives of 4; peace negotiations and 180–2; tensions in 3–6; truth and reconciliation in 5
transitional justice agreement: forced disappearances addressed in 71; guarantees of non-repetition 73; guiding principles of 68–73; justice component of 75–7; measures for comprehensive reparation for peacebuilding 72–3; recognizing clarification of truth, coexistence, and non-repetition *69*, 70–1
transitional justice mechanisms: as complementary 68; implementing 51–4; land restitution and 94–5; peace agreements and 220
Treaty of Extradition with the USA 21
Truth, Clarification, Coexistence, Justice and Non-Repetition Commission 173
Truth and Reconciliation Commission (TRC): in Peruvian society 207–9, 212, 214; in South African society 190, 193–4, 199
truth and reconciliation processes 5, 245
truth-building, as essential for peacebuilding 70–1
truth commissions: as alternative to trials 5; as mechanism to peace 70; objectives of 155; perpetrators' accounts in 124; in Peruvian society 214; psychology and 156–8; reconciliation and 155–6; transforming social identities 158–9; truth-telling/seeking practices in 160–2; use of testimony by 159; from victim to survivor 159. *See also* Truth and Reconciliation Commission (TRC)
truth-seeking 160–2, 165n11
truth-telling mechanisms 70
Tudman, Franjo 223
Turbay goverment 20–1
Tutu, Desmond 198

Unidad de Atención y Reparación Integral a las Víctimas (UARIV) 145
Unión Patriótica (UP) party 21–2, 42
United Nations: High Commissioner for Human Rights 224; Observer Group in Central America 53; Security Council 105–6; Sri Lankan model 242
United Self-Defence Forces of Colombia 30–1n22

Unit for the Search for Disappeared Persons in the Context and as a Result of the Conflict 71
Uprimny, R. 93
Uribe, Álvaro 35, 40, 56, 67, 120
Uribe agreements 21, 30n9
Uribe Government 27–8, 56, 59
Uyangoda, J. 235, 241

Valencia, León 19–20
Van Der Merwe, H. 236
Vargas, Guillermo León Sáenz 36–7
Vargas, Virgilio Barco 21–2
vertical violence 124
victims: assistance to 55; co-ordination mechanisms **144**; defined 55, 57; dignity of 255; emotional reconciliation between perpetrator and 159–60; of land dispossession 91, 95; Law 418 and 55; material reparations for 72–3; participatory process for 226; public testimony of 162–3; role in agreements 7; students as 176–7; transitional justice and 44. *See also* reparations
Victims and Land Restitution Law (LVRT) 60–3, 88–9, 92–7, 110, 258
Victims' Law 6, 143–5, 171
victim's participation mechanisms 140–5, **144**, 147–8
victor's peace 236, 246n1

Vielille, S. 229
violence: actors of war 180; causes of conflict *180*; educational institutions and 171–2; exteriorized 177–8; imagined geographies of *178*; land dispossession and 92; main actors of *181*; making meaning of 160; narratives of 177; origins of conflict 179; psychosocial trauma of 160; sustained 168–9; textbook treatment of 173–4. *See also* sexual violence against women
Volkan, Vamik 247n7
voluntary declarations 131n10
vulnerable groups, land restitution and 97

Walton, O. 241
war. *See* violence
war crimes probe 242
War Crimes section, Bosnia and Herzegovina 227
war criminals, sheltering 253
Weldon, G. 183
women: land tenure and 111–14; peace and security 105–6; sexual violence against 105, 107–10, 112, 216, 227, 256; subordination of 104. *See also* Creole radical feminism
women's movement 106–7